Unlock the Bible:
Keys to Understanding the Scripture

Other Unlock the Bible Titles

Unlock the Bible: Keys to Discovering the People and Places

Unlock the Bible: Keys to Exploring the Culture and Times

Unlock the Bible

Keys to Understanding the Scripture

General Editor
Ronald F. Youngblood

General Editor of Original Edition
Herbert Lockyer, Sr.

Consulting Editors
F. F. Bruce   R. K. Harrison

THOMAS NELSON
Since 1798

NASHVILLE   DALLAS   MEXICO CITY   RIO DE JANEIRO

Published in Nashville, Tennessee, by Thomas Nelson. Thomas Nelson is a registered trademark of Thomas Nelson, Inc.

Book design and composition by Upper Case Textual Services, Lawrence, Massachusetts.

Thomas Nelson, Inc., titles may be purchased in bulk for educational, business, fund-raising, or sales promotional use. For information, please e-mail SpecialMarkets@ ThomasNelson.com.

978-1-4185-4682-3

Printed in the United States of America

11 12 13 14 15 RRD 6 5 4 3 2 1

Contributors

Robert L. Alden
  Conservative Baptist Seminary, Denver, Colorado

Leslie C. Allen
  Fuller Theological Seminary, Pasadena, California

Ronald B. Allen
  Christian Theological Seminary, Indianapolis, Indiana

Timothy R. Ashley
  Acadia Divinity College, Wolfville, Nova Scotia, Canada

David W. Baker
  Ashland Theological Seminary, Ashland, Ohio

John J. Bimson
  Trinity College, Bristol, England

E. M. Blaiklock
  Auckland, New Zealand

Gerald Borchert
  Southern Baptist Theological Seminary, Louisville, Kentucky

Stephen G. Brown
  Shasta Bible College, Redding, California

F. F. Bruce
  University of Manchester, Manchester, England

John A. Burns
  Retired from Criswell Center for Biblical Studies,Dallas, Texas

Newton L. Bush
  Lima, Ohio

G. Lloyd Carr
  Retired from Gordon College, Wenham, Massachusetts

E. Clark Copeland
  Reformed Presbyterian Theological Seminary, Pittsburgh, Pennsylvania

Leonard J. Coppes
    Denver, Colorado

Walter M. Dunnett
    Retired from Northwestern College, St. Paul, Minnesota

Kendell H. Easley
    Mid-America Baptist College, Memphis, Tennessee

Kermit A. Ecklebarger
    Conservative Baptist Seminary, Denver, Colorado

James R. Edwards
    Jamestown College, Jamestown, North Dakota

John M. Elliott
    Aurora, Illinois

Millard J. Erickson
    Bethel Theological Seminary, St. Paul, Minnesota

Harvey E. Finley
    Retired from Nazarene Theological Seminary, Kansas City, Missouri

Royce G. Gruenler
    Gordon-Conwell Theological Seminary, South Hamilton, Massachusetts

Timothy Hadley
    Lubbock Christian University, Lubbock, Texas

Donald A. Hagner
    Fuller Theological Seminary, Pasadena, California

R. K Harrison
    Wycliffe College, Toronto, Canada

Harvey Hartman
    Liberty Baptist College, Lynchburg, Virginia

Robert Hendren
    Donelson, Tennessee

Herschel H. Hobbs
    Oklahoma City, Oklahoma

Harold W. Hoehner
    Dallas Theological Seminary, Dallas, Texas

John J. Hughes
    Whitefish, Montana

Robert Hughes
    Miami Christian College, Miami, Florida

Harry B. Hunt, Jr.
    Southwestern Baptist Theological Seminary, Fort Worth, Texas

W. Bingham Hunter
    Trinity Evangelical Divinity School, Deerefield, Illinois

David K. Huttar
Nyack College, Nyack, New York

William W. Klein
Conservative Baptist Seminary, Denver, Colorado

Woodrow M. Kroll
Back to the Bible, Lincoln, Nebraska

Alvin S. Lawhead
Nazarene Theological Seminary, Kansas City, Missouri

Gordon Lewis
Conservative Baptist Seminary, Denver, Colorado

Jack P. Lewis
Harding Graduate School of Religion, Memphis, Tennessee

Walter L. Liefeld
Trinity Evangelical Divinity School, Deerfield, Illinois

G. Herbert Livingston
Retired from Asbury Theological Seminary, Wilmore, Kentucky

Tremper Longman, III
Westminster Theological Seminary, Philadelphia, Pennsylvania

Robert S. MacLennan
McAlester College, St. Paul, Minnesota

W. Harold Mare
Covenant Theological Seminary, St. Louis, Missouri

Elmer A. Martens
Mennonite Brethren Biblical Seminary, Fresno, California

Wayne O. McCready
University of Calgary, Alberta, Canada

Scot McKnight
Trinity Evangelical Divinity School, Deerfield, Illinois

Janet McNish
Nashville, Tennessee

Robert R. Moore
Asbury College, Wilmore, Kentucky

William Mounce
Azusa Pacific College, Azusa, California

John Nolland
Regent College, Vancouver, Canada

Dave O'Brien
St. Paul Bible College, Bible College, Minnesota

Vernon S. Olson
St. Bonifacius, Minnesota

Grant R. Osborne
 Trinity Evangelical Divinity School, Deerfield, Illinois

Mildred Ottinger
 Nashville, Tennessee

Arthur G. Patzia
 Fuller Seminary, Pasadena, California

Gary Pratico
 Gordon-Conwell Divinity School, South Hamilton, Massachusetts

Richard A. Purdy
 West Norwalk, Connecticut

Robert V. Rakestraw
 The Criswell College, Dallas, Texas

John Rasko
 Alaska Bible College, Glennallen, Alaska

Richard O. Rigsby
 Talbot Theological Seminary, La Mirada, California

Allen P. Ross
 Dallas Theological Seminary, Dallas, Texas

Glenn E. Schaefer
 Simpson College, San Francisco, California

Stephen R. Schrader
 Liberty Baptist Seminary, Lynchburg, Virginia

Jack B. Scott
 Decatur, Georgia

Martin J. Selman
 Spurgeon's College, London, England

Norman Shepherd
 Minneapolis, Minnesota

Gary V. Smith
 Bethel Theological Seminary, St. Paul, Minnesota

Douglas K. Stuart
 Gordon-Conwell Theological Seminary, South Hamilton, Massachusetts

Robert L. Thomas
 Talbot Theological Seminary, La Mirada, California

Willem A. VanGemeren
 Reformed Theological Seminary, Jackson, Mississippi

Dolores Walker
 Walla Walla, Washington

Larry L. Walker
 Mid-America Baptist Seminary, Memphis, Tennessee

Daniel B. Wallace
   Mukilteo, Washington
Forest Weddle
   Fort Wayne Bible College, Fort Wayne, Indiana
Tom Wells
   Cincinnati, Ohio
Stephen Westerholm
   Toronto, Canada
Frederick E. Young
   Central Baptist Seminary, Kansas City, Kansas
Ronald F. Youngblood
   Bethel Theological Seminary, West San Diego, California

ABBA [AB ah] (*father*)—an Aramaic word that corresponds to our "Daddy" or "Papa." It is found three times in the New Testament: in the Garden of Gethsemane, Jesus prayed, "Abba, Father" (Mark 14:36); the apostle Paul linked the Christian's cry of "Abba, Father" with the "Spirit of adoption" (Rom. 8:15); and, again, Paul writes, "Because you are sons, God has sent forth the Spirit of His son into your hearts, crying out, 'Abba, Father!'" (Gal. 4:6). What a blessed privilege it is to be given the right to call the great Creator, "Our Father"!

ACTS OF THE APOSTLES—the one historical book of the New Testament, which traces the development of the early church after the ascension of Jesus. Standing between the Gospels and the Epistles, the Book of Acts is a bridge between the life of Jesus and the ministry of the apostle Paul. As such, it offers invaluable information about the development of the early church.

The title of Acts is somewhat misleading, for only a few of the apostles of Jesus are mentioned in the book. In reality, Acts relates some acts of some of the apostles, primarily Peter and Paul, and involves a time-span of about 32 years—from the ascension of Jesus (about A.D. 30) to Paul's imprisonment in Rome (about A.D. 62).

Structure of the Book.

The Acts of the Apostles is like a drama with two main characters, Peter and Paul. This drama portrays the spread of the gospel from Jerusalem—the city where Jesus was crucified—to Rome, the capital of the Roman Empire.

Authorship and Date.

There can be little doubt that the Book of Acts and the Gospel of Luke come from the same author. Each book is the length of a scroll (about 35 feet), and each is addressed to the same individual, Theophilus. The similarities between the Gospel of Luke and the Book of Acts in literary style, vocabulary, and theological ideas are unmistakable. Although the author does not identify himself by name, scholars have ascribed the authorship of both books to Luke, the companion of Paul.

It is difficult to say when Acts was written. We know only that it follows the Gospel: "The former account [Gospel of Luke] I made, O Theophilus" (Acts 1:1). If the Gospel were written in the early 70s, Acts would have been composed shortly thereafter. Many scholars date Acts as early as A.D. 62 because it ends abruptly with Paul's imprisonment in Rome.

Luke is a reliable historian, in part because of the sources he used. He was closely associated with many events of Paul's mission, and this results in greater vividness in the latter half of Acts. At three places in Acts (16:10–17, 20:5–21:18, and 27:1–28:16) the narrative changes to the first person plural ("we"), indicating that Luke was personally present. Luke also may have had access to written documents (for example, the decree of the Council of Jerusalem, Acts 15:23; or letters from early Christian leaders).

Above all, Luke had the benefit of a wide circle of contacts. In the Book of Acts he mentions 95 different persons from 32 countries, 54 cities, and 9 Mediterranean islands. From these he gathered information for the first part of Acts (especially chaps. 1–12) and for the gospel. Luke, however, writes selective history, focusing only on the course of the gospel from Jerusalem to Rome.

Historical Setting.

As in the Gospel of Luke, Luke writes to Gentiles. He wants his audience to know the truthful and triumphant course of the gospel, beginning in Jesus and continuing in the church (Acts 1:1).

This is his primary motive for writing the Book of Acts. In addition, however, Luke defends, where possible, the Christian faith from suspicion of sedition or superstition. The "Way" (9:2) is not a secret, subversive cult (26:26). On the contrary, it is proclaimed in the city squares for all to hear and judge. This is one reason the many public speeches were included in Acts. Neither is Christianity politically dangerous. If Christians are suspected of sedition against Rome, Luke shows that in each instance where they are brought before Roman authorities they are acquitted (Acts 16:39; 17:6; 18:12; 19:37; 23:29; 25:25; 26:31). Luke devotes nearly one third of Acts (chaps. 21–28) to Paul's imprisonment. He does this not only to show that the gospel reaches its destination in spite of insurmountable obstacles, but also to show that Paul and his message are not politically subversive.

Theological Contribution.

The Acts of the Apostles could justly be entitled "The Acts of the Holy Spirit," for the Spirit is mentioned nearly 60 times in the book. In His parting words, Jesus reminds the disciples of the promise of the Father (1:4–8); ten days later the power of the Spirit descends at Pentecost (2:1–4). Persons "from every nation under heaven" (2:5) are enabled by the Holy Spirit to hear "the wonderful works of God" (2:11), and so the Christian church was born.

Pentecost was a reversal of the Tower of Babel, where language became confused and nations were separated by misunderstanding (Gen. 11:1–9). At Pentecost, the Holy Spirit gathered persons from every nation into one united fellowship. From Pentecost onward, the Holy Spirit directs the unfolding drama of the growth of the church.

Acts contains portraits of many outstanding Christians of the early church. Barnabas exemplifies generosity (4:36–37), Stephen forgiveness (7:60), Philip and Paul obedience (8:26; 26:19), Cornelius piety (10:2), and the witness of the early church vibrates with boldness (2:29; 4:13, 29, 31; 28:31). Ordinary people are empowered to perform extraordinary feats. A faltering apostle is empowered to address multitudes (2:14) or make a defense before rulers (4:8). A prayer fellowship is shaken (4:31); a deacon defends his faith by martyrdom (7:58). The despised Samaritans receive the Spirit (8:4–8), as does a Gentile soldier (10:1–48). A staunch persecutor of the gospel is converted (9:1–19), and through him the gospel reaches the capital of the world!

Paul reaches Rome in chains. Circumstances, too, may be adverse: persecutions (8:3–4; 11:19), famines (11:27–30), opposition (13:45), or violent storms (27:1–44). Through it all, however, the Holy Spirit directs the drama so that "all things work together for good" (Rom. 8:28) to further the cause of Christ.

Special Considerations.

Nearly one fifth of Acts consists of speeches, primarily from Peter, Stephen, and Paul. Common to each of the speeches is a basic framework of gospel proclamation. This proclamation can be outlined as follows:

1. The promises of God in the Old Testament are now fulfilled.

2. The Messiah has come in Jesus of Nazareth.
   a. He did good and mighty works by the power of God.
   b. He was crucified according to the purpose of God.
   c. He was raised from the dead by the power of God.
   d. He now reigns by the power of God.
   e. He will come again to judge and restore all things for the purpose of God.
3. All who hear should repent and be baptized.

This outline is our earliest example of the gospel proclaimed by the early church. It is the "foundation of the apostles and prophets, Jesus Christ Himself being the chief cornerstone" (Eph. 2:20), upon which the church is built. In this sense, the Book of Acts is not yet completed, for each generation is enabled by the Holy Spirit to add its chapters by proclaiming the "wonderful works of God" (2:11).

ALLEGORY—a symbolic representation of a truth about human conduct or experience. The word "allegory" is found only once in the King James Version. In Galatians 4:24 it translates the Greek verb *allegoreo*, which means to say something different from what the words normally imply. The NKJV translates it by the word "symbolic."

As a literary device, an allegory may consist of only a few lines or it may be sustained through an entire book. According to traditional Jewish and Christian interpretation, the entire book of the Song of Solomon is an allegory: of God and his wife, Israel (Jewish), or of Christ and his bride, the church (Christian). Other examples of allegory in the Old Testament are Psalm 80:8–19 and Ecclesiastes 12:3–7. In Psalm 80 the pronouns "we" and "us" identify the vine as Israel (vv. 18–19).

In the New Testament, Jesus' parable of the wheat and the tares (Matt. 13:24–30, 36–43) is a good example of allegory. The apostle Paul also used allegories when writing. In Ephesians

6:11–17 he urges his readers to "put on the whole armor of God" and then gives the symbolic spiritual designation for each article worn by the Christian soldier. And in 1 Corinthians 10:1–4, Paul gives an allegory that compares the experience of Moses and the Israelites to Christian baptism and the Lord's Supper.

Perhaps the most memorable of Paul's allegories, however, is found in Galatians 4:21–31: Hagar and Sarah, Ishmael and Isaac. One of them (Ishmael) was born to the bondwoman Hagar; the other (Isaac) was born to a freewoman, Sarah. Hagar and Ishmael are symbolic of the Old Covenant: the law from Mount Sinai that brings all people into bondage. Sarah and Isaac are symbolic of the New Covenant: the gospel of grace from Mount Calvary that gives spiritual freedom. When Paul concluded by saying, "So then, brethren, we are not children of the bondwoman but of the free [woman]," he was urging his readers to reject the bondage of legalism—salvation by keeping the law—and to live by faith in Christ.

A MOS, BOOK OF—a prophetic book of the Old Testament noted for its fiery denunciation of the northern kingdom of Israel during a time of widespread idol worship and indulgent living. The book is named for its author, the prophet Amos, whose name means "burden bearer." Amos lived up to his name as he declared God's message of judgment in dramatic fashion to a sinful and disobedient people.

Structure of the Book.

The nine chapters of the Book of Amos emphasize one central theme: The people of the nation of Israel have broken their Covenant with God, and His judgment against their sin will be severe. After a brief introduction of Amos as the prophet (1:1–2), the book falls naturally into three major sections: (1) judgment against the nations, including Judah and Israel (1:3–2:16); (2) sermons of judgment against Israel (3:1–6:14); and (3) visions of God's judgment (7:1–9:10). The book concludes with a promise of Israel's restoration (9:11–15), ultimately fulfilled in the church's mission to the Gentiles (Acts 15:15–21).

In the first major section of the book Amos begins with biting words of judgment against the six nations surrounding the lands of Judah and Israel. These nations (or their capitals) are Damascus (1:3–5), Gaza (1:6–8), Tyre (1:9–10), Edom (1:11–12), Ammon (1:13–15), and Moab (2:1–3). Next he announces God's judgment against Judah, Israel's sister nation to the south (2:4–5). Because of Israel's bitterness toward Judah, Amos' listeners must have greeted this cry of doom with pleasant agreement.

But Amos was only warming up to the main part of his sermon. Suddenly he launched into a vivid description of God's judgment against the nation of Israel. With biting sarcasm, Amos condemned the citizens of Israel for their oppression of the poor (2:7), worship of idols (2:8), rejection of God's salvation (2:9, 2:12), and defilement of the Lord's holy name (2:7). Hypocrisy, greed, and injustice prevailed throughout the land. True worship had been replaced by empty ritualism and dependence on pagan gods. And Amos made it plain that Israel would be judged severely unless the people turned from their sin and looked to the one true God for strength and guidance.

In the second major section of his book (3:1–6:14), Amos preached three biting sermons of judgment against the nation of Israel. He referred to the wealthy, luxury-seeking women of Samaria—the capital city of Israel—as "cows of Bashan" (4:1). He also attacked the system of idol worship that had been established in the cities of Bethel and Gilgal (4:4; 5:5).

Following these sermons of judgment, Amos moved on in the third major section of his book (7:1–9:10) to present five visions of God's approaching judgment. The prophet's vision of a basket of fruit is particularly graphic. He described the nation of Israel as a basket of summer fruit, implying that it would soon spoil and rot in the blistering sun of God's judgment (8:1–14).

Following these messages of judgment, the Book of Amos ends on a positive, optimistic note. Amos predicted that the people of Israel would be restored to their special place in God's service after their season of judgment had come to an end (9:11–15). This note of hope is characteristic of the Hebrew prophets. They pointed to a glorious future for God's people, even in the midst of dark times. This positive spirit, which issued from Amos' deep faith in God, sustained the prophet and gave him hope for the future.

Authorship and Date.

The author of this book was the prophet Amos, since it is clearly identified in the introduction as "the words of Amos" (1:1). Amos was a humble herdsman, or shepherd, of Tekoa (1:1), a village near Jerusalem in the southern kingdom of Judah. But God called him to deliver His message of judgment to the people who lived in Israel, Judah's sister nation to the north. Amos indicated in his book that he prophesied during the reigns of King Uzziah (Azariah) in Judah and King Jeroboam II in Israel (1:1). This places his prophecy at about 760 B.C. He must have written the book some time after this date, perhaps after returning to his home in Tekoa.

In one revealing passage in his book, Amos indicates that he was "no prophet, nor was I a son of a prophet, but I was a herdsman and a tender of sycamore fruit" (7:14). In spite of this humble background, he was called by God to preach His message of repentance and judgment to a rebellious nation (7:15–16). His unquestioning obedience and his clear proclamation of God's message show that he was committed to the Lord and His principles of holiness and righteousness. Amos' keen sense of justice and fairness also comes through clearly in the book.

Historical Setting.

Amos prophesied during the reign of Jeroboam II of Israel (793–753 B.C.), a time of peace and prosperity. The prophet speaks of the excessive luxury of the wealthy (6:3–7), who had no concern for the needs of the poor. Religiously, the nation had departed from the worship of the one true God. Jeroboam encouraged the practice of fertility cults, mixing an element of Baal worship with Israel's faith in their Lord of the Covenant. The situation clearly called for a courageous prophet who could call the nation back to authentic faith as well as a policy of fairness and justice in their dealings with their fellow citizens.

Theological Contribution.

Amos is known as the great "prophet of righteousness" of the Old Testament. His book underlines the principle that religion demands righteous behavior. True religion is not a matter of observing all the right feast days, offering burnt offerings, and worshiping at the sanctuary. Authentic worship results in changed behavior—seeking God's will, treating others with justice, and following God's commands. This great insight is summarized by these famous words from the prophet: "Let justice run down like water, and righteousness like a mighty stream" (5:24).

Special Considerations.

Although Amos was a shepherd by occupation, his book gives evidence of careful literary craftsmanship. One technique that he used was puns or plays on words to drive home his message. Unfortunately, they do not translate easily into English. In his vision of the summer fruit, for example, Amos spoke of the coming of God's judgment with a word that sounds very similar to the Hebrew word for fruit (8:1–2). The "summer fruit" (*qayits*) suggested the "end" (*qets*) of the kingdom of Israel (NRSV). Like "ripe" summer fruit, Israel was "ripe" for God's judgment.

Another literary device that Amos used in his sermons of judgment against the nations is known as numerical parallelism: "For three transgressions ... and for four ..." (1:3). He repeated this phrase seven times as he covered the sins of the various nations around Israel (1:3, 6, 9, 11, 13; 2:1, 4). The reader can almost feel the suspense building until the prophet reaches the dramatic climax of his sermon: "For three transgressions of Israel, and for four, I will not turn away its punishment, because they sell the righteous for silver, and the poor for a pair of sandals" (2:6).

The Book of Amos is one of the most eloquent cries for justice and righteousness to be found in the Bible. And it came through a humble shepherd who dared to deliver God's message to the wealthy and influential people of his day. His message is just as timely for our world, since God still places a higher value on justice and righteousness than on silver and gold and the things that money will buy.

APOCALYPTIC LITERATURE [a pock uh LIP tik]—a certain type of Jewish and Christian literature written in Egypt and Palestine during the period from 200 B.C. to A.D. 200. The word *apocalypsis* is a Greek word meaning "revelation." Therefore, apocalyptic literature is a special kind of writing that arose among the Jews and Christians to reveal certain mysteries about heaven and earth, humankind and God, angels and demons, the life of the world today, and the world to come.

Apocalyptic literature probably arose in the tradition of the Prophets of Israel, but it came several centuries after their time. The last prophet of Israel, Malachi, wrote about 450 B.C. Two books in the Bible—the Book of Daniel in the Old Testament and the New Testament Book of Revelation—are good examples of the apocalyptic literary form.

The following additional Jewish and Christian books are also classified as apocalyptic by most Bible scholars:

Apocalypse of Abraham, Apocalypse of Baruch, Ascension of Isaiah, Assumption of Moses, 2 Baruch, Book of Jubilees, 1 and 2 Enoch, Life of Adam and Eve, the Sybilline Oracles, Testament of Abraham, and the Testaments of the 12 Patriarchs. Most of these books are found in the Pseudepigrapha of the Old Testament.

In 1974 several apocalyptic books and fragments were found among the Dead Sea Scrolls, including the War Scroll and Book of Mysteries. In the second and third century A.D., Christian writers produced a number of apocalypses, including The Revelation of Peter, The Revelation of Paul, and The Revelation of Thomas. All these writings are included in a collection known as the New Testament Apocrypha.

Most of the apocalyptic books were written by Jews in reaction to the oppression of their people by foreign powers. Often they wrote to explain why evil seemed to prosper while the righteous suffered. The Christian apocalyptic writings were influenced by these earlier Jewish works. The Book of Revelation in the New Testament uses symbols and images that occur in the Book of Enoch, and the book known as 4 Ezra, written about A.D. 100, seems to parallel the New Testament book of Revelation in several ways. The close similarities between Jewish and Christian apocalyptic literature explains why scholars group them into one category and study both Jewish and Christian apocalyptic literature together.

Characteristics.

Apocalyptic literature has certain literary devices or styles that set it apart from other literature.

Visions—Although other types of literature use visions to communicate (see Isaiah 6), apocalyptic literature uses visions as a way of revealing secrets from heaven about the present and the future of humankind. Often these visions are caused by some trauma or major personal or social event that created a crisis in the writer's experience (compare Rev. 1:10 with 4 Ezra

3:1). These visions lead in turn to further explanations about coming events or other visions and dreams.

Ethics—As a result of these visionary experiences, the writer draws ethical conclusions. In Revelation 2–3, John writes seven letters to seven churches in western Asia Minor. Each letter is addressed to specific issues facing the church. These letters were written after John saw a vision and was commissioned by God to write (Rev. 1:19). They call the churches to specific ethical or moral decisions.

Pseudonymous authorship—The Book of Revelation in the New Testament is the only book of apocalyptic literature that gives the name of the author. All other apocalyptic books are attributed to famous prophets of the past, such as Ezra, Enoch, Baruch, Jeremiah, Abraham, Moses, and Adam. The reason why these authors identified their writings with great persons in Israel's history probably was to add credibility to their work. A vision from Enoch, for example, would carry more weight than if it were from some contemporary writer.

Powerful symbolism—Each of the apocalyptic books is rich in symbolism. The reader's imagination is stretched. Those who read the apocalyptic books just after they had been written knew the meaning of the symbols used by the author. The events of the time, evil rulers, and pagan nations are symbolized by distorted animals and beasts, horrible signs from heaven, or a chaotic flowing of waters. But the people who are faithful to God are portrayed as majestic animals, like a lion, or a well kept plant. The purpose of this symbolism was to make the contrast between good and evil obvious to the reader.

Messages.

Through the apocalyptic books, the authors communicated several important messages to their readers. The following themes occur in all the apocalyptic writings.

The end is coming soon—Throughout these books the authors write about the arrival of the end times within the near future: "For the youth of this world is past, and the strength of the creation already exhausted and the advent of the times is very short, yea, they have passed by: and the pitcher is near to the cistern, and the ship to the port, and the course of the journey to the city, and life to its consummation" (2 Baruch 85:10).

In the other books various images are used to spell out the coming end. This apocalyptic view of the last days gives a certain urgency to these writings.

The whole universe involved—The end of the world is not a solitary event for the earth alone; it extends to the whole universe. This planet is only a part of a greater tragedy. An awful time is in store, for all nations of the earth will "be seized with great panic" (4 Ezra 5:1).

History divided into fixed segments—Along with a pessimistic view of history, the apocalyptic books declare that history has been determined by God before creation. World history is divided into fixed time periods. These fixed segments have been established, and mankind simply lives out the already established drama.

History may be divided into two periods—this age, which is ruled by Satan and his legions, and the age to come, in which wickedness will be abolished and God will rule supreme.

Angels and demons—Apocalyptic literature is filled with angels and demons who are actively involved in the drama of events. The problem of evil is explained by pointing to the demons and Satan himself as the forces that cause evil. Angels who have not fallen (1 Enoch 6–36) are used by God to protect and serve his faithful people. The Books of Enoch, Testament of the Twelve Patriarchs, and Jubilees give detailed descriptions of the task of angels and demons. These truths are also echoed by the Book of Revelation in the New Testament.

The New Heaven and the New Earth.

The end times as portrayed in the apocalyptic writings return to the beginning of creation. Out of heaven will come a new heaven and a new earth. The old will be destroyed, replaced by a new creation where God will rule (Revelation 20–22; 2 Enoch 65:7–10; 2 Baruch 48). Only those who have been faithful to God's law will be saved.

The Kingdom of God.

Enoch 41 describes the place from which all the world will be judged. Other apocalyptic books describe the Kingdom of God as the ultimate rule in the new creation (Enoch 84:3; Rev. 11:15; Dan. 4:17). All through the apocalyptic literature the image of the Kingdom or rule of God is central. All events are determined from God's throne.

A Messiah.

A Messiah or mediator between God and humankind appears in most of the apocalyptic writings as one who accomplishes the final salvation of the world. This figure appears either as a Messiah, a son of man, a chosen one, or a mediator.

Glory.

The righteous have suffered in this world because it has been ruled by Satan. But this situation will change in the future. This vision of glory appears as a word of hope or encouragement to the faithful—those who trust in God. Glory will come to God's people. They have the power necessary to live full and meaningful lives in this world now.

A POCRYPHA, THE [A POCK rih fuh]—a group of books written during a time of turmoil in the history of the Jewish people, from about 190 B.C. to about A.D. 210. These books fall into two main divisions, Old Testament apocryphal books and New Testament apocryphal books.

The Old Testament books, 15 in number, were written during the period from about 190 B.C. to about A.D. 70, when the Jewish people were in rebellion against the repression of foreign military rulers. These books were excluded from some early versions of the Old Testament but included in others. This explains why Bibles used by Roman Catholics contain the Old Testament Apocrypha, while they are not included in most Protestant editions of the Bible.

The books known as the New Testament Apocrypha were written during the second and third centuries A.D., long after the death of the apostles and other eyewitnesses to the life and ministry of Jesus. None of these books were included in the New Testament because they were judged as unworthy and not authoritative by officials of the early church.

The Old Testament Apocrypha.

The series of events that led to the writing of the Old Testament apocryphal books began in 167 B.C., when the Jews revolted against the king of Syria, Antiochus IV Epiphanes. A pious Jewish priest, Mattathias, and his sons led the rebellion. Mattathias refused to obey Antiochus' command that the Jews worship his gods and offer a pagan sacrifice. Mattathias killed the Syrian official as well as a fellow Jew who was offering the sacrifice and declared: "Follow me, every one of you who is zealous for the law and strives to maintain the covenant. He and his sons took to the hills, leaving all their belongings behind in the town" (1 Macc. 2:27–28, REB).

Guerrilla warfare against the Syrians followed, until the Jews established control of Palestine. Early in the revolt one of the sons of Mattathias, Judas Maccabeus (Maccabeus means "hammerer"), cleansed the Temple in Jerusalem from the pollution of the Syrian sacrifices. This day has been celebrated annually by the Jews since that time in the festival known as Chanukah (or Hanukkah), the Feast of Dedication (John 10:22).

These events helped stir the Jewish people to rededicate themselves to the law of Moses. In the fight to establish their independence and uphold their traditions, some Jewish authors wrote to encourage their own people. The apocryphal books show clearly that the authors were enthusiastic for faith in God and the study of His Word.

From 142 to 63 B.C. the Jews were led in their rebellion against foreign oppression by the family of Mattathias, known as the Hasmoneans. Simon Asamonaios was the grandfather of Mattathias, and his name was applied to all the members of this great family. In spite of the respect given to the Hasmoneans in the early years of their influence, civil strife again plagued the Jews. The Syrians continued to fight for power over the land of Israel. Judas Maccabeus finally made an agreement with Rome that the Romans would come to the aid of the Jews if they should need assistance in their struggle. About a century later some of the Jews did appeal to Rome for help. Pompey, a powerful Roman general, brought order to Jerusalem and made Judea part of a Roman province.

In 37 B.C. the land of Israel, called Palestine, was placed under the rule of a Roman official, Herod the Great (37–4 B.C.). Herod was actually a Roman vassal and was hated by most of the Jews. In spite of this hostility, Herod managed to launch an ambitious building program in Palestine. He created the magnificent port city of Caesarea on the Mediterranean Sea and improved the Temple in Jerusalem. The western wall still stands today in Jerusalem as evidence of Herod's skill as a builder.

After Herod's death (4 B.C.), his sons divided Palestine into four regions, ruling the land with varying degrees of success. In A.D. 66 the Jews again grew angry over the foreign domination of their land. Under the encouragement of radical freedom fighters known as Zealots, the Jews started a disastrous war with the Romans. This led to the destruction of Jerusalem and the Temple in A.D. 70 and the end of the Jewish nation.

This brief historical sketch provides the background for the Old Testament apocryphal writings. The Jewish people were continually wondering what God was saying to them through their struggles. Out of their experiences arose the books of the Apocrypha. Following are brief descriptions of the books in this Old Testament collection.

Baruch—This book is a collection of materials written during the period from 150 B.C. to 60 B.C. Set in the period of the prophet Jeremiah and his secretary Baruch around 585 B.C., it actually speaks to Jews who were living during the period of the Hasmoneans (142–63 B.C.). It was written originally in Hebrew and later was translated into Greek.

Baruch contains a letter (1:1–14), a prayer-sermon (1:15–3:8), a hymn (3:9–4:4), and a lament (4:5–5:9). Jerusalem had fallen into the hands of the enemy, but this book declared that God will not forget His people. The refrain, "Take courage, my children, Cry out to God, and he will deliver you from the power and hand of the enemy." (4:21, REB), echoes throughout Baruch. Some scholars believe Baruch was reworked many times and then was put into its final form by a rabbi in Palestine after the destruction of the Temple in A.D. 70.

Bel and the Dragon—This book is an addition to the Old Testament's Book of Daniel and was written by a Jew in Palestine around 50 B.C. The author used Babylonian mythology to declare that the God of the Hebrews can outwit the tricks of the priests of Babylon through the faith of the prophet Daniel. Daniel demonstrated that there is no God other than the Lord God of the Hebrews and that Bel, the supposed God of Babylon, does not exist. In this book Daniel also killed a dragon in a clever way. This was the author's way of showing that pagan gods are worshiped because the priests deceive the people. Only God is worthy of our praise, because He is a living God.

Ecclesiasticus, or the Wisdom of Jesus, Son of Sirach—This is a book of wisdom teachings in the Apocrypha. It should not be confused with the Book of Ecclesiastes in the Old Testament. The word Ecclesiasticus means "The Church Book" in Latin. But the title of the Book of Ecclesiastes comes from a Greek word that means "assembly" or "gathering."

Ecclesiasticus is a masterpiece of wisdom literature, organized into teachable units. Many subjects are contained in this work, including faith in God as Creator and Sustainer of life, love of wisdom and ethical conduct, virtue and good deeds, the value of the tradition of the past, proper behavior in eating and drinking, work and commerce, study and teaching, poverty and wealth, and health and sickness. It was written by Jesus ben Eleazar ben Sira, a Jew living in Jerusalem around 190 B.C.

The author of Ecclesiasticus upholds Israel's traditions as a channel through which God's Word is communicated. His essay on the great people in Israel's history gives the reader an appreciation for the kind of people who make our world pleasant and worthwhile. The righteous person receives a reward from God, while the sinner and unbeliever will be punished. The final chapter, 51, contains a beautiful prayer.

Esdras, Books of—The First Book of Esdras is a historical narrative taken from 2 Chronicles 35:1; 36:23; Ezra 1:1–11; 2:1–3:13; 4:1–10:44; and Nehemiah 7:73–8:12 of the Old Testament. It begins with the Passover celebrated by Josiah, the king of Judah (640–609 B.C.). Then the book discusses Josiah's death in the battle of Megiddo and continues with the story of the events leading up to the fall of Jerusalem and the deportation of the Jews to Babylon (586 B.C.). Cyrus, the great king of the Medes who freed the Jews from bondage in Babylon in 539 B.C., is also described.

Included in the Book of 1 Esdras is a description of the building of the Temple by the returned exiles in Jerusalem and the problems encountered in its reconstruction. An interesting part of the story is the trouble that the Jews had with the Samaritans. Thus, 1 Esdras provides an excellent background for a better understanding of the conflict between the Jews and Samaritans—a problem mentioned throughout the four gospels in the New Testament.

The story of the three young men (1 Esdras 3:1–5:6) who guarded the Persian King Darius I (522–486 B.C.) is an interesting drama. The guards were instructed to write down what they considered to be the most powerful thing on earth. Their answers and the surprise fourth answer (trust) make this book a delightful contribution to the wisdom writings of the Jewish people.

The purpose of the book of 1 Esdras was to promote the value of worship of the Lord among Jews. It was probably written during the time of the Hasmoneans, about 150 B.C., by a zealous Jew who held to this worship tradition and encouraged others to do the same.

The Second Book of Esdras was probably written during the same period as the Book of Revelation in the New Testament, around A.D. 96, by a Palestinian Jew who was disillusioned over the destruction of the Temple of Jerusalem in A.D. 70. He was puzzled by the apparent evil in a world where God was supposed to be in control.

The word "Babylon" in 2 Esdras is a code name for Rome. According to the writer, Rome had become evil in A.D. 96–100. The book is a good example of Jewish Apocalyptic Literature. In many ways it is like the Book of Revelation in the New Testament. The revelations in the book lament the destruction of Jerusalem and deal with the questions of the reward of the righteous, the punishment of the wicked, and the end of the age.

This gloomy book is tied together with a thread of hope. Deliverance for God's people is assured. God is ultimately in control of history, and His Word (in written form) will never disappear.

Esther, Additions to—The Old Testament Book of Esther does not mention the name of God or any worship rituals. Most scholars agree that these apocryphal additions to the Book of Esther were written to connect Esther to the traditions of Israel's faith in a more explicit way.

Jeremiah, Epistle of—This letter is a sermon against idolatry. It asks the readers to beware of false gods. The date of its writing is unknown, although some scholars have suggested a date as early as 541 B.C. Others believe it was written during the time of the invasion of Palestine by the Romans in 63 B.C. Some fragments of the letter were discovered among the Dead Sea Scrolls in the caves of Qumran.

Judith—This book contains one of the most delightful stories in the Apocrypha. A wise and intelligent Jewish woman, Judith was devoted to observing the law of Moses. The story takes place during the reign of a king of Assyria named Nebuchadnezzar. His general, Holophernes, was about to destroy the Jewish inhabitants of the city of Bethulia when Judith came to the aid of her fellow Jews. The people prayed to God for help, allowing Him five days in which to help them, or they would surrender (1:1–7:32). Judith went to the enemy camp and beheaded Holophernes, bringing his head back to the Jews of the city. Terrified, the Assyrians fled (8:1–16:25), and the Jews were saved.

Judith appealed to Jews living during a time of discouragement and defeat. It was probably written during the Hasmonean period (142–63 B.C.). Judith emphasized the importance of faithfulness to the law of Moses and the power of God in the lives of His people.

Maccabees, Books of—The First Book of Maccabees is a history of the struggle of the Jews in Judea under the leadership of one family, the Hasmoneans, from about 175 to 135 B.C. Judas Maccabeus was the family's most famous leader. Most of the action took place in and around Jerusalem. The book includes speeches, prayers, laments, and psalms of victory, all woven into a beautiful history of the Jews of that period. The author was probably a Jew living in Jerusalem who supported the Maccabean revolt and the importance of the law of Moses. Some scholars suggest that one of the members of the family of the Maccabees wrote the book, some time during the period from 103 to 63 B.C. The theme of the book is that faithful obedience to the law brings success by God's standards.

The Second Book of Maccabees is a two-part work that describes the events that occurred in Judea from 191 to 162 B.C. In a sense, it serves as a prelude to the Book of 1 Maccabees. The first part of the book (1:1–2:18) consists of two letters. One of the letters (1:1–10) was from Jews in Jerusalem to Jews in Egypt, telling them how to observe the Jewish holiday of Chanukah (or Hanukkah) which celebrates the cleansing of the Temple under Judas Maccabeus in 164 B.C. The other letter (1:10–2:18) was sent by the same group of Jews in Jerusalem to Aristobulus, a Jewish teacher in Egypt, encouraging him to celebrate the Temple festival.

The second section of the Second Book of Maccabees (2:19–15:39) describes events in Judea from 191 to 162 B.C. A good description of the celebration of Chanukah (Hanukkah) appears in 10:1–9. The entire book is important because of its teaching that the world was created "out of nothing" (7:28), and its clear statement of belief in the resurrection of the dead (7:9, 14, 23, 29).

Prayer of Azariah and the Song of the Three Young Men— This brief book is included in the Apocrypha because it represents an addition to the Old Testament Book of Daniel. It probably was written about 150 B.C. by a pious Jew who expanded the famous story in Daniel 3 about Shadrach, Meshach, and Abed-Nego—the three young Jews who were thrown into the fiery furnace by the king of Babylon. According to this addition to the biblical account, Azariah (Abed-Nego) began to pray while they were in the fire (vv. 1–22). After the prayer, all three began to sing as they stood in the flames

(vv. 28–68). Their songs came from various psalms of the Jewish people.

Prayer of Manasseh—This book is an addition to the Old Testament Book of 2 Chronicles. Manasseh was one of the most wicked kings in Israel's history. He burned his sons as offerings (2 Chr. 33:6) and practiced magic. After a humiliating defeat in battle, Manasseh repented of his sin, and God forgave him (2 Chr. 33:10–13). The Prayer of Manasseh was probably written later by a pious Jew who blended various psalms and prayers into this beautiful prayer of repentance.

The outline of the prayer follows a typical outline for a worship service: invocation and praise to God (vv. 1–7), confession of sins (vv. 8–12), a request for forgiveness (v. 13), and a concluding thanksgiving (vv. 14–15).

Song of the Three Young Men (see Prayer of Azariah).

Susanna—This book is an addition to the Old Testament Book of Daniel. It is full of suspenseful tragedy and wisdom. Written around 110–60 B.C. by a Jew in Palestine, the story is about a woman named Susanna, who was nearly sexually abused by two respected elders of the community. Susanna was brought to court by the elders on a charge of adultery. She stood condemned and sentenced to death until Daniel raised an objection and proved that the two elders had lied.

This is a powerful story that challenges the normal method of taking evidence in Jewish courts during the first century B.C. Susanna is important because it gives insights into the Jewish legal process during that time and because it supports another view of how evidence can be taken from a witness.

Tobit—This book is a narrative about Tobit, a Jew who was taken into captivity to Nineveh, the capital of Assyria, after the defeat of Israel in 722 B.C. Tobit was a strict observer of the law of Moses who met with unfortunate circumstances. One night he was blinded by droppings from a swallow that fell into his eyes. God heard the prayers of Tobit and another Jew, Sarah, who was living to the east in Babylon or Media. God sent his angel, Raphael, to save them both. Through Tobit's son Tobias and the angel Raphael, God was able to help Tobit and Sarah. The story ends happily as Tobias marries Sarah and defeats a demon named Asmodeus and the two reestablish order in their lives. Tobit was written to show the place of fasting and prayer in the lives of the faithful. It teaches that God breaks into human history, using His angels to rescue people.

Wisdom of Solomon—This book, along with the Book of Ecclesiaticus in the Apocrypha, is similar to the Book of Proverbs in the Old Testament. Classified as wisdom books, all these works are profound in their understanding and insight into practical matters of daily life. The Wisdom of Solomon was named after the great wise man of Israel, King Solomon, who reigned from 970 to 931 B.C. Solomon was the model for all wise people who followed him. Many proverbs or wise sayings written many centuries after Solomon, such as this book, were attributed to him. It was composed some time around 100 to 50 B.C.

The Wisdom of Solomon is organized into various topics for convenient use by those who study the book. The first section (1:1–5:23) declares that wisdom is given only to a righteous person. The second section (6:1–9:18) deals with political issues, such as God's part in judging the wicked rulers. The third section (10:1–19:21) deals with the actions of God among His people, His protection of Israel, and His punishment of their enemies.

The whole book assumes that as Creator, God is actively involved in human affairs. Wisdom comes from God and is necessary for preservation and creativity in this world. Immortality awaits those who live by this wisdom.

Remains of Antioch of Syria, capital of the dynasty that ruled Palestine during the era of the Maccabees and the writing of much of the Old Testament Apocrypha.

The New Testament Apocrypha.

The New Testament Apocrypha contains several writings that were similar to New Testament books but were not included as a part of the New Testament. These writings were greatly influenced by the philosophies and religions of the cities or nations out of which they came. Some of the apocryphal gospels were written to replace the gospels of the New Testament but were declared false writings by officials of the early church.

Often the apocryphal books from the early history of the church present stories and legends meant to fill in information about the apostles and Jesus that is lacking in the New Testament. For example, some New Testament apocryphal works claim to give details on the childhood of Jesus (Protevangelium of James, The Gospel of Thomas) as well as a description of how Jesus was raised from the dead (The Gospel of Peter). These writings expand on the accounts found in the New Testament.

Other apocryphal writings that expand or explain the gospel stories include The Gospel of the Egyptians, The Gospel of Truth, The Gospel of the Twelve, The Gospel of Philip, The Gospel of Judas, The Gospel of Bartholomew, The Gospel According to Mary, The Gospel of Nicodemus, and The Questions of Bartholomew. These are only a few of the 59 fragments and gospel-related writings in the New Testament Apocrypha.

The Acts of the Apostles in the New Testament is also paralleled by several apocryphal books. These include stories about the apostles themselves written in the second and third century. Titles of some of these books are The Acts of John, The Acts of Peter, The Acts of Paul, The Acts of Andrew and The Acts of Thomas.

The Acts of John, for example, tells the story of the disciple, John, his journey from Jerusalem to Rome, and his imprisonment on an island off the coast of modern-day Turkey called Patmos (see Rev. 1:9). Other travels of this apostle appear in the book, and he finally dies in Ephesus. Some scholars believe these second-century books may be based on some historical facts. They do give Bible researchers a better understanding of the origin of the early church.

The last group of New Testament apocryphal writings consists of Apocalyptic books. The New Testament Book of Revelation inspired the early Christians to write their own books that were similar in content and style. Probably the most popular of the apocryphal apocalypses are the Apocalypse of Peter, the Apocalypse of Paul, and the Apocalypse of Thomas. These apocalypses give Bible scholars a clear picture of the early Christian's view of heaven and hell, since they emphasize the state of sinners after death.

While these apocryphal New Testament books are interesting and informative, none are considered authoritative like the books of the New Testament. For various reasons, these books were judged unworthy and were not accepted as authoritative when the New Testament took its final form in the third century A.D. Thus, God has worked throughout history not only to inspire the Bible but also to preserve its authenticity and integrity so it can serve as a standard and guide for all believers.

The individual books of the Old Testament Apocrypha are arranged in alphabetical order in the accompanying article. But here is the order in which these 15 books are generally arranged in Bibles that contain the Apocrypha:

1. First Esdras
2. Second Esdras
3. Tobit
4. Judith
5. The Additions to Esther
6. The Wisdom of Solomon
7. Ecclesiasticus, or the Wisdom of Jesus, the Son of Sirach
8. Baruch

9. The Letter of Jeremiah
10. The Prayer of Azariah and the Song of the Three Young Men
11. Susanna
12. Bel and the Dragon
13. The Prayer of Manasseh
14. First Maccabees
15. Second Maccabees

B

BIBLE, THE—the sacred Book, or collection of books, accepted by the Christian church as uniquely inspired by God, and thus authoritative, providing guidelines for belief and behavior.

Major Divisions.

The Bible contains two major sections known as the Old Testament and the New Testament. The books of the Old Testament were written over a period of about 1,000 years in the Hebrew language, except for a few selected passages, which were written in Aramaic. The Old Testament tells of the preparation that was made for Christ's coming.

The New Testament was written over a period of about 60 years. The original language in which it was written was Greek. This portion of the Bible tells of Christ's coming, His life and ministry, and the growth of the early church.

The English word "testament" normally refers to a person's will, the document that bequeaths property to those who will inherit it after the owner's death. But the meaning of "testament" from both the Hebrew and the Greek languages is "settlement," "treaty," or "covenant." Of these three English words, Covenant best captures the meaning of the word "testament." Thus, the two collections that make up the Bible can best be described as the books of the old covenant and the books of the new covenant.

The old covenant is the covenant sealed at Mount Sinai in the days of Moses. By this covenant, the living and true God, who had delivered the Israelites from slavery in Egypt, promised to bless them as His special people. They were also to worship Him alone as their God and to accept His law as their rule for life (Ex. 19:3–6; 24:3–8).

The new covenant was announced by Jesus as he spoke to His disciples in the upper room in Jerusalem the night before His death. When He gave them a cup of wine to drink, Jesus declared that this symbolized "the new covenant in My blood" (Luke 22:20; 1 Cor. 11:25).

Between the times of Moses and Jesus, the prophet Jeremiah foresaw a day when God would make a new covenant with His people. Under this new covenant, God would inscribe His laws on the hearts of people rather than on tablets of stone (Jer. 31:31–34). In the New Testament, this new covenant of which Jeremiah spoke is identified with the covenant inaugurated by Jesus (Heb. 8:6–13).

While these two covenants, the old and the new, launched great spiritual movements, Christians believe these movements are actually two phases of one great act through which God has revealed His will to His people and called for their positive response. The second covenant is the fulfillment of what was promised in the first.

In the form in which it has been handed down among the Jewish people, the Old Testament, or Hebrew Bible, contains three divisions: the Law, the Prophets, and the Writings. The Law consists of Genesis, Exodus, Leviticus, Numbers, and Deuteronomy; this section of the Old Testament is also known as the Pentateuch. The Prophets fall into two subdivisions: the former prophets (Joshua, Judges, First and Second Samuel, and First and Second Kings) and the latter prophets (Isaiah,

Jeremiah, Ezekiel, and the Book of the Twelve Prophets—Hosea through Malachi). The rest of the books are gathered together in the Writings: Psalms, Proverbs, Job, Song of Solomon, Ruth, Lamentations, Ecclesiastes, Esther, Daniel, Ezra–Nehemiah (counted as one book), and First and Second Chronicles.

The arrangement of the Old Testament with which readers today are most familiar has been inherited from the pre-Christian Greek translation of the Old Testament (the Septuagint), an arrangement that was also followed by the later Latin Bible (the Vulgate). This arrangement has four divisions: the Pentateuch, the historical books, poetry, and prophecy. The 39 books in this latter arrangement, however, are exactly the same as the 24 of Jewish tradition.

The New Testament opens with five narrative books—the four gospels and the Acts of the Apostles. The gospels deal with the ministry, death, and resurrection of Jesus. The Book of Acts continues the story of the development of the early church across the next 30 years. Acts serves as a sequel to the gospels in general; originally it was written as a sequel to the Gospel of Luke in particular.

Twenty-one letters, or epistles, follow the historical narratives. Thirteen of these letters bear the name of the apostle Paul as writer, while the remaining eight are the work of other apostles or of authors associated with apostles. The last book in the New Testament, the Revelation of John, portrays through visions and symbolic language the accomplishment of God's purpose in the world and the ultimate triumph of Christ.

Authority of the Bible.

The authority of the Bible follows naturally from its inspiration. It is implied by its title, "the Word of God." It is the written record of the Word of God that came to prophets, apostles, and other spokesmen, and that "became flesh" in Jesus Christ. Christians believe Jesus Christ was the Word of God in a unique sense. Through Jesus, God communicated the perfect revelation of Himself to mankind (Heb. 1:1–3). For Christians the authority of the Bible is related to the authority of Christ. The Old Testament was the Bible that Jesus used—the authority to which He made constant appeal and whose teachings He followed and proclaimed. When Jesus was arrested in the Garden of Gethsemane and led away to His execution, He submitted with the words, "The Scriptures must be fulfilled" (Mark 14:49). He saw His mission in the world as a fulfillment of the predictions of the Old Testament.

The New Testament presents the record of Jesus' life, teachings, death, and resurrection; a narrative of the beginning of the Christian church with the coming of the Holy Spirit; and the story of the extension of the gospel and the planting of the church during the following generation. It also contains the written teachings of Jesus' apostles and other early Christians who applied the principles of His teaching and redemptive work to their lives.

Revelation and Response.

According to the Bible, God has made Himself known in a variety of ways. "The heavens declare the glory of God" (Ps. 19:1). "For since the creation of the world His invisible attributes are clearly seen, being understood by the things that are made, even His eternal power and Godhead" (Rom. 1:20). But while God is revealed in His creation and through the inner voice of human conscience, the primary means by which He has made Himself known is through the Bible.

God has revealed Himself through His mighty acts and in the words of His messengers, or spokesmen. Either of these ways is incomplete without the other. In the Old Testament record, none of the mighty acts of God is emphasized more than the Exodus—God's deliverance of the Israelites from Egyptian bondage. As He delivered His people, God repeatedly identified Himself as their redeemer God: "I am the LORD your God, who brought you out of the land of Egypt, out of the house of bondage. You shall have no other gods before Me" (Ex. 20:2–3).

If they had been delivered with no explanation, the people of Israel would have learned little about the God who redeemed His people. The Israelites might have guessed that in such events as the plagues of Egypt and the parting of the waters of the Red Sea, some supernatural power was at work on their behalf. But they would not have known the nature of this power or God's purpose for them as a people.

God also communicated with His people, the nation of Israel, through Moses, to whom He had already made Himself known in the vision of the burning bush. God instructed Moses to tell his fellow Israelites what had been revealed to him. This was no impersonal force at work, but the God of their ancestors, Abraham, Isaac, and Jacob. In fulfillment of His promises to them, God was acting now on behalf of their descendants.

In communicating with His people, God revealed both His identity and His purpose. His purpose was to make the Israelites a nation dedicated to His service alone. This message, conveyed to the Israelites through Moses, would have been ineffective if God had not delivered them personally. On the other hand, His deliverance would have been meaningless without the message. Together both constituted the Word of God to the Israelites— the saving message of the God who both speaks and acts.

This pattern of God's mighty acts and the prophetic word interacting with each other continues throughout the course of biblical history. The Babylonian Captivity is a good example of this process. A succession of prophets warned the people that if they did not mend their ways, Captivity would come on them as judgment. But even during the years of the Captivity the prophets continued to speak, encouraging the captives and promising that God would deliver them from their plight.

The prophets were God's primary spokesmen to the people of Israel in Old Testament times. But they were not His only messengers. Priests and sages, or wise men, were other agents through whom God's will was made known. The teachings of many of these messengers are preserved in the Bible.

In addition to God's revelation of Himself through the Bible, God's Word also records the response of those to whom the revelation was given. Too often the response was unbelief and disobedience. But at other times, people responded in faith and obedience. The Psalms, especially, proclaim the grateful response of people who experienced the grace and righteousness of God. These faithful people sometimes voiced their appreciation in words addressed directly to God. At other times they reported to others what God had come to mean to them.

In the New Testament writings, revelation and response came together in the person of Jesus Christ. On the one hand, Jesus was God's perfect revelation of Himself—He was the divine Word in human form (John 1:1, 14). His works of mercy and power portrayed God in action, especially His supreme act of sacrifice to bring about "the redemption that is in Christ Jesus" (Rom. 3:24). His teaching expressed the mind of God.

The words and acts of Jesus also proclaimed the meaning and purpose of His works. For example, His act of casting out demons "with the finger of God" (Luke 11:20) was a token that the kingdom of God had come upon them. He also declared that His death, which he interpreted as the fulfillment of prophetic Scripture (Mark 14:49), was "a ransom for many" (Mark 10:45).

In his life and ministry, Jesus also illustrated the perfect human response of faith and obedience to God. Jesus was "the Apostle [God's Messenger to us] and High Priest [our Representative with God] of our confession" (Heb. 3:1). Thus, Jesus performed the mighty acts of God and He spoke authoritatively as God's Messenger and Prophet.

Preservation of the Bible.

The Bible is a written, authoritative record by which any teaching or theory may be judged. But behind the writing lay periods of time when these messages were circulated in spoken form. The stories of the patriarchs were passed from generation to generation by word of mouth before they were written. The messages of the prophets were delivered orally before they were fixed in writing. Narratives of the life and ministry of Christ were repeated orally for two or three decades before they were given literary form. But in part, the Bible owes its preservation to the fact that oral narratives were eventually reduced to writing. Just as God originally inspired the Bible, He has used this means to preserve His Word for future generations.

The first person in the Bible to write anything down was Moses. God instructed Moses to write as a permanent memorial the divine vow that the name of Amalek would be blotted out (Ex. 17:14). From that time until the end of the New Testament age, the writing of the many books and parts of the Bible continued.

None of the original biblical documents—referred to by scholars as the "original autographs"—has survived. No scrap of parchment or papyrus bearing the handwriting of any of the biblical authors has been discovered. But before the original documents disappeared, they were copied. Scribes exercised the utmost care as they laboriously and lovingly copied the Scriptures and handed them down from generation to generation. Their best copies are the texts on which current translations of the Bible are based.

The process of copying and recopying the Bible has continued to our time. Until the middle of the 15th century A.D., all the copying was done by hand. Then, with the invention of printing in Europe, copies could be made in greater quantities by using this new process. Each copy of the Bible had to be produced slowly by hand with the old system, but now the printing press could produce thousands of copies in a short time. This made the Scriptures available to many people, rather than just the few who could afford handmade copies.

The older handwritten copies of Bible texts are called manuscripts. Early manuscripts for the books of the Bible were written on papyrus or skin. Papyrus was a type of ancient paper manufactured from a reed plant that grew in the Nile Valley and similar environments. Papyrus was inexpensive, but it was not very durable. It rotted quickly when exposed to dampness.

The ancient papyrus manuscripts that have been discovered were found in the dry sands of Egypt and other arid places. Great quantities of inscribed papyri have been recovered from the Egyptian sands during the last hundred years dating from the period shortly before and after the beginning of the Christian era, about A.D. 30. A few scraps of papyri containing ancient texts of the Bible have been among the recovered manuscripts.

The skins of animals proved to be a much more durable writing material than papyrus. Many different writing materials were manufactured from such skins. Some were a coarse form of leather. Others were subjected to a special refining process, emerging as a writing material known as parchment. Vellum, another valued writing material, was made from calfskin. Some of the most important manuscripts of the Bible were written on vellum.

The Canon of the Bible.

The word "canon" means a "rod"—specifically, a rod with graduated marks used for measuring length. This word refers to the list of individual books that were eventually judged as authoritative and included in the Old Testament and the New Testament.

The early formation of the canon of the Old Testament is not easy to trace. Its threefold division in its early history—the Law, the Prophets, and the Writings—may reflect the three stages of its formation. From the beginning, the Law was accepted, even if it was not always obeyed. Evidence of its acceptance would include Moses' reading of "the Book of the Covenant" to the people at Mount Sinai and the people's response, "All that the LORD has said we will do, and be obedient" (Ex. 24:7).

Further evidence of acceptance of the Law includes the discovery of the "Book of the Law," probably the Book of Deuteronomy, in the Temple of Jerusalem during King Josiah's reign and the religious reform that followed the discovery (2 Kin. 22:8–23:25). Also, following the return of the Jewish people from the Babylonian Captivity, "the Book of the Law of Moses" was read to the people of Jerusalem under Ezra's direction. This book became the constitution of their new nation (Neh. 8:1–18).

The second division of the Old Testament accepted by the Jewish people was the Prophets. The prophets' words were preserved from the beginning by their disciples, or by others who recognized the prophets as messengers of God. In general, their words were probably written shortly after they were spoken, for their authority as God's messengers came before their widespread acceptance by the Jewish people. The words of the prophets were not regarded as authoritative because they were included in the Old Testament; they were included because they were considered to be authoritative.

The third division of the Hebrew Old Testament, the Writings, may have remained "open" longer than the first two. Scholars know less about the formation of this division than the first two.

The "Bible" Jesus used was the Hebrew Old Testament. He left no instructions about forming a new collection of authoritative writings to stand beside the books that He and His disciples accepted as God's Word. The Old Testament was also the Bible of the early church, but it was the Old Testament as fulfilled by Jesus. Early Christians interpreted the Old Testament in the light of His person and work. This new perspective controlled the early church's interpretation to such a degree that, while

Jews and Christians shared the same Bible, they understood it so differently that they might almost have been using two different Bibles.

The works and words of Jesus were first communicated in spoken form. The apostles and their associates proclaimed the gospel by word of mouth. Paul taught the believers orally in the churches he founded when he was present. But when he was absent, he communicated through his letters.

Quite early in its history, the church felt a need for a written account of the teachings of Jesus. His teachings did provide the basis for the new Christian way of life. But the church grew so large that many converts were unable to rely on the instructions of those who had heard and memorized the teachings of Jesus. From about A.D. 50 onward, probably more than one written collection of sayings of Jesus circulated in the churches. The earliest written gospel appears to have been the Gospel of Mark, written about A.D. 64.

An individual gospel, a letter from an apostle, or even several works circulating independently, would not amount to a canon, or an authoritative list of books. A canon implies a collection of writings. There is evidence that two collections of Christian writings circulated among the churches at the beginning of the second century. One of these was the gospel collection—the four writings commonly called the four gospels. The other collection was the Pauline collection, or the letters of the apostle Paul. The anonymous letter to the Hebrews was added to this second collection at an early date.

Early Christians continued to accept the Old Testament as authoritative. But they could interpret the Old Testament in the light of Jesus' deeds and words only if they had a reliable record of them. So, alongside Moses and the prophets, they had these early writings about Jesus and letters from the apostles, who had known Jesus in the flesh.

When officials of the early church sought to make a list of books about Jesus and the early church that they considered authoritative, they retained the Old Testament, on the authority of Jesus and His apostles. Along with these books they recognized as authoritative the writings of the new age—four gospels, or biographies on the life and ministry of Jesus; the 13 letters of Paul; and letters of other apostles and their companions. The gospel collection and the apostolic collection were joined together by the Book of Acts, which served as a sequel to the gospel story, as well as a narrative background for the earlier epistles. The whole was concluded by the Book of Revelation.

The primary standard applied to a book was that it must be written either by an apostle or by someone close to the apostles. This guaranteed that their writing about Jesus and the early church would have the authenticity of an eyewitness account. As in the earliest phase of the church's existence, "the apostles' doctrine" (Acts 2:42) was the basis of its life and thought. The apostolic writings formed the charter, or foundation documents, of the church.

None of the books written after the death of the apostles were included in the New Testament, although early church officials recognized they did have some value as inspirational documents. The fact that they were written later ruled them out for consideration among the church's foundation documents. These other writings might be suitable for reading aloud in church because of their edifying character, but only the apostolic writings carried ultimate authority. They alone could be used as the basis of the church's belief and practice.

Behind the Bible is a thrilling story of how God revealed Himself and His will to human spokesmen and then acted throughout history to preserve His Word and pass it along to future generations. In the words of the prophet Isaiah, "The grass withers, the flower fades, but the word of our God stands forever" (Is. 40:8).

BIBLE, INTERPRETATION OF THE, OR HERME-NEUTICS—the science and art of biblical interpretation. Correct Bible interpretation should answer the question, "How can I understand what this particular passage means?" Because there are rules that govern its use, it is a science. Because knowing the rules is not enough, it also is an art. Practice to learn how to use the rules is also required.

The question of how to interpret the Bible is not a minor issue. It is, in a sense, one of the battlegrounds for our souls. If Satan had a list of what he does not want us to do, Bible study would be at the top, along with prayer and worship. Through study of Scripture we learn who Jesus is and are enabled to become like Him. How can we become like Him, if we do not know what He is like? Devotional studies are important, but they must result from a serious study of Scripture. The apostle Paul prayed that the Colossians might be "filled with the knowledge of His will in all wisdom and spiritual understanding" (Col. 1:9).

Knowing Scripture as well as obeying it are the twin foundations of a godly life. A godly life produces the further desire to study God's Word. Bible interpretation done properly, therefore, takes the student from study to application back to study and on to further application in a mounting spiral toward God. Satan's attempt to take away our desire to study Scripture is nothing less than an attempt to remove the basis of our spiritual growth and stability.

The Basic Principles of Bible Study.

Six basic principles are at the heart of a sound method of biblical interpretation.

1. Because Scripture is a divine Book, and because of our limitation as humans, prayer is an absolute necessity as we study the Bible. Paul teaches that the non-Christian and the spiritually immature Christian are limited in their ability to know Christian things (1 Cor. 2:14–3:3). Therefore, we must pray that

God will bridge the gap that separates us from understanding spiritual things, by having the Holy Spirit teach us (John 14:26; 16:13). Without this illumination or insight from God's Spirit, we cannot learn. This need for insight was the concept Paul referred to when he told Timothy to "reflect on what I am saying, for the Lord will give you insight into all this" (2 Tim. 2:7, NIV).

2. The Bible is also a human book and, to a degree, must be interpreted like any other book. This brings us to the principle of common sense. For example, the grammatical-historical method of studying the Bible instructs us (a) to look at the grammar of a passage carefully to see what it says, and (b) to understand a biblical statement in light of its historical background. We understand a historical statement as a straightforward statement and do not change its literal, grammatical sense. This is "common sense."

Another example of the common sense principle is illustrated when Jesus says Christians can have anything for which they ask (John 15:7). Common sense tells us that there must be some limitation on this statement because we realize that Christians in fact do not have whatever they would like. (First John 5:14 confirms that the limitation is God's will.) Using the common sense principle in this way can be dangerous because it could become an excuse for cutting out any portion of Scripture we do not happen to like. But if our common sense is controlled by God, it is a valid principle to use for interpreting the Bible.

3. We interpret the Bible properly when we learn to ask the right questions of the text. The problem here is that many people do not know what the right questions are, or they are too lazy to learn. Biblical interpretation is a science, and the rules it uses take time, energy, and a serious commitment to learn. But when learned, there is much more satisfaction in asking the right questions than in merely guessing.

4. The primary rule of biblical interpretation is "context." This cannot be emphasized too strongly. If the Bible student would merely let a passage speak for itself within the context of the paragraph, chapter, or book, the majority of all errors in interpretation would be avoided.

The problem is our bias, or our subjectivity. Many times we approach a passage thinking we already understand it. In the process we read our own meaning into the passage. This is called eisegesis. (*Eis* is a Greek preposition meaning "into.") But interpreting the Bible correctly demands that we listen to what the text itself is saying, and then draw the meaning out of the passage. This is called exegesis. (*Ex* is a Greek preposition meaning "out of.") If we let a passage be defined by what it and the surrounding verses say, then we have taken a large step toward interpreting the Bible properly. Only by watching the context carefully and by letting the passage speak for itself do we give Scripture the respect it deserves.

Of course, it is impossible to dismiss totally our own bias and subjectivity. Our interpretation will always be colored by our culture and our opinions about the passage, or perhaps by our theological beliefs, which are partially based on the passage. But this should not discourage our attempt to let the passage speak for itself as freely as possible, without being weighed down with our personal opinions and views.

5. These four key words—*observation, interpretation, evaluation,* and *application*—are the heart of all approaches to finding out what the Bible means. They provide the structure of what questions you ask of the text, and when.

Observation:
> Do I understand the basic facts of the passage such as the meaning of all the words?

Interpretation:
> What did the author mean in his own historical setting?

Evaluation:

What does this passage mean in today's culture?

Application:

How can I apply what I have learned to how I live my life?

6. Interpreting the Bible correctly is a two-step process. We must first discover what the passage meant in the day and age of the author. Then we must discover its message for us in today's culture. *Observation* and *interpretation* apply to the first step; *evaluation* and *application* apply to the second.

Why are these two steps important? First, the Bible was not actually written directly to us, and it makes sense to put ourselves in the shoes of the original audience if we are to understand its message properly. Second, these steps force us to *understand* the meaning of the passage before we *apply* it to our lives. Surprisingly, this step is often overlooked. Third, the two steps separate us from the text, thereby helping to prevent eisegesis, since it separates what the text says from how it affects us today.

The Four Stages of Biblical Interpretation.

Using the four key words in their proper sequence, we are ready to interpret the Bible correctly.

1. *Stage one: observation*—The questions asked in this stage are, Do I understand all the facts in this passage? Do I know the context before and after this passage? Do I know the meanings of all the words? Do I understand the general flow of the discussion? Do I understand the cultural background? It is necessary to clear up all the factual problems before moving into the theological meaning of the passage.

For example, in 1 Corinthians 8 the apostle Paul discusses eating meat that had been offered to idols. What is the background? When meat was sacrificed to an idol, that which was not eaten by the priests was sold at the market. Some Corinthian

Christians said it was permissible to eat the meat since idols are nothing but wood and stone. Others thought it was not permissible because it might appear they were still involved in pagan worship. Only after we understand these facts may we go on to the next stage of interpretation.

2. *Stage two: interpretation*—The basic question asked in this stage is, What did the author mean in his own historical setting? We must put ourselves in the shoes of Scripture's original audience. To answer this question, there are two further questions we may ask. The first is, What does the passage actually say? Many times we forget to look carefully at what a passage says. Some cite Matthew 5:21–22 as proof that to think bad is just as wrong as doing it. Is anger as bad as murder? Of course not. (Common sense tells us that, if nothing else.) But the text does not actually say they are the same. It says the law against murder is not fully obeyed by mere outward obedience, but by maintaining the proper attitude of not being angry, which in turn prohibits the outward act of murder.

The second question is, Does the context help define the meaning of the passage? For example, what does Scripture mean when it says, "There is no God" (Ps. 53:1)? Context shows this is a statement made by a fool. What does Paul mean when he says Jesus will return like "a thief in the night" (1 Thess. 5:2)? Context shows it means His coming will be sudden (v. 3). Should women remain totally silent in the church (1 Cor. 14:34)? No, since the context of 1 Corinthians 11:5 shows that women may pray or prophesy.

Does Jesus' statement, "When you fast, do not be like the hypocrites" (Matt. 6:16) demand that His disciples fast? No, because Matthew 9:14 shows that Jesus' disciples did not fast while He was alive. (The beauty of using Scripture to interpret Scripture is that when the Bible answers its own questions, then we know the answer is correct.) The twin matters of what the text actually says and the passage's context help complete the second stage of interpretation.

There are times when even these two questions will not help us understand the meaning of a passage. Sometimes we have to read between the lines and make an educated guess as to what the passage means. This is fine when necessary. But we must remember that we are guessing, and we must keep an open mind to other possible interpretations.

Integrity is also a necessary element in all biblical interpretation. If we tell someone about what a friend said, we should try to be as accurate as possible. If we are not sure about a certain point, we should say, "I think this is what he said." We all do this with our friends. So why then, when we interpret Scripture, do many of us lose that integrity? Why do we not read the text carefully? Why do we read between the lines, make fanciful interpretations that are more a product of our imagination than reverent study, and then insist that this is what the text actually says?

In interpreting the Bible, we must never forget whose letters we are reading. They have come from God Himself, and they demand respect. They demand to speak for themselves. They demand that we be honest and have integrity. We must not put our guesswork on the same level as the words of God.

How do we interpret 1 Corinthians 8? Once we understand the facts and background of the passage, once we have asked what the passage actually is saying and what is its context, then we see that Paul is teaching the principle of voluntarily refraining from a practice that, although not wrong in and of itself, might be harmful to a fellow Christian. We have completed the first step of interpretation. We have seen what the passage meant in the day and age of the author.

3. *Stage three: evaluation*—The stage of evaluation asks, What does the passage signify in today's culture? It is the issue

of whether a passage of Scripture applies to us today, or whether it is limited to the culture in which it was originally written.

The question raised by the evaluation process is answered one of two ways. Either the passage is applied directly to our culture, or it must be reapplied because of cultural differences. The vast majority of New Testament teaching can be applied directly to 20th-century culture. If we love God, regardless of when or where we live, then we must obey His commandments (John 14:15). This teaching is true in any culture for all times.

But sometimes a biblical teaching is directed so specifically to the culture of the ancient world that another culture cannot understand it. For example, Western culture today generally does not sacrifice meat to idols, and therefore the meaning of 1 Corinthians 8 may be lost. How then do we evaluate its meaning for us?

It is helpful at this point to define two terms. A "cultural expression" is a statement that can be understood only within a certain cultural context. An "eternal principle" is a principle that God uses to govern the world regardless of culture. "I will never again eat meat, lest it make my brother stumble" (1 Cor. 8:13), is a cultural expression because it is understandable only within those cultures that offer meat to idols. "God is love" (1 John 4:8) is an eternal principle because it is understandable in all cultures.

But we should clearly understand that every cultural expression in the Bible is the result of some eternal principle. And even though a cultural expression cannot be carried over directly to another culture, the eternal principle behind it can. Just because it is cultural does not mean it can be ignored.

A good example of this important principle might be the teaching that we should always be polite when we are guests for dinner. In America, this principle could express itself as "Eat all the food on the table lest you insult your host's cooking." But in Uganda it is important that food be left on the serving plates lest it appear your host has not sufficiently provided for you.

Therefore, whereas the principle shows itself in America as "Eat all the food," the same principle shows itself in Uganda as "Leave some of the food on the serving plates." *The task of the Biblical interpreter is to look through any cultural expression to the eternal principle that gave rise to it, and to reapply the principle in his own culture.* This is the process of evaluation. Is it cultural? If it is, how does the eternal principle that gave rise to the cultural expression reapply in the new culture?

Two implications can be drawn from this. First, if a statement is cultural, then there must be a principle that gave rise to the cultural statement. But if no principle can be found, then what was thought to be cultural must in fact be an eternal principle. Second, if the interpreter is not sure whether a statement is cultural, would it not be better to be safe and view the statement as eternal, lest a command of God be ignored?

We should also remember that just as a biblical passage can be set in its culture, so interpreters are likewise controlled to some extent by their own culture. Many people today do not believe that the biblical accounts of miracles are true. For example, some scholars argue that miracles were a part of first-century culture and were believed by the people in Jesus' day. But this is the 20th century and people do not believe in miracles in this culture. But these scholars' views on the impossibility of the supernatural are likewise influenced by the materialistic, science-oriented culture in which they live. We must be careful not to allow our own culture to influence our view of Scripture.

4. *Stage four: application*—Up to this point, the process of interpreting the Bible has been academic. But it is absolutely essential to recognize that the purpose and goal of Bible study is a godly life. Study is not complete until we put into practice what we have learned.

The question to ask at this stage of interpretation is, "How can I apply what I have learned to how I live my life?" The academic and the practical are thus fused into a meaningful approach to the Bible's message. Some people dismiss the academic as boring and trivial. Others reject the application as unnecessary. Both extremes are equally wrong. The Bible interpreter must walk the tightrope between these approaches. A three-act play is unsatisfying without the final act. The last act, without the first two, does not make sense. Sometimes in Bible study it is necessary to emphasize the academic when the passage is difficult to understand, or to emphasize the application when the passage's practical relevance is confusing. But one of these approaches should never be used to the exclusion of the other.

Special Problems in Interpreting the Bible.

Scripture, like any other book, uses figures of speech and different types of literature that can be difficult to understand. These call for special rules for the Bible interpreter.

1. *Hyperbole*—A hyperbole is an exaggeration used for effect—an overstatement. "I'm so hungry I could eat a horse" obviously is not literally true. It is an exaggeration used to convey the idea of extreme hunger. Most hyperboles are easily recognized because we use them all the time. But sometimes they are not. For example, the apostle John made a statement something like this in his gospel: If everything Jesus ever did were written down, the world could not hold all the books that would be written (John 21:25). Surely John expected us to see that he was overstating his point. It is a graphic picture of how much Jesus did, but one painted in hyperbolic fashion.

2. *Metaphor*—A simile makes a comparison by using a word such as "like": "Life is like a circus." A metaphor is a similar comparison, except that it omits the word "like": "The world is a stage." Metaphors such as "I am the door" (John 10:9) are easily recognized. But what about Jesus' words at the Last Supper:

"This is My body" (Luke 22:19)? Jesus probably intended this statement to be understood metaphorically rather than literally or physically.

3. *Anthropomorphism*—Do rivers have hands to clap (Ps. 98:8)? Does God have eyes (Ps. 33:18), although He is spirit (John 4:24)? Anthropomorphisms in the Bible describe nonhuman objects as though they have human characteristics. But how do we understand those verses that say God "repents" (Ex. 32:12; Jer. 18:8; relents, regrets, NKJV)? Does God change His mind? Or do these verses describe God from a human point of view?

4. *Parable*—"Once upon a time in a far-away land there lived a fairy princess." We do not understand this sentence in a scientific or literal sense. We recognize that it comes from a certain type of literature, and thus we do not interpret it historically. Different types of literature fall into different categories, each of which has its own rules of interpretation.

Parables are one type of literature in the Bible. We interpret them properly by picturing the story in our minds as if we lived in Jesus' day, finding the one main point, and not giving meaning to all the details. The difference between allegory and parable is important to understand. An allegory is a totally made-up story. Even the details of an allegory may be significant.

Pilgrim's Progress is the classic example of allegory in which even minute details refer to other things. But a parable is a story taken from everyday life. In a parable the speaker may not treat the details as important. They may be given to help the reader picture the situation more clearly.

Although a few parables have allegorical elements, most parables teach only one main point. The parable of the sower (Matt. 13:3–23) is part allegory because the sower, seed, ground, birds, sun, and weeds all stand for something else: Jesus, the

Word, Jesus' audience, Satan, persecution, and the cares of the world. But what about the parable of the judge (Luke 18:1–14)?

If the woman represents the disciple, is God the unjust judge? Is the purpose of the parable of the rich man and Lazarus (Luke 16:19–31) to teach that you cannot travel between heaven and hell? The standard procedure for interpreting parables is to find the one main point and to view the details of the story simply as illustrations, but not as the direct teaching of the parable.

5. *Prophecy*—There are two points to remember when interpreting prophecy. The first is that what the prophet foresaw as one event may actually be two or more. The Old Testament thought of the "Day of the Lord" (Is. 2:12) as one event. But the last days actually began at Pentecost (Acts 2:20) and will conclude at Christ's return (2 Thess. 2:2).

The second point to remember is that although much Old Testament prophecy is fulfilled in the New Testament, much was fulfilled in the Old Testament and then again in the New. Isaiah's prophecy in 7:14 was fulfilled in Isaiah's day (Is. 8:8), and again by Jesus' birth (Matt. 1:23). Isaiah's prophecy had a more complete meaning in that it was to be fulfilled again at a more distant time in the future.

6. *Poetry*—Hebrew poetry does not concentrate on rhythm or rhyme. It expresses itself by parallelism. Two phrases are joined so that the second repeats the first with different words (Ps. 95:2), or the second states the opposite of the first (Prov. 15:5), or the second adds a new thought to the first (Prov. 15:3). Sometimes the couplet will be arranged with the second phrase reversing the order of the first (Prov. 15:21). Therefore, when interpreting poetry, the Bible student must recognize the type of parallelism being used, since the phrases interpret each other. In addition, poetry often stresses emotional flow rather than logical precision.

7. *Apocalyptic*—This type of literature in the Bible is the most misunderstood by interpreters today because it is no

longer used. It has specific rules of interpretation. Its most noticeable characteristic is its use of strange, symbolic figures, such as those in the Book of Revelation.

The key to interpreting these figures lies in the Book of Revelation itself. In 1:20 the seven stars are interpreted as representing the seven angels, and the seven lampstands stand for the seven churches. In 17:9–10 the seven-headed beast stands for the seven hills, and in 17:18 the woman is identified as the city that rules the earth. Therefore, to understand Apocalyptic Literature, and Revelation in particular, we must interpret the imagery as very figurative. The images are describing things and spiritual realities in figurative language.

Some might object that this is not understanding the Bible literally. But since the Book of Revelation interprets its own images in figurative terms, the images must serve as figurative descriptions of real things. Therefore, to understand the book literally, we must understand it figuratively.

8. *Wisdom*—Old Testament wisdom literature is found mainly in Job, Proverbs, and Ecclesiastes. Since wisdom gives practical hints on how to cope with life and its problems, it often consists of rules of thumb rather than universally applicable promises. For example, "Train up a child in the way he should go, and when he is old he will not depart from it" (Prov. 22:6) is not a categorical imperative that works in every situation. Biblical wisdom sayings must therefore be used with due caution and great discernment (Prov. 1:1–6).

In interpreting the Bible, we must remember from Whom it comes. We are handling the Lord's message. This demands an attitude of respect and our willingness to subject ourselves to its authority.

The Jordan River valley south of Jericho near the Dead Sea.

BIBLE VERSIONS AND TRANSLATIONS—The Bible was written across a period of several centuries in the languages of Hebrew and Aramaic (Old Testament) and Greek (New Testament). With the changing of nations and cultures across the centuries, these original writings have been translated many times to make the Bible available in different languages. Following are the major versions and translations of the Bible that have been issued during the past 2,200 years. Just as God inspired people to write His Word, He also has preserved the Bible by using human instruments to pass it on to succeeding generations.

Ancient Versions.

Ancient versions of the Bible are those that were produced in classical languages such as Greek, Syriac, and Latin. The following ancient versions were issued during a 600-year period from about 200 B.C. to A.D. 400.

Greek—The oldest Bible translation in the world was made in Alexandria, Egypt, where the Old Testament was translated from Hebrew into Greek for the benefit of the Greek-speaking Jews of that city. A Jewish community had existed in Alexandria almost from its foundation by Alexander the Great in 331 B.C.

In two or three generations this community had forgotten its native Palestinian language. These Jews realized they needed the Hebrew Scriptures rendered into the only language they knew—Greek. The first section of the Hebrew Bible to be translated into Greek was the Pentateuch, or the first five books of the Old Testament, some time before 200 B.C. Other parts were translated during the next century. This version is commonly called the Septuagint, from *septuaginta,* the Latin word for 70 (LXX). This name was selected because of a tradition that the Pentateuch was translated into Greek by about 70 elders of Israel who were brought to Alexandria especially for this purpose.

Only a few fragments of this version survive from the period before Christ. Most copies of the Greek Old Testament belong to the Christian era and were made by Christians. The

John Rylands University Library, Manchester, England, owns a fragment of Deuteronomy in Greek from the second century B.C. Another fragment of the same book in Greek dating from about the same time exists in Cairo. Other fragments of the Septuagint have been identified among the texts known as the Dead Sea Scrolls, discovered in 1947.

When Christianity penetrated the world of the Greek-speaking Jews, and then the Gentiles, the Septuagint was the Bible used for preaching the gospel. Most of the Old Testament quotations in the New Testament are taken from this Greek Bible. In fact, the Christians adopted the Septuagint so whole-heartedly that the Jewish people lost interest in it. They produced other Greek versions that did not lend themselves so easily to Christian interpretation.

The Septuagint thus became the "authorized version" of the early Gentile churches. To this day it is the official version of the Old Testament used in the Greek Orthodox Church. After the books of the New Testament were written and accepted by the early church, they were added to the Old Testament Septuagint to form the complete Greek version of the Bible.

The Septuagint was based on a Hebrew text much older than most surviving Hebrew manuscripts of the Old Testament. Occasionally, this Greek Old Testament helps scholars to reconstruct the wording of a passage where it has been lost or miscopied by scribes as the text was passed down across the centuries. An early instance of this occurs in

Genesis 4:8, where Cain's words to Abel, "Let us go out to the field," are reproduced from the Septuagint in the NRSV, NIV, and other modern versions. These words had been lost from the standard Hebrew text, but they were necessary to complete the sense of the English translation.

Aramaic targums—The word targum means "translation." After their return from Captivity in Babylonia, many Jews spoke Aramaic, a sister language, instead of the pure Hebrew of their ancestors. They found it difficult to follow the reading of the Hebrew Scriptures at worship. So they adopted the practice of providing an oral paraphrase into Aramaic when the Scriptures were read in Hebrew. The person who provided this paraphrase, the Turgeman, was an official in the synagogue.

One of the earliest examples of such a paraphrase occurs in Nehemiah 8:8. Because of the work of Ezra, the Pentateuch, or the first five books of the Old Testament, was officially recognized as the constitution of the Jewish state during the days of the Persian Empire. This constitution was read publicly to the whole community after their return to Jerusalem. The appointed readers "read distinctly [or, *with interpretation*] from the book, in the Law of God; and they gave the sense, and helped them understand the reading."

The phrase "with interpretation" appears as a marginal reading in several modern versions (for example, the RSV), but it probably indicates exactly what happened. The Hebrew text was read, followed by an oral paraphrase in Aramaic so everyone would be sure to understand.

This practice continued as standard in the Jewish synagogue for a long time. The targum, or paraphrase of the Hebrew, was not read from a written document, lest some in the congregation might think the authoritative law was being read. Some religious leaders apparently held that the targum should not be written down, even for use outside the synagogue.

In time, all objections to a written targum disappeared. A number of such paraphrases began to be used. Official Jewish recognition was given to two in particular—the Targum of Onkelos on the Pentateuch and the Targum of Jonathan on the Prophets. Some were far from being word-for-word translations. As expanded paraphrases, they included interpretations and comments on the biblical text.

Some New Testament writers indicate knowledge of targumic interpretations in their quotations from the Old Testament.

For example, "Vengeance is Mine, I will repay" (Rom. 12:19; Heb. 10:30) is a quotation from Deuteronomy 32:35; but it conforms neither to the Hebrew text nor to the Greek text of the Septuagint. This particular phrase comes from the Targum. Again, the words of Ephesians 4:8, "When He ascended on high, He led captivity captive, and gave gifts to men," are taken from Psalm 68:18. But the Hebrew and Septuagint texts speak of the *receiving* of gifts. Only the Targum on this text mentions the giving of gifts.

Syriac—The term Syriac describes the Eastern Aramaic language spoken in Northern Mesopotamia, the land between the Tigris and Euphrates Rivers northeast of the land of Palestine. Large Jewish settlements were located there. At some point, the Old Testament must have been translated into Syriac for their benefit.

As Christianity expanded, this area became an important center of Christian life and action. The Christians in northern Mesopotamia inherited the Syriac Old Testament and added a Syriac translation of the New Testament to it. This "authorized version" of the Syriac Bible is called the Peshitta (the "common" or "simple" version). In its present form, it goes back to the beginning of the fifth century A.D. But there were earlier Syriac translations of parts of the New Testament. Two important manuscripts of the Gospels exist in an Old Syriac version, which probably goes back to about the second century A.D. The Syriac-speaking church was very missionary-minded. It carried the gospel into Central Asia, evangelizing India and parts of China. It translated portions of the Bible from Syriac into the local languages of the areas it evangelized. The earliest forms of the Bible in the languages of Armenia and Georgia (north of Armenia) were based on the Syriac version.

Coptic—Coptic was a highly developed form of the native language of the ancient Egyptians. Christianity was planted in Egypt while some of the twelve apostles were still alive, although there is no record of how it was carried there. With the development of a Christian community in Egypt, the need arose for a Bible in the Coptic tongue. To this day the Coptic Church of Egypt uses the Bohairic version of the Coptic Bible, translated in the early centuries from the Septuagint and the Greek New Testament into the dialect of Lower Egypt. Earlier still is the Sahidic version, in the dialect of Upper Egypt.

Gothic—Across the Rhine and Danube frontiers of the Roman Empire lived a race of people known as the Goths. The evangelization of the Ostrogoths, those who lived north of the Danube River, began in the third century. About A.D. 360 Bishop Ulfilas, "the apostle to the Goths," led his converts south of the Danube to settle in what is now Bulgaria. There he translated the Bible into their language. The Gothic version was the first translation of the Bible into a language of the Germanic family. English, German, Dutch, and Scandinavian belong to this language group.

Latin—The need for a Latin Bible first arose during the second century A.D., when Latin began to replace Greek as the dominant language of the Roman Empire. The first Old Testament sections of the Latin Bible were considered unreliable, since they were actually a translation of a translation. They were based on the Septuagint, which, in turn, was a translation of the Hebrew Bible into Greek. Since the New Testament was written originally in Greek, it was translated directly into the Latin language. Several competing New Testament translations were in use throughout the Latin-speaking world as early as about A.D. 250.

The task of producing one standard Latin Bible to replace these competing translations was entrusted by Damasus, bishop of Rome (366–384), to his secretary Jerome. Jerome undertook the task unwillingly, knowing that replacing an old version with a new is bound to cause offense, even if the new is better. He began with a revision of the gospels, followed by the

Psalms. After completing the New Testament, Jerome mastered the Hebrew language in order to translate the Old Testament into Latin. He completed this work in A.D. 405.

Jerome's translation of the Bible is known as the Latin Vulgate. It did not win instant acceptance. Many were suspicious of it because it varied so much from the version with which they were familiar. But in time its superior merits caused it to gain popularity.

The best surviving manuscript of the Latin Vulgate, the Codex Amiatinus, is now in the Laurentian Library of Florence, Italy. Written in a monastery in Northumbria, England, it was presented to Pope Gregory II in 716.

The Latin Vulgate is especially important because it was the medium through which the gospel arrived in Western Europe. It remained the standard version in this part of the world for centuries. In 1546 the Council of Trent directed that only "this same ancient and vulgate edition ... be held as authentic in public lecture, disputations, sermons and expository discourses, and that no one make bold or presume to reject it on any pretext." Until the 20th century no translations of the Bible except those based on the Vulgate were recognized as authoritative by the Roman Catholic Church.

The Old English Versions.

Until the beginning of the 16th century, all Bible versions in the languages of the masses of Western Europe were based on the Latin Vulgate. Among these, the Old English versions are of special interest. Most of these versions consisted of only parts of the Bible, and even these had limited circulation. In this period few of the people of ancient England could read. Many of the familiar stories of the Bible were turned into verse and set to music so they could be sung and memorized.

Caedmon, the unlettered poet of Whitby, is said to have turned the whole history of salvation into song in the seventh century. Bede, the monk of Jarrow, the most learned man of his day in Western Europe, devoted the last ten days of his life to turning the gospels into English so they could be read by the common people.

Alfred the Great, king of a large part of southern and western England, defeated the Danish invaders in 878. He published a code of laws that was introduced by an Old English translation of the Ten Commandments and other brief passages from the Bible.

The parts of the Bible most favored for translating during this period were those often read or recited during worship services, especially the Psalms and the gospels. An Old English version of the Psalms by Bishop Aldhelm dates from soon after 700. A manuscript called the Wessex Gospels dates from the middle of the tenth century.

Some of the earliest Old English versions of Scripture were written between the lines of Latin-language manuscripts. The manuscript known as the Lindisfarne Gospels (now in the British Museum, London) was produced originally in Latin shortly before 700. Two and a half centuries later a priest named Aldred wrote between the lines of the text a literal translation in the Northumbrian dialect of Old English. Bible texts of this type, with some letters decorated in gold and silver, are known as illustrated manuscripts.

William Tyndale, shown seated in this painting, translates the New Testament into English—one of the first versions to be published in the language of the common people.

Wycliffe's Versions.

In the early Middle Ages, parts of the Bible were translated from Latin into several of the dialects of Western Europe. These included versions in the Bohemian, Czech, and Italian languages, as well as the Provencal dialect of southeastern France. But none of these compare in importance with the work of John Wycliffe, pioneering reformer who translated the entire Bible from Latin into the English language.

Wycliffe (c. 1330–1384), master of Balliol College, Oxford, was a distinguished scholar and preacher. But he was also a social reformer who wanted to replace the feudal organization of state and church with a system that emphasized people's direct responsibility to God. The constitution of this new order would be the law of God, which Wycliffe equated with the Bible. Before this could happen, the law of God had to be accessible to the laity as well as the clergy, the unlearned as well as the learned. This called for a Bible in English as well as Latin, so Wycliffe and his associates undertook the task of translating the entire Bible from the Latin Vulgate into contemporary English.

There were actually two Wycliffe versions of the Bible—an earlier one, produced between 1380 and 1384 during Wycliffe's lifetime, and a later version completed in 1395, 11 years after his death.

The earlier version is a thoroughly literal translation. Wycliffe followed the Latin construction without attempting to render the meaning into good English idiom. The translators produced a literal version because it was intended to serve as the lawbook of the new order. The Latin text of the lawbook was already established, and the English text had to follow it word for word. About two thirds of this version was produced by one of Wycliffe's supporters, Nicholas of Hereford. Wycliffe himself may have done some of the translation work on the remaining portion. By the time this first translation was completed, the movement with which this English social reformer was associated was condemned by the authorities.

The second Wycliffe version was the work of his secretary, John Purvey. It was based on the earlier version, but it rendered the text into idiomatic English. Purvey's version became very popular, although its circulation was restricted by church officials. It was suppressed in 1408 by a document known as the "Constitutions of Oxford," which forbade anyone to translate or even to read any part of the Bible in English without the

permission of a bishop or a local church council. These constitutions remained in force for more than a century.

From Wycliffe to King James.

More than 200 years passed from the time that Wycliffe's
second English version was issued (1395) until the historic King
James Version was published in 1611. These were fruitful years
for new versions of the Bible. The stage was set for the monu-
mental King James Bible by five different English translations
that were issued during these years.

Tyndale—The years from about 1450 onward brought
exciting cultural changes in Western Europe. The revival of
interest in classical and biblical learning was already under way
when it received a stimulus from the migration of Greek
scholars to the West after the fall of Constantinople to the Turks
in 1453. With the invention of printing in Germany, the
promoters of the new learning found a new technology at their
disposal.

Among the first products of the printing press were editions
of the Bible. The first major work to be printed was the famous
Gutenberg edition of the Latin Bible, in 1456. The following
decades brought printed editions of the Hebrew Bible, the
Greek New Testament, and the Septuagint. The leaders of the
Protestant Reformation were quick to take advantage of this
new invention to help advance their efforts in church reform.

Making the Bible available in the tongue of the common
people was a major strategy in the Reformers' policy. Martin
Luther, leader of the Reformation, translated the New Testament
from Greek into German in 1522 and the Old Testament from
Hebrew into German the following years. What Luther did for
the Germans, William Tyndale did for the people of England.

After completing his studies at the Universities of Oxford
and Cambridge, William Tyndale (c. 1495–1536) devoted his
time and talents to providing his fellow Englishmen with the
Scriptures in their own language. He hoped that Bishop Tunstall

of London would sponsor his project of translating the Bible, but the bishop refused to do so. Tyndale then went to Germany in 1524 to undertake his project. By August of 1525 his English New Testament was complete.

Tyndale began printing his new version at Cologne, but this was interrupted by the city authorities. The printing work was then carried through by Peter Schoeffer in Worms, who produced an edition of 6,000 copies. Soon this new Bible was selling in England, although it had been officially banned by the church.

Tyndale's translation differed in two important respects from the versions of Wycliffe. It was rendered not from the Latin language but from the Greek original, and it circulated in printed form, not as a handcopied manuscript. From the New Testament, Tyndale moved to the Old, issuing an edition of the Pentateuch, then the Book of Jonah, and a revision of Genesis. Later, in 1534, Tyndale issued a revision of his New Testament, justly described as "altogether Tyndale's noblest monument." A further revision of the New Testament appeared in 1535. In May of that year Tyndale was arrested. After an imprisonment of 17 months, he was sentenced to death as a heretic; he was strangled and burned at the stake at Vilvorde, near Brussels, on October 6, 1536.

Tyndale started a tradition in the history of the English Bible that has endured to this day. What is commonly called "Bible English" is really Tyndale's English. His wording in those portions of the Bible which he translated was retained in the King James Version to a great degree. The latest in the succession of revisions that stand in the Tyndale tradition is the New King James Version. But even those versions that did not set out to adhere to his tradition, such as the New International Version, show his influence.

Coverdale and Matthew—At the time of Tyndale's death, a printed edition of the English Bible, bearing a dedication to

King Henry VIII, had been circulating in England for nearly a year. This was the first edition of the Bible issued by Miles Coverdale (1488–1568), one of Tyndale's friends and associates. This English version reproduced Tyndale's translation of the Pentateuch and the New Testament; the rest of the Old Testament was translated into English from Latin and German versions.

Coverdale's Bible of 1535 was the first complete English Bible in print. A second and third edition appeared in 1537. The title page bore the words: "Set forth with the King's most gracious licence." But this was not the only English Bible to appear in 1537 with these words on the title page. Another of Tyndale's associates, John Rogers, published an edition of the Bible that year under the name, "Thomas Matthew." "Matthew's Bible" was similar to Coverdale's with one exception: its translation of the historical books from Joshua to 2 Chronicles was one that Tyndale had finished without publishing before his death.

The Great Bible—Official policy toward the translation and circulation of the Bible in England changed quickly. King Henry's break with the Roman Catholic pope in Rome in 1534 had something to do with it, but deeper factors were also involved. A landmark in the history of the English Bible was the royal injunction of September 1538, directing that "one book of the whole Bible of the largest volume in English" should be placed in every parish church in England where the people could have access to it. When this decree was issued, another version of the Bible—the "Great Bible"—was being prepared so this commandment could be followed.

Publication of the Great Bible was delayed because French officials halted its production in Paris, where it was being printed. The printing was then transferred to London, where the Great Bible appeared in 1539. The Great Bible was Coverdale's revision of Matthew's Bible, which means that it was essentially a copy of Tyndale's translation. It quickly became the "authorized version" of the English Bible.

One part of the Great Bible remained in use long after the version as a whole had been replaced by later and better versions. To this day the Psalter in the Book of Common Prayer that is sung in the services of the Church of England is the Psalms contained in the Great Bible.

The Geneva Bible—During the reign of Mary Tudor of England (1553–1558), many English Reformers sought refuge in other parts of Europe because of her policy of persecution. One community of English refugees settled in Geneva, Switzerland, where John Knox was pastor of the English congregation and where John Calvin dominated theological study. Many of these English refugees were fine scholars, and they began work on a new English version of the Bible. A preliminary edition of the New Testament (Whittingham's New Testament) was published in 1557. This was the first edition of any part of the English Bible to have the text divided into verses. The whole Bible appeared in 1560.

This "Geneva Bible" was the first English Bible to be translated in its entirety from the original biblical languages. Widely recognized as the best English version of the Bible that had yet appeared, it quickly became the accepted version in Scotland. In England it also attained instant popularity among the people, although it was not accepted by church officials. After the publication of the King James Version in 1611, the Geneva Bible remained popular. This was the Bible which the Pilgrims took with them to the New World in 1620; to them the King James Version was a compromise and an inferior production. The Geneva Bible was printed until 1644 and was still found in use 30 years later.

The Bishops' Bible—The rival version to the Geneva Bible sponsored by church leaders in England was published in 1568. It was called the Bishops' Bible because all the translators were either bishops at the time or became bishops later. It was a good translation, based throughout on the original languages; but it was not as sound in scholarship as the Geneva Bible.

The King James Version—Shortly after James VI of Scotland ascended the throne of England as James I (1603), he convened a conference to settle matters under dispute in the Church of England. The only important result of this conference was an approval to begin work on the King James Version of the English Bible (KJV).

A group of 47 scholars, divided into six teams, was appointed to undertake the work of preparing the new version. Three teams worked on the Old Testament; two were responsible for the New Testament; and one worked on the Apocrypha. They used the 1602 edition of the Bishops' Bible as the basis of their revision, but they had access to many other versions and helps, as well as the texts in the original biblical languages. When the six groups had completed their task, the final draft was reviewed by a committee of 12. The King James Version was published in 1611.

The new version won wide acceptance among the people of the English-speaking world. Nonsectarian in tone and approach, it did not favor one shade of theological or ecclesiastical opinion over another. The translators had an almost instinctive sense of good English style; the prose rhythms of the version gave it a secure place in the popular memory. Never was a version of the Bible more admirably suited for reading aloud in public.

Although there was resistance to the King James Version at first, it quickly made a place for itself. For more than three centuries it remained "The Bible" throughout the English-speaking world.

Catholic Versions.

A generation before the appearance of the King James Bible, an English version of the Bible for Roman Catholics was undertaken by the faculty of the English College at Douai, France. Unlike the Geneva Bible, which was translated from the original languages, the Douai (or Douay) Bible was translated from the Latin Vulgate. The translator of the Douai Bible was Gregory Martin, formerly an Oxford scholar, who translated two chapters a day until the project was finished. Each section was then revised by two of his colleagues. The New Testament portion of this version was issued in 1582 and the Old Testament in 1609–10.

The Douai Bible was scholarly and accurate, but the English style and vocabulary were modeled on Latin usage. It would not have become popular among the Catholic laity if it had not been for the work of Richard Challoner (1691–1781), who revised it thoroughly between 1749 and 1772. What has generally been called the Douai Bible since Challoner's day is in fact the Douai Bible as revised by Challoner. In several respects it was a new version. Until 1945 this Douai revision by Challoner remained the only version of the Bible officially sanctioned for English-speaking Catholics.

Nineteenth-Century Revisions.

During the 18th century and the earlier part of the 19th century, several private attempts were made at revising the King James Version. The reasons for revision included the outdated English of the KJV, the progress made by scholars in understanding the original languages of the Bible, and the availability of better texts in the original biblical languages, especially the Greek text of the New Testament.

One of the most influential private revisions was Henry Alford's *New Testament* (1869). In the preface to this translation, Alford expressed the hope that his work would be replaced soon by an official revision of the KJV. This hope was fulfilled in 1870 when the Church of England initiated plans for a revision. Two groups of revisers were appointed, one for the Old Testament and one for the New. Representatives of British churches other than the Church of England were included on these committees. Before long, parallel companies of revisers were set up in the United States. At first these groups worked under the hope that one version might be produced for both England and the United States. But this was not to be. The American scholars, conservative as they were in their procedure, could not be bound by the stricter conservatism of their British counterparts. The three installments of the British revision (RV) appeared in 1881, in 1885, and in 1894. The American revision, or American Standard Version (ASV), was released in 1901, but did not include the Apocrypha.

The RV and ASV were solid works of scholarship. The Old Testament revisers had a much better grasp of Hebrew than the original translators of the King James Bible. The New Testament revision was based on a much more accurate Greek text than had been available in 1611. Although the RV and ASV were suitable for Bible study, they did not gain popular acceptance, mainly because their translators paid little attention to style and rhythm as they rendered the biblical languages into English.

Twentieth-Century Private Translations.

The first half of the 20th century was marked by a succession of brilliant private enterprises in translation—both for the New Testament alone and for the whole Bible.

Twentieth Century New Testament—The earliest of these was the Twentieth Century New Testament, a project conducted by a group of intelligent laypersons who used Westcott and Hort's edition of the Greek New Testament (1881) as their basic text. They were concerned that no existing version (not even the RV) made the Bible plain to young people, and they set out to supply this need. They completed their work in 1901; a revised edition appeared in 1904.

Weymouth—Richard Francis Weymouth, a Greek scholar, published an edition of the Greek New Testament called *The*

Resultant Greek Testament in 1886. Later he issued a modern translation of this text, *The New Testament in Modern Speech,* which appeared in 1903, shortly after his death. The "modern speech" into which this translation was rendered was dignified contemporary usage and it paid special attention to accuracy in the translation of details such as the definite article and tenses.

Moffatt—Much more colloquial than Weymouth's version was *The New Testament: A New Translation* (1913) by James Moffatt. Moffatt was a Scot, and his translation bore traces of the idiom of his native land. While his unique expressions shocked some readers accustomed to more dignified Bible English, they brought home the meaning of the text with greater clarity than ever before.

In 1924 Moffatt added *The Old Testament: A New Translation;* in 1928 the whole work appeared in one volume, entitled *A New Translation of the Bible.* In both Testaments Moffatt occasionally took greater liberties with the wording and order than was proper for a translator; yet to this day one of the best ways to get a quick grasp of the general sense of a book of the Bible is to read it through in Moffatt's translation.

Goodspeed—Edgar J. Goodspeed of the University of Chicago produced *The New Testament: An American Translation* in 1923. He was convinced that most Bible versions were translated into "British English"; so he tried to provide a version free from expressions that might be strange to Americans. A companion work, *The Old Testament: An American Translation,* edited by J. M. Powis Smith and three other scholars, was issued in 1927. In 1938 Goodspeed's translation of the Apocrypha appeared. This was the final contribution to *The Complete Bible: An American Translation.*

The Revised Standard Version.

The Revised Standard Version (RSV) is one of the last versions in the long line of English Bible translations that stem from William Tyndale. Although it is a North American production, it has been widely accepted in the whole English-speaking world.

The RSV was launched as a revision of the KJV (1611), RV (1885), and ASV (1901). Authorized by the International Council of Religious Education, it is copyrighted by the Division of Christian Education of the National Council of Churches in the USA. The New Testament first appeared in 1946, the two Testaments in 1952, and the Apocrypha in 1957. A new edition in 1962 incorporated 85 minor changes in wording.

A Catholic edition of the RSV New Testament appeared in 1964, followed by the whole Bible in 1966. In 1973 a further edition of the RSV appeared (including revisions made in the 1971 edition of the New Testament). This version of the Bible was approved for use by Protestants, Roman Catholics, and the Greek Orthodox Church, making it an English Bible for all faiths. A completely revised edition (NRSV) was published in 1990.

New Catholic Versions.

Several new versions of the English Bible designed especially for Catholic readers have appeared during the 20th century.

Knox—In 1940 Ronald Knox, an English priest with exceptional literary gifts, was commissioned by his superiors to undertake a new Bible translation. At that time it was out of the question for a translation for Catholic readers to be based on anything other than the Latin Vulgate. The Vulgate served as the base of Knox's version, but he paid attention to the original Greek and Hebrew texts. His New Testament appeared in 1945, followed by the Old Testament in 1949.

Knox had a flair for adapting his English expressions to the rigid restrictions of the Latin Vulgate style. But the progress of the biblical movement in the Catholic Church in recent years has made his translation outdated. No longer must all Catholic versions of the Bible be based on the Latin Vulgate.

The Jerusalem Bible—The Jerusalem Bible was originally a French translation of the Bible, sponsored by the Dominican faculty of the Ecole Biblique et Archeologique in Jerusalem. A one-volume edition of the work, with fewer technical notes, was issued in 1956. The English counterpart to this volume, prepared under the editorship of Alexander Jones, was published in 1966. The biblical text was translated from the Hebrew and Greek languages, although the French version was consulted throughout for guidance where variant readings or interpretations were involved.

The Jerusalem Bible is a scholarly production with a high degree of literary skill. While it is the work of Catholic translators, it is nonsectarian. Readers of many religious traditions use the Jerusalem Bible. The *New Jerusalem Bible* (NJB) is now available.

The New American Bible—The New American Bible (NAB) was launched as a revision of the Douai (or Douay) Bible for American readers. In the beginning the revision was sponsored by the Episcopal Confraternity of Christian Doctrine, and the resulting work was called the Confraternity Version. The translators were scholars who belonged to the Catholic Biblical Association of America.

The New Testament of this translation first appeared in 1941. While it was a revision of the Douai text, which was based in turn on the Latin Vulgate, the translators at times went back to the Greek text behind the Latin. They drew attention in their notes to places where the Greek and Latin texts differed.

As the project progressed, the translators moved away from the Latin Vulgate as their text, basing it instead on the Greek and Hebrew text. So radical was this fresh approach that a new name seemed appropriate for the version when the entire Bible was completed in 1970. It was no longer called the Confraternity Version but the New American Bible. This new name may have been influenced also by the title of the New English Bible, which had appeared earlier in the same year.

The New English Bible—When the copyright of the British Revised Version was about to expire (1935), the owners of the copyright, the Oxford and Cambridge University Presses, consulted scholars about the possibility of a revision to bring this translation up to date. Later the scope of the project changed so that an entirely new translation, rather than a revision of an old translation, was commissioned.

The initiative in this enterprise was taken by the Church of Scotland in 1946. It approached the British churches, and a joint committee was set up in 1947 to make plans for a new translation of the Bible into modern English. The joint committee included representatives of the principal non-Roman churches of Great Britain and Ireland, agents of Bible societies, and officials of Oxford and Cambridge University Presses. The translators' goal was to issue a version "genuinely English in idiom ... a 'timeless' English, avoiding equally both archaisms and transient modernisms." The New Testament of the New English Bible (NEB) was published in March 1961; the whole Bible, together with the Apocrypha, appeared in March 1970. Between 1961 and 1970 the New Testament received some further revision. A thoroughly revised edition, the Revised English Bible (REB) was published in 1989.

In one respect the New English Bible reverted to the policy of the translators of the King James Version; sometimes they rendered the same Hebrew or Greek word with different English words. This means the student who cannot use the Hebrew or Greek texts will be unable to use this version for detailed word study. Sometimes the NEB makes a useful distinction in its selection of words, as when "church" is reserved for the universal company of Christian believers and "congregation" is used for a local group of believers. But a useful distinction made by the RV, ASV, and RSV is sometimes obscured by the NEB. A good example is when the same word, "devil or devils," is used by the NEB for Satan as well as the beings that should more correctly be called "demons." Two different Greek words for these beings are used in the original texts, and there is no good reason why they should be called the same thing by the NEB.

Paraphrases and Simplified Versions.

Some translators have attempted to bring out the meaning of the biblical text by using either simplified or amplified vocabularies. Other translations that fall into this category are those that use lists of words considered basic to the English language.

Williams—Charles B. Williams, in *The New Testament in the Language of the People* (1937), tried to express the more delicate shades of meaning in Greek tenses by using a fuller wording. Thus, the command of Ephesians 4:25, "Let every one speak the truth with his neighbor" (RSV), is expressed, "You must ... each of you practice telling the truth to his neighbor."

Wuest—What Williams did for Greek tenses, Kenneth S. Wuest did for all parts of speech in his *Expanded Translation of the New Testament* (1956–59). In this translation, the familiar Bible phrase, "Husbands, love your wives" (Eph. 5:25), appears as, "The husbands, be loving your wives with a love self-sacrificial in its nature."

Amplified Bible—In *The Amplified Bible* (1958–65), a committee of 12 editors working for the Lockman Foundation of La Habra, California, incorporated alternative translations or additional words that would normally appear in margins or footnotes into their translation of the text. One fault of this translation is that it gives the reader no guidance to aid in choosing the proper alternative reading for specific passages.

New Testament in Basic English—Basic English is a simplified form of the language, created by C. K. Ogden, which attempts to communicate ideas with a simplified vocabulary of 850 words. In the 1930s Ogden's foundation, the Orthological

Institute, commissioned an English biblical scholar, S. H. Hooke, to produce a Basic English version of the Bible. For this purpose the basic vocabulary of 850 words was expanded to 1,000 by adding special Bible words and others helpful in the reading and understanding of poetry. *The New Testament in Basic English* appeared in 1940; the complete Bible was published in 1949.

Williams—Charles Kingsley Williams, who had experience in teaching students whose native tongue was not English, produced *The New Testament: A New Translation in Plain English* in 1952. He used a "plain English" list of less than 1,700 words in this translation.

Phillips—J. B. Phillips, an Anglican clergyman, relieved the tedium of fire-watching and similar nighttime duties during World War II by turning Paul's letters into English. This work was not a strict translation but a paraphrase that made the apostle's arguments meaningful for younger readers. He published *Letters to Young Churches* in 1947, and it became an instant success. The style was lively and forceful; the apostle Paul came across as a real man who had something important to say.

Phillips followed up on his initial success by releasing other parts of the New Testament. *The Gospels in Modern English* followed in 1952; *The Young Church in Action* (the Book of Acts) appeared in 1955; and *The Book of Revelation* was published in 1957. In 1958 the whole work appeared in one volume, *The New Testament in Modern English*. A completely revised edition of this paraphrase was issued in 1972, but many readers prefer the earlier edition.

The Living Bible—Like J. B. Phillips' work, *The Living Bible* is a paraphrase that began with a rendering of the New Testament letters—*Living Letters* (1962). The translator, Kenneth N. Taylor, prepared this paraphrase initially for his own children, who found it difficult to follow the apostle Paul's thought when his letters were read in family worship. Taylor went on to paraphrase the rest of the New Testament, then the Old Testament, until *The Living Bible* was published complete in 1971. This paraphrase is especially popular with young people. Many adults have also found that it brings the message of the Bible home to them in language they can understand.

The Good News Bible—In 1966 the American Bible Society issued *Today's English Version* (also entitled *Good News for Modern Man*), a translation of the New Testament, in simple, contemporary English. The aim of this version was similar to the preceding basic English and plain English versions, but *The Good News Bible* used no limited vocabulary list. In 1976 the entire *Bible in Today's English Version* was published. The translators of *The Good News Bible* worked to achieve "dynamic equivalence." They wanted this translation to have the same effect on modern readers that the original text produced on those who first read it. The *Good News Bible* has gained wide acceptance, and similar translations have been produced in a number of other languages.

Miscellaneous Simplified Versions—Other simplified translations of the Bible include Clarence Jordan's *Cotton Patch Version* (1968–70), which renders portions of the New Testament into the unique idiom of the American South. Also included in this category is Carl Burke's *God Is For Real, Man* (1967) and *Treat Me Cool, Lord* (1969). These were written in the unique language of prison inmates while Burke was serving as a jail chaplain.

Prominent Recent Translations.

Three versions in particular fall into this category.

New American Standard Bible—An editorial board of 54 scholars began work on this translation in the 1960s. They were determined to issue a new and revised translation based on the American Standard Version of 1901 in order to keep that version alive and usable among the Bible-reading public. Sponsored by the Lockman Foundation, the complete Bible of the NASB was published in 1971 after 11 years of careful, scholarly work. The translators used the most dependable Hebrew and Greek texts available. The editorial board has continued to function since publication of the Bible, making minor revisions and refinements in the translation as better texts of the original languages of the Bible became available.

New International Version—The New International Version (NIV) is a completely new translation of the Bible, sponsored by the International Bible Society. It is the work of an international and transdenominational team of scholars, drawn mainly from the United States but also including scholars from Canada, Britain, Australia, and New Zealand. The sponsors of the NIV claim it is "written in the language of the common man," but its language is more literary than the "common English" of the Good News Bible.

The translators of the NIV were familiar with traditional Bible English. They used the language of the King James Version where it was "accurate, clear, and readable." But they made many significant changes. Unlike the RSV and NEB (which retained "thee," "thou," and "thy" when God was being addressed), the NIV uses "you" and "your." The New Testament of this version was published in 1973; the whole Bible appeared in 1978. It underwent a modest revision in 1983.

New King James Version—The original King James Version, first published in 1611, has been the favorite translation among English-speaking peoples for more than three centuries. During its long history, the King James Bible has been updated and revised several times to reflect changes in speech as well as growing knowledge of the original text of the Scriptures. Previous major revisions of this translation were issued in 1629, 1638, 1762, and 1769.

During the 1970s, Thomas Nelson Publishers of Nashville, Tennessee, sensed the need for a fifth major revision. Over 130

Bible scholars were selected to work on the New King James Version. The translators worked from the earliest and most trustworthy Hebrew and Greek texts available and also used the 1769 King James revision as a general guide to make sure the new edition preserved the majestic style and devotional quality of the original King James.

The most noticeable change in the New King James is replacement of "thee's" and "thou's" and other archaic pronouns with their modern English equivalent. The "-est" and "-eth" verb endings also were eliminated in favor of more contemporary English idioms. The New Testament with Psalms was released in 1980, followed by the Old Testament in 1982.

New Century Version—Word Publishing's easy-to-read translation seeks to maintain faithfulness to the original languages while using a simplified vocabulary. The NCV provides clarity with regard to ancient customs, words that have changed in meaning, and difficult figures of speech, and is appropriate for use by children as well as adults.

Contemporary English Version—In 1995, the American Bible Society and Thomas Nelson Publishers introduced a new dynamic equivalent translation of the Bible, that uses clear, contemporary vocabulary to express complex ideas—making it valuable for evangelistic outreach and discipleship—especially when readers are new to the Bible, or those to whom English is a second language. The CEV is particularly good for reading aloud, as God's Word is expressed in clear and simple English.

Miscellaneous Translations.

Many English translations have not been mentioned in this article. Among Jewish translations of the Hebrew Bible, special reference should be made to *A New Translation of the Holy Scriptures according to the Masoretic Text,* produced in installments since 1963 by a committee working under the chairmanship of H. M. Orlinsky.

The Authentic New Testament (1955) is a translation by a well-known Jewish scholar, Hugh J. Schonfield. Brief mention should also be made of the following translations: The Penguin Classics edition of *The Four Gospels,* by E. V. Rieu (1952) and *The Acts of the Apostles,* by C. H. Rieu (1957); the *Berkeley Version* (New Testament, 1945; Bible, 1959), revised as *The Modern Language Bible* (1969); the *New World Translation* of Jehovah's Witnesses (1961); *The New Testament in the Language of Today,* by William F. Beck, a Lutheran scholar (1963); and *The New Testament* in the translation of William Barclay (1968–69).

BIBLICAL CRITICISM—the application of one or more techniques in the scientific study of the Bible. These techniques are not peculiar to Bible study; they would be equally helpful in the study of the writings of Homer or Shakespeare. Their primary intention is to help the reader of the Bible understand it better; for that reason biblical criticism examines the Greek and Hebrew texts (textual criticism), the historical setting of the various parts of the Bible (historical criticism), and various literary questions regarding how, when, where, and why the books of the Bible were first written (literary criticism). These methods of study, when done with reverence for Scripture, should assist a student's appreciation for the Inspiration of the Bible.

Textual Criticism.

This is the attempt to determine, as accurately as possible, the wording of the text of the Bible as first written down under the inspiration of the Holy Spirit. Since none of the original documents has survived and the text is available only in copies, it is necessary to compare the early copies with each other. This allows the textual critic to classify these early copies into groups exhibiting certain common features and to decide why their differences occurred and what the original wording most likely was.

The early copies on which textual critics work consist mainly of manuscripts in the original languages, translations into other languages, and biblical quotations made by Jewish and Christian writers.

Historical Criticism.

The examination of the Bible in light of its historical setting. This is particularly important because the Bible was written over a period of more than one thousand years. The story the Bible records extends from the beginning of civilization in the ancient world to the Roman Empire of the first century A.D. Historical criticism is helpful in determining when the books of the Bible were written. It is also helpful in determining a book's "dramatic date"—that is, when the people it describes lived and its events happened. The dramatic date of Genesis, for instance, is much earlier than the date when it was written. Historical criticism asks if the stories of the patriarchs—Abraham, Isaac, Jacob and Joseph—reflect the conditions of the times in which they lived.

The consensus is that these stories better reflect their dramatic date than the dates of their writing, just as the picture presented in the New Testament best reflects what is known about the early part of the first century A.D.

Literary Criticism.

The study of how, when, where, and why the books of the Bible were written. Literary criticism may be divided into questions concerning sources, tradition, redaction, and authorship.

1. *Source criticism* attempts to determine whether the writers of the books of the Bible used earlier sources of information and, if so, whether those sources were oral or written. Some biblical books clearly indicate their dependence on earlier sources: 1 and 2 Chronicles, Luke, and Acts. Some of the sources for the Chronicles are still available to us in 1 and 2 Samuel and 1 and 2 Kings, which were written earlier. The author of Luke and

Acts says that much of his information was handed on by "those who from the beginning were eyewitnesses and ministers of the word" (Luke 1:2).

However, these sources usually have not survived independently and their identification and reconstruction cannot be certain. It is fairly clear, however, that the Gospels of Matthew, Mark, and Luke draw on common sources; their two most widely agreed sources are one that related the story of Jesus and one that contained a collection of His teachings.

2. *Tradition criticism* (including form criticism) studies how information was passed from one generation to another before it was put in its present form. Tradition is simply that which is handed down; it may be divinely authoritative, or it may be merely "the tradition of men" (Mark 7:8; Col. 2:8). Sometimes a tradition was handed on by word of mouth for several generations before it was written down, as in the record of the patriarchs in Genesis. Sometimes a tradition was handed on by word of mouth for only 20 or 30 years, as in the records of the works and words of Jesus before the gospels were written.

Tradition criticism attempts to trace the stages by which these traditions were handed down, the forms they took at those various stages, and the forms in which they reached the people who committed them to writing.

Form criticism is the branch of tradition criticism that examines the various "forms"—e.g. parables, miracles, discourses—by which the traditions took shape. Form criticism has been applied to many areas of the biblical literature, such as the composition of the Psalms, the prophet's calls to their ministries, and the contents of the gospels. Some scholars have, for instance, classified various psalms as "Royal" psalms, "Lament" psalms, "Torah" (Law) psalms, "Praise" psalms, etc.

Classifying sections of the Bible according to the form they take can provide an additional perspective from which one can better understand the text of Scripture. However, this method must be used with great caution and restraint to avoid imposing the interpreter's own assumptions on the Bible.

3. *Redaction criticism* attempts to understand the contribution to the finished manuscript made by the person who finally committed the oral or written traditions to writing. This may be illustrated from the Gospel of Luke. Luke makes no claim to have been an eyewitness of the events of Jesus' ministry; everything he records in the Gospel was received from others. Tradition criticism studies what Luke received and the state in which he received it. Redaction criticism studies what he did with what he received. Luke (and the same can be said of the other evangelists) was a responsible author who set the stamp of his own personality on what he wrote.

It is important to remember that an author's personal contribution to the finished book was no less reliable (and, hence, no less authoritative) than the tradition which he received. Unfortunately, some redaction critics make the error of assuming that the author's work is inauthentic, ignoring the work of the Holy Spirit in inspiring the writers of the Bible.

4. *Authorship and destination criticism* involve the attempt to determine the authorship of a work, as well as the person, group, or wider public for whom it was written. Sometimes there is no need for inquiry into these matters; Paul's letter to the Romans, for example, is clearly the work of the apostle Paul and was sent by him to the Christians in Rome. But the judicious use of literary criticism will throw further light on the circumstances that led to the writing of the book and the purpose for which Romans was sent. When, however, a work is anonymous, critical inquiry may help us to discover what sort of person the author was. For example, we do not know for certain who wrote the letter to the Hebrews. However, by looking critically at Hebrews we can learn much about the character of the author and a little about the character and situation of the people to whom the letter was written.

BIBLICAL ETHICS—living righteously—doing what is good and refraining from what is evil—in accordance with the will of God. The term refers not to human theories or opinions about what is right and wrong but to God's revealed truth about these matters. Questions of human conduct prevail throughout the Bible. God's revelation through His written Word narrates the story of ethical failure on the part of human beings, God's redeeming grace, and the ethical renewal of His people.

God's people are called to holiness because they are God's people: "You shall therefore be holy, for I am holy" (Lev. 11:45). The New Testament counterpart to this principle is found in Matthew 5:48: "Therefore you shall be perfect, just as your Father in heaven is perfect."

God gave the Law to the nation of Israel as a standard of righteousness. This was the revealed will of God for His people. But His commandments were given in a context of Grace. When the Ten Commandments were given through Moses, they were introduced with a statement supporting the relationship that had already been established between God and His people whom He delivered from Egypt (Ex. 20:2; Deut. 5:6). God's commandments are always given to those who are already His people by grace.

This truth carries through to the New Testament. Jesus' ethical teaching in the Sermon on the Mount was preceded by the Beatitudes, which reminded Jesus' disciples that God's grace comes before His commands (Matt. 5:3–12).

This connection between God's demands and His grace means that biblical ethics must always be understood in terms of what God has already done for His people. Grace precedes Law, just as doctrine always precedes ethics in the letters of the New Testament. So ethics should not be regarded as the center of the Christian faith. Correct behavior is the outflow or product of grace—the proper response in those who have experienced God's grace.

For the Christian the ultimate standard of ethics is Jesus Christ and His teachings. The Christian is not under the Law of the Old Testament (Eph. 2:14–16). But since the ethical teachings of Jesus sum up the true meaning of the Old Testament Law, following His teachings fulfills the Law. So there is a direct relationship between the concept of righteousness as revealed in the Old Testament and later in the New.

The Ten Commandments, for example, are referred to as positive ethical instruction in the New Testament (Rom. 13:9). Yet the commandment concerning the Sabbath is no longer in force (Col. 2:15–16). And the ceremonial law, involving sacrificial rituals in the Temple, no longer is in effect because of the ultimate sacrifice of Christ (Heb. 10:12–18).

Jesus' commandment to love is the essence of Christian ethics. When a Pharisee asked Jesus to identify "the great commandment in the law," Jesus answered, " 'You shall love the Lord your God with all your heart, with all your soul, and with all your mind.' This is the first and great commandment. And the second is like it: 'You shall love your neighbor as yourself.' On these two commandments hang all the Law and the prophets" (Matt. 22:37–40). The apostle Paul also declared that all the commandments are "summed up in this saying, namely, 'You shall love your neighbor as yourself.' Love does no harm to a neighbor; therefore love is the fulfillment of the Law" (Rom. 13:9–10). This great love commandment summarizes and fulfills the intention of the Old Testament Law.

While love is the summary of Christian ethics, the New Testament contains many specific ethical instructions. A basic pattern for this ethical teaching is the contrast between our old existence before faith in Christ and our new existence in Him. Christians are called to leave behind their old conduct and to put on the new (Eph. 4:22–24), to walk in newness of life (Rom. 6:4), and to exhibit the fruit of the Spirit (Gal. 5:22–23).

Although as Christians we are free from the Law, we are not to use that liberty "as an opportunity for the flesh, but through love" to "serve one another" (Gal. 5:13). Love is best expressed through service and self-giving (Matt. 20:26–27). These points lead naturally to the observation that Jesus Himself is the supreme example of righteousness. Christian ethics are summed up not only in His teaching, but in His life as well. So true discipleship consists of following Jesus (Eph. 5:2) and being conformed to His image (Rom. 8:29).

The call for righteousness is directed to the individual, but ethics also has an important social dimension. The centrality of love indicates this very clearly. The prophets of the Old Testament emphasized the connection between righteousness and social justice (Amos 2:6–8; 5:24). The ethical teachings of the Bible as followed by Christians will have an impact on the world (Matt. 5:13–16). But in spite of all these truths, the Bible does not call for a social program to be imposed upon the world. The ethics of the Bible are for the people of God. The Sermon on the Mount is for disciples of Christ. As Christians follow biblical ethics, the world will be affected for good by them.

BIBLICAL THEOLOGY—theology as it is understood from the perspective of the biblical writers themselves. This category of theology must be carefully distinguished from systematic theology, which systematizes and re-expresses the teachings of the Bible through the use of modern concepts and categories. Biblical theology is *biblical* because it states the theology of the Bible by limiting itself to the language, categories, and perspectives of the biblical writers. It attempts to arrive at this understanding without modern theological biases or assumptions.

Biblical theology is historical in its orientation. It attempts to get into the minds of the authors of Scripture in order to arrive at the meanings they intended for their original readers. This means that biblical theology is dependent upon careful interpretation of the biblical texts in their original languages. But biblical theology is much more complex than merely compiling Bible verses on various themes or subjects in the Bible, followed by a summary of this material. This approach would not be sensitive to the various historical contexts and specific emphases of the biblical writers.

Biblical theology does attempt to systematize, but only to the extent that this can be done without imposing an artificial structure upon the biblical writers. The biblical theologian will go no further than these writers went in systematizing their material. Biblical theology wants to represent their perspectives as clearly and as faithfully as possible.

Unity and Diversity.

Biblical theology is divided into Old Testament theology and New Testament theology, although the relation between the two also concerns biblical theologians. Further specialization also occurs within both Old Testament and New Testament theologies. Biblical theologians often speak of the theologies of Deuteronomy, Isaiah, Paul, or Matthew. This is in keeping with the emphasis of biblical theology upon the distinctives of the individual biblical writers.

But a big part of the task of biblical theology is to pull together the common emphases of the biblical writers and to seek the unity of their writings. Although these inspired writers have different contributions to make to the subject of God and His revelation, their writings are compatible with each other. Thus biblical theology focuses on the diversity that exists within the larger unity of Scripture, and tries to set forth that which unifies, without ignoring the diversity.

Method.

As long as the interpreter gives sufficient attention to the distinctives of the various writers, biblical theology can organize its work topically, according to main subjects. But because biblical theology is primarily interested in historical understanding, it is better to proceed chronologically. Thus, biblical theologians work their way progressively through the Bible, tracing the progress of revelation and the development of theological thought, from the earliest writers to the latest. Biblical theology thus becomes the history of progressive revelation progressively set forth. The focus is not on the religious experience of the people, but on the revelation of God and His people's understanding of His acts.

History of Salvation.

Biblical theologians seek to find the best organizing principle or idea that serves as the center of a biblical theology. Old Testament theologians have suggested such ideas as the covenant, the Lordship of God, the presence of God, and the people of God. New Testament theologians have mentioned the kingdom of God, grace, salvation, resurrection, and kerygma (a summary of the main points in the preaching of the earliest Christians in the Book of Acts).

Any of these concepts can be used as an organizing principle, for all the central concepts of the Bible are related. But certainly one of the most helpful suggestions to come from biblical theologians is the idea of "salvation history." This refers to the saving acts of God in history. It is an ideal organizing principle for both Old and New Testaments.

Many biblical theologians believe the most effective way to look at the Bible is in terms of God's special acts of salvation on behalf of His people Israel and the church. But they see these various individual events as a unity, moving from promise to completion. Thus, "salvation history" is a single great plan of salvation that finds its ultimate fulfillment in the work of

Christ. Following is a broad overview of the events in this salvation history.

The Old Testament as Promise: Israel.

Two basic theological truths of the Old Testament are God as Creator and God as Redeemer. The created order is God's not only because He created it, but also because He is in the process of redeeming it from its rebellion and sin. The Bible is the story of God setting right what went wrong with His creation because of the fall of Adam.

The history of salvation begins with the call of Abraham and the covenant between Abraham and God (Gen. 12:1–3). This story reaches its conclusion in the coming of Jesus Christ. The election of the nation of Israel as God's special people is not for their sake alone, but for the sake of all the peoples of the world ("in you all the families of the earth shall be blessed," Gen. 12:3). This blessing is ultimately experienced by the church through faith in Jesus Christ.

The great redemptive act of the Old Testament is the Exodus, the deliverance of God's people from bondage in Egypt. This is the Old Testament counterpart to the deliverance brought about by Christ through His death on the cross. Through the Exodus, God revealed not only His sovereign power, but also his faithfulness and the depth of His covenant love for Israel. This was followed immediately by the covenant between God and His people renewed at Mount Sinai and the giving of the Law. God had already entered into covenant relationship with His people and had miraculously delivered them. This means that obedience to the Law cannot be understood as a requirement for becoming the people of God and enjoying His favor. The Law was given in the context of God's grace.

From the perspective of the New Testament, the Law may be interpreted as having several purposes. It was given to instruct the people about the absolute holiness of God and the sinfulness of humanity. The Law also set Israel apart from the surrounding nations in order that its people might be the pure channel by which the Messiah could come and accomplish His saving work for all humanity.

Through the prophets of the Old Testament the work of Christ was anticipated most clearly. They cautioned the people against presuming upon their relationship with God, as though being a member of the chosen race were a virtue in itself (Amos 3:1–2). And they tried to lift the people's eyes from their national and political concerns to God's love for all nations. God's intent was to transform the entire fallen creation; He was not concerned only with the political sovereignty of the nation of Israel.

All along God was up to something far greater than Israel realized. He was planning to do a new thing (Is. 42:10; 65:17). The prophet Jeremiah expressed this truth by referring to a "new covenant" that God would establish in the future (Jer. 31:31–34). The old covenant, particularly the Law, could not accomplish the goal that God had for His people and His creation. In the new covenant His Law would be written on the hearts of His people, and they would enjoy the lasting forgiveness of their sins.

God preserved His people through the experiences of the division of the kingdom, the destruction of the nations of Israel and Judah, the Captivity, and the resettlement of His people in Jerusalem. He continued to reveal Himself and His purposes through the prophets, who increasingly spoke of what God would do in the near future. In this spirit of anticipation His people entered the New Testament era with its great announcement of fulfillment and hope in Jesus Christ.

The New Testament as Fulfillment: the Church.

The New Testament announced the ministry of Jesus as the turning point of the ages, the beginning of the great fulfillment proclaimed by the prophets. It is impossible to exaggerate the centrality of this theme of fulfillment in the New Testament.

The use of more than 300 quotations from the Old Testament in the New Testament clearly demonstrates this point.

According to the first three gospels, the message of Jesus was that the kingdom of God had arrived. The kingdom was expressed in both the words and deeds of Jesus. The presence of the kingdom depends directly on the presence of the Messianic King. With His arrival, the fulfillment of the end time has already begun, although it is clear that the final realization of God's purpose remains yet in the future.

The death of Jesus was important as the basis of the kingdom. The rule of God in the human heart cannot be experienced in any age, present or future, without the atoning sacrifice that reconciles sinners with a holy God. Thus the death of Jesus became central for the theology of the New Testament. But the resurrection was equally important. In this event, the new order of the new creation broke directly into the present age. The resurrection of Christ was assurance of the truths He had proclaimed, as well as the resurrection of the dead at the end of time.

The pouring out of the Holy Spirit at Pentecost depended on the finished work of Christ in His death and resurrection. This was a certain sign of the new age brought by Christ and the mark of the new people of God, the church. The ministry of the Spirit guarantees that the results of Christ's work are experienced in the believer's life until Jesus returns to earth.

In the sermons preached by the first Christians (in the first half of the Book of Acts), we see the main points of the faith of the early church. In fulfillment of prophecy, Jesus was born of the line of David, was crucified, died, and was buried. But He arose from the dead and will return some day as Judge. The possibility of repentance and salvation is thus founded directly on these saving acts of God in His Son.

The letters of the New Testament contain interpretation and application of these events. Many of the letters, or epistles, are divided into two main sections—doctrine and ethics. In the doctrinal sections of these letters, the meaning of Christ's work is described. The ethical sections always build on the doctrinal foundations, instructing Christians on how to live the Christian life.

In both the doctrinal and ethical sections of the epistles, the excitement of the fulfillment experienced through Jesus Christ is always foremost. The work of Christ, particularly in the Cross and the Resurrection, is considered the saving act of God. These are compared to the saving acts of God in the Old Testament. Thus, in biblical theology, the promises of God in the Old Testament are fulfilled in God's great act of redemption through His Son in the New.

CATHOLIC EPISTLES—the traditional designation of seven letters in the New Testament: James; 1 and 2 Peter; 1, 2, and 3 John; and Jude. The word "catholic" means "general, worldwide, universal" (in contrast to specific). When applied to these non-Pauline epistles, it means they were circulated generally throughout the whole of Christendom and not just sent to a specific local church.

CHRONICLES, BOOKS OF FIRST AND SECOND—two historical books of the Old Testament that may be characterized as "books of hope." In broad, selective strokes, these books trace the history of humankind from Adam to the Captivity and Restoration. Much of this material is a repetition of that found in the books of 1 and 2 Samuel and 1 and 2 Kings. But the writer of Chronicles apparently wrote his history to encourage the exiles who had returned to Jerusalem after 70 years of captivity in Babylon. This selective history reminded them of Israel's glorious days from the past and gave them hope for the future as they pondered God's promises to His Covenant People.

Structure of the Book.

The books of 1 and 2 Chronicles were written originally as one unbroken book. In later translations of the Bible, however, this long narrative was divided into two shorter books. Each of these books falls naturally into two major divisions.

The first nine chapters of 1 Chronicles contain long genealogies, or family histories, that are composed of information from the earliest historical books of the Bible. These genealogies take the reader from the descendants of Adam up through the ancestors of King David. Special attention is given to the families of priests and Levites (6:1–81; 9:1–34), Saul's family, and particularly to the family of David (chaps. 2–3). The second major section of the book (chaps. 10–29) focuses on the reign of King David. This long account begins with the death of Saul (chap. 10), omitting the historical facts that preceded this event. Saul's death is reported to establish the fact that he was unqualified for office and that David was God's choice for this responsibility (10:14).

The account of David's reign is presented in a positive light, with all the details about David's great sin omitted. First Chronicles also lists the names of all those associated with him as mighty men (chaps. 11–12), and records his great victories (chaps. 14, 18–20). This section of the book also lists the names of the Levites, priests, and musicians in David's administration (chaps. 23–26), as well as other state officials (chap. 27). Also included is David's work in establishing Jerusalem as his capital city (11:4–9), and as the center of worship (chaps. 13, 15–16, 22, 28–29).

The Book of 2 Chronicles also contains two major sections. Chapters 1–9 focus on the rule of King Solomon, whose greatest accomplishment was the building of the Temple in Jerusalem. Included is correspondence between Solomon and Hiram, king of Tyre, about building materials (chap. 2), as well as a full account of the dedication service when the Temple was completed (chaps. 5–7). The second major section (chaps. 10–36) is a highly selective account of the kings of Judah—from Rehoboam (chaps. 10–12) until the time of the Captivity (chap.

36). Kings given prominence in this narrative include Abijah (chap. 13), Asa (chaps. 14–16), Jehoshaphat (chaps. 17–20), Joash (chaps. 23–24), Amaziah (chap. 25), Uzziah or Azariah (chap. 26), Hezekiah (chaps. 29–32), and Josiah (chaps. 34–35). The book ends with the proclamation of King Cyrus of Persia allowing the return of the Jews to rebuild their Temple in Jerusalem (36:22–23).

One particularly interesting fact about the Book of 2 Chronicles is that it includes little information about the kings of the Northern Kingdom, Israel. And the facts it gives about the kings of Judah are mostly positive. This indicates the author was interested in tracing the line of David and showing that Judah was the nation that remained faithful to the covenant between God and His people. This fact would have been encouraging to the exiles who returned to Jerusalem to rebuild the Temple. They felt they were continuing the forms and traditions that set them apart as the true worshipers of God and gave them a sense of identity as God's Covenant People.

Authorship and Date.

The author of the Books of 1 and 2 Chronicles is unknown, although Ezra the priest and scribe (Ezra 7:1–6, 10–11) seems the most likely possibility. As in 1 and 2 Chronicles, the Books of Ezra and Nehemiah were written originally as one unbroken book in the Hebrew language. And the last two verses of 2 Chronicles are repeated in the first three verses of the Book of Ezra, probably indicating that the latter was originally a continuation of the former. Most scholars agree that these four books were written and compiled by the same person, but not all accept the theory of Ezra's authorship.

Ezra, however, remains the best candidate for this honor because of his important role among the community of exiles in Jerusalem. After leading a group to return to their homeland, he worked with another Jewish leader, Nehemiah, to strengthen the people's commitment to God's law (Ezra

10:17–19; Neh. 8:1–8; 9:1–3). He must have written all four of these books—1 and 2 Chronicles, Ezra and Nehemiah—some time after he arrived in Jerusalem about 458 B.C. and led the reforms among the people.

The Chronicler used many sources in writing his book, including the Books of Samuel and Kings. He also used court histories, as did earlier writers, and prophetic narratives. One illustration of this procedure can be observed in 2 Chronicles 9:29, at the end of the story of Solomon.

Historical Setting.

The Books of 1 and 2 Chronicles cover several centuries of the history of God's Covenant People—from the founders of the nation until the end of their captivity in Babylonia and Persia about 538 B.C. But the books were written with a specific purpose in mind—to give comfort and hope to those who returned to Jerusalem.

The stage was set for the return of the Jewish people to Jerusalem after the Persians defeated Babylonia and became the dominant power of the ancient world. The Babylonians had held the Jewish people captive for 70 years, but the Persians had a different foreign policy. They believed in letting their subject nations live in their own native regions under the authority of a ruling governor. They allowed the Jewish people to return to Jerusalem in several different stages, beginning with the first wave under Zerubbabel in 538 B.C. (2 Chr. 36:22–23).

After they returned to Jerusalem and rebuilt the Temple, the remnant of God's Covenant People needed constant encouragement. Keeping their faith and traditions alive required continual struggle. The situation called for determination and a strong sense of hope—hope that the promises of God to David would not be forgotten, and that a king from this royal line would rule again one day among God's people. This was the unique situation to which the Books of 1 and 2 Chronicles were addressed.

Theological Contribution.

The Books of 1 and 2 Chronicles tie the entire sweep of the Old Testament together into one great affirmation of hope. These books should not only be read as histories, but for their insights into how God has kept faith with His Covenant People across the centuries. By selecting events that show how God has kept His promises, the author presents a beautiful doctrine of hope that begins with Adam (1 Chr. 1:1) and stretches to the end of the Captivity of God's people thousands of years later (2 Chr. 36:23). The clear implication for Christians today is that He is still a God of hope whose ultimate purpose will prevail in the world and in the lives of His people.

The Books of 1 and 2 Chronicles emphasize such priestly interests as genealogies, the offices and duties of priests and Levites, the building and dedication of the Temple and its furnishings, and the organization of Temple leadership and worship. They virtually ignore the apostate rulers of the Northern Kingdom of Israel, giving at least minimal attention to each of the 20 rulers of the Southern Kingdom of Judah. Positive aspects of rule in the south are stressed, with the reigns of David the ideal king and Solomon his successor receiving the most attention. Honoring David and his dynasty is clearly high on the chronicler's agenda. As the last book in the Hebrew canon, Chronicles thus prepares the way for the book of "the genealogy of Jesus Christ, the Son of David" (Matt. 1:1).

COLOSSIANS, EPISTLE TO THE—one of four shorter epistles written by Paul while he was in prison, the others being Philippians, Ephesians, and Philemon. The Epistle to the Colossians focuses on the person and work of Jesus Christ. It reaches heights of expression that rival anything said of Christ elsewhere in Scripture. Colossians shares many similarities in style and content with Ephesians. Colossians probably was written as a companion to the brief letter to Philemon (compare Col. 4:7–13 and Philem. 12, 24).

Structure of the Epistle.

Colossians is nearly divided, as are most of Paul's epistles, into doctrinal (chaps. 1–2) and practical (chaps. 3–4) sections. Following the opening address (1:1–2), Paul expresses his thankfulness for the faith, love, hope, and example of the Colossians (1:3–8). He then develops a majestic hymn to Christ, emphasizing His role in both creation and redemption (1:15–23). In light of the surpassing worth of Christ and His work, Paul willingly accepts the obligation to proclaim Christ and to suffer for Him (1:24–2:5). He also appeals to the Colossians to take root in Christ rather than in confusing speculations (2:6–23).

In the second section, Paul urges the Colossian Christians to mold their behavior to fit their beliefs. Since believers share in Christ's resurrection (3:1–4), Paul encourages them to continue living to please God. He urges them to "put to death" various vices and to "put on" the character of Christ (3:5–17). True Christianity also works itself out in social relationships between wives and husbands (3:18–19), children and parents (3:20–21), and slaves and masters (3:22–4:1). Paul concludes with a note on witnessing to unbelievers (4:2–6) and his customary greetings (4:7–18).

Authorship and Date.

Colossians was written by Paul (and Timothy, 1:1) to a Christian community (perhaps "house churches," 1:2; 4:15) that he had not visited (2:1). Paul had established a resident ministry in Ephesus, 100 miles west of Colosse. For more than two years the influence of his ministry reached "all who dwelt in Asia" (Acts 19:10). Epaphras must have heard Paul in Ephesus and then carried the gospel to Colosse (1:7–8; 4:12–13).

Paul wrote the epistle from prison (4:3, 10, 18), but he did not indicate where he was imprisoned. Caesarea and Ephesus have been suggested, but the most probable place is Rome (Acts 28:30). This would date the epistle in the late 50s or early 60s.

Historical Setting.

False teaching had taken root in Colosse. This teaching combined Jewish observances (2:16) and pagan speculation (2:8); it is possible that this resulted in an early form of Gnosticism. This teaching pretended to add to or improve upon the gospel that, indirectly at least, had come from Paul. Some of the additions Paul mentions are feasts and observances, some of them related to astrology (2:16), plus a list of rules (2:20). These practices were then included within a philosophy in which angels played a leading role (2:18); Paul calls this philosophy "the basic principles of the world" (2:8).

Theological Contribution.

Paul unmasks the false teaching as "empty deceit ... of men" (2:8), having the "appearance of wisdom" (2:23), but useless in fact. He declares that the addition of such things dilutes rather than strengthens the faith (2:20).

But Paul does more than denounce false teaching. The best corrective is a firm grip on who Jesus Christ is and what He did for our salvation. In Christ "are hidden all the treasures of wisdom and knowledge" (2:3), and "in Him all fullness" dwells (1:19). In fact, "He is the image of the invisible God" (1:15). He has stripped every power opposed to Him (2:15), wiped out every accusation against us (2:14), and actually "reconciled all things to Himself" (1:20). He is not only head of the church (1:18); but He stands before all time and above every power, and at the end of all history (1:16).

This beautiful epistle on the majesty of Jesus Christ speaks to us today as much as to the Colossians. It reminds us that Jesus Christ is sufficient for every need and is still the most powerful force in the world.

CORBAN [KAWR bahn] (*an offering brought near*)—a word applied to a gift or offering in the Temple that declared that gift dedicated to God in a special sense. Once a gift was offered under the special declaration of Corban, it could not be withdrawn or taken back; it was considered totally dedicated for the Temple's special use.

Jesus condemned the Pharisees for encouraging the people to make such gifts to the Temple while neglecting their responsibility to care for their parents (Mark 7:11–13). According to Jesus, this was a clear violation of a higher commandment, "Honor your father and your mother" (Mark 7:10).

CORINTHIANS, EPISTLES TO THE—two letters of the apostle Paul addressed to the church in Corinth. First Corinthians is unique among the Pauline letters because of the variety of its practical concerns. Second Corinthians is one of Paul's most personal letters, containing a wealth of insights into the heart of Paul the pastor. Both letters reveal the degree to which Paul identified with his churches, suffering in their shortcomings and celebrating their victories. The Corinthian correspondence draws us into a world much like our own. Paul the anxious pastor wrote to young Christians who were concerned with problems involved in living the Christian life in a non-Christian environment.

Structure of the Epistles.

Following the introduction (1 Cor. 1:1–9), Paul appealed to the Corinthians to mend the divisions within the church (1:10–4:21). Paul reminded the Corinthians that they were united by the simple, but life-changing, preaching of the cross (1 Cor. 1:18–2:16). Indeed, each church leader builds on the one foundation of Jesus (chap. 3), and consequently labors in behalf of Christ (chap. 4). In chapters 5 and 6 Paul took up two moral abuses in Corinth. He judged a man who had sexual intercourse with his father's wife (chap. 5), and he reproved the believers for generating arguments that wound up in court before nonbelieving judges (1 Cor. 6:1–11).

Paul then addressed certain questions which were brought to him by the Corinthians: about sexuality (6:12–20), marriage (chap. 7), and eating food offered previously to idols (chap. 8). On such matters Paul appealed for a responsible use of Christian freedom—not for self-gain, but in consideration for the other. He reminded them that he conducted his own ministry in this way (chap. 9), and he warned against becoming fixed on anything that could lead to idolatry (chap. 10).

Paul then returned to other abuses, especially involving church order. In chapter 11 he developed the correct teaching on the Lord's Supper; in chapter 12 on spiritual gifts; in chapter 13 on love; in chapter 14 on the charismatic gifts of tongues and prophecy, and in chapter 15 on the resurrection. Finally, he reminded the Corinthians of the weekly collection for the saints in Jerusalem (16:1–4). He concluded with travel plans and greetings (16:5–24).

Second Corinthians is closely related to the circumstances that occasioned its writing. The letter begins with reference to a painful experience of rejection at Corinth (Paul's third visit). Paul gave thanks that the Corinthians were now reconciled to him (chap. 1), but he recalled his torment over their stubbornness (chap. 2). Chapters 3 and 4 are theological reflections on ministry, and chapters 5 and 6 on reconciliation. In chapter 7 Paul shared his joy at the church's repentance. paul changed perspective in chapters 8 and 9 by turning to the matter of the collection for the church in Jerusalem.

The tone of 2 Corinthians changes in chapters 10–13. These chapters are laced with warnings to the Corinthians and Paul's opponents, defenses of his apostleship, and a rehearsal of Paul's sufferings as an apostle. If chapters 1–9 reveal Paul's joy and relief, chapters 10–13 let us see the wounds, both physical and emotional, which he bore as an apostle. The letter closes with the only trinitarian benediction in the Bible (2 Cor. 13:14).

Authorship and Date.

First and Second Corinthians bear unmistakable marks of Pauline authorship (1 Cor. 1:1; 2 Cor. 2:1). The first epistle was written from Ephesus (1 Cor. 16:8) during Paul's third missionary journey, perhaps in A.D. 56. The second letter followed some 12 to 15 months later from Macedonia, where Paul met Titus and received news of the church's repentance (2 Cor. 2:12–17).

Historical Setting.

Acts 18:1–18 records the founding of the Corinthian church. During his second missionary journey, Paul went alone from Athens to Corinth in about A.D. 51. There he labored with a Jewish–Christian couple, Aquila and Priscilla, who recently had been expelled from Rome by the emperor Claudius because they were Jews. Silas and Timothy also joined Paul in Corinth. When Paul left Corinth 18 months later, a Christian congregation flourished. The congregation was composed primarily of former pagans (1 Cor. 12:2), most of them apparently from the lower classes (1 Cor. 1:26–28). Some were slaves (1 Cor. 7:21). A few wealthier persons (1 Cor. 11:22–32) and Jews, however (8:1–13), were among the believers.

A bit of detective work enables us to reconstruct the circumstances of the Corinthian correspondence. It is reasonably certain that Paul wrote four letters and paid perhaps three visits to the church in Corinth.

During his third missionary journey, Paul received word about immorality in the young congregation at Corinth. He wrote a letter (which has since been lost) against mixing with fornicators (1 Cor. 5:9). The letter apparently failed to achieve its purpose. Some time later Paul learned (1 Cor. 1:11; 16:17) that the sexual problems persisted, along with others. Paul responded by writing a second letter (probably 1 Corinthians), in which he referred to various points raised by the Corinthians (see the sections beginning, "Now concerning," 1 Cor. 7:1, 25; 8:1; 12:1; 16:1). In addition, he condemned the Corinthians for their divisions (1 Cor. 1:10) and their gross sexual violations (1 Cor. 5:1).

This letter also failed to correct the abuses at Corinth. Paul then apparently made a visit to Corinth, during which he was rebuffed (2 Cor. 2:1). From Ephesus Paul then wrote a third letter in which he spared no punches in his contest with the willful Corinthians. This letter, which he sent by Titus, has also been lost. Many scholars believe it has been attached to 2 Corinthians and preserved as chapters 10–13 of his epistle.

In anxiety over the possible effect of this drastic letter, and impatient over Titus' delay in returning, Paul traveled north from Ephesus to Macedonia. There Titus met him and, to Paul's relief and joy, reported that the Corinthians had punished the ringleader of the opposition and repented (2 Cor. 2:5–11). Paul then wrote a fourth letter (2 Corinthians), recounting his former anxiety and expressing his joy over the reform in Corinth.

Theological Contribution.

The problems Paul faced in the church at Corinth were complex and explosive. The correspondence that resulted is rich and profound in theological insight. While addressing the problems in Corinth, the apostle reaches some of the most sublime heights in all New Testament literature.

Corinth, like its neighboring city of Athens, symbolized Greek culture in its desire for wisdom and power. Paul must have been tempted to write to the Greeks as a Christian philosopher (1 Cor. 2:4). He rejected this tendency, however, and relied instead on the irony of the cross, "to the Jews a stumbling block and to the Greeks foolishness" (1 Cor. 1:23). The foolishness of the gospel—indeed, its offensiveness to cultured Greeks—was indication of its power to save. To those who respond, "Christ is the power of God and the wisdom of God" (1 Cor. 1:24). According to Paul, the preaching of the cross is not a human teaching but a revelation of the Spirit, who makes known the mind of Christ (1 Cor. 2:10–16). The centrality of the cross overcomes all divisions within the church.

Since many of the problems arising in Corinth concerned behavior and morals, Paul majored on ethical advice in his correspondence. The leading principle he uses is that "all things are lawful for me, but not all things are helpful" (1 Cor. 6:12; 10:23). Christians ought to use their freedom not for self-advantage, but for the glory of God and the good of their neighbors. This principle goes beyond legislating simple "dos and don'ts." Instead, it cultivates a mature and responsible faith that will provide guidance for every moral problem.

First Corinthians is also important because of its teaching on the gifts of the Spirit (chap. 12) and the resurrection of the dead (chap. 15). Paul recognized a variety of gifts (12:4–10), but insisted that "one and the same Spirit" gives them. The body consists of different parts, but remains one organism. Likewise, Christ's body of believers consists of members with different gifts, each given by the one Spirit.

First Corinthians 15 is our earliest record of the resurrection in the New Testament. Unless Christ has been resurrected, Paul maintained, the faith of Christians is empty (15:12–19). As death came through Adam, so new life comes through Christ (15:21, 45). The resurrection of Jesus is the "firstfruits" (15:20) of the victory to come. Because of the resurrection the believer can confess, "O death, where is your sting?" (15:55).

Second Corinthians is probably best known for its teaching on Christian ministry. Chapters 4 and 5 are unrivaled for their beauty of expression and grandeur of thought. Paul marvels at the treasure of the gospel that God entrusts to human servants. Indeed, the weakness of the servant only highlights the message of salvation (4:1–15). This message finds its most famous expression in 2 Corinthians 5:17, "If anyone is in Christ, he is a new creation; old things have passed away; behold, all things have become new." The voltage of this truth transforms Christian messengers into ambassadors for Christ.

Special Considerations.

As in the case with the resurrection, Corinthians also contains the earliest record of the Lord's Supper (1 Cor. 11:23–26). The immortal last words of Christ, "This cup is the new covenant in my blood" (11:24–25), recall his past death and anticipate his future return.

First Corinthians also contains one of the best-known chapters in the New Testament. In poetic cadence Paul proclaims "the more excellent way" of *agape* (chap. 13). Love is not merely a feeling, but an attitude committed to patience, hope, and stability in the face of problems. Such love will outlast the world itself. Agape love is the greatest characteristic of Christian life and experience.

COVENANT—an agreement between two people or two groups that involves promises on the part of each to the other. The Hebrew word for "covenant" probably means "betweenness," emphasizing the relational element that lies at the basis of all covenants. Human covenants or treaties were either between equals or between a superior and an inferior. Divine covenants, however, are always of the latter type, and the concept of covenant between God and His people is one of the most important theological truths of the Bible. Indeed, the word itself has come to denote the two main divisions of Christian Scripture: Old Covenant and New Covenant (traditionally, Old Testament and New Testament).

By making a covenant with Abraham, God promised to bless His descendants and to make them His special people. Abraham, in return, was to remain faithful to God and to serve as a channel through which God's blessings could flow to the rest of the world (Gen. 12:1–3). God's covenant with Abraham was made (Gen. 15:18) and confirmed (Gen. 17:2) to guarantee that Abraham's descendants would be innumerable and that they would receive the Promised Land. The Abrahamic covenant sign is circumcision (Gen. 17:11).

Even before Abraham's time, God also made a covenant with Noah. It illustrates three important principles: (1) All divine covenants originate with God (Gen. 9:9); (2) all of them are everlasting (Gen. 9:16); (3) all of them are memorialized with a visible sign, in this case the rainbow (Gen. 9:13). The purpose of the Noahic covenant was the divine promise that God would never again destroy all sinful humanity by a flood (Gen. 9:11).

Another famous covenant was between God and David, in which David and his descendants were established as the royal heirs to the throne of the nation of Israel (2 Sam. 7:12; 22:51). This covenant agreement reached its highest fulfillment when Jesus the Messiah, a descendant of the line of David, was born in Bethlehem about a thousand years after God made this promise to David the king (Matt. 1:1; 2:4–6; Luke 1:29–33).

God's covenant with Israel through Moses is the "old" or "first" covenant as contrasted with the "new" (Jer. 31:31–34; 2 Cor. 3:6–17; Gal. 4:24–31; Heb. 8:3–9:22). Its establishment (Ex. 19:3–25), stipulations (Ex. 20:1–17), exposition (Ex. 20:22–23:33), and confirmation (Ex. 24:1–12) constituted the formal basis of the redemptive relationship between the Lord and His Chosen People until it was superseded by the new covenant (Heb. 8:3). The Mosaic covenant sign is the Sabbath (Ex. 31:13, 16–17). Israel's pledge to obey the Lord (Ex. 19:8; 24:3, 7), on the basis of which Moses sprinkled the "blood of the covenant" on them (Ex. 24:8), was broken soon (Ex. 32:1–31) and often (Jer. 31:32).

All biblical covenants were solemnized by slaying one or more animals and shedding their blood (Gen. 8:20; 15:9–10; Ex. 24:5; Jer. 34:18–20), the importance of which is reflected in the Hebrew idiom "cut a covenant" (Gen. 15:18; Jer. 34:18), uniformly translated "made a covenant." The blood-bought ratification of the earlier covenants prefigured the "new covenant in [Jesus'] blood" (Luke 22:20; 1 Cor. 11:25), shed as the sign and seal of our redemption once for all people and for all time (Heb. 10:5–19).

A covenant, in the biblical sense, implies much more than a contract or simple agreement. A contract always has an end date, while a covenant is a permanent arrangement. Another difference is that a contract generally involves only one part of a person, such as a skill, while a covenant covers a person's total being.

The Old Testament contains many examples of covenants between people who related to each other as equals. For example, David and Jonathan entered into a covenant because of their love for each other. This agreement bound each of them to certain responsibilities (1 Sam. 18:3). The striking thing about God's covenants with His people is that God is holy, all-knowing, and all powerful; but He consents to enter into covenants with people who are weak, sinful, and imperfect.

The New Testament makes a clear distinction between covenants of Law and covenants of Promise. The apostle Paul spoke of these "two covenants," one originating "from Mount Sinai," the other from "the Jerusalem above" (Gal. 4:24–26). Paul also argued that the covenant established at Mount Sinai, the Law, is a "ministry of death" and "condemnation" (2 Cor. 3:7, 9)—a covenant that cannot be obeyed because of human weakness and sin (Rom. 8:3).

But the "covenants of promise" (Eph. 2:12) are God's guarantees that He will provide salvation in spite of people's inability to keep their side of the agreement because of sin. The provision of a Chosen People through whom the Messiah would be born is the promise of the covenants with Adam and David (Gen. 3:15; 2 Sam. 7:14–15). The covenant with Noah is God's promise to withhold judgment on nature while salvation is occurring (Gen. 8:21–22; 2 Pet. 3:7, 15). In the covenant with Abraham, God promised to bless Abraham's descendants because of his faith (Gen. 12:1–3).

These many covenants of promise may be considered one covenant of grace, which was fulfilled in the life and ministry of Jesus. His death ushered in the new covenant under which we are justified by God's grace and mercy rather than our human attempts to keep the law. And Jesus Himself is the Mediator of this better covenant between God and humankind (Heb. 9:15).

Jesus' sacrificial death served as the oath, or pledge, that God made to us to seal this new covenant. He is determined to give us eternal life and fellowship with Him, in spite of our unworthiness. As the Book of Hebrews declares, "The word of the oath, which came after the law, appoints the Son who has been perfected forever" (Heb. 7:28). This is still God's promise to any person who turns to Him in repentance and faith.

DANIEL, BOOK OF—a major prophetic book of the Old Testament that emphasizes the truth that God is in control of world history. The book is named for Daniel, its author and central personality, who was rescued miraculously from a den of lions after he refused to bow down and worship a pagan king.

Structure of the Book.

Daniel's 12 chapters may be divided naturally into three major sections: (1) introductory information about Daniel (chap. 1); (2) narratives about Daniel and his friends during their days of captivity among the Babylonians and the Persians (chaps. 2–7); and (3) Daniel's dreams and visions concerning the future of Israel and the end of time (chaps. 8–12).

The first chapter sets the stage for the rest of the book by introducing Daniel and his three friends, Hananiah, Mishael, and Azariah. These four young Hebrew men were taken captive in one of the Babylonian raids against Judah in 605 B.C. Intelligent and promising, they were placed in special training as servants in the court of King Nebuchadnezzar; then their names and diets were changed to reflect Babylonian culture in an attempt to take away their Jewish identity. But Daniel and his friends rose to the challenge, proving their Jewish food was superior to the diet of the Babylonians. The young men increased in wisdom and knowledge, gaining favor in the king's court.

In the second major section of the book (chaps. 2–7), Daniel and his friends met several additional tests to prove that although they were being held captive by a pagan people, the God whom they worshiped was still in control. Daniel's three friends (renamed Shadrach, Meshach, and Abed–Nego) refused to worship the pagan Babylonian gods. Cast into the fiery furnace, they emerged unharmed because of God's miraculous protection. Daniel, refusing to bow down and worship Darius, the king of Persia, was thrown into a den of lions. But he was also saved by God's direct intervention. These tests proved that the God whom they served was superior to the pagan gods of their captors.

Daniel's skill as an interpreter of dreams is also well established in this second section of his book. He interpreted several visions and dreams for King Nebuchadnezzar of Babylonia. As he revealed the meaning of the mysterious "handwriting on the wall" to Nebuchadnezzar's successor Belshazzar, he made it plain that the Babylonian Empire would be defeated by the Medes and the Persians. This happened exactly as Daniel predicted (5:13–31), and he continued as a servant in the court of the conquering Persian king.

The final section of Daniel's book (chaps. 8–12) consists of a series of visions about succeeding kingdoms and the end of time. These visions came to the prophet during his years in captivity. Standing by the Tigris River in one of these visions, he saw a goat attack a ram. The goat symbolized the Greeks, who would defeat the Medes and Persians (Dan. 8:20–21). This goat had several different horns, representing the subsequent division of the Greek Empire among the four generals of Alexander the Great.

Daniel had another unusual look into the future known as the Prophecy of Seventy Weeks (Dan. 9:24–27). In this vision, the angel Gabriel revealed to Daniel that the nation of Israel would be restored to its homeland after their period of captivity. This would be followed many years later by the coming of the Messiah and then, finally, the final judgment and the end of time.

Daniel's spectacular book closes with a vision of the final judgment, when the righteous will receive everlasting life and the wicked will receive God's condemnation. But not even Daniel was blessed with perfect understanding of this mystery of the ages. "My Lord, what shall be the end of these things?" (12:8), he asked. To this God replied, "Go your way, Daniel, for the words are closed up and sealed till the time of the end" (12:9).

Authorship and Date.

Most conservative scholars believe the Book of Daniel was written by the prophet and statesman of that name who lived as a captive of Babylonia and Persia for almost 70 years after he was taken into captivity in 605 B.C. But this theory is rejected by some scholars, who object to the specific details of the prophetic visions that Daniel records.

Daniel predicted that the empires of Babylonia and Persia, for example, would be succeeded by the Greeks under Alexander the Great. He also foresaw that the Greek Empire would be divided among the four generals of Alexander upon his death. Daniel also predicted that the Jewish people would suffer great persecution under an official who would come into power some time after Alexander's death.

Most interpreters identify this ruler, who would "destroy the mighty, and also the holy people" (8:24), as Antiochus Epiphanes, the Greek ruler of Syria. Antiochus persecuted the Jewish people unmercifully from 176–164 B.C. because of their refusal to adopt heathen religious practices. According to this line of thinking about Daniel and his prophecies, the book was written not by Daniel the prophet but by an unknown author about 400 years later than Daniel's time. This anonymous writer, according to this theory, wrote the book during the persecution of Antiochus Epiphanes to give the Jewish people renewed hope and religious zeal as they stood against their oppressors. Daniel's prophecies, according to these critics, are not "prophecies" at all, but were written after these events and were attributed to Daniel to show that these great events of world history would eventually happen.

Those who attack the authenticity of the Book of Daniel do not have enough evidence to support their charge. The speculation that it was written by zealous Jews to mobilize their countrymen in opposition to Antiochus Epiphanes is far-fetched and unconvincing. There is no valid reason to abandon the traditional view that it was written by the prophet Daniel. According to evidence in the book itself, Daniel's captivity lasted from the time of Nebuchadnezzar's reign in Babylon (1:1–6) into the reign of Cyrus of Persia (10:1), about 536 B.C. He must have written his book some time during this period or shortly thereafter.

Historical Setting.

The Book of Daniel clearly belongs to that period among God's Covenant People known as the Babylonian Captivity . Nebuchadnezzar took captives from Judah on four separate occasions, beginning in 605 B.C. Among this first group taken were Daniel and his companions. Their courageous acts must have been a great encouragement to the other captives.

Daniel's own interest in the forthcoming close of the captivity is supported by his prophecy in chapter 9 . His prayer to God appears to be dated in 538 B.C., the very year that Cyrus of Persia issued his decree making it possible for some of the captives to return to Jerusalem to restore their land and rebuild the Temple (Ezra 1:1–4). The fact that some did choose to return may be a tribute to the effectiveness of Daniel's book. He wrote it to show that God was in charge of world history and that He had not yet finished with His Covenant People.

Theological Contribution.

The major contribution of the Book of Daniel arises from its nature as apocalyptic prophecy. Highly symbolic in language, the prophecy was related to the events of Daniel's near future, but even today it contains a message for the future.

In apocalyptic prophecy, these close-at-hand and further-removed dimensions of the future often blend into each other. An example of this is the figure of Antiochus Epiphanes, prominent in chapters 8 and 11 of the book. In these passages the prophet Daniel moves from the nearer figure, who was to desecrate the Jewish Temple in 168 B.C., to his appearance at a remote time in the future as the Antichrist (8:23–26; 11:36–45; Rev. 13:1–10). This interplay between the near future and the distant future makes it difficult to interpret the book correctly.

In addition to its prophetic contribution, the Book of Daniel portrays a time in biblical history when miracles were abundant. Other periods when miracles were commonplace included the times of Moses, Elijah and Elisha, Jesus Christ, and the early church. In each of these periods, God was working in a spectacular manner to show His power and bring about a new era in His saving relationship to mankind.

Special Considerations.

Chapter 9 of Daniel is a fascinating passage; it combines the best of biblical piety and biblical prophecy. Daniel's study of the prophecy of the 70 years of captivity from the prophet Jeremiah (Jeremiah 25) led him to pray for God's intervention on behalf of His people. He called on God to shorten the time of their grief (9:1–19). The Lord's answer came through the angel Gabriel, who gave Daniel the prophecy of the Seventy Weeks, or 70 sevens (9:24–27). The 70 sevens as envisioned by the prophet are usually interpreted as years. Thus, the prophecy deals with the next 490 years in the future of God's Covenant People. These 490 years are divided into three groups: 7 weeks (49 years), 62 weeks (434 years), and 1 week (7 years).

Various methods have been used to calculate these periods of years in this prophecy. Here is a general scheme of how it may be done:

> During the first seven weeks (49 years), the returned exiles will complete construction of the city of Jerusalem.
>
> The passing of the next 62 weeks (434 years) will mark the time for the cutting off of the Messiah (9:26).
>
> The final or 70th week will bring the making and breaking of a covenant by a mysterious prince and the time of the Abomination of Desolation (9:27).

These verses contain a full scheme for the history of Israel from Daniel's time to the age of the Messiah. During the first period, the city of Jerusalem will be rebuilt. Then the Messiah will come, but He is destined to be cut off by a mysterious "people of the prince who is to come" (9:26). This prince will have authority during the final period; but his rule will then end, and God's purposes for His people will be realized.

Some scholars believe the 70 weeks or 490 years of this prophecy began with the decree of Ezra 7:11–26, in 458 B.C., when some of the exiles returned to rebuild the city of Jerusalem. They also believe the first 69 weeks (483 years) of this prophecy end roughly at the time of the beginning of the ministry of Christ, in A.D. 26. Others follow more complex schemes and arrive at different conclusions.

Perhaps the round numbers in this prophecy (70 sevens) should be our clue that it is dangerous to try to pin its fulfillment to a specific day or year. But we can say for sure that the end of the 483 years spoken of by Daniel would bring us to the general period of the ministry of the Lord Jesus Christ. The final week in the prophecy is symbolic of the age between the Ascension of Jesus and His Second Coming. This part of

Daniel's prophecy is yet to be fulfilled in the future Tribulation described so graphically in the Book of Revelation.

DAY OF THE LORD, THE—a special day at the end of time when God's will and purpose for mankind and His world will be fulfilled. Many Bible students believe the Day of the Lord will be a long period of time rather than a single day—a period when Christ will reign throughout the world before He cleanses heaven and earth in preparation for the eternal state of all mankind. But others believe the Day of the Lord will be an instantaneous event when Christ will return to earth to claim His faithful believers while consigning unbelievers to eternal damnation.

Amos 5:18–20 is probably the earliest occurrence in Scripture of the phrase, "day of the LORD ." According to Amos, that day would be a time of great darkness for any in rebellion against God, whether Jew or Gentile. The day would be a time of judgment (Is. 13:6, 9; Jer. 46:10), as well as restoration (Is. 14:1; Joel 2:28–32; Zeph. 1:7, 14–16; 1 Thess. 5:2; 2 Peter 3:10).

DEAD SEA SCROLLS—the popular name for about 800 scrolls and fragments of scrolls that were found in 11 caves near Khirbet ("ruin of") Qumran on the northwest shore of the Dead Sea in 1947 and shortly thereafter. Taken together, these leather and papyrus (primitive paper) manuscripts were a find without precedent in the history of modern archaeology. The Dead Sea Scrolls have helped scholars to: (1) establish the date of a Hebrew Bible no later than A.D. 70; (2) reconstruct various details of the history of the Holy Land from the fourth century B.C. to A.D. 135; and (3) clarify the relationship between Jewish religious traditions and early Christianity.

The Dead Sea Scrolls were discovered when a Bedouin shepherd, who was looking for a stray goat, discovered several large clay pots containing ancient scrolls on the floor of a cave above Wadi Qumran. After some delay, several scholars were shown the manuscripts by dealers in antiquities. When it was determined that these manuscripts were extremely old, scholars began their search in earnest. Slowly other valuable scrolls were found, gathered, carefully unrolled, and published. It took 20 years (1947–1967) to bring together the various texts of the Dead Sea Scrolls. Because the Scrolls were written between 250 B.C. and A.D. 68, they offer an invaluable source for understanding the beliefs, community life, and use of the Bible of one group of Jews, probably the Essenes, who were active during the time Jesus lived. Jericho, a town Jesus visited, is only 13 kilometers (8 miles) north of Khirbet Qumran. Some scholars believe that some of the early followers of Jesus or John the Baptist may have come from the Qumran Community. Some of the writings of this community remind the reader of the themes of "repentance" and the "coming of the new age" that were preached by John the Baptist and Jesus. However, there is no evidence that the followers of John or Jesus joined the Qumran group.

The writings are the work of Jewish sectarians, written mainly in Hebrew, with a few in Aramaic and some fragments in Greek. Some of the scrolls were written to protest the lawless priest who was in charge of the Temple worship in Jerusalem. It is likely that the main reason for building this monastic-like community near the Dead Sea was to get away from the "wicked priest" and to hear the words of the "teacher of righteousness." Not all of the Dead Sea Scrolls have been translated or published. Probably the most interesting ones were found in Cave I not far from Qumran. Seven scrolls were found preserved in fairly good condition. They had been carefully stored in large clay jars and include:

1. A complete manuscript of the Book of Isaiah in Hebrew.

2. A partial manuscript of Isaiah in Hebrew. (The two Isaiah scrolls are easy to read, even after more than 2000 years, and are the earliest copies of Isaiah in existence.)

3. *The Community Rule,* or *The Manual of Discipline,* containing the laws that governed the life of the Qumran community.

4. *The Thanksgiving Psalms* are similar to the biblical psalms. They praise God the Creator for His protection against evil: "I give thanks unto Thee, O Lord, for Thou hast put my soul in the bundle of life and hedged me against all the snares of corruption."

5. *The War Scroll* is an interesting collection of plans for the final battle between the "sons of light" and the "sons of darkness," or between the "army of God" and the "army of Belial" (the Evil One). Such information as that of religious offices during wartime, recruitment, the sequence of campaigns, and the order of deploying battle squadrons is included.

6. A commentary on the Book of Habakkuk known as the *Pesher on Habakkuk* was written to demonstrate how the prophet Habakkuk, who lived in the seventh century B.C., was actually writing for the battle of the last days, when the wicked would be defeated by the righteous. The author of the *Pesher on Habakkuk* made direct references from Habakkuk to his own day. One section has the following commentary: "And God told Habakkuk to write down that which would happen to the final generation, but He did not make known to him when time would come to an end. And as for that which He said, 'That he who reads may read it speedily' (Hab. 2:2); interpreted, this concerns the Teacher of Righteousness, to whom God made

known all the mysteries of the words of His servants the prophets."

7. *The Genesis Apocryphon,* a "commentary" on the Book of Genesis, is only partially preserved. Written around 50 B.C. in Aramaic, the common language of the Jews, it begins with the birth of Noah and documents the life and adventures of Abraham.

These seven manuscripts are typical of the scrolls found in the other caves on the west side of the Dead Sea. The material discovered includes various kinds of literature. There are numerous biblical fragments, such as commentaries on Isaiah, Hosea, Micah, Nahum, Habakkuk, Psalm 37, Psalm 45, and Genesis. Except for Esther, all the books of the Old Testament were found in part or in full.

This cave at Qumran, designated as Cave 4 by archaeologists, contained thousands of manuscript fragments.

Apocryphal and pseudepigraphal writings were found scattered in various caves. Fragments of Tobit and Ecclesiasticus from the Apocrypha give evidence of the importance of these works for the community. The Book of Jubilees, the Book of Enoch, some of the Testaments of the Twelve Patriarchs, the Sayings of Moses, the Vision of Amram, the Psalms of Joshua, the Prayer of Nabonidus, and the Book of Mysteries are a few of the pseudepigraphal works discovered. A number of hymns or psalms that were found and are included in this category are: The Hymn of the Initiates, The Book of Hymns (The Thanksgiving Hymns), Psalm 151, Poems from a Qumran Hymnal, Lament for Zion, and Hymns of Triumph.

The writings that were found can be listed under the following categories:

Biblical Manuscripts:

Isaiah scroll (complete), Exodus, Leviticus, Numbers, and Deuteronomy, among many others. Some are represented by multiple copies.

Commentaries:

Genesis Apocryphon, Job, Isaiah, Hosea, Micah, Habakkuk, Psalm 37, and Psalm 45.

Apocrypha:

Epistle to Jeremiah, Tobit, and Ecclesiasticus.

Pseudepigrapha:

Book of Jubilees, Book of Enoch, and The Testaments of the Twelve Patriarchs (fragments).

Previously Unknown Pseudepigrapha:

Sayings of Moses, Vision of Amram, Psalms of Joshua, Daniel cycle (The Prayer of Nabonidus), and Book of Mysteries.

Community Documents:

The Manual of Discipline, Damascus Document, Thanksgiving Psalm, and War Scroll.

The examples listed here are meant to be suggestive, and not exhaustive, of the archaeological finds. Other manuscripts discovered in the Judean Wilderness, for instance, deal with a later era.

Although many fragments have yet to be published, photographs of all the Dead Sea Scrolls, whether complete or fragmentary, have now been released and made available for scholarly research.

DEUTERONOMY, BOOK OF—an Old Testament book commonly identified as the farewell speech of Moses to the people of Israel just before his death. The title of the book, from the Greek word *Deuteronomion,* means "second law" and comes from the Septuagint text of Deuteronomy 17:18 ("a copy of this law"). In his address, Moses underscored and repeated many of the laws of God that the people received at Mount Sinai about 40 years earlier. He also challenged the people to remain faithful to their God and His commands as they prepared to enter the Promised Land.

Structure of the Book.

Because it is written in the format of a series of warmhearted speeches, Deuteronomy is unique among the books of the Bible. Following a brief introduction of Moses as the speaker, the book begins with a series of speeches and addresses from Moses to the people. These speeches continue through chapter 31, with only brief narrative interruptions of his spoken words. Chapter 32 records the Song of Moses, while the Blessing of Moses constitutes chapter 33. The final chapter departs from the speech format to report on Moses' death and the selection of Joshua as his successor.

In his addresses, Moses reminded the people of their days of slavery in Egypt and how God had delivered them safely through the wilderness to the borders of the Promised Land. He also restated the Ten Commandments and indicated that these great moral principles should direct their lives. As God's special people, they were to be holy and righteous as an example for surrounding pagan nations. Moses also warned Israel of the perils of idolatry and called the people to worship the one true God, who demanded their total commitment: "Hear, O Israel: The LORD our God, the LORD is one! You shall love the LORD your God with all your heart, with all your soul, and with all your might" (6:4–5).

As he spoke to the people, Moses also repeated many of the laws and regulations that dealt with observance of the Sabbath, proper forms of worship, treatment of the poor, religious feasts and festivals, inheritance rights, sexual morality, property rights, treatment of servants, and the administration of justice.

Authorship and Date.

Conservative Bible students are united in their conviction that Moses wrote this book. But many liberal scholars theorize that Deuteronomy was written several centuries after Moses' time by an unknown author who wanted to bring about the religious reforms of the nation of Judah under King Josiah (2 Kin. 22–23). These sweeping reforms began when a copy of the "Book of the Law" (Deut. 22:8) or "Book of the Covenant" (23:2)—thought to be all (or parts) of Deuteronomy—was discovered as workmen repaired the Temple in Jerusalem. According to this theory, Deuteronomy had been written during, or shortly before, Josiah's reign (640–609 B.C.).

This theory unfortunately overlooks the statement of the book itself that Moses wrote much if not most of Deuteronomy and directed that it be read regularly by the people (31:9–13). The first-person pronouns "I" and "we" appear throughout the book as Moses refers to himself and his people and their experiences. The logical conclusion is that Moses wrote the first 33 chapters of the book. Chapter 34, about his death, probably was added by his successor Joshua as a tribute to Moses. The date of the writing must have been some time around 1400 B.C.

Historical Setting.

The Book of Deuteronomy marks a turning point in the history of God's Chosen People. For the previous 40 years, they had been through many unforgettable experiences under the leadership of Moses. He had led them out of enslavement in Egypt and through the wilderness to receive God's laws at Mount Sinai. Then, because of their rebellion and unfaithfulness, they had wandered aimlessly in the desert for almost 40 years. Now they were camped on the eastern border of Canaan, the land God had promised as their homeland.

Moses sensed that the people would face many new temptations as they settled in the land and established permanent dwellings among the pagan Canaanites. He also realized that his days as their leader were drawing to a close. He used this occasion to remind the people of their heritage as God's special people and to challenge them to remain faithful to God and His laws. Thus, the Book of Deuteronomy becomes a stirring conclusion to the life of this great statesman and prophet. One of the final verses of the book pays this fitting tribute to Moses' visionary leadership: "Since then there has not arisen in Israel a prophet like Moses, whom the LORD knew face to face" (34:10).

Theological Contribution.

The New Testament contains more than 80 quotations from Deuteronomy, so it must be rated as one of the foundational books of the Bible. Jesus Himself often quoted from Deuteronomy. During His temptation, He answered Satan with four quotations from Scripture. Three of these came from this key Old Testament book (Matt. 4:4; Luke 4:4—Deut. 8:3; Matt. 4:7, Luke 4:12—Deut. 6:16; Matt. 4:10, Luke 4:8—Deut. 6:13).

When Jesus was asked to name the most important commandment in the Law, He responded with the familiar call from Deuteronomy: "You shall love the Lord your God with all your heart, with all your soul and with all your might" (Matt. 22:37; Mark 12:30; Luke 10:27; Deut. 6:5). He then added some other important words from Leviticus to show that He was carrying the law one step further: "The second [commandment] is like it: 'You shall love your neighbor as yourself'" (Matt. 22:39; Mark 12:31; Luke 10:27; Lev. 19:18).

Another great truth underscored by the Book of Deuteronomy is that God is faithful to His Covenant People, those whom He has called to carry out His purpose of redemption in the world. The Hebrews were chosen as God's instruments not because they were a worthy, powerful people, but because He loved them and desired to bless the rest of the world through their influence (7:6, 11). This is still God's purpose as He continues to call people to follow Him and commit themselves to His purpose in their lives.

Special Considerations.

Some people look upon the laws of God in the Old Testament as burdensome and restrictive. The Book of Deuteronomy, however, teaches that God's laws are given for our own good to help us stay close to Him in our attitudes and behavior. Thus, Moses called on the people to keep God's statutes, "which I command you today for your good" (10:13). The intention of God's law is positive; passages in the New Testament that seem to condemn the law must be interpreted in this light. It is the misuse of the law—trusting it rather than God's mercy as the basis of our salvation—that we should avoid. God's law is actually fulfilled in the person of our Lord and Savior Jesus Christ (Matt. 5:17, 20).

ECCLESIASTES, BOOK OF—a wisdom book of the Old Testament that wrestles with the question of the meaning of life. It takes its name from the Greek word, *ekklesiastes,* meaning "convener of an assembly." The book is often referred to by its Hebrew name, *qoheleth,* which means "preacher" or "speaker."

Theme of the Book.

The second verse of Ecclesiastes, "Vanity of vanities, all is vanity" (1:2), eloquently summarizes the underlying theme of the book—that all human achievements are empty and disappointing when pursued as ends in themselves. Many passages in Ecclesiastes appear to be as pessimistic and depressing as this statement because they point out the folly of pursuing selfish goals. One after the other, the author shows how wisdom, pleasure, hard work, popularity, wealth, and fame fail to bring lasting satisfaction. But the book ends on a triumphant note as the reader is asked to consider life's highest good: "Fear God and keep His commandments, for this is the whole duty of man" (12:13).

Authorship and Date.

King Solomon of Israel, a ruler noted for his great wisdom and vast riches, has traditionally been accepted as the author of Ecclesiastes. Evidence for this is strong, since Solomon fits the author's description of himself given in the book: "I, the Preacher, was king over Israel in Jerusalem. And I set my heart to seek and search out by wisdom concerning all that is done under heaven" (1:12–13). But some scholars claim that Solomon could not have written the book because it uses certain words and phrases that belong to a much later time in Israel's history. These objections by themselves are not strong enough to undermine Solomon's authorship, however. The book may have been written some time during his long reign of 40 years, from 970 to 931 B.C.

Historical Setting.

King Solomon amassed great riches during his reign. He also developed a great reputation as a man of wisdom. He must have written Ecclesiastes as he looked back over his life and reflected on the meaning of all his accomplishments.

Theological Contribution.

The Book of Ecclesiastes has a powerful message for our selfish, materialistic age. It teaches that great accomplishments and earthly possessions alone do not bring lasting happiness. True satisfaction comes from serving God and following His will for our lives.

But another important truth from Ecclesiastes is that life is to be enjoyed. The Preacher repeats this truth several times so it does not escape our attention: "There is nothing better for them than to rejoice, and to do good in their lives, and also that every man should eat and drink and enjoy the good of all his labor—it is the gift of God" (3:12–13; see also 2:24–25; 5:18; 8:15; 9:7–10). Our grateful acceptance of God's daily blessings can bring a sense of joy and fulfillment to our lives.

Special Considerations.

One of the most moving passages in the Bible is the poem from Ecclesiastes on the proper time for every activity (3:1–8). This text, if taken seriously, can restore balance to our living. Another powerful passage is the figurative description of the aging process (12:1–7). The Preacher realizes that old age with its afflictions looms ahead for every person. So he counsels his audience, "Remember now your Creator in the days of your youth, before the difficult days come" (12:1).

EPHESIANS, EPISTLE TO THE—one of four shorter epistles written by the apostle Paul while he was in prison, the others being Philippians, Colossians, and Philemon. Ephesians shares many similarities in style and content with Colossians; it may have been written about the same time and delivered by the same person.

In the Epistle to the Ephesians, Paul is transported to the limits of language in order to describe the enthroned Christ who is Lord of the church, the world, and the entire created order. As the ascended Lord, Christ is completing what He began in His earthly ministry, by means of His now "extended body," the church. Christ's goal is to fill all things with Himself and bring all things to Himself.

Structure of the Epistle.

Ephesians divides naturally into two halves: a lofty theological section (chaps. 1–3), and a section of ethical appeal and application (chaps. 4–6). Paul begins by greeting his readers and assuring them that they have been blessed with God's gracious favor—redemption in Christ—from before the foundation of the world (1:1–14). Paul then prays that God may grant them an even greater measure of spiritual wisdom and revelation (1:15–23). Chapter two begins with perhaps the clearest statement of salvation by grace through faith in all the Bible (2:1–10). Although the Ephesians were once alienated from God, now they are reconciled both to God and to one another by Christ, who is "our peace" (2:11–22). Paul was made an apostle to proclaim the "mystery of Christ"—the inexhaustible riches of the gospel to the Gentiles (3:1–13). Paul brings the first half of the epistle to a close with a prayer that the Ephesians may understand the depth of Christ's love (3:14–19). A benediction concludes the doctrinal section (3:20–21).

An appeal to adapt one's life to one's faith (4:1) marks the transition to the second half of the epistle. The Christian fellowship should pattern itself after the unity of the Godhead (4:1–16), and Christians should pattern themselves after the example of Christ (4:17–5:21). As new people in Christ they should walk in love, light, and wisdom. Paul cites Christ's relationship with the church as a model for wives and husbands (5:22–33), children and parents (6:1–4), and servants and masters (6:5–9). The epistle ends with an appeal to put on the whole armor of God and to stand against the forces of evil (6:10–20), followed by final greetings (6:21–24).

Authorship and Date.

Ephesians bears the name of Paul (1:1; 3:1), and it sets forth many of the great Pauline themes, such as justification by faith (2:1–10) and the body of Christ (4:15–16). Nevertheless, Ephesians has a number of notable differences from the undisputed letters of Paul. We know, for instance, that Paul spent three years in Ephesus (Acts 19:1–40), and it is clear that the Ephesians cherished his ministry among them (Acts 20:17–38). Strangely, however, Paul writes to the Ephesians as though they knew of his ministry only by hearsay (3:2). Moreover, with the exception of Tychicus (6:21), Paul mentions no one by name in Ephesians. Because of the impersonal nature of the epistle, plus the fact that it contains a number of words and phrases not characteristic of Paul, some scholars suspect that Ephesians was written by someone other than the apostle Paul.

Although this is possible, it is not likely. If Ephesians were not written by Paul, then it was written by someone who understood Paul's thinking as well as the apostle himself. Moreover, it is unlikely that a person capable of writing Ephesians could have remained unknown to the church. Many scholars have resolved the problems of authorship by suggesting that while Ephesians was indeed written by Paul, it was intended as a circular letter, or "open letter," to a number of communities surrounding Ephesus.

In the oldest manuscripts of the epistle, the phrase "in Ephesus" (1:1) is absent. Perhaps this phrase was omitted to leave space in copies of the letter for the insertion of different place names. Paul is known to have used circular letters on occasion (Col. 4:16), and the circular theory would account for the general tone of the letter.

If Paul was the author of Ephesians, then he probably wrote it about the same time as the Epistle to the Colossians. Both Ephesians and Colossians agree to a large extent in style and content. Both letters were delivered by Tychicus (Eph. 6:21; Col. 4:7). Furthermore, Paul was in prison at the time, presumably in Rome. This would suggest a date in the late 50s or early 60s.

Historical Setting.

The general nature of Ephesians makes it difficult to determine the specific circumstances that gave rise to the epistle. It is clear, however, that the recipients were Gentiles (3:1) who were estranged from citizenship in the kingdom of Israel (2:11). Now, thanks to the gracious gift of God, they enjoy the spiritual blessings that come from Christ.

Theological Contribution.

The theme of Ephesians is the relationship between the heavenly Lord Jesus Christ and His earthly body, the church. Christ now reigns "far above all principality and power and might and dominion" (1:21) and has "put all things under His feet" (1:22). Exalted though He is, He has not drifted off into the heavens and forgotten His people. Rather, so fully does He identify with the church that He considers it His body, which He fills with His presence (1:23; 3:19; 4:10).

The marriage relationship between husband and wife is a beautiful analogy for expressing Christ's love, sacrifice, and lordship over the church (5:22–32). The enthroned Christ has reinvested Himself in the hearts of believers through faith (3:17) so they can marvel at His love. Absolutely nothing exists beyond His redeeming reach (1:10; 3:18; 4:9).

Christ's bond with His church is also portrayed in the oneness of believers. Those who were once "far off" and separated from God "have been made near by the blood of Christ" (2:13). In fact, believers are now raised with Christ and seated with Him in the heavenly places (2:5–6). Since believers are with Him, they are accordingly to be like Him—"endeavoring to keep the unity of the Spirit in the bond of peace" (4:3). "He [Christ] Himself is our peace" (2:14), says Paul, and He removes the walls and barriers that formerly divided Jews and Gentiles, and draws them together in one Spirit to the Father (2:14–22).

Having spoken of these marvelous spiritual blessings, Paul then appeals to believers "to have a walk worthy of the calling with which you were called" (4:1). This appeal is a helpful insight on Christian ethics. Rather than setting down laws and regulations, Paul says, in effect, "Let your life be a credit to the One who called you." The Christian is set free by Christ; yet he is responsible to Christ. Paul makes several statements about how believers can honor Christ (4:17–5:9), but the goal is not to earn merit through morality. Instead of looking for nice people, Paul envisions new persons, the "perfect person," remade according to the stature of Christ Himself (4:13). This maturity could refer to the desired, and still unattained, unity of the church.

Special Considerations.

The term "heavenly places" (1:3; 1:20; 2:6; 3:10; 6:12) is not the same as heaven, for in one instance Paul speaks of "spiritual hosts of wickedness in the heavenly places" (6:12). "Heavenly places" implies the unseen, spiritual world beyond our physical senses. It is the region where the most difficult, and yet authentic, Christian discipleship is lived out—the world of decisions, attitudes, temptations, and commitments. It is the battleground of good and evil (6:12).

Christ has raised believers to the heavenly places with the assurance that the One in whom we hope is more powerful, real, and eternal than all of the forces of chaos and destruction that threaten our world.

EPISTLE—a letter of correspondence between two or more parties; the form in which several books of the New Testament were originally written. Epistle is generally synonymous with letter, although epistle sometimes is regarded as more formal correspondence, and letter as more personal.

There is no real precedent for the New Testament epistles in the Old Testament or Jewish literature. Rather, its 21 epistles (Romans through Jude) follow the general custom and form of letters, which became an important form of communication in the Greek-speaking world about 300 years before the birth of Jesus.

Greek letters may be roughly divided into six classes: (1) private letters, averaging slightly less than a hundred words in length, and written on papyrus (an early form of paper); (2) correspondence between government officials; (3) letters intended for publication, such as the correspondence of the church fathers in the fourth century A.D.; (4) letters written to communicate ideas; (5) letters attributed to famous personalities; and (6) imaginary letters, somewhat like our modern historical novels, which were designed to entertain.

Ancient letters were written with a reed pen on either papyrus or parchment (scraped animal skins). A sheet of papyrus normally was about 10 to 12 inches in size, and accommodated about 200 words. For sending, it was folded or rolled, tied, and often sealed to insure privacy.

The Roman government provided postal service only for official documents. Private letters had to be sent by special messengers or friendly travelers. Letters normally were sent to designated parties, although some were "open" or circular letters. Paul's letters, with the possible exception of Ephesians, were addressed to specific congregations; but the non-Pauline letters, usually called "general" epistles, included some letters that were circulated to several churches.

Most ancient letters were dictated to a secretary, or scribe. In Romans 16:22, Paul's secretary identifies himself as Tertius. When receiving dictation, a scribe could use a form of shorthand, in either Greek or Latin, which would later be converted to script and submitted to the author for approval. In addition to dictation, on occasion an author might provide a secretary with a summary of ideas and allow him to draft the epistle. This practice may have been followed in the case of 1 Peter.

Ancient letters normally followed a pattern that included: (1) an introduction, listing the names of sender and recipient, followed by a formal greeting inquiring about the recipient's health and a thanksgiving formula; (2) a body, or purpose for writing; and (3) a conclusion, consisting of appropriate remarks and a farewell. The farewell was normally written in the hand of the sender to show the recipient it was an authentic letter.

The apostle Paul's epistles follow this pattern, with only a few exceptions. Paul replaced the bland greeting of inquiry about health with a salutation combining Christian grace and Hebrew peace. His thanksgiving was likewise more than a formality; it was a sincere expression of gratitude for the well-being of his congregations. He also omitted the farewell in favor of personal greetings or a benediction.

Paul's epistles were letters written to communicate ideas. But they were more than abstract essays. With the exception of Romans, Paul's letters were written as follow-ups to his missionary activity. Their purpose was to further the spiritual growth of the churches he founded. The body of the Pauline epistles consisted of two parts: a theological or doctrinal section, and an ethical or practical section. These two sections flowed together in the same way that justification leads to sanctification in the life of the believer.

Paul's epistles illustrate his personality. Perhaps the most prominent impression Paul leaves with his readers is his pastoral concern. His life was intimately involved in the struggles of his churches. His sense of divine calling (Rom. 1:1–6; Gal. 1:12) shines through in every epistle. This leads Paul to assume a posture of authority when addressing his congregations. His authority, however, is not rooted in a superiority complex but in his Christlike devotion to his converts and churches.

The Pauline epistles are arranged in the New Testament according to length, from the longest (Romans) to the shortest (Philemon), and not by their importance or by the dates when they were written.

E STHER, BOOK OF—a historical book of the Old Testament that shows how God preserved His Chosen People. The book is named for its main personality, Queen Esther of Persia, whose courage and quick thinking saved the Jewish people from disaster.

Structure of the Book.

The Book of Esther reports on actual events, but it is written like a short story. The main characters in this powerful drama are King Xerxes of Persia; his wife Queen Esther, a Jewish woman; his second in command, Haman, recently promoted by the king; and Mordecai, a leader among the Jewish people who are scattered throughout the Persian Empire. In an attempt to stamp out the Jews, Haman manipulates the king into issuing an order calling for their execution. But Esther uses her royal favor to intervene and expose Haman's plot. Ironically, in a dramatic twist of plot, Haman is hanged on the gallows he built for Mordecai's execution, and Mordecai is promoted to prime minister. The Jewish people are granted revenge against their enemies. They also celebrate by instituting the Feast of Purim to mark their miraculous deliverance.

Authorship and Date.

For centuries scholars have debated the question of who wrote the Book of Esther. The Jewish historian Josephus claimed it was written by Mordecai. But many modern scholars dispute this because Mordecai is mentioned in the past tense in the final chapter of the book. Until new evidence emerges, the author must remain unknown.

The question of date can be answered with greater certainty. The reign of the Persian king Xerxes (Esth. 1:1, NIV) lasted for about 20 years, beginning about 485 B.C. So Esther must have been written some time shortly after 465 B.C., since an obituary formula is used of Xerxes in Esther 10:2.

Historical Setting.

The Book of Esther is valuable historically because it gives us a view of the Jewish people who were scattered throughout the ancient world about 475 B.C. The events in the book occurred about 100 years after the leading citizens of the Jewish nation were carried into exile by Babylon in 587 B.C. Shortly after the Persians overthrew the Babylonians, they allowed the Jewish exiles to return to their native land. Many did return to Jerusalem, but thousands of Jewish citizens chose to remain in Persia, probably because this had become home to them during their long separation from their native land. Thus, this book shows clearly that God protects His Chosen People, even when they are scattered among the nations of the world.

Theological Contribution.

The Book of Esther is a major chapter in the struggle of the people of God to survive in the midst of a hostile world. Beginning with the Book of Genesis, God had made it clear that he would bless His Covenant People and bring a curse upon those who tried to do them harm (Gen. 12:1, 3). The Book of Esther shows how God has kept this promise at every stage of history. Just as Haman met his death by execution, we can trust God to protect us from the enemy, Satan, and to work out His ultimate purpose of redemption in our lives.

Special Considerations.

One unusual fact about this book is that it never mentions the name of God. For this reason some people believe Esther has no place in the Bible. They see it as nothing but a fiercely patriotic Jewish book that celebrates the victory of the Jews over their enemies.

This harsh criticism is unfair to Esther. A careful reading will reveal that the book does have a spiritual base. Queen Esther calls the people to fasting (4:16), and God's protection of His people speaks of His providence (4:14). The book also teaches a valuable lesson about the sovereignty of God: although the enemies of the Covenant People may triumph for a season, He holds the key to ultimate victory.

EXODUS, BOOK OF—key Old Testament book about Israel's beginning and early years as a nation. It takes its name from the event known as the Exodus, the dramatic deliverance of the Hebrew people from enslavement in Egypt under the leadership of Moses. Throughout Exodus we meet a God who is the Lord of history and the Redeemer of His people.

These themes, repeated throughout the rest of the Bible, make Exodus one of the foundational books of the Scriptures.

Structure of the Book.

Exodus begins where the Book of Genesis leaves off—with the descendants of Joseph who moved to Egypt to escape famine and hardship in their own land. For many years the Hebrew people grew and prospered under the blessings of the Egyptian ruler. But then with one transitional verse, Exodus explains the changing political climate that brought an end to their favored position: "Now there arose a new king over Egypt, who did not know Joseph" (1:8). The Hebrews were reduced to the status of slaves and put to work on the Pharaoh's building projects.

The Book of Exodus falls naturally into three major divisions: (1) Israel in Egypt (1:1–13:21); (2) Israel in the wilderness (15:22–18:27); and (3) Israel at Mt. Sinai (19:1–40:38).

Some of the major events covered by this rapidly moving book include God's call of Moses through the burning bush to lead His people out of bondage (3:1–4:17); the series of plagues sent upon the Egyptians because of Pharaoh's stubbornness (7:14–11:10); the release of the captives and their miraculous crossing of the Red Sea, followed by the destruction of Pharaoh's army (13:17–15:21); God's provision for the people in the wilderness through bread, quail, and water (16:1–17:7); the giving of the Ten Commandments and other parts of the Law to Moses at Mt. Sinai (20:1–23:33); and the renewal of the covenant between God and His people (24:1–8).

The book ends as Moses and the workmen under his supervision build a tabernacle in the wilderness near Mt. Sinai at God's command. A cloud, symbolizing God's presence, rests on the tabernacle; and the entire building is filled with His glory (35:1–40:38).

Authorship and Date.

Exodus is one of the first five books of the Old Testament—books that have traditionally been assigned to Moses as author. But some scholars insist that Exodus was compiled by an unknown writer or editor who drew from several different historical documents. There are two sound reasons why Moses can be accepted without question as the divinely inspired author of this book.

First, Exodus itself speaks of the writing activity of Moses. In Exodus 34:27 God commands Moses to "write these words." Another passage tells us that "Moses wrote all the words of the LORD" in obedience to God's command (24:4). It is reasonable to assume that these verses refer to Moses' writing of material that appears in the Book of Exodus. Second, Moses either observed or participated in the events described in Exodus. He was well qualified to write about these experiences, since he had been educated in the household of the Pharaoh during his early life (Ex. 1:10–11).

Since Moses wrote Exodus, it must be dated some time before his death about 1400 B.C. Israel spent the 40 preceding years wandering in the wilderness because of their unfaithfulness. This is the most likely time for the writing of the book.

Historical Setting.

Exodus covers a crucial period in Israel's early history as a nation. Most conservative scholars believe the Hebrews left Egypt about 1446 B.C. Some believe it took place much later, around 1290 B.C. About two-thirds of the book describes Israel's experiences during the two years after the Exodus itself. This was the period when Israel traveled through the wilderness toward Mt. Sinai and received instructions from God through Moses as he met with God on the mountain.

Theological Contribution.

The Book of Exodus has exercised much influence over the faith of Israel, as well as Christian theology. The Bible's entire message of redemption grows out of the covenant relationship between God and His people first described in this book. In addition, several themes in the book can be clearly traced in the life and ministry of Jesus. Moses received the Law on Mt. Sinai; Jesus delivered the sermon on the mount. Moses lifted up the serpent in the wilderness to give life to the people; Jesus was lifted up on the cross to bring eternal life to all who trust in Him (John 3:14).

The Passover (Ex. 12), instituted by God for the deliverance of the Hebrews from slavery, became one of the focal points of Israel's faith. It also served as the base on which Jesus developed the Last Supper as a lasting memorial for His followers. With clear insight into Exodus, the message of the Bible and the meaning of the life of Jesus dawns with greater understanding for Christian believers.

Special Considerations.

The Book of Exodus is a dramatic testimony to the power of God. The signs and plagues sent by God to break Pharaoh's stubbornness are clear demonstrations of His power. In addition to setting the Israelites free, they also dramatize the weakness of Egypt's false gods. The puny idols of Egypt are powerless before the mighty God of Israel.

The crossing of the Red Sea is one of the most dramatic events in all of the Bible; the biblical writers repeatedly refer to it as the most significant sign of God's love for Israel. A helpless slave people had been delivered from their enemies by their powerful Redeemer God. They celebrated their victory with a song of praise (Ex. 15:1–18) that emphasizes the theme of the Book of Exodus:

> I will sing to the LORD,
> For He has triumphed gloriously!

The horse and its rider
  He has thrown into the sea!
The LORD is my strength and my song,
  And He has become my salvation.

EZEKIEL, BOOK OF—a prophetic book of the Old Testament with vivid, symbolic language much like that in the Book of Revelation in the New Testament. The Book of Ezekiel is named for its author, the prophet Ezekiel, who received his prophetic messages from God in a series of visions. He addressed these prophecies to the Jewish exiles in Babylonia, where he lived among them.

Structure of the Book.

Although Ezekiel is a long book of 48 chapters, it has a logical, orderly structure that makes it easy to analyze. After a brief introductory section about Ezekiel and the nature of his mission, the book falls naturally into three main divisions: (1) judgment on the nation of Judah (chaps. 4–24); (2) judgment on the surrounding nations (chaps. 25–32); and (3) the future blessing of God's Covenant People (chaps. 33–48).

Ezekiel was a priest who lived among the other citizens of the nation of Judah as a captive of Babylonia during the years of the Captivity. In the first chapter of the book, he describes an amazing vision of God that came to him at the beginning of his ministry. He saw four living creatures, each of which had the faces of a man, a lion, an ox, and an eagle. Clearly visible above these strange creatures was the likeness of a throne, symbolizing the might and power of God. The glory of the Lord was clearly visible to Ezekiel as He called the prophet to proclaim His message of judgment. This vision sets the tone for the rest of Ezekiel. In other encounters with strange visions throughout the book, Ezekiel proclaims God's message for His Covenant People, as well as the Gentile nations surrounding the land of Israel.

In the first major section of the book (chaps. 4–24) Ezekiel describes God's judgment on the nation of Judah because of its rampant idolatry. Chapters 8–11 are especially interesting because their prophecies were delivered by Ezekiel in the city of Jerusalem after God transported him there during one of his visions (8:3). At the end of chapter 11, Ezekiel was taken back to Babylonia, where he continued his messages (11:24–25).

The next major division of the book (chaps. 25–32) proclaims God's judgment against the nations surrounding Israel. Included are judgments against Ammon, Moab, Edom, Philistia, Tyre and Sidon, and Egypt.

The final section of the book (chaps. 33–48) speaks of the future restoration of the people of Israel. It includes Ezekiel's famous vision of the valley of dry bones (chap. 37). At God's command, Ezekiel spoke to the bones and they arose. Then God declared to the bones, "I will put My Spirit in you, and you shall live, and I will place you in your own land" (37:14). This was a clear promise from God that His Covenant People would be restored to their homeland after their period of exile in Babylon. This same theme is continued in chapters 40–48, which describe the restoration of the Temple in Jerusalem and the renewal of sacrifices and authentic worship. These chapters are similar in tone and content to the closing chapters of the Book of Revelation. Ezekiel points forward to the ultimate glorious kingdom of Jesus the Messiah.

Authorship and Date.

The author of this book was the prophet Ezekiel, a spokesman for the Lord who lived among the Jewish captives in Babylonia. Some scholars have questioned Ezekiel's authorship, claiming instead that it was compiled by an unknown author from several different sources. But the book itself clearly states that Ezekiel delivered these prophecies. The prophet refers to himself with the personal pronoun "I" throughout the book. The uniformity of style and language in the book—including such phrases as "son of man" (2:1) and "as I live, says the Lord GOD" (5:11)—is also a convincing proof of authorship by a single person. There is no good reason to doubt the traditional theory that Ezekiel wrote the book.

The prophet identifies himself in the book as "Ezekiel the priest, the son of Buzi" (1:3). He also tells us he began his prophetic ministry "in the fifth year of King Jehoiachin's captivity" (1:2). He was the king of Judah who was taken captive by Babylon in 597 B.C. This would place the beginning of Ezekiel's prophecies at about 593 B.C. The last dates that he mentions in the book are the "twenty-seventh year" (29:17) and "the twenty-fifth year of our captivity" (40:1). So Ezekiel must have prophesied for at least 22 years among the captives, until 571 B.C. He probably wrote the Book of Ezekiel some time shortly after 570 B.C.

Historical Setting.

The Book of Ezekiel belongs to the early years of the Babylonian captivity of God's Covenant People. The Babylonians took captives from Jerusalem in three stages. In an early campaign about 605 B.C., the prophet Daniel was among the Jews taken to Babylon. A second attack against the city occurred in 597 B.C., when many additional captives were taken. Ezekiel must have been among those carried away at this time. Then in the extensive campaign of 588–586 B.C., Nebuchadnezzar destroyed Jerusalem and took most of the remaining inhabitants into exile.

In the early prophecies of the Book of Ezekiel, the author wrote as a captive in Babylon who expected Jerusalem to be destroyed. Chapter 24 describes the beginning of the final siege of the city. This date was so important that the Lord had the prophet write it down as a memorial of the dreaded event (24:2). This was followed by the symbol of the cooking pot with scum rising from the boiling meat, a clear judgment against Judah. On this day also the prophet's beloved wife died. Ezekiel was forbidden to mourn her death as a symbol of God's wrath upon the wayward nation (24:15–24).

Portions of the Book of Ezekiel were written during the long siege of Jerusalem. While Ezekiel and the other captives lived in Babylon, they must have heard of the suffering of their fellow citizens back home. At last they received word that the city had fallen, and Ezekiel translated this event into an unforgettable message for the people (33:21–29). Such were the perilous times in which Ezekiel prophesied.

Theological Contribution.

One of the greatest insights of the Book of Ezekiel is its teaching of individual responsibility. This prophet proclaimed the truth that every person is responsible for his own sin as he stands exposed before God. In Ezekiel's time the Jewish people had such a strong sense of group identity as God's Covenant People that they tended to gloss over their need as individuals to follow God and His will. Some even believed that future generations were held accountable for the sins of their ancestors. But Ezekiel declared: "The soul who sins shall die. The son shall not bear the guilt of the father, nor the father bear the guilt of the son. The righteousness of the righteous shall be upon himself, and the wickedness of the wicked shall be upon himself" (18:20). This underscores the need for every person to make his own decision to follow the Lord. None of us can depend on the faith of our ancestors to gain entrance into God's kingdom.

Ezekiel also paints a beautiful picture of the future age in which God will rule triumphantly among His people. Although God's people were suffering at the hands of a pagan nation when Ezekiel prophesied, better days were assured. God would establish His universal rule among His people through a descendant of David (37:24–25). This is a clear reference to the Messiah, a prophecy fulfilled when Jesus was born in Bethlehem more than 500 years later. The followers of Jesus became the "new

Israel," or the church—those who seek to follow God and carry out His purpose in the world.

Special Considerations.

In his use of parables, symbolic behavior, and object lessons to drive home his messages, the prophet Ezekiel reminds us of the prophet Jeremiah. Through the use of parables, Ezekiel portrayed God's Covenant People as a helpless newborn child (16:1–12), as a lioness who cared carefully for her cubs (19:1–3), as a sturdy cedar (17:1–3), and as a doomed and useless vine (chap. 15). He also used a clay tablet to portray the Babylonian siege against the city of Jerusalem (4:1–2), ate his bread "with quaking" and drank his water "with trembling and anxiety" (12:17) to symbolize God's wrath, and carried his belongings about to show that God would allow His people to be carried into exile by the Babylonians (12:1–16).

Ezekiel may have picked up this technique of acting out his messages from Jeremiah himself. For about 40 years before Jerusalem's fall in 586 B.C., Jeremiah prophesied in the capital city. As a young resident of Jerusalem, Ezekiel probably heard and saw this great prophet at work. When he was called to prophesy to the exiles in Babylon beginning about 593 B.C., he may have used Jeremiah's methods as a way to get attention and win a hearing for God's message.

EZRA, BOOK OF—a historical book of the Old Testament that describes the resettlement of the Jewish people in their homeland after their long exile in Babylonia. The book is named for its author and central figure, Ezra the priest, who led the exiles in a new commitment to God's Law after their return.

Structure of the Book.

The ten chapters of this book fall naturally into two main divisions, chapters 1–6, which report the return of the first wave of exiles to Jerusalem under the leadership of Zerubbabel, about 538 B.C., and chapters 7–10, which describe the return of a second group under Ezra's leadership, about 458 B.C.

One of the most unusual facts about the Book of Ezra is that its two major sections are separated by a time gap of about 80 years. The book opens with a brief introduction that explains how the first return from exile happened. Cyrus, king of Persia, issued a proclamation allowing the Jewish people to return to Jerusalem to rebuild their Temple and resettle their native land. About 50,000 of the people returned under the leadership of Zerubbabel, a Jewish citizen appointed by Cyrus as governor of Jerusalem (2:64–67). Arriving in about 538 B.C., they set to work on the rebuilding project. In spite of some shrewd political maneuvering by their enemies, the work moved forward in fits and starts until the Temple was completed in about 515 B.C. (6:13–15).

The second major section of the book (chaps. 7–10) reports on the arrival of Ezra in Jerusalem with another group of exiles about 60 years after the Temple had been completed. Just as Zerubbabel had led the people to rebuild God's house, Ezra's mission was to lead his countrymen to rebuild the Law of God in their hearts. Ezra worked with another Jewish leader, Nehemiah, to bring about several reforms among the Jewish people in Judah during this period. From the Book of Nehemiah (Neh. 8:1–8), we learn that Ezra read the books of the Law (Genesis, Exodus, Leviticus, Numbers, and Deuteronomy) aloud to the people. This led to a great religious revival throughout Jerusalem as the people committed themselves again to God's Law, confessed their sins (Neh. 9:1–3), and renewed the covenant with their Redeemer God (Nehemiah 10).

We also learn from the final two chapters of his book that Ezra was distressed at the Jewish men who had married non-Jewish women. He led these men to repent of their sin and divorce their pagan wives (10:6–44).

Authorship and Date.

Ezra has traditionally been accepted as the author of this book that bears his name, as well as the companion book of Nehemiah. In the Hebrew Old Testament, Ezra and Nehemiah appeared as one unbroken book, closely connected in theme and style to the books of 1 and 2 Chronicles. The last two verses of 2 Chronicles are repeated in the first three verses of the Book of Ezra, probably indicating that they belonged together in the original version. For this reason, many scholars believe Ezra served as writer and editor-compiler of all four of these books: 1 and 2 Chronicles, Ezra, and Nehemiah. He probably drew from official court documents as sources for his writings.

This compilation theory also helps explain the strange 80-year gap between the two major sections of Ezra's book. He wrote about Zerubbabel's return many years after it happened, drawing from official court records or some other account of the event. To this he added his own personal memoirs, now contained in chapters 7–10 of the Book of Ezra as well as chapters 8–10 of the Book of Nehemiah. The rest of the material in the Book of Nehemiah may have come from Nehemiah's memoirs, which Ezra incorporated into the book of Ezra-Nehemiah. The time for the final writing and compilation of all this material must have been some time late in the fifth century B.C.

Historical Setting.

The Book of Ezra belongs to the post-exilic period. These were the years just after a remnant of the nation returned to Jerusalem following their exile of several decades in Babylonia. The return came about after the capture of Babylonia by the Persian Empire. Unlike the Babylonians, the Persians allowed their subject nations to live in their own native regions under the authority of a ruling governor. The Persians also practiced religious tolerance, allowing each nation to worship its own god. This explains the proclamation of Cyrus of Persia, which allowed the Jewish people to return to Jerusalem and rebuild their Temple. Cyrus even returned the Temple treasures that the Babylonians took when they destroyed Jerusalem about 50 years earlier (1:7–11).

Theological Contribution.

The theme of the Book of Ezra is the restoration of the remnant of God's Covenant People in Jerusalem in obedience to his Law. The book shows clearly that God had acted to preserve His people, even when they were being held captives in a pagan land. But in their absence, the people had not been able to carry on the true form of Temple worship. Only in their Temple in Jerusalem, they believed, could authentic worship and sacrifice to their Redeemer God be offered. This is why the rebuilding of the Temple was so important. Here they could restore their worship of God and find their true identity as God's people of destiny in the world.

The Book of Ezra also teaches a valuable lesson about the providence of God. Several different Persian kings are mentioned in this book. Each king played a significant role in returning God's Covenant People to their homeland and helping them restore the Temple as the center of their religious life. This shows that God can use pagans as well as believers to work His ultimate will in the lives of His people.

Special Considerations.

Many scholars believe the Jewish people in Babylonia must have numbered many times the 50,000 or so who chose to return to Jerusalem with the first group under Zerubbabel (2:64–67). This indicates that most of them probably had become comfortable with their lives in these foreign lands. Or perhaps the certainties of their present existence were more appealing than the uncertainties of life in Jerusalem—a city most of them had never seen.

Some Bible readers are bothered by Ezra's treatment of the pagan women whom the Jewish men had married (10:10–19).

How could he be so cruel as to insist that these wives be "put away" (divorced) with no means of support? His actions must be understood in light of the drastic situation that faced the Jewish community in Jerusalem following the Exile. Only a small remnant of the Covenant People had returned, and it was important for them to keep themselves from pagan idolatry and foreign cultural influences at all costs. Ezra must have realized, too, that this was one of the problems which had led to their downfall and captivity as a people in the first place. Yet even the horrors of defeat and exile by the Babylonians had failed to teach the people a lesson. Ezra was determined to stamp out the problem this time before it became a widespread practice among God's Covenant People.

GALATIANS, EPISTLE TO THE—a brief but energetic letter from the apostle Paul to the Christians of Galatia. Galatians is one of Paul's most commanding epistles; its importance far exceeds its size. It provides valuable information about Paul's life between his conversion and missionary journeys (1:11–2:14). Beyond its autobiographical value, however, Galatians ranks as one of Paul's great epistles; in it he forcefully proclaims the doctrine of justification by faith alone. Martin Luther, the Reformer, claimed Galatians as "my epistle." So wedded was Luther to Galatians, both in interest and temperament, that, together, they shaped the course of the Reformation. Galatians has been called the "Magna Charta of Christian Liberty." The peals of its liberating truth have thundered down through the centuries, calling people to new life by the grace of God.

Structure of the Epistle.

Galatians falls into three sections, each two chapters long. The first third of the letter is a defense of Paul's apostleship and gospel (chaps. 1–2). The middle section (chaps. 3–4) is devoted to the question of salvation. In it Paul uses a variety of means—logic (3:15–20), quotations from the Old Testament (3:7–14), metaphor (4:1–6), personal authority (4:12–20), and allegory

(4:21–31)—to argue that salvation comes not through obeying the Mosaic law, but by receiving the grace of God through faith. The third section of Galatians concerns the consequences of saving faith (chaps. 5–6). Christians are free to love (5:1–15); the Holy Spirit produces fruit in their lives (5:16–26); and the needs of others lay a rightful claim on them (6:1–10). Paul concludes by summing up the main points of the letter (6:11–16), along with a closing admonition that he bears the marks of Jesus in his body (6:17), and a blessing (6:18).

Authorship and Date.

No epistle in the New Testament has better claim to come from Paul than does Galatians. The epistle bears his name (1:1), tells his story (1:11–2:14), and expounds the truth that occupied his life—justification by faith in Jesus Christ (2:16).

The date of the epistle is less certain. It depends on another question: to whom is the epistle addressed? This question is difficult because the word Galatia (1:2) is ambiguous. Ethnically, the word refers to a people of Celtic stock living in northern Asia Minor. Politically, however, it refers to the region throughout central Asia Minor, including various districts in the south, that were annexed to Galatia when it was made a province by the Romans in 25 B.C. It is impossible to say for sure which use of the term Paul intended, although the broader political usage seems more probable.

Paul was well acquainted with southern Galatia (Acts 13–14; 16:1–5), and we have no certain evidence that he ever visited northern Galatia (unless Acts 16:6 and 18:23 refer to that area). Moreover, it seems unlikely that Paul would have addressed the Galatians in such a direct way unless he enjoyed a close relationship with them. These reasons indicate that the people to whom the letter was addressed probably lived in southern Galatia. If this is so, it probably was written before the Council of Jerusalem (Acts 15). If it had already occurred (about A.D. 49), Paul would undoubtedly have cited the decision of that council since it agreed with the thrust of his argument in the epistle. If this is so, Galatians may be Paul's earliest (surviving) epistle, written perhaps in A.D. 48.

If, on the other hand, "Galatia" refers to the northern ethnic region, which Paul could not have visited before his second (Acts 16:6) or third (Acts 18:23) missionary journeys, the letter could not have been written before the mid-fifties. But this viewpoint seems less likely to be true.

Historical Setting.

After Paul had evangelized the churches of Galatia, he received disturbing news that they were falling away from the gospel he had taught them (1:6). Certain religious activists had visited Galatia after Paul's departure and had persuaded the Christians there that the gospel presented by Paul was insufficient for salvation (1:7). In addition to faith in Jesus Christ, they insisted that a person must be circumcised according to the law of Moses (5:12) and must keep the Sabbath and other Jewish holy days (4:10), including the Jewish ceremonial law (5:3). These "troublers" (1:7), as Paul calls them, may have included some Gnostic ideas (4:3, 9) in their teachings. These teachers are sometimes referred to as Judaizers, since they taught that both faith and works—belief in Jesus and obedience to the Law—are necessary for salvation.

Theological Contribution.

News of the troublers' "perversion of the gospel" (1:7) was distressing to Paul. Paul quickly rose to the Judaizers' challenge and produced this letter. From the outset he was ready for battle; he abandoned his customary introduction and plunged immediately into the battle with the Judaizers. The Judaizers had suggested that Paul was an inferior apostle, if one at all, and that his gospel was not authoritative (1:10). Paul countered with an impassioned defense of his conversion (1:11–17) and of his approval by the leaders of the church at Jerusalem (1:18–2:10).

Indeed, the gospel that Paul had delivered to the Galatians was not his own, nor was he taught it; but it came "through the revelation of Jesus Christ" (1:11–12). Those who presumed to change it were meddling with the very plan of God (1:7–8).

God's plan is that Jews and Gentiles are justified before God by faith alone. This plan can be traced to the beginning of Israel's history, for Abraham "believed God, and it was accounted to him for righteousness" (Gal. 3:6; also Gen. 15:6). The law, which did not come until 430 years after Abraham (3:17), was never intended to replace justification by faith. Rather, the law was to teach us of our need for Christ (3:24–25). Christ, therefore, is the fulfillment of the promise to Abraham.

The result of justification by grace through faith is spiritual freedom. Paul appealed to the Galatians to stand fast in their freedom, and not get "entangled again with a yoke of bondage [that is, the Mosaic law]" (5:1). Christian freedom is not an excuse to gratify one's lower nature; rather, it is an opportunity to love one another (5:13; 6:7–10). Such freedom does not insulate one from life's struggles. Indeed, it may intensify the battle between the Spirit and the flesh. Nevertheless, the flesh (the lower nature) has been crucified with Christ (2:20); and, as a consequence, the Spirit will bear its fruit—such as love, joy, and peace—in the life of the believer (5:22–23).

Special Considerations.

The letter to the Galatians was written in a spirit of inspired agitation. For Paul, the issue was not whether a person was circumcised, but whether he had become "a new creation" (6:15). If Paul had not been successful in his argument for justification by faith alone, Christianity would have remained a sect within Judaism, rather than becoming the universal way of salvation. Galatians, therefore, is not only Luther's epistle; it is the epistle of every believer who confesses with Paul: "I have been crucified with Christ; it is no longer I who live, but Christ lives in me; and the life which I now live in the flesh I live by faith in the Son of God, who loved me and gave Himself for me" (Gal. 2:20).

GENESIS, BOOK OF—the first book of the Bible. Placed at the opening of the Hebrew Scriptures, Genesis is the first of the five books of Moses, known as the Pentateuch. Genesis is the book of beginnings. The word Genesis means "the origin, source, creation, or coming into being of something." The Hebrew name for the book is *bereshith,* the first word in the Hebrew text, which is translated as "in the beginning" (Gen. 1:1). Genesis describes such important beginnings as the Creation, the fall of man, and the early years of the nation of Israel.

The beginning of salvation history—the story of God and man, sin and grace, wrath and mercy, covenant and redemption—also begins in the Book of Genesis. These themes are repeated often throughout the rest of the Bible. As the Book of Revelation is the climax and conclusion of the Bible, so the Book of Genesis is the beginning and essential seedplot of the Bible. Thus, Genesis is an important book for understanding the meaning of the entire Bible.

Structure of the Book.

The Book of Genesis may conveniently be divided into four major parts: (1) the Creation and the early days of mankind (Gen. 1:1–11:9); (2) the story of Abraham and Isaac (Gen. 11:10–25:18); (3) the story of Jacob and Esau (Gen. 25:19–36:43); and (4) the story of Joseph and his brothers (Gen. 37:1–50:26).

The first major part of the Book of Genesis (chaps. 1–11) contains five great events: (1) the history of creation and a description of life in the Garden of Eden before the Fall (Gen. 1:1–2:25); (2) the story of Adam and Eve in the Garden of Eden: the temptation and Fall of humankind (Gen. 3:1–24); (3) the story of Cain and Abel (Gen. 4:1–16); (4) the story of Noah and the Flood: the wickedness and judgment of man (Gen. 6:1–9:29); and (5) the story of the Tower of Babel: the proud presumption of human beings, the confusion of tongues, and the scattering of humankind upon the earth (Gen. 11:1–9). Each of these great events relates to the whole of humanity, and each is filled with significance that continues throughout Scripture.

The rest of the Book of Genesis (chaps. 12–50) relates the narrative of the four great patriarchs of Israel: Abraham, Isaac, Jacob, and Joseph. The theme of these chapters is God's sovereignty in calling out a Chosen People who would serve and worship Him.

Authorship and Date.

The Book of Genesis gives no notice about its author. The early church, however, held to the conviction that Moses wrote the book, as did the Jerusalem Talmud and the first-century Jewish historian Josephus. In spite of the number of modern scholars who reject the Mosaic authorship of Genesis, the traditional view has much to commend it. Both the Old Testament and the New Testament contain frequent testimony to the Mosaic authorship of the entire Pentateuch (Lev. 1:1–2; Neh. 13:1; Matt. 8:4; Acts 26:22).

It would be difficult to find a person in Israel's life who was better prepared or qualified than Moses to write the history recorded in the Book of Genesis. A man who "was learned in all the wisdom of the Egyptians" (Acts 7:22), Moses was providentially prepared to understand and integrate, under the inspiration of God, all the available records, manuscripts, and oral narratives. Moses may have written the book during the years of the wilderness wandering to prepare the new generation to enter the land of Canaan.

As a prophet who enjoyed the unusual privilege of unhurried hours of communion with God on Mount Sinai, Moses was well equipped to record for all generations this magnificent account of God's dealings with the human race and the nation of Israel.

Historical Setting.

Moses may have finished writing the Book of Genesis not long before his death on Mount Nebo (Deuteronomy 34). During this time the children of Israel, now led by Joshua, were camped east of the Jordan River, poised for the invasion of Canaan. In such a crucial historical context, the message of the Book of Genesis would have been of tremendous spiritual help to its first hearers. The creation of the world, the beginnings of sin and disobedience, the principle of judgment and deliverance, the scattering of the nations, the call and covenant God made with Abraham, the checkered careers of the first descendants of Abraham—all of these accounts would bear directly on the attitudes and faith of the new community.

The first readers, or hearers, of the Book of Genesis were the covenant community, the Chosen People of God. Like Abraham, they were on a journey—a great venture of faith into the unknown (Gen. 12:1–9). Like Abraham, they needed to respond to God in wholehearted faith and in the fear of the Lord (Gen. 22:1–19). They needed to hear such words as were spoken to Isaac: "I am the God of your father Abraham; do not fear, for I am with you. I will bless you and multiply your descendants for My servant Abraham's sake" (Gen. 26:24).

Theological Contribution.

The Book of Genesis is a primary source for several basic doctrines of the Bible. The book focuses on God primarily in two areas: He is the Creator of the universe, and He is the one who initiates covenant with His people. Genesis ties creation and covenant together in a stunning manner: the God who initiates covenant is the same God who has created the entire universe. The eternal God and almighty Creator enters into covenant with His people (Gen. 1:1; John 1:1).

God's covenant with Abraham begins the basic plot of Scripture. God's work from that day forward was to accomplish His plan for the nations of the world through His people Israel, the descendants of Abraham. God's covenant with Abraham (Gen. 12:1–3; 15:1–21) contains a number of personal blessings on the father of the faith. But the climax of the text is in words of worldwide import: "And in you all the families of the earth shall be blessed" (Gen. 12:3).

This promise is realized in the person of the Lord Jesus Christ, the Seed of Abraham (Gal. 3:16, 19), through whom peoples of all nations and families may enter into the joy of knowing the God of Abraham. God's promise is realized also in the church, in those who believe in Christ, which the apostle Paul calls "the Israel of God" (Gal. 6:16). The true "seed," or descendants, of Abraham, Paul argued, are not Abraham's physical descendants but those who have the same faith as Abraham (Rom. 9:7–8; Gal. 3:29).

Genesis presents the creation of human beings as male and female in the image of God (Gen. 1:26–27; 5:3; 9:6), their fall and ruin, their judgment, and their possible triumph in God's grace. In the context of their judgment came the first whisper of the gospel message of the final triumph of Christ over Satan: "And I will put enmity between you [the serpent] and the woman, and between your seed and her seed; He shall bruise your head, and you shall bruise His heel" (Gen. 3:15). This prophecy was fulfilled by the death of Jesus on the cross, a sacrifice that destroyed the works of the devil (1 John 3:8).

The apostle Paul referred to the story of Adam's fall (Genesis 3) by comparing Adam to Christ (Rom. 5:12, 18). Christ is portrayed as a "second Adam" who, by His atonement, reverses the effects of the Fall. Some scholars see another type, or foreshadowing truth, of Calvary in the fact that God, in order to cover the nakedness of Adam and Eve (symbolic of sin, guilt, and shame), killed an animal (thereby shedding blood) and made garments of skin with which to clothe them (Gen. 3:21). For, as the writer of the Book of Hebrews says, "Without shedding of blood there is no remission [of sin]" (Heb. 9:22).

Special Consideration.

Some scholars organize the literary structure of the Book of Genesis around the Hebrew word *toledoth* (literally, genealogy), which Moses seems to use ten times in Genesis to indicate major blocks of material. The NKJV translates *toledoth* as "this is the history of" (Gen. 2:4) and "this is the genealogy of" (Gen. 5:1; 6:9; 10:1; 11:10; 11:27; 25:12; 25:19; 36:1; 37:2).

The Book of Genesis takes the reader to the moment when the Creator spoke into being the sun, moon, stars, planets, galaxies, plants, moving creatures, and mankind. Those who seek to discredit the Book of Genesis by pointing to alleged discrepancies between religion and science are blind to the exalted spiritual content of this work. If a student expects to find in Genesis a scientific account of how the world came into existence, with all questions concerning primitive life answered in technical language, he will be disappointed. Genesis is not an attempt to answer such technical questions.

Genesis is marked by exquisite prose, such as chapter 22 (the account of the binding of Isaac) and chapters 37–50 (the Joseph narrative). Literary critics often point to Genesis 24, the story of a bride for Isaac, as a classic example of great narrative style. Genesis also has poetic sections such as the solemn curses by God (Gen. 3:14–19) and the prophetic blessing of Jacob (Gen. 49:3–27). Genesis 1, the account of creation, is written in highly elevated prose with a poetic tone.

At times attention is focused on the men in the Book of Genesis. But women of major significance also appear in the book: Eve is the mother of all living (Gen. 3:20); Sarah had a faith that was complementary to Abraham's (Gen. 21:1–7); and Leah, Rachel, Bilhah, and Zilpah are the mothers of the 12 patriarchs of Israel (Gen. 29:31–30:24; 35:23–26).

Genesis is also a book of firsts. Genesis records the first birth (Gen. 4:1), the first death (Gen. 4:8), the first musical instruments (Gen. 4:21), and the first rainbow (Gen. 9:12–17).

Genesis is indeed the book of beginnings. As the children of Israel read this book in the wilderness, or after they crossed the Jordan River, they knew that their experiences with God were just beginning.

GOD, NAMES OF—the titles or designations given to God throughout the Bible. In the ancient world, knowing another's name was a special privilege that offered access to that person's thought and life. God favored His people by revealing Himself by several names that offered special insight into His love and righteousness.

Jehovah/Yahweh.

One of the most important names for God in the Old Testament is Yahweh, or Jehovah, from the verb "to be," meaning simply but profoundly, "He Is." His full name is found only in Ex. 3:14 and means "I am who I am" or "I will be who I will be." The four-letter Hebrew word YHWH was the name by which God revealed Himself to Moses at the burning bush (Ex. 3:14). This bush was a vivid symbol of the inexhaustible dynamism of God who burns like a fire with love and righteousness, yet remains the same and never diminishes. Some English translations of the Bible vocalize the word as Jehovah, while others use Yahweh.

God is the author of life and salvation. His "I am" expresses the fact that He is the infinite and original personal God who is behind everything and to whom everything must finally be traced. "I am who I am" signals the truth that nothing else defines who God is but God Himself. What He says and does is who He is. The inspired Scriptures are the infallible guide to understanding who God is by what He says about Himself and what He does. Yahweh is the all-powerful and sovereign God who alone defines Himself and establishes truth for His creatures and works for their salvation.

Moses was called to proclaim deliverance to the people and was told by God, "Thus you shall say to the children of Israel, 'I AM has sent me to you'" (Ex. 3:14). In the deliverance of the Hebrew people from slavery in Egypt, God revealed a deeper significance to His name. But He had already disclosed Himself to Abraham, Isaac, and Jacob as Yahweh. Each of them had called on the name of the Lord (Yahweh) (Gen. 12:8; 13:4; 26:25; Ex. 3:15) as the God who protects and blesses. Yet Exodus 6:3 shows that Abraham, Isaac, and Jacob did not know the fuller meaning of Yahweh, which was to be revealed to Moses and the Hebrew people in His role as Redeemer during the Exodus experience.

The divine name Yahweh is usually translated "LORD" in English versions of the Bible, because it became a practice in late Old Testament Judaism not to pronounce the sacred name YHWH, but to say instead "my Lord" (Adonai)—a practice still used today in the synagogue. When the vowels of Adonai were attached to the consonants YHWH in the medieval period, the word Jehovah resulted. Today, many Christians use the word Yahweh, the more original pronunciation, not hesitating to name the divine name since Jesus taught believers to speak in a familiar way to God.

The following are other names in honor of the Lord in the Old Testament that stem from the basic name of Yahweh:

Jehovah-jireh—This name is translated as "The-LORD-Will-Provide," commemorating the provision of the ram in place of Isaac for Abraham's sacrifice (Gen. 22:14).

Jehovah-nissi—This name means "The-LORD-Is-My-Banner," in honor of God's defeat of the Amalekites (Ex. 17:15).

Jehovah-shalom—This phrase means "The-LORD-Is-Peace," the name Gideon gave the altar that he built in Ophrah (Judg. 6:24).

Jehovah-shammah—This phrase expresses the truth that "The-Lord-Is-There," referring to the city which the prophet Ezekiel saw in his vision (Ezek. 48:35).

Jehovah-tsebaoth—This name, translated "The-Lord-of-hosts," was used in the days of David and the prophets, witnessing to the Almighty God of sovereign power who is surrounded by His heavenly hosts (1 Sam. 1:3).

Jehovah Elohe Yisrael—This name means "The-Lord-God-of-Israel," and it appears in Isaiah, Jeremiah, and the Psalms. Other names similar to this are Netsah Yisrael, "The Strength of Israel" (1 Sam. 15:29); and Abir Yisrael, "The Mighty One of Israel" (Is. 1:24).

El.

Another important root name for God in the Old Testament is El. By itself it refers to a god in the most general sense. It was widely used in ancient eastern cultures whose languages are similar to Hebrew and therefore may refer either to the true God or to false gods. The highest Canaanite god was El, whose son was Baal. In the Bible the word is often defined properly by a qualifier like Jehovah: "I, the Lord (Jehovah) your God (Elohim), am a jealous God (El)" (Deut. 5:9).

Abraham planted a tamarisk tree at Beersheba "and there called on the name of the Lord (Yahweh), the Everlasting God (El Olam) (Gen. 21:33). Jacob built an altar on a piece of land he purchased at Shechem and called it El Elohe Israel ("God, the God of Israel"), commemorating his wrestling with the angel at the place he called Peniel ("the face of God"), and receiving his new name Israel (*Yisrael*, "God strives") (Gen. 32:28–30; 33:20).

El Shaddai (God Almighty), signifying God as a source of blessing, is the name with which God appeared to Abraham, Isaac, and Jacob (Ex. 6:3).

Elohim.

Elohim is the plural form of El, but it is usually translated in the singular. Some scholars have held that the plural represents an intensified form for the supreme God; others believe it describes the supreme God and His heavenly court of created beings. Still others hold that the plural form refers to the triune God of Genesis 1:1–3, who works through Word and Spirit in the creation of the world. In any event, Elohim conveys the idea that the one supreme being, who is the only true God, is in some sense plural.

Several important names of God identify Him as Branch, King, Wisdom, Shepherd, and Servant:

Branch of Righteousness—Jeremiah 23:5–6 names the coming messianic figure, the "Branch of righteousness," who will descend from David and be raised up to reign as King to execute judgment and righteousness in the earth. Christians see in this linkage a prophecy about God the Son taking on human flesh to serve as righteous King.

King—This descendant of David will have several divine qualities. He will be a Branch of Righteousness, a King, and His name will be called "The Lord Our Righteousness" (*Jehovah-tsidkenu*).

Wisdom—In Proverbs 8:1–36 Wisdom, who always says and does what is righteous, works with God in the creation of the universe. Paul describes Christ in similar terms in Colossians 1:13–19; 2:1–3.

Shepherd—God is also described in prophecy as the Shepherd who will feed His flock, gather the lambs in His arms, carry them in His bosom, and gently lead those with young (Is. 40:11; Jer. 31:10; Ezek. 34:11–16). Jesus applied this name to Himself (Luke 15:4–7; John 10:11–16), making Himself equal to God; and Jesus Christ is so named by His followers (Heb. 13:20; 1 Pet. 5:4; Rev. 7:17).

Servant—The name of Servant also identifies the divine Messiah and His saving ministry on behalf of His people. God's Servant is described in terms that apply to Jesus. He is upheld and chosen by God; He delights in God; He receives God's Spirit. Like Wisdom in Proverbs 8, He is holy, just, and righteous. He will bring Jacob back to Him and will be a light to the nations since He is an offering for sin (Is. 42:1–4; 49:1–7; 53:1–12).

Word of God.

The Word of God figures prominently in Scripture as another name of God. The Word is not as clearly a person in the Old Testament as in the New Testament where Jesus Christ is identified as the personal Word of God (John 1:1, 14). But it is evident from Psalm 33:4, 6, and 9 that the Word should be understood in a personal sense, for "the word of the Lord is right" indicates a personified Word. "By the Word of the Lord the heavens were made" (v. 6), echoes the creation in Genesis 1:3, 6. In the New Testament Jesus is seen to be both Word and Law personified.

Glory.

God is described as Glory in Exodus 16:7; Psalm 104:31; and Isaiah 60:1. In the New Testament Jesus shares the glory of God (Matt. 25:31; 1 Cor. 2:8; Heb. 1:3).

When the new age arrives with the birth of Jesus Christ, the names of the three persons who comprise the Trinity are made more explicit. These names fulfill the deeper meanings of the Old Testament names for God.

In the New Testament God is known as Father (Matt. 5:16; 28:19) and Abba (Mark 14:36; Gal. 4:6). Jesus is known as Son (Matt. 11:27), Son of God (John 9:35), Son of man (Matt. 8:20), Messiah (John 1:41), Lord (Rom. 14:8), Word (John 1:1), Wisdom (1 Cor. 1:30), Bridegroom (Mark 2:19), Shepherd (John 10:11), Vine (John 15:1), Light (John 1:9), and "I am" (John 8:12, 58). The Holy Spirit is known as the Helper (John 14:16).

GOSPEL—the joyous good news of salvation in Jesus Christ. The Greek word translated as "gospel" means "a reward for bringing good news" or simply "good news." In Isaiah 40:9, the prophet proclaimed the "good tidings" that God would rescue His people from captivity. In His famous sermon at the synagogue in Nazareth, Jesus quoted Isaiah 61:1 to characterize the spirit of His ministry: "The Spirit of the Lord is upon Me, because He has anointed Me to preach the gospel [good news] to the poor" (Luke 4:18).

The gospel is not a new plan of salvation; it is the fulfillment of God's plan of salvation that was begun in Israel, was completed in Jesus Christ, and is made known by the church. The gospel is the saving work of God in His Son Jesus Christ and a call to faith in Him (Rom. 1:16–17). Jesus is more than a messenger of the gospel; He *is* the gospel. The good news of God was present in His life, teaching, and atoning death. Therefore, the gospel is both a historical event and a personal relationship.

Faith is more than intellectual agreement to a theoretical truth. Faith is trust placed in a living person, Jesus Christ. When the apostle Paul warned Christians of the dangers of following "another gospel" (2 Cor. 11:4), he was reminding them that any gospel different than the one he preached was no gospel at all.

In the second century, the word "gospel" came to be used for certain writings in which the "good news" or story of Jesus Christ was told. These writings were written in the first century, but they became known as "gospels" much later. Mark was the first to write such a story (Mark 1:1), and in so doing he invented a literary form that we call a "gospel." The New Testament has four versions of the one gospel: the Gospels of Matthew, Mark, Luke, and John.

A gospel is more than a biography intended to provide information about a historical character. It is the presentation of the life of Jesus to show His saving significance for all people and to call them to faith in Him.

GOSPELS—the four accounts at the beginning of the New Testament about the saving work of God in His Son Jesus Christ. The writers of the four gospels introduced a new literary category into literature. The gospels are not true biographies, because apart from certain events surrounding His birth (Matt. 1–2; Luke 1–2) and one from His youth (Luke 2:41–52), they record only the last two or three years of Jesus' life.

Moreover, the material included is not written as an objective historical survey of Jesus' ministry. The gospels present Jesus in such a way that the reader realizes that God acted uniquely in Him. The authors of the gospels wrote not only to communicate knowledge about Jesus as a person, but also to call us to commitment to Him as Lord.

The gospels produce four distinctive portraits of Jesus rather than exact photographic likenesses. Thus, there are four gospels (accounts) of the one gospel (the good news of salvation in Jesus Christ).

The Gospel in Four Editions.

Why, though, are there four versions of the same story? Why not one account? This question is as old as the church itself. Around A.D. 150, Tatian compiled a life of Christ, called the Diatessaron, by harmonizing the four gospels. His contemporary, the heretic Marcion, attempted to resolve the problem by choosing one gospel, Luke, and discounting the others.

The church, however, resisted Tatian's artificial life of Jesus and Marcion's choice of one gospel to the exclusion of the other three. Prior to Tatian and Marcion, the church had accepted each of the four gospels as a faithful and complementary witness to Jesus Christ. The church adopted symbols for the gospels—Matthew a lion, Mark an ox, Luke a man, John an eagle (or variations thereof)—from the fourfold witness to God in Scripture (Ezek. 1:5; 10:14; Rev. 4:7). At an early date the church realized that the combined witness of the four gospels was required to declare the full significance of Christ.

The Synoptic Problem.

If one sets the four gospels side by side, it becomes apparent that Matthew, Mark, and Luke have much in common. Each gospel arranges its material in a similar fashion, and each gospel casts the life of Jesus within the framework of a Galilean ministry that extended from Jesus' baptism to His death, with emphasis on His final days.

The similarity of the gospels also includes their content. The first three gospels recount many of the same incidents or teachings, and often in the same or related wording. A glance, for example, at the baptism of Jesus as related by Matthew (3:13–17), Mark (1:9–11), and Luke (3:21–22) will quickly demonstrate their agreement. Because of this similarity in arrangement, content, and wording, the first three gospels are called synoptic gospels (from the Greek *synopsis,* "a seeing together").

The Gospel of John presents a more independent account of Christ. John's relationship to the first three gospels can be considered only after a thorough discussion of Matthew, Mark, and Luke.

The synoptic problem arises from the attempt to explain the general similarity of Matthew, Mark, and Luke, while accounting for their individual differences. Two of the four gospel writers (Mark and Luke) were not eyewitnesses of the events they relate, and some question remains about the other two. This means we cannot assume that the similarities and differences among the gospels come solely from their personal perspectives as interpreters of Jesus and His ministry. Other sources also probably contributed to the composition of the four gospels.

In the past 200 years, a great deal of scholarship has been devoted to recovering such possible sources, though it is doubtful whether the puzzle has been fully resolved. The theories advanced generally fit one of two categories. One possibility is that the synoptics depend on a prior source that is now lost, except as it is preserved in the synoptics themselves. A second possibility is that two of the synoptic gospels depend on the other gospel. Until about 1800, the church generally accepted the view, first advanced by Augustine, that Matthew wrote the first gospel, Mark abbreviated Matthew, and Luke used both to compose the third gospel.

Mark as a Source.

Most scholars now agree that at least two, and perhaps as many as four, sources lie beneath the synoptic gospels. The first and most important of these is the Gospel of Mark—and not Matthew, as the church long assumed. Mark contains 666 verses (excluding 16:9–20, which many scholars consider later additions to the text). A total of 606 of these verses reappear in full or in part in Matthew's Gospel of 1,071 verses; 350 of Mark's verses reappear in Luke's Gospel of 1,151 verses. This means that more than one-half of Matthew and one-third of Luke are composed of material from Mark. Only 31 verses in Mark have no parallel in Matthew or Luke.

A number of observations show that Mark, and not Matthew or Luke, is the prior source. First, Matthew and Luke never agree in arrangement of material when compared against Mark. When either Matthew or Luke disagree in the sequence of events, the other follows Mark.

Second, certain details in Mark's gospel are either omitted or reworked in Matthew and Luke. The latter often refine Mark's awkward expressions; for example, compare Mark 4:1 with Matthew 13:1–2 and Luke 8:4 . Inconsistencies in Mark are omitted by Matthew and Luke; for example, compare Mark 2:26 with Matthew 12:3 and Luke 6:3. Mark's frank assessments of the disciples (6:52; 9:32) are omitted by Matthew and Luke, apparently out of respect for their importance as apostles. Mark's references to Jesus' human emotions—for example, grief (14:34), exasperation (8:12), anger (10:14), amazement (6:6), and fatigue (4:38)—are softened by the other synoptics; and examples of

Jesus' ability to perform certain actions (Mark 6:6) are deleted by them, too (Matt. 13:58; Luke 4:23).

On the other hand, Matthew and Luke on occasion heighten Jesus' accomplishments in comparison with Mark (Mark 1:32, 34; Matt. 8:16). If we assume that Matthew and Luke reworked Mark in these instances, it is possible to explain the differences; but it is practically impossible to do so if we assume otherwise.

Q Source.

When the remaining material in Matthew and Luke is examined, the reader discovers that more than 200 verses appear in them, while they have no parallel in Mark. This material, which consists mainly of Jesus' teachings, can be grouped into four categories: (1) Jesus and John the Baptist, (2) Jesus and His disciples, (3) Jesus and His opponents, and (4) Jesus and the future. Scholars assume that this material must have come from a source known only to Matthew and Luke.

For purposes of identification, this source is assigned the name "Q" (from the German, *Quelle*, "source"). Since Q passages agree closely, sometimes to the point of exact wording, it is reasonable to assume that this source was written rather than oral. Q material occurs scattered throughout Matthew 5–7; 10–11; 18:10, 23; and 24:37; but it is centralized in two sections of Luke (6:20–7:35; 9:57–13:34). Luke, therefore, probably more nearly preserves the original sequence of Q.

The "Q" document, of course, is theoretical, since no copy of it is known to exist. It is likely, however, that a document preserving the sayings of Jesus and fitting the description of Q was known to the early church. The church father, Papias, writing about A.D. 130, records, "Matthew collected the oracles in the Hebrew language, and each interpreted them as best he could." It is unlikely that these "oracles" are our present Gospel of Matthew, though it may be that they served as a source for the Gospel of Matthew (and Luke?). The sayings of Jesus were highly esteemed in the early church, especially for the instruction of converts; and it is possible that the more than 200 verses that Matthew and Luke have in common depend on a sayings source compiled by Matthew and known to Papias as "oracles."

Special M and Special L.

When Mark and Q are accounted for, there remain more than one-fifth of Matthew and one-third of Luke for which there is no parallel in other gospels. Where each writer obtained this information is uncertain, although much of Luke's special material probably came from sources associated with his Pauline journeys, particularly in Caesarea. At any rate, each writer appears to have used unique materials in writing his gospel. These sources are sometimes labeled Special M (Matthew) and Special L (Luke).

Form Criticism.

Following World War I, a new approach to gospel research arose in Germany. Its goal was to get behind the written sources (Mark, Q, L, or M) and investigate the forms (hence, form criticism) in which the gospel was transmitted by word of mouth in the period between the death of Jesus (A.D. 30) and the appearance of the first Christian writings of Paul (A.D. 50).

This school of thought rests on several assumptions. One assumption is that the tradition that was handed down about Jesus tended to become grouped into a number of broad categories: miracle stories, parables, pronouncements (Mark 2:27; 3:35), sayings of various kinds (Matt. 6:19–34), and most importantly, accounts of the death of Jesus.

Another assumption of form criticism is that the early church remembered, shaped, and passed on those aspects of Jesus' teachings and ministry that were relevant to its circumstances. This means that, in addition to telling us about Jesus, the gospels tell us something about the early church that passed on the stories about Jesus.

This assumption has resulted in the important awareness that the early church did not look upon Jesus merely as an historical figure of the past, but as the living Lord of the present. This second assumption is especially evident in the Gospel of John, which blends the remembrances called to mind by the Holy Spirit (John 14:26) with the events of Jesus' life. Since the early church maintained its treasure of tradition about Jesus primarily through preaching, the contents of the gospels are shaped significantly by the faith of the early church.

This is not to say that stories were "made up" by the early church in order to preach about a Jesus who was a figment of someone's vivid imagination. It means, instead, that the early church kept some memories about Jesus alive, while it did not continue others; and one of the reasons for this is that certain events and sayings were much more important in the early church's eyes than others were.

Although form criticism is still in its infancy stages, it has increased our appreciation of the role the early church played in the formation of the gospels. Some form critics, however, have erred in overstating the influence of the church on the gospel tradition, sometimes even implying that the gospels mirror the church instead of the Lord.

Is it possible to know whether the early church distorted or preserved the intent of the historical Jesus? Fortunately, the New Testament contains certain checks that provide reasonable certainty of careful handling on the part of the early church. We may be assured that eyewitnesses, including some of the apostles, were alive when the gospels appeared in writing. Such eyewitnesses would have encouraged historical accuracy and prevented distortion in the gospels.

Another important fact is that rabbis of Jesus' day trained their disciples to commit their teachings to memory, in fact, to the point of perfect recitation of long passages. We have no reason to assume that Jesus was less diligent about the transmission of His teaching than the rabbis were about theirs.

We also may be assured that the early church did not project upon the gospels any teachings or concerns foreign to Jesus. The synoptic gospels, for example, record more than 50 parables of Jesus, but not one parable is recorded in the remainder of the New Testament. This observation demonstrates that Jesus—and only Jesus—taught in parables, and the church was faithful to record them.

Expressed respect for the words of Jesus can also be found in the apostle Paul, who distinguishes between "commands of the Lord" and his own opinion (1 Cor. 7:10, 12, 25). In a similar vein, we have no instances where the words of Paul, Peter, John, or any of the "pillars" of the church (Gal. 2:9) are placed in Jesus' mouth. Nor do we find the teachings of the apostles included in the gospels. Jesus commands center stage, and He has no successors.

Furthermore, we know that the early church faced a series of crises as it began to evangelize the Gentile world. One such crisis concerned the conditions of accepting Gentiles into the church, and especially circumcision. But such questions are scarcely mentioned in the gospels (Matt. 8:10).

Finally, inclusion in the gospels of confusing statements (such as the second coming; Mark 9:1), or matters unimportant to the early church (little children; Mark 10:13–16), or even embarrassing remembrances (Peter's denial; Mark 14:66–68), indicate that the early church was more intent on preserving the tradition it received than on improving its own image.

Redaction Criticism.

Since World War II, some scholars have done gospel research in another area. These scholars focus on the role of the gospel writers as editors of the material received from the early church, and hence the name redaction criticism (from the German, *Redaktion*, "editing"). Whatever sources and traditions the writers may have inherited, redaction studies have revealed that the gospel writers were more than chroniclers or witless transmitters of the material they received. Each is an important link in the chain connecting us with Jesus. Each offers a unique and complementary portrait of Jesus, because each writes to a different audience and emphasizes different aspects of Jesus' life.

For Mark, Jesus is the Suffering Servant who reveals His divine Sonship on the cross. Matthew's major concern is to present Jesus as a teacher who is greater than Moses and continually present with the disciples. For Luke, Jesus is the keystone in the history of salvation, beginning with Israel, fulfilled in Jesus, and com-municated by the church. The fourth gospel writer penetrates the mystery of the incarnation (Jesus as God in human form; John 1:14), who brings life to the world through trust in Him.

The Synoptics and the Gospel of John.

It would be a mistake to imply that John is radically different from the other gospels and deserves no consideration with them. All four gospels portray Jesus Christ through selected events in His life, climaxing in His death and resurrection. But John features an independent, unique presentation of Jesus. In the synoptics, Jesus' ministry lasts less than a year, and is conducted mainly in Galilee; in John it extends to three or more years and centers more often in Judea.

The synoptics present Jesus as a man of action who paints word pictures for His hearers; John, however, portrays longer, less picturesque, and more speculative discourse coming from Jesus, and comparatively little action. In the synoptics, Jesus teaches in parables—nearly 60 in all—but in John no parables exist. In the synoptics, Jesus teaches mainly about the kingdom of God, whereas in John he teaches about Himself. In the synoptics, Jesus often demands silence of those who behold His miracles, but in John miracles are signs revealing Jesus and His mission.

These facts are sufficient to indicate that the synoptics present basically one perspective on the life of Jesus and that the Gospel of John presents another perspective, achieved most probably by profound meditation on the meaning of Jesus Christ.

The importance of the gospels for the early church may be indicated by noting that these four, which were collected perhaps as early as A.D. 125, were the first books of the New Testament to be accepted as authoritative by the early church. Today the four gospels remain our only reliable source of information about the central figure of the human race.

We may never fully understand how the gospels originated and what sources each writer used for his account. But a more important challenge than solving the literary mysteries of the gospels is learning to appreciate the unique portrait that each writer offers of Jesus and growing in our love and devotion to Him.

HABAKKUK, BOOK OF—a short prophetic book of the Old Testament that deals with the age-old problems of evil and human suffering. The book is named for the prophet Habakkuk.

Structure of the Book.

Habakkuk's book contains only three short chapters, but they present a striking contrast. In the first two, Habakkuk protests, complains, and questions God. But the final chapter is a beautiful psalm of praise. Habakkuk apparently used this complaining and questioning technique to drive home his powerful message about the approaching judgment of God.

Habakkuk begins his book with a cry of woe. Injustice is rampant, the righteous are surrounded by the wicked, the law is powerless, and God doesn't seem to care about the plight of His people (1:1–4). Habakkuk wonders why God is allowing these things to happen.

God's reply brings little comfort to the prophet. He explains that the armies of Babylon are moving throughout the ancient world on a campaign of death and destruction. At the time when Habakkuk received this vision, the Babylonians had already defeated Assyria and Egypt. The implication is that Habakkuk's nation, Judah, will be the next to fall.

The prophet was shocked at the news. He reminded God of His justice and holiness (1:12–13). How could He use the wicked Babylonians to destroy His Chosen People? Surely He realized the sins of His people were as nothing, when compared to the pagan Babylonians. "Why do you ... hold your tongue when the wicked devours one more righteous than he?" he asks (1:13). This direct question indicates Habakkuk's great faith. Only a person very close to God would dare question the purposes of the Almighty so boldly. God assures Habakkuk that the Babylonians will prevail not because they are righteous but because they are temporary instruments of judgment in His hands (2:4). Then he pronounces five burdens of woe against the Babylonians (2:6, 9, 12, 15, 19). God will not be mocked; the end of the Babylonians is as certain as the judgment they will bring on Judah. In all of this, God will vindicate His righteous character: "For the earth will be filled with the knowledge of the glory of the LORD, as the waters cover the sea" (2:14).

After this assurance, Habakkuk breaks out with the beautiful psalm of praise to God contained in chapter 3. This is one of the greatest testimonies of faith in the Bible.

Authorship and Date.

Nothing is known about the prophet Habakkuk except his name. But he was surely a sensitive poet as well as a courageous spokesman for God. His little book is a literary masterpiece that points people of all ages to faith in God and His eternal purpose. Since the book speaks of the coming destruction of Judah, it had to be written some time before Jerusalem was destroyed by the Babylonians in 586 B.C. The most likely time for its composition is probably about 600 B.C.

Historical Setting.

The Book of Habakkuk belongs to that turbulent era in ancient history when the balance of power was shifting from the Assyrians to the Babylonians. Assyria's domination came to an end with the destruction of its capital city, Nineveh, by the invading Babylonians in 612 B.C.

Less than 20 years after Habakkuk wrote his book, the Babylonians also destroyed Jerusalem and carried the leading citizens of Judah into captivity. God used this pagan nation to punish His Covenant People for their unfaithfulness and worship of false gods.

Theological Contribution.

The question-and-answer technique of the prophet Habakkuk teaches a valuable lesson about the nature of God. That God allows Himself to be questioned by one of His followers is an indication of His long-suffering mercy and grace.

The theme of God's judgment against unrighteousness also is woven throughout the book. God soon will punish His wayward people for their transgression, but He also will punish the pagan Babylonians because of their great sin. God always acts in justice. He will not forget mercy while pouring out his wrath (3:2). His judgment will fall on the proud, but the just will live in His faithfulness (2:4). God's acts of judgment are in accord with His holiness, righteousness, and mercy.

Special Considerations.

The Protestant Reformation under Martin Luther was influenced by the Book of Habakkuk. Luther's discovery of the biblical doctrine that the just shall live by faith came from his study of the apostle Paul's beliefs in the Books of Romans and Galatians. But Paul's famous declaration, "The just shall live by faith" (Rom. 1:17), is a direct quotation from Habakkuk 2:4. Thus, in this brief prophetic book, we find the seeds of the glorious gospel of our Lord and Savior Jesus Christ.

HAGGAI, BOOK OF—a short prophetic book of the Old Testament written to encourage the people of Israel who had returned to their native land after the captivity in Babylon.

Structure of the Book.

The two short chapters of Haggai contain four important messages, each dated to the very month and day it was delivered. He called on the people to rebuild the Temple, to remain faithful to God's promises, to be holy and enjoy God's great provisions, and to keep their hope set on the coming of the Messiah and the establishment of His kingdom.

Authorship and Date.

This book was written by the prophet Haggai, whose name means "festive." Like those whom he encouraged, he probably spent many years in captivity in Babylon before returning to his native land. A contemporary of the prophet Zechariah, he delivered these messages of encouragement "in the second year of King Darius" (1:1), a Persian ruler. This dates his book precisely in 520 B.C.

Historical Setting.

Haggai takes us back to one of the most turbulent periods in Judah's history—their captivity at the hands of a foreign power, followed by their release and resettlement in Jerusalem. For more than 50 years they were held captive by the Babylonians. But they were allowed to return to their native land, beginning in 538 B.C., after Babylon fell to the conquering Persians. At first, the captives who returned worked diligently at rebuilding the Temple, but they soon grew tired of the task and gave it up altogether. Haggai delivered his messages to motivate the people to resume the project.

Theological Contribution.

Haggai urged the people to put rebuilding the Temple at the top of their list of priorities. This shows that authentic worship is a very important matter. The rebuilt Temple in Jerusalem was important as a place of worship and sacrifice. Centuries later, at the death of Jesus "the veil of the Temple was torn in two" (Luke

23:45), demonstrating that He had given Himself as the eternal sacrifice on our behalf.

Special Considerations.

The Book of Haggai ends with a beautiful promise of the coming of the Messiah. Meanwhile, God's special servant, Zerubbabel, was to serve as a "signet ring" (2:23), a sign or promise of the glorious days to come. As the Jewish governor of Jerusalem under appointment by the Persians, Zerubbabel showed there was hope for the full restoration of God's Covenant People in their native land.

HAGIOGRAPHA [HAG ee AHG ruh fuh] (*holy writings*)—the third division of the Hebrew Old Testament. The other two divisions are the Law and the Prophets. Also known as the Writings, the Hagiographa contained 11 books (13 in the English Bible), usually in the following order in the Hebrew Bible: Psalms, Job, Proverbs, Song of Songs, Ruth, Lamentations, Ecclesiastes, Esther, Daniel, Ezra–Nehemiah, and 1 and 2 Chronicles.

HEBREWS, EPISTLE TO THE—the 19th book in the New Testament. Hebrews is a letter written by an unknown Christian to show how Jesus Christ had replaced Judaism as God's perfect revelation of Himself. Hebrews begins with a marvelous tribute to the person of Christ (1:1–3), and throughout the epistle the author weaves warning with doctrine to encourage his readers to hold fast to Jesus as the great High Priest of God. The author makes extensive use of Old Testament quotations and images to show that Jesus is the supreme revelation of God and the all-sufficient Mediator between God and humankind. Because of its literary style and the careful way it develops its argument, Hebrews reads more like an essay than a personal letter.

Structure of the Epistle.

The letter begins by showing that Jesus is the Son of God and, therefore, is superior to angels (1:1–2:18) and to Moses (3:1–6). This section contains a warning not to lose the blessings, or "rest," of God because of unbelief, as the Israelites did under Moses (3:7–4:13).

The second section of the letter (4:14–10:18) attempts to show that Christ is the perfect High Priest because of His unmatched compassion for people and complete obedience to God (4:14–5:10). Following an additional warning against renouncing the faith (5:11–6:20), the author then describes Jesus as a priest according to the order of Melchizedek (7:1–28). The emphasis on Melchizedek, who is mentioned only twice in the Old Testament (Gen. 14:18–20; Ps. 110:4), may seem farfetched to modern readers. However, there is a good reason for comparing Christ to Melchizedek; it is to show that Melchizedek, unlike Aaron, was unique. He had no recorded predecessors or successors. He was, therefore, a priest forever, like the Son of God (7:1–3). As a consequence of His being like Melchizedek, Jesus inaugurated a new and better covenant (8:1–13) because His sacrifice of Himself replaces the sacrifice of "bulls and goats" (9:1–10:18).

The final section of the epistle appeals to the readers not to give up the benefits of Christ's work as High Priest (10:19–13:17). In an attempt to offset spiritual erosion (10:19–39), the author recalls the heroes of faith (11:1–40). Let their example, he says, encourage the readers to "run with endurance the race that is set before us" (12:1). The letter closes with various applications of faith to practical living (13:1–19), a benediction (13:20–21), and greetings (13:22–25).

Authorship and Date.

Other than 1 John, the Epistle to the Hebrews is the only letter in the New Testament with no greeting or identification of its author. Although the King James Version entitles the book "The Epistle of Paul the Apostle to the Hebrews," this title stems from later manuscripts which came to include it. It is highly doubtful, however, that Paul wrote Hebrews. The language, vocabulary, and style of Hebrews differ from Paul's genuine letters. Such typically Pauline expressions as "Christ Jesus," "in Christ," or "the resurrection" are all but absent in Hebrews. When Hebrews and Paul treat the same subjects, they often approach them differently. For example, in Hebrews the "law" means the ritual law, whereas for Paul it means the moral law; "faith" in Hebrews is belief in the trustworthiness of God, whereas for Paul it is a personal commitment to a living Lord. The author of Hebrews sounds more like a Platonic philosopher than Paul when he speaks of the old covenant (8:5) and the law (10:1) as "shadows" of their originals.

There has been no shortage of suggestions concerning who the author may have been. The list includes Luke, Priscilla, Aquila, Clement of Rome, Silvanus, and Philip. The two most likely candidates are Apollos and Barnabas. Both have characteristics that commend them, Apollos because he was an eloquent Alexandrian Jew who knew the Scriptures well (Acts 18:24), and Barnabas because he was a Levite (Acts 4:36). As with the others, however, these suggestions are only possibilities. The writer of the epistle remains anonymous.

One can only make an educated guess about the date and place of composition. Since the author's purpose was to show that Christianity had replaced Judaism, to have been able to point to the destruction of the Temple (which occurred in A.D. 70) as an indication that God had no further use for it would have been a decisive argument. Since the author does not make use of this information, it is reasonable to assume the destruction of the Temple had not happened yet, thus dating the letter sometime before A.D. 70. The only clue about where Hebrews was written is found in the closing remark, "Those from Italy greet you" (13:24). This may indicate that the author was writing from Italy, presumably Rome.

Historical Setting.

The repeated use of Old Testament quotations and images in Hebrews suggests that the people who received this book had a Jewish background. The repeated warnings against spiritual unbelief reveal that the readers of this epistle were on the verge of renouncing the Christian faith and returning to their former Jewish ways (2:1–4; 3:7–4:14; 5:12–6:20; 10:19–39; 12:12–29). Negligence in good deeds and sloppy attendance at worship services (10:23–25) were evidence of a cooling in their faith. In an effort to rekindle the readers' flame of commitment to Christ, the author urges his readers not to retreat from persecution (10:32–39), but to hasten to the front lines. He calls for a new exodus (3:7–19); he holds before them examples of a pilgrim faith (chap. 11); and he tells them not to "draw back" (10:39), but to "go forth to Him, outside the camp, bearing His reproach" (13:13).

Theological Contribution.

In a spirit similar to Stephen's defense before the Jewish Sanhedrin (Acts 7), Hebrews sets out to show that Christianity is superior to Judaism because of the person of Jesus Christ, who is the Son of God, the Great High Priest, and the Author of salvation. Christ stands as the peak of revelation, superior to angels (1:1–2:9) and to Moses (3:1–6). He is the Son of God, the reflection of God's own glory and, indeed, the very character and essence of God (1:3). Whatever revelations appeared before Jesus were but shadows or outlines of what was to appear in Him.

Christ is also the Great High Priest (4:14). Whereas earthly priests inherited their office, Christ was appointed by the direct call of God (5:5–6). Whereas earthly priests followed in the lineage of Aaron, Christ, who has no successors, is a priest forever, according to the order of Melchizedek (7:17). Whereas earthly priests ministered within temples made with human hands, Christ ministers within the true sanctuary—the eternal house of God (8:2; 9:24). Whereas earthly priests offered animal sacrifices for their sins as well as for those of the people, Christ offered the one perfect sacrifice that never need be offered again—His sinless self (5:3; 10:4–14).

As the unique Son of God who made the supreme sacrifice of Himself to God, Jesus is described by the author of the book of Hebrews as the "author of their salvation" (2:10), the "finisher of our faith" (12:2), and the "great Shepherd of the sheep" (13:20). Christ saves His people *from* sin and death, and He saves them *for* fellowship with God. In Hebrews salvation is called the "rest" of God (4:1), "eternal inheritance" (9:15), the "Most Holy Place" (9:12). These three emphases—Jesus as Son, High Priest, and Savior—are drawn together in one key passage: "Though He was a *Son*, yet He learned obedience by the things which He suffered. And having been perfected, He became the *author of eternal salvation* to all who obey Him, called by God as *High Priest* 'according to the order of Melchizedek' " (5:8–10). In light of Christ's preeminence, the author urges his readers to hold fast to the true confession and endure whatever suffering or reproach is necessary on its behalf (4:14; 6:18; 13:13).

Special Considerations.

Two passages in Hebrews often trouble Christians. In 6:4–6 and 10:26 the author warns that if a person willingly turns from fellowship with Christ, he can no longer be forgiven. The intent of these verses is to cause Christians to remember the great cost of God's grace and to take their profession of faith seriously. The intent of these verses is not to cause believers to doubt their salvation. There is no example in the Bible where anyone who desired the forgiveness of Christ was denied it.

The backbone of this epistle is the finality of Christ for salvation. This wonderful truth is no less urgent for us today than it was for the original readers of Hebrews. The rise of cults, with their deceptive claims of security, is but one example of the many things that appeal for our ultimate loyalty. Hebrews reminds us that "Jesus Christ is the same yesterday, today, and forever" (13:8). Because of His perfect sacrifice of Himself, He is still the only Mediator between us and God. Only Jesus is the true Author of our salvation.

HERMENEUTICS [**hur meh NEWT icks**]—the principles and methods used to interpret Scripture. Bible scholars believe a biblical text must be interpreted according to the language in which it was written, its historical context, the identity and purpose of the author, its literary nature, and the situation to which it was originally addressed.

HEXATEUCH—a term for the first six books of the Old Testament (Genesis, Exodus, Leviticus, Numbers, Deuteronomy, and Joshua), viewed as a unit. The first five books of the Old Testament, known as the Pentateuch, have traditionally been regarded as the first division of the Hebrew Old Testament. However, since the early 19th century many scholars who specialize in the literary criticism of the Old Testament have preferred to think in terms of a Hexateuch, or six-volumed book, as forming the first division. These scholars view the book of Joshua as closely linked with the preceding five, arguing that it came from the same sources.

While Joshua is similar in some ways to the books that precede it, many scholars disagree with the concept of a Hexateuch. They argue that Joshua belongs with the Former Prophets, which includes Judges, Samuel, and Kings, rather than with the Law.

HOSEA, BOOK OF—a prophetic book of the Old Testament that emphasizes God's steadfast love for His Covenant

People, in spite of their continuing sin and rebellion. The book is named for its author, the prophet Hosea, who demonstrated God's steadfast love in dramatic fashion through his devotion to his own unfaithful wife.

Structure of the Book.

Hosea contains 14 chapters that are filled with some of the most powerful truths in all the Bible. After a brief introduction of himself as God's prophet, Hosea tells about his unusual family situation. God appeared to Hosea, instructing him, "Go, take yourself a wife of harlotry and children of harlotry" (1:2). The reason for this unusual request was to demonstrate that God's Covenant People, the nation of Israel, had been unfaithful to God because of their worship of false gods.

Hosea did as the Lord commanded, taking a prostitute named Gomer as his wife. The first three chapters of the book report their stormy relationship as husband and wife. Soon after their marriage, Gomer bore three children. Hosea gave them symbolic names—Jezreel (*God scatters*), Lo-Ruhamah (*not pitied*), and Lo-Ammi (*not my people*)—to show that God was about to bring His judgment upon the nation of Israel because the people had fallen into worship of false gods. Just as the nation rejected God, Gomer eventually left Hosea and the children to return to her life of prostitution. But Hosea's love for his wife refused to die.

He searched until he found her at the slave market. Then he bought her back and restored her as his wife. This tender picture showed clearly that God had not given up on Israel, although the people had "played the harlot" many times by returning to their old life of pagan worship and enslavement to sin.

The second major division of Hosea's book, chapters 4–14, contains the prophet's messages of judgment against the nations of Israel and Judah. The northern kingdom of Israel, Hosea's homeland, is singled out for strong rebuke because of its gross sin and immorality. But the book ends on a positive note. In tender language, the prophet reminds the nation of God's undying love. In spite of their unfaithfulness, He is determined to redeem them and restore them to their favored place as His Covenant People.

Authorship and Date.

The undisputed author of this book is the prophet Hosea, who identifies himself in the book as "the son of Beeri" (1:1). His name, a shortened form of "Joshua" and "Jesus," means "salvation." The prophet also says that he lived and prophesied during the reign of King Jeroboam II of Israel while four successive kings—Uzziah, Jotham, Ahaz, and Hezekiah—were ruling in Judah. This means his prophetic ministry covered a period of about 40 years, from about 755 B.C. to about 715 B.C. His book was written some time during these years.

Historical Setting.

Hosea prophesied during the twilight years of the northern kingdom of Israel, a time of rapid moral decline. Worship of false gods was mixed with worship of the one true God. Ritualism rather than righteousness was the order of the day as even the priests lost sight of the real meaning of worship. Although King Jeroboam II was the instigator of many of these policies, at least his 40-year reign (793–753 B.C.) brought a measure of political stability to the nation. This stability came to an end when he died. In rapid succession, six different kings ruled Israel during the next 25 years; four were eliminated by assassination. Weakened by internal strife, Israel collapsed in 722 B.C. when the nation of Assyria destroyed Samaria, Israel's capital city. Hosea was probably an eyewitness to many of these events as his prophecy about God's judgment on Israel was fulfilled.

Theological Contribution.

Through his marriage and prophetic message, Hosea presents a vivid picture of the steadfast love of God for His people. Because they have sinned and broken the covenant, God's people deserve His certain judgment. But because of His undying love for them, His mercy and lovingkindness will prevail. Many people believe the Old Testament portrays God's wrath, while the New Testament pictures his love. But the Book of Hosea includes tender expressions of deep love among this prophet's descriptions of judgment. Hosea ranks with Deuteronomy and the Gospel of John as major biblical treatises on the love of God. This love is not mere sentiment; it is rooted in compassion and bound in holiness. God's love makes demands, but it is also willing to forgive.

Special Considerations.

The Book of Hosea is noted for its many references to the history of Israel, as well as its vivid poetic images. Throughout the book the prophet speaks tenderly of the nation of Israel as "Ephraim." This is a reference to the largest of the ten northern tribes of Palestine that made up the nation of Israel. Because of their superior numbers, Ephraim was a symbol of power and strength. This tribal name also reminded the nation of its history and tradition. Ephraim, after whom the tribe was named (Gen. 48:17–22), was the son of Joseph.

Few events in the Bible have been debated as strongly as Hosea's marriage. The command for a man of God to marry a harlot is so startling that interpreters have offered many different explanations. Some suggest that the story is meant to be read only as an allegory. Others believe Gomer was faithful at first but went astray after their marriage. Still others believe she was a prostitute from the very beginning but that Hosea did not learn this until later.

All of these approaches to the passage issue from our offended sense of right and wrong. The plain meaning of the text is that Hosea married a prostitute at God's direct command. In this way, through his own tormented life Hosea could present a striking picture of the pain in God's heart because of the harlotries of His Covenant People.

I

IMPRECATORY PSALMS—individual psalms in the Book of Psalms in which the authors call for misfortune and disaster to strike their enemies. The writers of the psalms were often persecuted by ungodly people, so they prayed that God would pour out His wrath and righteous judgment upon their foes. Only by doing so, they believed, could God's love and justice strike a proper balance. Some examples of imprecatory psalms are Psalms 5, 11, 17, 35, 55, 59, 69, 109, 137, and 140.

INSPIRATION—a technical term for the Holy Spirit's supernatural guidance of those who received special revelation from God as they wrote the books of the Bible. The end result of this inspiration is that the Bible conveys the truths that God wanted His people to know and to communicate to the world.

The primary purpose of the Bible is to lead people to a personal relationship with God as Savior. But everything taught by the Bible on any subject is helpful and instructive for the complete Christian life (2 Tim. 3:16–17). Because Christianity relates to the real world, the Bible's declarations about the earth and history are completely trustworthy.

Two terms often used in discussion of the inspiration of the Bible are "plenary" and "verbal." "Plenary," a term meaning full or complete, means that each book, chapter, and paragraph of the Bible is equally derived from God. "Verbal" inspiration emphasizes the truth that the wording of the text, as well as the ideas conveyed, is supernaturally inspired by God through the Holy Spirit.

"Inerrancy" is a term used along with plenary verbal inspiration to convey the view that the Bible's teaching is true on everything of which it speaks. The words of Scripture, in the original writings, teach the truth without any admixture of error. The Bible is not just a useful body of human ideas. It makes clear the mind of God Himself.

"Infallibility" is a term often used as a synonym for inerrancy. However, the root meaning of infallibility is "not liable to fail in achieving its purpose." Truth, or inerrancy, is affirmed of the content of the Bible; infallibility refers to the effectiveness of the wording in conveying reliable ideas, as well as the effectiveness of those ideas when used by the all-powerful Holy Spirit (Is. 55:11).

Important as biblical infallibility is, it is not enough without inerrancy. The reason why the Spirit can use Scripture so effectively is that He directed its production from the beginning so that all of it is God's reliable information.

Inspiration, then, is a statement about God's greatness. God is intelligent and able to communicate with human beings, whom He created in His image. God knows everything about all reality in creation and is absolutely faithful and true (Rev. 3:7; 21:5). it follows that ideas communicated by divine revelation are true and conform to reality as God knows it. God overruled human limitations and sinful biases so that His human agents were able to write what He wanted written. God guided the thought conveyed so that it was without error, accomplishing the objectives He intended.

Exactly what role did the human writers of the Bible play in their transmission of God's message? They were not totally passive as those whose hands move automatically in an unconscious state. Their distinctive ways of writing stand out, as in the four gospels, which describe the life and ministry of Jesus Christ. Luke, the beloved physician, used many medical terms not found in Matthew, Mark, or John. Some biblical writers, like Moses and Paul, were highly educated; others were not.

Although some passages of Scripture may have been received by audible dictation (Ex. 4:12; 19:3–6; Num. 7:89), many were guided by a silent activity of the Holy Spirit (Luke 1:1–4). To err is human, and the conscious participation of finite, sinful authors would have led to error if not for this supernatural guidance by the Spirit.

God gave these people the distinctive functions of prophets and apostles, originated what they wrote, and kept them from error in all the writing processes. All of Scripture has prophetic authority. None of it originated in the will of human beings. It came about through the will of God (2 Pet. 1:20–21). All Scripture was given by inspiration of God (2 Tim. 3:16).

Clear standards tested whether a person who claimed to speak for God was a true prophet or a false prophet (Deut. 13:1–5; 18:20–22). People who spoke out of their hearts and by their own independent wills were subject to the death penalty (Deut. 13:6–10). Genuine prophets were inspired by the Holy Spirit as authentic speakers for God.

Although the Bible does not tell exactly how God inspired its writers, it was certainly not in a mechanical way. God the Holy Spirit is the third person of the Trinity who is working with persons. How does one person influence another person? Why do some have a more powerful impact upon people than others? Many factors are involved. We do know for certain that the Scriptures originated with God and that the writers were "moved" or carried along by the Holy Spirit (2 Pet. 1:20–21) as they recorded God's message.

The Holy Spirit's work in the life of the Virgin Mary is a good example of how the Spirit worked with the biblical writers. A fully human, sinful woman bore a sinless child who would be called the Holy One, the Son of God (Luke 1:35). How could that be? The power of the Highest "overshadowed" her so that she conceived Jesus. Likewise, the power of the Highest "overshadowed" the biblical writers so that what they wrote could be called the Holy Bible, the Word of God.

Followers of Jesus Christ as Savior and Lord will follow Him in His view of the Old Testament Scriptures and the entire Bible. He endorsed all three sections of the Hebrew Bible: the Law, the Prophets, and the Psalms (Writings). He accepted as fact some of the most controversial historical details: Adam and Eve at the beginning of time (Matt. 19:4); Abel's murder of Cain (Luke 11:51); Noah, the ark, and the Flood (Matt. 24:37–39); the destruction of Sodom and Gomorrah and of Lot's wife (Luke 17:28–30); and Moses' authorship of the Pentateuch (John 5:46). "All things must be fulfilled," He said, "which were written in the Law of Moses and the Prophets and the Psalms concerning Me" (Luke 24:44). People were mistaken, Jesus said, "not knowing the Scriptures nor the power of God" (Matt. 22:29). He expressed His concern for unbelievers: "O foolish ones, and slow of heart to believe in all that the prophets have spoken!" (Luke 24:25).

The view that God's great mind had to accommodate itself to human errors in the production of the Bible does not fit the high view of Scripture that Jesus had. God certainly adapted His truth to a human level of understanding. But a person can adapt truth about the origin of human life to a child's level of understanding without teaching errors about storks. In a similar way, God adapts His truth in part to our limited understandings, but neither He, nor His Son, nor His Spirit taught error in the name of God.

Belief in the Bible's inerrancy and infallibility best fits the claims of Jesus about the Bible and the claims the Bible makes for itself. Salvation is the primary purpose of Scripture, but this is not its only function. It teaches truth about the world's origins, history, and the future.

Those who believe all that the Bible affirms should live faithfully according to its instruction in all personal relationships. Central to the Bible's teaching is love for God and love for neighbor. If believers in biblical inerrancy do not love God and their neighbors, their defense of scriptural authority will become "a resounding gong or a clanging cymbal" (1 Cor. 13:1, NIV).

ISAIAH, BOOK OF—a major prophetic book of the Old Testament, noted for its description of the coming Messiah as God's Suffering Servant. Because of its lofty portrayal of God and His purpose of salvation, the book is sometimes called "the fifth gospel," implying it is similar in theme to the gospels of the New Testament. The book is named for its author, the great prophet Isaiah, whose name means "The Lord has saved."

Structure of the Book.

With its 66 chapters, Isaiah is one of the longest prophetic books of the Old Testament. Most scholars agree that the book falls naturally into two major sections, chapters 1–39 and chapters 40–66. One good way to remember the grand design of the book is to think of the sections as parallel to the two main parts of the Bible. The first section of Isaiah contains the same number of chapters as the number of books in the Old Testament (39). The second part of the book parallels the New Testament in the same way—27 chapters for the 27 books of this section of the Bible.

The general theme of the first part of Isaiah's book is God's approaching judgment on the nation of Judah. In some of the most striking passages in all the Bible, the prophet announces that God will punish His people because of their sin, rebellion, and worship of false gods. But this message of stern judgment is also mingled with beautiful poems of comfort and promise. Although judgment is surely coming, better days for God's Covenant People lie just ahead. This section of Isaiah's book refers several times to the coming Messiah. His name will be called Immanuel (7:14). As a ruler on the throne of David, he will establish an everlasting kingdom (9:7).

Other significant events and prophecies covered in the first section of Isaiah's book include his call as a prophet (chap. 6), God's judgment against the nations surrounding Judah (chaps. 13–23), and a warning to Judah not to seek help through vain alliances with Egypt (chaps. 30–31).

During Isaiah's time, Judah's safety was threatened by the advancing Assyrians. When the king of Judah sought to protect the nation's interests by forming an alliance with Egypt to turn back the Assyrians, Isaiah advised the nation to look to their God for deliverance—not to a pagan nation led by an earthly ruler. He also prophesied that the Assyrian army would be turned back by God before it succeeded in overthrowing the nation of Judah (30:27–33).

The second major section of Isaiah's book (chaps. 40–66) is filled with prophecies of comfort for the nation of Judah. Just as Isaiah warned of God's approaching judgment in the first part of his book, the 27 concluding chapters were written to comfort God's people in the midst of their suffering after His judgment had fallen. The theme of this entire section may be illustrated with Isaiah's famous hymn of comfort that God directed the prophet to address to the people: "'Comfort, yes, comfort My people!'" says your God. "'Speak comfort to Jerusalem, and cry out to her, that her warfare is ended, that her iniquity is pardoned; for she has received from the LORD's hand double for all her sins'" (40:1–2).

Isaiah's message in this part of his book is that after their period of judgment has passed, God's Covenant People will be restored to their place of responsibility in God's plan for the salvation of the world. The great suffering through which they were passing was their period of captivity as exiles in the pagan nation of Babylonia. This theme of suffering on the part of God's people is demonstrated dramatically by Isaiah's famous description of the Suffering Servant. The nation of Israel was God's suffering servant who would serve as God's instrument of blessing for the rest of the world after their release from captivity and restoration as His Chosen People (42:1–9).

But Isaiah's prophecy also points beyond the immediate future to the coming of Jesus Christ as the Messiah several centuries later. The heart of this stunning prophecy occurs in chapter 53, as Isaiah develops the description of God's Servant to its highest point. The Servant's suffering and death and the redemptive nature of His mission are clearly foretold. Although mankind deserved God's judgment because "we have turned, every one, to his own way" (53:6), God sent His Servant to take away our sins. It is through His suffering that we are made right with God, since "the LORD has laid on Him the iniquity of us all" (53:6). Isaiah closes his book with a beautiful description of the glorious age to come (chaps. 58–66). In that day the city of Zion, or Jerusalem, will be restored. God's people will gather there to worship Him in all His majesty and glory. Peace and justice will reign, and God will make all things new.

Authorship and Date.

The question of who wrote the Book of Isaiah is a matter of much disagreement and debate among Bible scholars. In one camp are those who insist the entire book was written by the famous prophet Isaiah who ministered in the southern kingdom of Judah for 40 years, from about 740–700 B.C.

But other scholars are just as insistent that the entire book was not written by this prophet. They agree that chapters 1–39 of the book belong to Isaiah, but they refer to chapters 40–66 as "Second Isaiah," insisting it was written by an unknown author long after the ministry of this famous prophet of Judah.

Those who assign chapters 40–66 to a "Second Isaiah" point out that the two major sections of the book seem to be set in different times. Chapters 1–39 clearly belong to the eighth century B.C., a turbulent period in the history of Judah. But Isaiah 40–66, according to these scholars, seems to be addressed to the citizens of Judah who were being held as captives in Babylon about 550 B.C. This was two centuries after Isaiah lived and prophesied. In addition, these scholars point to the differences in tone, language, and style between these two major sections as proof that the book was written by two different authors.

But the traditional view cannot be dismissed so easily. Conservative scholars point out that the two sections of the book do have many similarities, although they are dramatically different in tone and theme. Many phrases and ideas that are peculiar to Isaiah appear in both sections of the book. A good example of this is Isaiah's unique reference to God as "the Holy One of Israel" (1:4; 17:7; 37:23; 45:11; 55:5; 60:14). The appearance of such words and phrases can be used to argue just as convincingly that the book was written by a single author.

Conservative scholars also are not convinced that the two major sections of the book were addressed to different audiences living in different times. In the second section of his book, they believe Isaiah looked into the future and predicted the years of the Captivity and the return of the Covenant People to their homeland after the Captivity ended. If the prophet could predict the coming of the Messiah over 700 years before that happened, he could certainly foresee this major event in the future of the nation of Judah.

After all the evidence is analyzed, there is no convincing reason to question the traditional view that the entire book was written by the prophet whose name it bears. Perhaps chapters

1–39 were written early in Isaiah's ministry and chapters 40–66 were written near its end.

Isaiah gives us few facts about himself, but we do know he was "the son of Amoz" (1:1). The quality of his writing indicates he was well educated and that he probably came from an upper-class family. Married, he had two children to whom he gave symbolic names to show that God was about to bring judgment against the nation of Judah. He was called to his prophetic ministry "in the year that King Uzziah [Azariah] died" (6:1)—about 740 B.C.—through a stirring vision of God as he worshiped in the Temple. He prophesied for about 40 years to the nation of Judah, calling the people and their rulers to place their trust in the Holy One of Israel.

Historical Setting.

Isaiah delivered his prophecies during a time of great moral and political upheaval. In the early part of his ministry, about 722 B.C., Judah's sister nation, the northern kingdom of Israel, fell to the invading Assyrians. For a while, it looked as if Judah would suffer the same fate. But Isaiah advised the rulers of Judah not to enter alliances with foreign nations against the Assyrian threat. Instead, he called the people to put their trust in God, who alone could bring real salvation and offer lasting protection for the perilous times.

Theological Contribution.

The Book of Isaiah presents more insights into the nature of God than any other book of the Old Testament.

To Isaiah, God was first of all a holy God. His holiness was the first thing that impressed the prophet when he saw Him in all His glory in the Temple (6:1–8). But God's holiness also reminded Isaiah of his own sin and weakness. "Woe is me," he cried, "for I am undone! Because I am a man of unclean lips, and I dwell in the midst of a people of unclean lips" (6:5). After this confession, Isaiah's lips were cleansed by a live coal from the altar, and he agreed to proclaim God's message of repentance and judgment to a wayward people.

Isaiah also tells us about a God who is interested in the salvation of His people. Even the prophet's name, "The Lord has saved," emphasizes this truth. He uses the word "salvation" 28 times in his book, while all the other Old Testament prophets combined mentioned this word only 10 times. In Isaiah's thought, salvation comes from God, not from human beings. God is the sovereign ruler of history and the only one who has the power to save.

The Book of Isaiah also reveals that God's ultimate purpose of salvation will be realized through the coming Messiah, our Lord and Savior Jesus Christ. No other book of the Bible contains as many references to the coming Messiah as this magnificent book. Isaiah points us to a loving Savior who came to save His people from their sins. When Jesus began His public ministry in His hometown of Nazareth, He quoted from one of these beautiful messianic passages from Isaiah (61:1–2) to show that this prophecy was being fulfilled in His life and ministry. His purpose was "to set at liberty those who are oppressed, to preach the acceptable year of the LORD" (Luke 4:18–19).

Special Considerations.

One unusual passage in the Book of Isaiah gives us a clue about how God views His work of judgment and salvation. The prophet describes God's judgment as "His awesome work, and bring to pass His act, His unusual act" (28:21). If judgment is God's unusual act, does this not imply that salvation is the work more typical of Him as a loving God? It is an interesting question to think about as we express thanks to God for the marvelous insights of Isaiah and his important book.

J

JAMES, EPISTLE OF—a book characterized by its hard-hitting, practical religion. The epistle reads like a sermon and, except for a brief introduction, has none of the traits of an ancient letter. Each of the five chapters is packed with pointed illustrations and reminders designed to motivate the wills and hearts of believers to grasp a truth once taught by Jesus: "A tree is known by its fruit" (Matt. 12:33).

Authorship and Date.

The author identifies himself as "James, a servant of God and of the Lord Jesus Christ" (1:1). At least five personalities named James appear in the New Testament. None has a stronger claim to being the author of this epistle than James, the brother of the Lord. Apparently neither a disciple nor an apostle during Jesus' lifetime, he is first mentioned in Mark 6:3, where he is listed as the first (oldest) of Jesus' four younger brothers. After the ascension of Jesus, James emerged as a leader of the church in Jerusalem (Acts 15:13; 1 Cor. 15:7; Gal. 2:9)—a position he must have occupied for nearly 30 years, until his martyrdom, according to church tradition.

This James is probably the author of the epistle that bears his name. He refers to himself simply as "James," with no explanation added. This indicates he was well-known to his readers.

He calls himself a "servant" rather than an apostle; and he begins the epistle with the same "greetings" (1:1) with which he begins the apostolic decree following the Council of Jerusalem (Acts 15:23). These factors suggest one and the same James, the brother of the Lord.

The most important argument against authorship by the Lord's brother is that the Epistle of James was virtually unknown in the ancient church until the third century. It remains an unsolved mystery why it was neglected and then accepted into the New Testament canon at a relatively late date if James, the Lord's brother, were its author. Although this consideration cannot be overlooked, it does not overrule the Lord's brother as the most probable author of the epistle.

The Epistle of James gives few hints by which it might be dated. Estimates range from A.D. 45 to 150, depending on how one regards its authorship. If James, the Lord's brother, is its author, then it must have been written before A.D. 62 (the approximate time of his death). The epistle may have been written after Paul's letters were in circulation, because James' emphasis on works may be intended to offset Paul's emphasis on faith. This would date the epistle around A.D. 60.

Historical Setting.

James addresses the epistle "to the twelve tribes which are scattered abroad" (1:1). This implies a readership of Jewish Christians living outside Palestine. Elsewhere in the epistle, however, James refers to hired field labor (5:4), and this locates his audience inside Palestine. In James' day only in Palestine did farmers employ hired rather than slave labor, as was customary elsewhere. The epistle makes frequent references or allusions to the Old Testament. Its style and language are reminiscent of the Old Testament, especially wisdom literature and the prophet Amos. All these factors indicate that James was writing to persons of Jewish-Christian background. His emphasis was on the essentials of obedient living in accordance with the true intent of the law of God.

Theological Contribution.

The Epistle of James is a sturdy, compact letter on practical religion. For James, the acid test of true religion is in the doing rather than in the hearing, "believing," or speaking. James exalts genuineness of faith, and is quick to encourage the lowly that God gives grace to the humble (4:6), wisdom to the ignorant (1:5), salvation to the sinner (1:21), and the kingdom to the poor (2:5). He is equally quick to condemn counterfeit religion that would substitute theory for practice, and he does so with biting sarcasm. True religion is moral religion and social religion. True religion is doing the right thing in one's everyday affairs. In this respect James echoes clearly the ethical teaching of Jesus, especially as it is recorded in the Sermon on the Mount (Matthew 5–7). "Not everyone who says to Me, 'Lord, Lord,' shall enter the kingdom of heaven, but he who does the will of My Father in heaven" (Matt. 7:21).

Special Considerations.

Some Bible scholars suggest that James and Paul differ in their views on the saving significance of faith and works. Paul states, "A man is justified by faith apart from the deeds of the law" (Rom. 3:28), and James says, "A man is justified by works, and not by faith only" (James 2:19). A closer reading of the two, however, reveals that they differ more in their definition of faith than in its essence. James writes to readers who are inclined to interpret faith as mere intellectual acknowledgment (James 2:19). As a consequence he stresses that a faith that does not affect life is not saving faith; hence, his emphasis on works. Actually, this is quite close to Paul's understanding. For Paul, faith is the entrusting of one's whole life to God through Christ, with the result that one's life becomes renewed with the "fruit of the Spirit" (Gal. 5:22).

JEREMIAH, BOOK OF—a major prophetic book of the Old Testament directed to the southern kingdom of Judah just before that nation fell to the Babylonians. The book is named for its author and central personality, the great prophet Jeremiah, who faithfully delivered God's message of judgment in spite of fierce opposition from his countrymen.

Structure of the Book.

Jeremiah, consisting of 52 chapters, is one of the longest books in the Bible. It is also one of the hardest to follow and understand. Most of the other prophetic books have a chronological arrangement, but not the Book of Jeremiah. Prophecies delivered in the final years of his ministry may appear at any point in the book, followed by messages that belong to other periods in his life. Mingled with his prophecies of God's approaching judgment are historical accounts of selected events in the life of Judah, personal experiences from Jeremiah's own life, and poetic laments about the fate of his country. It is important to be aware of this if one wants to understand the message of this great prophetic book.

Basically, the first half of the book (chaps. 1–25) contains Jeremiah's prophecies of God's approaching judgment against Judah because of its sin and idolatry. The second half (chaps. 26–52) contains a few of his prophecies, but the main emphasis is on Jeremiah and his conflicts with the kings who ruled in Judah during his ministry. Also included near the end of his book is a report on the fall of Jerusalem and Judah's final days as a nation (chaps. 39–41; 52), along with a narrative about Jeremiah's flight into Egypt with other citizens of Judah following its fall (chaps. 42–44).

Authorship and Date.

Most conservative scholars agree that the author of the Book of Jeremiah was the famous prophet of that name who ministered in the southern kingdom of Judah during the final four decades of that nation's existence. But some scholars claim the book's disjointed arrangement proves it was compiled by an unknown author some time after Jeremiah's death. The book itself gives us a clue about how it may have taken its present form.

After prophesying against Judah for about 20 years, the prophet Jeremiah was commanded by God to put his messages in written form. He dictated these to his scribe or secretary, Baruch, who wrote them on a scroll (36:1–4). Because Jeremiah had been banned from entering the royal court, he sent Baruch to read the messages to King Jehoiakim. To show his contempt for Jeremiah and his message, the king cut the scroll apart and threw it in the fire (36:22–23). Jeremiah promptly dictated his book to Baruch again, adding "many similar words" (36:32) that had not been included in the first scroll.

This clear description of how a second version of Jeremiah came to be written shows the book was composed in two or more different stages during the prophet's ministry. The scribe Baruch was probably the one who added to the book at Jeremiah's command as it was shaped and refined over a period of several years. This is a possible explanation for the disjointed arrangement of the book. Baruch must have put the book in final form shortly after Jeremiah's death, presumably in Egypt.

We can learn a great deal about the prophet Jeremiah by reading his book. He was a sensitive poet who could weep over the sins of his nation: "Oh, that my head were waters, and my eyes a fountain of tears" (9:1). But he was also a courageous man of God who could endure persecution and affliction. He narrowly escaped death several times as he carried out God's command to preach His message of judgment to a wayward people. A patriot who passionately loved his nation, he drew the tough assignment of informing his countrymen that Judah was about to fall to a pagan power. Many of his fellow citizens branded him a traitor, but he never wavered from the prophetic ministry to which God had called him.

With the fall of Jerusalem in 586 B.C., most of the leading citizens of the nation were carried away as captives to Babylon. But Jeremiah was allowed to remain in Judah with other citizens who were placed under the authority of a ruling governor appointed by Babylon. When the citizens of Jerusalem revolted against this official, Jeremiah and others were forced to seek safety in Egypt, where he continued his prophetic ministry (chaps. 43–44). This is the last we hear of this courageous prophet of the Lord.

Historical Setting.

The Book of Jeremiah belongs to a chaotic time in the history of God's Covenant People. Jeremiah's native land, the southern kingdom of Judah, was caught in a power squeeze between three great powers of the ancient world: Egypt, Assyria, and Babylonia. As these empires struggled for dominance with one another, the noose grew tighter around Judah's neck.

To protect its borders, Judah entered into an alliance with Egypt against the Babylonians. But Jeremiah realized the alliance was too little and too late. For years his beloved nation had risked disaster as it rejected worship of the one true God and turned to pagan gods instead. Immorality, injustice, graft, and corruption prevailed throughout the land. God revealed to the prophet that he intended to punish His Covenant People by sending the Babylonians to destroy Jerusalem and carry the people into captivity. Jeremiah preached this message of judgment faithfully for about 40 years.

At the beginning of his prophetic ministry, it appeared briefly that conditions might improve. King Josiah (ruled 641/40–609 B.C.) began reforms based on God's Law, but at his death the dark days of paganism returned. Josiah's successors continued their reckless pursuit of idolatry and foolish alliances with Egypt against the Babylonians. At the decisive battle of Carchemish in 605 B.C., the Egyptians were soundly defeated. About 18 years later the Babylonians completed their conquest of Judah by destroying the capital city of Jerusalem. Just as Jeremiah had predicted, the leading citizens of Judah were carried to Babylonia, where they remained in captivity for half a century.

Theological Contribution.

Jeremiah's greatest theological contribution was his concept of the New Covenant (31:31–34). A new covenant between God and His people was necessary because the people had broken the old covenant; the captivity of God's people by a foreign power was proof of that. Although the old covenant had been renewed again and again throughout Israel's history, the people still continued to break the promises they had made to God. What was needed was a new type of covenant between God and His people—a covenant of grace and forgiveness written on the human heart, rather than a covenant of law engraved in stone.

As Jeremiah reported God's plan for this new covenant, he anticipated the dawning of the era of grace in the person of Jesus Christ more than 500 years in the future: "No more shall every man teach his neighbor, and every man his brother, saying, 'Know the LORD,' for they all shall know Me, from the least of them to the greatest of them," says the LORD. "For I will forgive their iniquity, and their sin I will remember no more" (31:34). So important is Jeremiah 31:31–34 in biblical theology that it is the longest continuous Old Testament passage to be quoted in full in the New Testament (Heb. 8:8–12).

Special Considerations.

Jeremiah was a master at using figures of speech, metaphors, and symbolic behavior to drive home his messages. He carried a yoke around his neck to show the citizens of Judah they should submit to the inevitable rule of the pagan Babylonians (27:1–12). He watched a potter mar a piece of clay, then reshape it into a perfect vessel. He applied this lesson to the nation of Judah, which needed to submit to the divine will of the Master Potter while there was still time to repent and avoid God's judgment (18:1–11).

But perhaps his most unusual symbolic act was his purchase of a plot of land in his hometown, Anathoth, about three miles northeast of Jerusalem. Jeremiah knew this land would be practically worthless after the Babylonians overran Jerusalem, as he was predicting. But by buying the plot, he symbolized his hope for the future. Even in Judah's darkest hour, Jeremiah prophesied that a remnant would return from Babylonia after their captivity to restore their way of life and to worship God again in the Temple (32:26–44). God directed Jeremiah to put the deed to the land in a clay vessel so it would be preserved for the future: "For thus says the LORD of hosts, the God of Israel:'Houses and fields and vineyards shall be possessed again in this land '" (32:15).

JOB, BOOK OF—an Old Testament book, written in the form of a dramatic poem, that deals with several age-old questions, among them the question of why the righteous suffer. The book takes its name from the main character in the poem, the patriarch Job. Because Job deals with a number of universal questions, it is classified as one of the Wisdom Books of the Old Testament. Other books of this type are Proverbs, Ecclesiastes, and the Song of Solomon.

Structure of the Book.

Job begins with two introductory chapters, in the form of a narrative or prologue, that set the stage for the rest of the book. Chapters 3 through 37 form the main body of the book. These chapters are poems in the form of dramatic dialogues between Job and his friends. Four additional chapters containing God's response to their arguments are also written in poetic form.

The book ends with a final narrative or epilogue (42:7–17) that tells what happened to Job after these discussions had ended.

This prologue–body–epilogue format was used often in writings in the ancient world. The author of Job was a literary craftsman who knew how to bring words together in dramatic fashion to drive home his message.

The story of Job opens with a brief description of the man, his possessions, and his family. "Blameless and upright" (1:1), he owned thousands of sheep, camels, oxen, and donkeys. He also had seven sons and three daughters. In simple terms, Job was considered a wealthy man in the tribal culture of the ancient world. But Satan insists that the integrity of this upright man has never been tested. He accuses Job of serving God only because God has protected him and made him wealthy. God grants permission for the testing to begin.

In rapid fashion, Job's sons and daughters are killed and all his flocks are driven away by his enemies. Finally, Job himself is stricken with a terrible skin disease. In his sorrow he sits mourning on an ash heap, scraping his sores with a piece of pottery while he laments his misfortune. This is when Job's three friends—Bildad, Eliphaz, and Zophar—arrive to mourn with him and to offer their comfort.

But instead of comforting Job, these friends launch into long lectures and philosophical debates to show Job the reason for his suffering. Their line of reasoning follows the generally accepted view of their time—that misfortune is always sent by God as punishment for sin. Job argues just as strongly that he is an upright man who has done nothing to deserve such treatment at the hand of God.

Finally, after Job and his friends have debated this question at length and have failed to arrive at a satisfactory solution, God himself speaks from a whirlwind. He does not enter their discussion about why the righteous suffer; He reveals Himself as the powerful, all-knowing God. God's message to Job is that He does not have to explain or justify His actions. He is the sovereign, all-powerful God who always does what is right, although His ways may be beyond human understanding.

Job is humbled by this outpouring of God's power, and he learns to trust where he cannot understand. This leads to his great affirmation of faith, "I have heard of You by the hearing of the ear, but now my eye sees You" (42:5). Then the book closes with the birth of more sons and daughters and Job's rise to a position of even greater wealth and prominence. Job lived out his additional years as a happy, contented man: "So Job died, old and full of days" (42:17).

Authorship and Date.

No one knows who wrote the Book of Job. A few scholars have taken the position that it may have been written by Moses. Others have suggested that the patriarch Job himself may have written this account of his experiences. But these theories have no solid evidence to support them. The only thing we can say for certain is that the book was written by an unknown author.

The exact date of the book's writing is still a mystery. Some believe its unknown author put it in writing as late as the second century B.C. Others insist it must have been written about 450 B.C., long after the Jews returned from the Captivity in Babylonia. But many conservative scholars assign the writing of the book to the time of King Solomon, about 950 B.C. Historical evidence favors this date, since this was the golden age of biblical Wisdom Literature.

Historical Setting.

The events described in the Book of Job must have occurred many centuries before they were finally written. Job may have lived during the time of the patriarch Abraham, about 2000 B.C. Like Abraham, Job's wealth was measured in flocks and herds. In patriarchal fashion, Job's married children were a part of his household, living in separate tents but subject to his rule as leader of the family clan.

This story of Job and his misfortunes was probably passed down by word of mouth from generation to generation for several hundred years. Finally, it was put in writing by an unknown writer during Solomon's time, thus assuring its preservation for all future generations.

Theological Contribution.

The Book of Job teaches us to trust God in all circumstances. When we suffer, it usually is a fruitless effort to try to understand the reasons for the difficulty. Sometimes the righteous must suffer without knowing the reason why; that it why it is important to learn to trust God in everything.

This masterful book also shows very clearly that God is not captive to His world, His people, or our views of His nature. God is free; he is subject to no will but His own. He is not bound by our understanding or by our lack of it. Job also discovered that God is a God of great power and majesty. When we see how great He is, we realize just how little we are. Like Job, we want to bow down in humble submission.

The Book of Job also teaches us that God is good, just, and fair in His dealings. He restored Job's fortunes and gave him more than he had ever enjoyed. God always replaces the darkness of our existence with the light of His presence when we remain faithful to Him.

Special Considerations.

The dialogue sections of the Book of Job are written in poetry. Great truths are often expressed in such poetic language. These great truths are worth the slow, reflective reading it sometimes takes to grasp their meaning. Great art like that in this book often challenges our understanding. That is why we need to come back to it again and again.

JOEL, BOOK OF—a brief prophetic book of the Old Testament that predicted the outpouring of the spirit of God on all people—a prophecy fulfilled several centuries later on the Day of Pentecost (Joel 2:28–32; Acts 2:14–21). The title of the book comes from its author, the prophet Joel.

Structure of the Book.

The three brief chapters of this book are divided into two major sections. In the first section (1:1–20) the prophet Joel introduces himself and speaks to his readers about their need to turn from their sins. For the most part, the speaker in the second part of the book (2:1–3:21) is the all-powerful God, who warns His people about the approaching day of judgment and assures them of His abiding presence, in spite of their unworthiness.

In the first section of the book, Joel calls attention to a devastating swarm of locusts that had recently swept through the land (1:4). These destructive locusts stripped the foliage from all trees, shrubs, and crops (1:7). The people and livestock of Judah were facing the threat of starvation because of the famine that followed this invasion (1:15–18). As bad as this natural catastrophe had been, the prophet declares it will be as nothing in comparison to the coming day of the Lord. This is the day of Judgment, when God will vent His wrath upon His sinful and disobedient people.

After Joel delivers his pleas for repentance, God Himself speaks to His wayward people. In spite of the famine, He declares that there will be plenty to eat in the days of blessing to come (2:18–19). This day of renewal will be marked by the outpouring of His spirit on all people (2:28–29). All the nations of the world will take notice as God gathers His people together in the holy city of Jerusalem to serve as their ruler: "Judah shall abide forever, and Jerusalem from generation to generation" (3:20).

Authorship and Date.

The author of this book was the prophet Joel, who identifies himself in the introduction as "the son of Pethuel" (1:1). This is all we know about this spokesman for the Lord. From evidence in the book itself, we can assume that he knew a great deal about Jerusalem, Judah's capital city, and the rituals associated with temple worship (2:15). But he probably was not a priest, since he called upon the priests to go into mourning because of the sins of the nation (1:13). Indeed, Joel's many references to agriculture (1:7, 10–12) may indicate he was a farmer or a herdsman, although this is not certain.

It is difficult to determine the exact date of this book's writing. Unlike most of the other Old Testament prophets, Joel mentions no kings of Judah or Israel and no historical events that might give us some indication about when he wrote his prophecy. The one strong clue is the similarity of Joel's concept of the day of the Lord to the language of the prophet Zephaniah (Joel 2:2; Zeph. 1:14–16). Zephaniah prophesied during the reign of Josiah, the king of Judah (640–609 B.C.). This also seems the most likely time for the writing of the Book of Joel.

Historical Setting.

If Joel did write his book about 600 B.C., he would have lived in the frantic final years of the nation of Judah. After the Babylonian army destroyed Jerusalem in 586 B.C. the leading citizens of Judah were carried into captivity in Babylonia. This invasion of the Babylonians must have given special significance to the terrible "day of the Lord" about which Joel warned his countrymen.

Theological Contribution.

The Book of Joel is remarkable because it shows that a message from God can often come packaged in the form of a natural disaster. The truth of the book is rooted in the disastrous invasion of locusts, which Joel describes in such vivid language. This prophet teaches us that the Lord may use a natural disaster to stir in His people a renewed awareness of His will. Any traumatic event of nature—flood, fire, storm, or earthquake—should motivate the sensitive ear to listen again to the words of the Lord.

Special Considerations.

Readers of Joel are always impressed with the prediction of the future outpouring of the Holy Spirit (2:28–32). The apostle Peter used this passage to explain the exciting events of Pentecost to his hearers (Acts 2:16–21). Just as Joel predicted, the Holy Spirit was poured out on all these early followers of Jesus who were gathered in Jerusalem seeking God's will and praying for His divine guidance.

But there is still a future dimension to Joel's prediction. The gifts of the Spirit that began to flow through the people of God on Pentecost were not exhausted on that day. They are still available to all who believe in the Lord Jesus Christ and who anxiously await His return and the final establishment of His kingdom.

JOHN, EPISTLES OF—three epistles—one longer (1 John) and two shorter (2 and 3 John)—written by the author of the Gospel of John. These epistles read like a love letter from an elderly saint who writes from long years of experience with Christ and His message. Although unnamed, the author addresses his readers intimately as "little children" (1 John 2:1, 18, 28; 3:7, 18; 4:4; 5:21) and "beloved" (1 John 3:2, 21; 4:1, 7, 11). His tone changes, however, when he bears down on his opponents for making light of the bodily existence of Jesus (1 John 2:18–23; 4:1–3, 20).

Structure of the Epistles.

None of the three epistles yields naturally to a structural outline. First John begins with an uncompromising testimony to the bodily existence of Jesus (1:1–4). Since God is light, fellowship with God must result in confession of our sin before Christ, our forgiveness, and our "walking in the light" (1:5–2:2). To know Christ is to keep His commandments, or "to walk just as He walked" (2:6). We cannot be in the light if we hate our brothers and sisters or love the world (2:7–17).

The presence of antichrists, who deny that Jesus is the Christ, is a sign of the end times. But true believers rest secure in the "anointing" of the Holy Spirit which they have from Christ (2:18–27). Since God is righteous, believers are to be righteous in their lives. When the Lord returns, His children will be like Him (2:28–3:3). Whoever abides in Christ does not continue to sin habitually or constantly (3:4–10).

Christian love is not something merely to talk about, but to do (3:11–18). Active love gives us confidence before God (3:19–24). A person must examine various spiritual manifestations to determine if they are of God; only teachers who confess that Jesus Christ has come in the flesh are of God (4:1–6). In His love God sent His Son as an atoning sacrifice for sin. As a consequence we are to love one another (4:7–21).

Faith is victory over the world (5:1–5), and there is a threefold witness to faith: the Holy Spirit, the water (baptism), and the blood (Holy Communion) (5:6–12). Christians may be assured that God hears and grants their requests (5:13–15). The letter concludes with assurance that the Son of God is sufficient to save (5:18–21).

Second John identifies its author as "the elder" and those to whom the letter is written as "the elect lady and her children" (v. 1). The "lady" and "children" are personified ways of referring to the church and its believers. Like 3 John, the letter has the character of a note from the elder, reminding his "children" to walk in truth and love (vv. 4–6). The elder also draws attention to false teachers who deny the bodily existence of Jesus Christ, and he warns against receiving them (vv. 7–11). He hopes to visit the church soon (vv. 12–13).

Third John, also from "the elder," is addressed to Gaius (v. 1), who has demonstrated his loyalty by offering hospitality to traveling missionaries (vv. 2–8). A certain Diotrephes had previously ignored a letter from the elder, and he receives some stiff criticism for doing so (vv. 9–11). In contrast to Diotrephes, a certain Demetrius is highly commended (v. 12). The elder expresses his hope to visit the church soon (vv. 13–14).

Authorship and Date.

Although these three epistles were written by an anonymous author, he wrote affectionately to his readers as "little children" and referred to himself as "the elder" (2 John 1; 3 John 1). He must have been well-known and well-loved by those to whom he wrote.

Eusebius, an early church leader, mentions a John the elder (presbyter) who was a disciple and companion of John the apostle in Ephesus. Although we cannot say for sure, it may be that John the elder is the same "elder" mentioned in 2 and 3 John. If so, then he wrote the Gospel of John as well as these three letters; the style and content in each are very similar.

The inclusion of personal testimony (1 John 1:1–4) indicates that John the elder depended directly on the testimony of the apostle John in writing these documents. The epistles were probably written from Ephesus toward the close of the first century A.D. *Historical Setting.*

First John has none of the usual features of an epistle: no salutation or identification of author; no greetings; and no references to persons, places, or events. Ironically, although its format is impersonal, like a sermon or treatise, its tone is warm and personal. This suggests that it was written to a broad audience (probably in and around Ephesus) that was very dear to the author.

All three epistles were written to deepen the spiritual life of the churches while guarding against false teaching. The false teachers had arisen within the church, although the content of their teaching betrayed that they were not part of the church (1 John 2:19; 4:4). John fears that such a splinter group will lead true believers astray (1 John 2:26–27; 3:7; 2 John 7). He calls them "antichrists" (1 John 2:18, 22; 4:3; 2 John 7) for denying that Jesus had come in the flesh (1 John 4:1–13; 2 John 7; also 1 John 2:18–25; 4:15).

By emphasizing the divine nature of Jesus, the false teachers appeared to be Christians; but they showed their true colors by denying that God became a true human in Jesus. Claiming to have the Spirit of God, they were actually false prophets (1 John 4:1–6).

Theological Contribution.

Like the Gospel of John, the epistles of John are built on the foundation blocks of love, truth, sin, world, life, light, and Paraclete. It emphasizes the great themes of knowing, believing, walking, and abiding. These words seem simple on the surface. But in the hands of one who had pondered the mystery and meaning of Jesus' existence in human form, they yield many deep truths.

For John, the keystone in the arch of the gospel is that God has appeared in human form (1 John 1:1–4). The Incarnation is life (1 John 1:2); and this life is available in the Son of God, Jesus Christ (1 John 5:11): "He who has the Son has life; he who does not have the Son of God does not have life" (1 John 5:12). The message of life is the alpha (1 John 1:2) and omega (1 John 5:20), the beginning and the end, of the epistle.

Jesus Christ has transferred us from death to life (1 John 3:14) by destroying the works of the devil (1 John 3:8). God made Jesus a "propitiation" (1 John 2:2; 4:10) in order to forgive sin (1 John 1:7–9; 2:12; 3:5). As a propitiation, Jesus is our "Advocate with the Father" (1 John 2:1) who takes away the guilt of our wrongdoing and gives us confidence to approach the judgment seat of God (1 John 2:28; 4:17). Jesus Christ is both the Son of God and the bearer of sin, the eternal demonstration of the love of God.

For John, love is not a feeling or attitude toward others. God is love (1 John 4:8, 16), and He acts in love on our behalf (1 John 4:9–10). Love, therefore, is something one does, by keeping God's commandments (1 John 2:2–5; 5:3), "in deed and in truth" (1 John 3:18), and, above all, by loving others (1 John 2:9–11; 3:10). John declares that it is hypocritical to profess love for God and to show hatred toward others (1 John 4:20). The love of God does not take us out of this world. Rather, it draws us into fellowship with God (1 John 1:3) and with others (1 John 1:7).

Fellowship with God is realized by knowing God and abiding in Him. To *know* God (the verb occurs 25 times in the epistles) is not to know about God, but to be joined to Him in righteousness (1 John 2:29), truth (1 John 3:19), and especially love (1 John 4:7–8). The permanence of such knowing is expressed in the word abide, which occurs 26 times in these epistles. To abide in God is to share the identity of Jesus Christ and to experience the characteristics of God: light (1 John 2:10), love (1 John 3:17; 4:12), and eternal life (1 John 3:15).

Special Considerations.

Many Christians wonder about John's declaration, "Whoever abides in Him [Jesus Christ] does not sin" (1 John 3:6). This does not mean that if someone sins he is not a Christian. Indeed, in the epistles we are told that Christ came to forgive sins; and we are admonished to confess our sins to Him (1 John 1:6–2:2; 3:5; 4:10). The statement means that Christ has transferred us from death to life and has caused us to share in the nature of God. Consequently, we are no longer confined to darkness because Jesus Christ has broken the power of sin in our lives (1 John 3:8).

John says that believers may pray to God on behalf of others (1 John 5:16–17), unless their sins "lead to death." The exact meaning of such sin is unclear, although it probably refers to a denial of the bodily existence of Jesus (1 John 2:22; 4:3; 5:12).

JOHN, GOSPEL OF—the fourth and most theological of the Gospels of the New Testament. The first three Gospels portray mainly what Jesus did and how He taught, but the Gospel of John is different. It moves beyond the obvious facts of Jesus' life to deeper, more profound meanings. Events and miracles are kept to a minimum in the Gospel of John. They are used as springboards or "signs" for lengthy discussions that reveal important truths about Christ. On the other hand, John uses a host of key words that symbolize who Jesus is and how we may know God. John is a "spiritual" gospel—not because it is more spiritual than the other three—but because it expresses spiritual ideas in spiritual language. Among the gospels, therefore, John offers a unique portrait of Christ that has been cherished by believers through the centuries.

Structure of the Gospel.

The fourth Gospel consists basically of two parts: a book of "signs" and a book of "glory." The signs reveal Jesus' person (chaps. 1–12), and the glory results from Jesus' passion (chaps. 13–20). A prologue (1:1–18) and epilogue (chap. 21) serve as an introduction and conclusion to the gospel. Within this two-part structure, the gospel follows a pattern already presented in the prologue: revelation (1:1–5), rejection (1:6–11), and reception (1:12–18). The corresponding divisions of the gospel are: revelation (1:19–6:71), rejection (chaps. 7–12), and reception (chaps. 13–21).

Authorship and Date.

Like the other gospels, John comes to us as an anonymous book. The question of authorship can be resolved only by observing clues within the gospel and by the tradition of the early church. Tradition agrees that the author was John the apostle, who was exiled to the island of Patmos in the Aegean Sea and who later died in Ephesus sometime after Trajan became emperor of Rome in A.D. 98. The gospel claims to come from an eyewitness (1:14; 1 John 1:1–4), and the author is familiar with the geography of Palestine. These external and internal evidences suggest that "the beloved disciple" (13:23; 19:26; 20:2; 21:7, 20), which appears as a title or nickname for John the apostle, composed the fourth gospel.

Other clues within the gospel and epistles of John, however, point beyond the apostle to another author. In 2 and 3 John, verses 1, the author identifies himself as "the elder." The similarities between the gospel and the epistles of John are too strong for us to conclude that the gospel was written by John the apostle and the epistles by John the elder. Early church tradition referred to an elder who was a disciple of John. Moreover, certain passages in the gospel of John tend to suggest that the writer was not the beloved disciple (19:35; 21:24).

Taking the evidence as a whole, it appears that the gospel was composed by a John the elder (*presbyter*), who was a disciple of John the apostle and who depended directly on the apostle's testimony for the content of the gospel. Both Johns are reputed to have lived in Ephesus. Some scholars identify John the elder with John the apostle and view the gospel as composed by the apostle. Ephesus, therefore, becomes the most likely place for the gospel's origin, sometime around the close of the first century.

Historical Setting.

It is difficult to say with certainty to whom this gospel was addressed. Unlike Luke (1:1–4), the author mentions no addressee. Unlike Matthew and Mark, he gives few hints of his intended audience. The gospel uses both Jewish and Greek thought forms in its presentation of Christ.

For John, Jesus goes beyond the bounds of Judaism. This gospel reports a fiercer conflict between Jesus and the Jews than the other gospels do. The gospel begins before time (1:1), and it shows that Jesus is timeless. Jesus speaks not to any one nation or ethnic group, but to the human condition. John portrays Jesus for the widest possible readership. This is one reason why the fourth gospel has spoken so deeply to Christians in all ages.

If there is doubt to whom John writes, there can be little doubt about why John writes. The gospel contains a clear statement of purpose: "These [signs] are written that you may believe that Jesus is the Christ, the Son of God, and that believing you may have life in His name" (20:31).

For John, the sole purpose of life is that "you may know and believe that the Father is in me and I in Him" (10:38). Thus, John writes that we might know the Father and experience life eternal through faith in the Son.

Theological Contribution.

John writes with a modest vocabulary, but his words are charged with symbolism. Terms like believe, love, truth, world, light and darkness, above and below, name, witness, sin, judgment (eternal) life, glory, bread, water, and hour are the key words of this gospel. In John 3:16–21, a passage of fewer than 150 words in Greek, seven of these terms occur.

The world is where God reveals truth (8:32), light (8:12), and life (14:6) in His Son Jesus Christ. The world is also where persons must decide for or against the witness of Christ, and the decision is judgment (3:18). Sin is to misjudge Jesus—to fail to receive Him as the bread of life (6:35), or not to walk in Him as the light of the world (8:12). The Son has come from above to glorify the Father (17:1), and He does so in His "hour" (12:23; 13:1)—through His suffering on the cross.

In the synoptic gospels—Matthew, Mark, and Luke—Jesus utters short sayings. Longer discourses, such as the Sermon on the Mount (Matthew 5–7), are either collections of sayings on various themes, or, like Matthew 13, mostly parables. John, on the other hand, records no parables and few of the brief sayings so common to the synoptics. Rather, he expands upon an incident; for example, Nicodemus (chap. 3), the woman at the well (chap. 4), the man born blind (chap. 9), Lazarus (chap. 11), or footwashing (chap. 13). Or he takes up an image; for example, bread (chap. 6), water (chap. 7), light (chap. 8), or shepherd (chap. 10). John then uses these words as symbols to reveal a fuller revelation of Christ. These discourses are blended so completely with John's own style that frequently the reader cannot tell whether it is John or Jesus speaking (3:16).

Why does John present such a different picture of Jesus? John may reveal Jesus as He taught in private, while the other three gospels may recall His public method of address (Mark 4:34). This may be a partial answer. A fuller explanation may be that the other gospels retain the actual form of Jesus' teaching, while John uncovers the essence of Jesus as a person.

This does not imply that John disregards historical truth. At some points his gospel probably preserves the facts of Jesus' life with greater precision than the other gospels do. For example, Matthew, Mark, and Luke leave the impression that Jesus ministered mainly in Galilee, making only one Passover journey to Jerusalem. This leads one to assume that Jesus' ministry lasted less than one year. John, however, mentions at least three Passover journeys (John 2:13, 23; 6:4; 12:1) and longer periods of ministry in Judea. The other gospels do hint of previous visits by Jesus to Jerusalem "O Jerusalem, Jerusalem.... How often I wanted to gather your children together" (Matt. 23:37; Luke 13:34).

Nevertheless, it is clear that John is guided more by theological than historical interests. The gospels of Matthew, Mark, and Luke begin by showing Jesus' role as the fulfiller of the Old Testament promises of salvation. But John begins with the preexistence of Jesus: "In the beginning was the Word" (1:1). Jesus is divine ("the Word was God," 1:1), but He is also human ("the

Word became flesh," 1:14). Only as such is He the revealer of the Father.

In the first chapter, John introduces Jesus by seven key titles: Word, Lamb of God, Rabbi, Messiah, King of Israel, Son of God, and Son of Man. Only in John do we find the "I am" sayings: "I am the bread of life" (6:35), "I am the light of the world" (8:12), "before Abraham was, I AM" (8:58), "I am the door of the sheep" (10:7), "I am the good shepherd" (10:11), "I and My Father are one" (10:30), "I am the way, the truth, and the life" (14:6), and "I am the vine" (15:5). In each of these sayings the "I" is emphatic in Greek. It recalls the name of God, "I AM," in the Old Testament (Ex. 3:14).

In the Old Testament God's words were to be reverently received. So it is with Jesus. In John He begins His messages by saying, "Truly, truly I say to you." Just as in the Old Testament God alone was to be worshiped, in John people are to believe in Jesus alone. Here John stresses his concept of "believing." The verb "to believe" is found nearly a hundred times in the gospel, though the noun "belief/faith" does not occur. For John, saving faith is a verb, carrying the sense of active trust in Jesus; it is not a static noun.

When one considers Jesus' moral teaching, another key word emerges. In John Jesus does not enter into questions of prayer, fasting, almsgiving, swearing, marriage, or wealth as he does in the other gospels. Rather, one's relationships to God, others, and the world are summed up in love. The love that God has for his beloved Son (3:35; 15:9) is passed on by the Beloved to "His own" (13:1). As recipients of God's love, Christians are to love God by loving one another (13:34). This love, which unites believers is also a testimony to the world. The key verse of John expresses the basic theological truth of the gospel: "For God so loved the world that He gave His only begotten Son, that whoever believes in Him should not perish but have everlasting life" (3:16).

The Gospel of John expresses the uniqueness of the Son's relationship with the Father. The Son existed before the world with the Father; He was sent into the world by the Father; and He goes out of the world to the Father.

Special Considerations.

Our present Gospel of John contains a story that probably was not written by the original author. The account of the woman caught in adultery (7:53–8:11) differs markedly in style from the rest of John. It is not found in the earlier and better manuscripts of the book. It was probably added at a later date by an unknown author under God's inspiration to express an important truth about Jesus and His attitude toward sinful people.

JONAH, BOOK OF—a short Old Testament book that emphasizes God's love for all people—pagans and Gentiles as well as his Chosen People, the Israelites. The book is named for its central figure, the prophet Jonah, who learned about God's universal love as he struggled with God's call to service.

Structure of the Book.

The book begins with God's call to Jonah to preach in the great city of Nineveh, capital of the Assyrian empire. As staunch political enemies of the Israelites and as worshipers of false gods, the Assyrians also were shunned as pagans and outcasts. But God's call to Jonah showed clearly that He had not given up on Assyria. The prophet was to call Nineveh to repentance, warning the nation of its approaching doom unless it turned to God.

Instead of obeying God's command and heading to Nineveh, Jonah caught a ship traveling in the opposite direction. At sea a great storm arose, and Jonah was tossed overboard by the superstitious sailors in an attempt to appease the prophet's God. Jonah escaped unharmed when he was swallowed by a great fish and was miraculously deposited on shore. This time he obeyed God's command and traveled to Nineveh to carry out his preaching assignment.

But the reluctant prophet was not prepared for the results of his message. The entire city repented, and Jonah sulked in anger because Nineveh escaped God's punishment.

To teach the prophet a lesson, God raised up a plant, perhaps a gourd vine, to shade Jonah from the sun, then allowed a worm to cut it down. A hot wind from the east added to Jonah's misery, and he whined and complained about the missing plant. Then God reminded Jonah that He was a God of compassion who had the right to love and forgive the pagan Assyrians or any other people who turned to Him in obedience and faith. Jonah had been fretting about a plant, while God had turned His attention to a much more important matter—the worth and salvation of people.

Authorship and Date.

The traditional view is that the prophet Jonah wrote this book. This would place its writing at about 760 B.C., since this prophet—"the son of Amittai" (1:1)—is the same Jonah who prophesied during the reign of Jeroboam II of Israel, from 793 to 753 B.C. (2 Kin. 14:25). The only other thing we know about Jonah is that he was a native of the village of Gath Hepher in Israel.

Some scholars insist the book was not written until about three centuries later by an unknown author. According to this theory, the writer composed the story of Jonah and his prophecy to combat the narrow-minded views of the Jewish people after their return to Jerusalem following their years of captivity in Babylonia. It is true that the Israelites went to extremes during these years as they tried to cast off all foreign influences and preserve the unique heritage of their faith. And Jonah certainly is a book that emphasizes the universal love of God. But the evidence put forth to support this theory is weak and inconclusive.

Thus, the traditional view that the prophet Jonah himself wrote the book after his visit to Nineveh about 760 B.C. has much to commend it.

Historical Setting.

The prophet Jonah visited Nineveh during the glorious days of the Assyrian empire. From about 885 to 625 B.C., the Assyrians dominated the ancient world. Numerous passages in the Old Testament report advances of Assyrian military forces against the neighboring kingdoms of Judah and Israel during these years. As early as 841 B.C., Jehu, king of Israel, was forced to pay tribute to the dominating Assyrian ruler, Shalmaneser III. This kind of harassment continued for over a century until Israel finally fell to Assyrian forces about 722 B.C.

No wonder Jonah was reluctant to go to Nineveh; God had called him to visit the very heartland of enemy territory and to give the hated Assyrians a chance to repent. It was a radical order that would have taxed the obedience of any prophet. Jonah's grudging attitude should not blind us to the fact that he did carry out God's command.

Theological Contribution.

One of the great truths emphasized by this book is that God can use people who do not want to be used by Him. Jonah was practically driven to Nineveh against his will, but his grudging message still struck a responsive chord in the Assyrians. This shows that revival and repentance are works of God's Spirit. Our task is to proclaim His message.

But the greatest insight of the book is that God desires to show mercy and grace to all the peoples of the world. No one nation or group can claim exclusive rights to His love. The task of the Hebrew people was to preach this message about God's universal love to all the world (Gen. 12:1–3). But they forgot this missionary purpose and eventually claimed God and His blessings as theirs alone. The Book of Jonah cries out against this narrow-minded interpretation of God and His purpose. In the last verse of the book, God makes it plain to Jonah that His mercy and compassion are as wide as the world itself: "And should I not pity Nineveh, that great city, in which are more than one hundred and twenty thousand persons who cannot discern between their right hand and their left, and also much livestock?" (4:11).

Special Considerations.

Too much attention has been focused on the "great fish" (1:17) that swallowed Jonah and then spat him out on the shore. We solve nothing by debating whether a fish could swallow a man or whether a person could remain alive for three days in the stomach of such a creature. The point of this part of the story is that God worked a miracle to preserve the life of His prophet so he could get to Nineveh to carry out God's orders. The text states that God "prepared" this fish specifically for that purpose (1:17). Other miracles that God "prepared" to teach Jonah His purpose for the city of Nineveh were the plant (4:6), the worm that cut the plant down (4:7), and the hot east wind that added to Jonah's misery (4:8).

Some Bible readers insist on interpreting this book as an allegory or a parable. But these approaches ignore Jesus' own literal interpretation of Jonah. In speaking of His death and resurrection, Jesus declared, "For as Jonah was three days and three nights in the belly of the great fish, so will the Son of Man be three days and three nights in the heart of the earth" (Matt. 12:40; also Luke 11:29–32). Thus, the Book of Jonah is much more than a fish story. It is a beautiful account of God's grace that lifts our sights to the greatest love story of all—the death of His Son Jesus Christ for the sins of the world.

JOSHUA, BOOK OF—an Old Testament book that describes the conquest and division of the land of Canaan by the

Hebrew people. The book is named for its central figure, Joshua, who succeeded Moses as leader of Israel.

Structure of the Book.

The Book of Joshua has a natural, flowing structure that makes it a joy to read and study. In a brief prologue, the warrior Joshua is introduced as the capable leader selected by God to lead the people. Then the book launches immediately into narratives about the military victories of the Hebrews as they drove the Canaanites out of the land. Joshua's strategy was to divide and conquer. He struck first in central Canaan by taking the city of Jericho and surrounding territory. Then he launched rapid attacks to the south and north. This strategy quickly gave the Covenant People a foothold in the land. After weakening the enemy's position with this strategy, Joshua led numerous minor attacks against them during the next several years.

These accounts of Joshua's military campaigns are followed by a long description of the division of the land among the 12 tribes of Israel. Finally, the book ends with the death of Joshua after he leads the people to renew the covenant and charges them to remain faithful to God.

Authorship and Date.

Early Jewish tradition credited Joshua with writing this book. But this is disputed by many modern scholars. One of the strongest objections to his authorship is the final section of the book, which describes Joshua's death and burial (24:29–33). Obviously, Joshua could not have written this material.

But other sections of the book strongly suggest that they were written by Joshua. One passage declares that after giving his farewell address, "Joshua wrote these words in the Book of the Law of God" (24:26). Some of the battle narratives are also written with vivid description and minute detail, suggesting that they may have been composed by the commander on the scene, Joshua himself (see especially chaps. 6–8).

The most logical and believable theory about authorship is that Joshua wrote a major part of the book. But it probably did not reach its finished form until several years after his death. An editor must have added some additional narratives, such as the one about Joshua's death and burial, to complete this important book about Joshua and his contribution. A commonly accepted date for the death of Joshua is about 1375 B.C., so the book may have been completed shortly after this date.

Historical Setting.

The Book of Joshua covers about 25 years in one of the most important periods of Israel's history—their conquest and final settlement of the land that God had promised to Abraham and his descendants many centuries earlier. The specific years for this occupation must have been from about 1400 to 1375 B.C.

Theological Contribution.

One important message of the Book of Joshua is that true and false religions do not mix. Joshua's orders were to destroy the Canaanites because of their pagan and immoral worship practices. But these people never were totally subdued or destroyed. Traces of their false religion remained to tempt the Israelites. Again and again throughout their history, the Hebrew people departed from worship of the one true God. This tendency toward false worship was the main reason for Joshua's moving farewell speech. He warned the people against worshiping these false gods and challenged them to remain faithful to the Lord, who had delivered them. The point of Joshua's message: You cannot worship these false gods and remain faithful to the Lord. "But as for me and my house, we will serve the Lord" (24:15).

Special Considerations.

Some people have difficulty with God's commanding Joshua to destroy the Canaanites. But behind this command lay God's concern for his Covenant People. He wanted to remove the Canaanites' idolatrous worship practices so they would not be a temptation to the Israelites. This command to Joshua also represented God's judgment against sin and immorality. God used Israel as an instrument of His judgment against a pagan nation.

JUDE, EPISTLE OF—the last of the general letters of the New Testament and the next to the last book of the Bible. Jude is a brief but hard-hitting epistle written by a man who believed in not allowing negative influences to destroy the church. Jude unmasks false teaching with pointed language and vivid images, while appealing to the faithful to remember the teachings of the apostles.

Structure of the Epistle.

A salutation (vv. 1–2) is followed by a warning that "licentiousness" has found its way into the church (vv. 3–4). Such blasphemies will receive the judgment of God, as did sinful Israel (v. 5), rebellious angels (v. 6), and Sodom and Gomorrah (v. 7). Verses 8 through 13 note that the outrage of the blasphemers exceeds that of Satan himself and is similar to the rebellions of Cain (Gen. 4:3–8), Balaam (Numbers 22–24), and Korah (Num. 16:19–35). Their schemes are nothing new; Enoch of old prophesied their punishment (vv. 14–16). Christians need not be victimized by such deceivers; their defense lies in remembering the words of the apostles and by working for the salvation of those caught in such errors (vv. 17–23). A famous benediction concludes the epistle (vv. 24–25).

Authorship and Date.

The author of the epistle introduces himself as "Jude, a servant of Jesus Christ, and brother of James" (v. 1). There is no further identification, and the James mentioned is probably the Lord's brother (Gal. 1:19). Jude, therefore, would also be a brother of Jesus (Judas, Mark 6:3; Matt. 13:55), although not an apostle (Jude 17). The emphasis on remembering "the words which were spoken before by the apostles" (v. 17) suggests that the epistle was composed sometime after the apostles had taught, thus favoring a date near the close of the first century.

Historical Setting.

The Epistle of Jude has the character of a tract or brief essay written for a general Christian audience (v. 1). The author set out to write about "our common salvation" (v. 3), but the more pressing issue of false teachers launched him into a bitter attack on the "ungodly" (v. 15). Their ungodliness took the form of denying the lordship of Jesus Christ and, in the name of grace (v. 4), justifying a life that included immorality of all sorts (vv. 4, 7, 16), mercenary interests (v. 11, 16), cheap talk (v. 16), and utter worldliness (v. 19).

The false teachers attacked by Jude seem to have separated "spiritual" matters from behavior. Apparently they taught that the world is evil, and therefore it makes little difference how one behaves. Like the Nicolaitans (Rev. 2:6, 15), the false teachers deserved the just punishment of God. They refused to recognize the implications of the incarnation—that if God cared enough to send His Son into the world, then He certainly cares how people behave in it.

Theological Contribution.

Jude writes as a defender of the faith who is "contending earnestly for the faith which was once for all delivered to the saints" (v. 3). The "ungodly" are not the heathen outside the church; they are the false teachers inside (v. 12). Their association with the faith, however, does not mean they live in the faith: the ungodly have not the Spirit (v. 19), whereas the faithful do (v. 20); the ungodly remain in eternal darkness (v. 13), but the saints have eternal life (v. 21). Condemning his opponents in sharp imagery, Jude calls them "raging waves of the sea, foaming up their own shame; wandering stars for whom is reserved the blackness of darkness forever" (v. 13). The saints, on the other hand, must set their anchor in the teaching of the apostles (v. 17), and in the love of God (v. 21). They must work to retrieve from certain destruction those who have been deceived (vv. 22–23).

Special Consideration.

Jude's last word on the problem of corruption in the church is preserved in a memorable benediction. Only God can keep us from error and bring us to Himself:

> "Now to Him who is able to keep you from stumbling, and to present you faultless before the presence of His glory with exceeding joy, to God our Savior, who alone is wise, be glory and majesty, dominion and power, both now and forever. Amen."

JUDGES, BOOK OF—a historical book of the Old Testament that covers the chaotic time between Joshua's death and the beginning of a centralized government under King Saul, a period of over 300 years. The "judges" for whom the book is named were actually military leaders whom God raised up to deliver His people from their enemies. Twelve of these heroic deliverers are mentioned in the book.

Structure of the Book.

The introduction to Judges (1:1–3:6) describes the period after Joshua's death as a time of instability and moral depravity. Without a strong religious leader like Joshua to give them clear direction, the people of Israel fell into the worship of false gods. To punish the people, God delivered them into the hands of enemy nations. In their distress the people repented and cried out to God for help, and God answered their pleas by sending a "judge" or deliverer. In each instance after a period of faithfulness and security, the people once again forgot God, renewing the cycle of unfaithfulness all over again. This theme of sin-punishment-repentance-deliverance runs seven times throughout the book; it is introduced by the refrain, "The children of Israel again did evil in the sight of the LORD " (4:1).

The three best-known judges or deliverers described in the book are Deborah (4:1–5:31), Gideon (6:1–8:32), and Samson (13:1–16:31). The other nine heroic figures from this period in Israel's history are, Ehud; Elon; Ibzan; Jair; Jephthah; Othniel; Shamgar; Tola, and Abdon.

The Book of Judges contains some of the best-known stories in the Bible. One judge, Gideon, routed a Midianite army of several thousand with a group of 300 warriors. Under the cover of darkness, Gideon and his men hid lighted torches inside empty pitchers, then broke the pitchers and blew trumpets to catch the army by surprise. The mighty Midianites fled in panic (7:15–25).

An interesting part of the Gideon story is the way in which this judge of Israel tested what he perceived to be God's call. First, Gideon spread a piece of wool on the ground and asked God to saturate it with dew but leave the ground around it dry if he wanted Gideon to deliver Israel. This happened exactly that way. Still not satisfied, Gideon asked God to reverse this procedure the second night—to leave the wool dry with wet ground all around it. After this happened, Gideon agreed to lead his band of warriors against the Midianites (6:36–40).

Another famous story in the Book of Judges is about Samson and Delilah. A judge of superhuman strength, Samson defeated superior forces of the Philistine tribe several times by himself. They finally captured him after Delilah betrayed him by cutting his long hair, which was the secret of his strength. In captivity, Samson took thousands of his enemies to their death by pulling down the pillars of the temple where the Philistines were worshipping their pagan god Dagon (16:1–31).

Authorship and Date.

Like the authors of several other historical books of the Old Testament, the author of Judges is unknown. But internal evidence gives us a clue about the probable date when it was written. The writer reminds us, "In those days there was no king in Israel; everyone did what was right in his own eyes" (17:6; 21:25). This statement tells us the book was written after the events described in Judges, probably during the days of King Saul or King David, about 1050 to 970 B.C.

Early Jewish scholars believed the book was written by Samuel, Israel's first prophet, who anointed Saul as the nation's first king. But this is impossible to determine from evidence presented by the book itself. The unknown writer may have been a contemporary of Samuel.

Historical Setting.

Israel's entry into the Promised Land under Joshua was not so much a total conquest as an occupation. Even after the land was divided among Israel's twelve tribes, the Israelites continued to face the possibility of domination by the warlike Canaanites who were never driven entirely out of the land. These were the enemies who threatened Israel repeatedly during the period of the judges, from about 1380 to 1050 B.C.

The Canaanite problem was intensified by Israel's loose form of tribal organization. The Israelites were easy targets for a well-organized enemy like the Canaanites. The first big task of the judges whom God raised up as deliverers was to rally the separate tribes behind them to rout the common enemy.

Mount Tabor rises 1,300 feet above the Plain of Jezreel. The Book of Judges mentions this mountain in the account of Barak's attack against the army of Sisera (Judg. 4:14, 15).

Theological Contribution.

The Book of Judges points out the problems of the nation of Israel when the people had a succession of "judges" or military leaders to deliver them from their enemies. This is a subtle way of emphasizing the nation's need for a king or a strong, centralized form of government. But even the establishment of kingship failed to lead to a state of perfection. Only after the right king, David, was placed on the throne did the nation break free of its tragic cycle of despair and decline. David, of course, as God's chosen servant, points to the great King to come, the Lord Jesus.

Judges also speaks of our need for an eternal deliverer or a savior. The deliverance of the human judges was always temporary, partial, and imperfect. Some of the judges themselves were flawed and misdirected. The book points forward to Jesus Christ, the great Judge (Ps. 110:6), who is King and Savior of His people.

Special Considerations.

Many readers are troubled by the rash vow of the judge Jephthah in the Book of Judges. He promised God that if he were victorious in battle, he would offer as a sacrifice the first thing to come out of his house to greet him on his return. The Lord did give Jephthah victory. On his return, his daughter came out of the house to greet him. And he was forced to carry out his terrible vow (11:29–40). This text is so troubling to some people that they seek to weaken it by claiming that Jephthah did not actually kill his daughter but only made her remain a virgin. This claim is based on the words, "She knew no man" (11:39). But the text indicates clearly that Jephthah did what he had vowed.

Human sacrifice was never sanctioned by the nation of Israel. Indeed, God condemned it as an evil of the surrounding nations. The point the author of Judges made in recording this deed is the same he had in mind as he recorded the sins and excesses of Samson. The period of the judges was a time of such religious and political chaos that even the best of God's servants were seriously flawed.

Deborah's song of victory (chap. 5) demonstrates a high degree of literary skill at this early period in Israel's history. It also shows clearly that women have made great contributions to God's work across the centuries. Another insight is that God deserves the praise when His people are victorious in battle.

KINGS, BOOKS OF—two Old Testament books that recount the history of God's chosen people during four turbulent centuries, from 970 to 586 B.C. The narratives in these books of history are organized around the various kings who reigned during these centuries, thus explaining the titles by which the books are known.

Structure of the Books.

As originally written in the Hebrew language, 1 and 2 Kings consisted of one unbroken book. It formed a natural sequel to the Books of 1 and 2 Samuel, which also appeared originally in the Hebrew Bible as a single book. The writer of Samuel traced the history of Israel up to the final days of David's reign. This is where the Book of 1 Kings begins—with the death of David and the succession of his son, Solomon, to the throne.

The first half of the Book of 1 Kings describes Solomon's reign. Included are accounts about his vast wealth, his great wisdom, his marriage to foreign wives, and his completion of the temple in Jerusalem. But 1 Kings also reveals that all was not well in Solomon's empire. Many of the people grew restless and rebellious because of the king's excesses and the high taxes required to support his ambitious projects. At his death the people in the northern part of the empire rebelled and formed their own nation, known as the Northern Kingdom of Israel. Those who remained loyal to the house of David and Solomon continued as the Southern Kingdom, or the nation of Judah.

From this point on in the Books of 1 and 2 Kings, the narrative grows complex and difficult to follow. The historical writer traces the history of a king of Israel, then switches over to touch on the high points in the administration of the parallel king of Judah. This can be very confusing to the Bible reader unless this parallel structure is known.

But we do these books a great injustice if we assume they are filled with nothing but dry historical statistics and minute details. First and Second Kings contain some of the most interesting stories in the Bible. Here we come face to face with the fiery prophet Elijah, who challenged the false god Baal and hundreds of his prophets in a dramatic showdown on Mount Carmel. The prophet's faith was verified as God proved himself superior to Baal by answering Elijah's fervent prayer.

In these books we also meet a proud Syrian commander, Naaman the leper, who almost passed up his opportunity to be healed by his reluctance to dip himself in the waters of the Jordan River. Fortunately, his servants convinced him to drop his pride, and he emerged from the river with his skin restored "like the flesh of a little child" (2 Kin. 5:14).

During the four centuries covered by these books, a total of 19 different kings ruled the nation of Israel, while 22 different kings (if David and Solomon are included) occupied Judah's throne. The writer covers some of these kings with a few sentences, while he devotes several pages to others. Apparently, this author selected certain kings for major attention because they illustrated the conditions that led to the eventual collapse of the nations of Judah and Israel.

Some of these kings were honest, ethical, and morally pure. But the good kings always were the exception. The majority of the rulers led the people astray, some even openly encouraging them to worship false gods. Thus, the most familiar refrain in 1 and 2 Kings is the phrase, "He did evil in the sight of the Lord" (2 Kin. 8:18).

Israel was the first nation to collapse under the weight of its disobedience and depravity. This kingdom ended in 722 B.C. with the fall of its capital city, Samaria, to the Assyrians. The citizens of the Southern Kingdom of Judah struggled on for another 136 years under a succession of kings before their nation was overrun by the Babylonians in 586 B.C. The Book of 2 Kings comes to a close with the leading citizens of Judah being held captive in Babylon.

Authorship and Date.

These books cover, in chronological fashion, about 400 years of Judah and Israel's history. The last event mentioned in this chronology is the captivity of Judah's citizens by the Babylonians. This means the book had to be compiled in its final form some time after the Babylonians overran Jerusalem in 586 B.C.

Early tradition credited the prophet Jeremiah with the writing of these two books. Whether this is correct is uncertain. We do know that this famous prophet preached in Jerusalem before and after the fall of the city. Two chapters from 2 Kings also appear in the Book of Jeremiah (compare 2 Kings 24–25 and Jeremiah 39–42; 52). This led many scholars to the natural assumption that Jeremiah had written the book.

Most scholars today no longer hold to the Jeremiah theory. The evidence points to an unknown prophet who worked at the same time as Jeremiah to compile this long history of his nation's religious and political life. His purpose was to show that the two kingdoms fell because of their unfaithfulness and to call the people back to renewal of the covenant.

While this prophet–writer is not named in the Books of 1 and 2 Kings, he does reveal the sources he used. He speaks of "the chronicles of the kings of Israel" (1 Kin. 14:19) and "the chronicles of the kings of Judah" (1 Kin. 14:29). These were probably the official court documents and historical archives of the two nations. He must have drawn from them freely as he wrote.

Historical Setting.

The four centuries covered by 1 and 2 Kings were times of change and political upheaval in the ancient world as the balance of power shifted from one nation to another. Surrounding nations that posed a threat to Israel and Judah at various times during this period included Syria, Assyria, and Babylonia.

The Assyrian threat was particularly strong during the last 50 years of the Northern Kingdom. Under Tiglath–Pileser III, this conquering nation launched three devastating campaigns against Israel in 734, 733 and 732 B.C. It was a blow from which Israel never recovered, and the nation fell to Assyrian forces just 10 years later in 722 B.C.

While Syria and Assyria were threats to Judah at various times, their worst enemy turned out to be the nation of Babylon. The Babylonians took captives and goods from Jerusalem in three campaigns—in 605 and 597 B.C. and in a two-year siege beginning in 588 B.C. Jerusalem finally fell in 586 B.C. The Temple was destroyed, and thousands of Judah's leading citizens were carried into captivity in Babylon.

Theological Contribution.

The Books of 1 and 2 Kings present an interesting contrast between King David of Judah and King Jeroboam I, the first king of the northern kingdom of Israel.

Jeroboam established a legacy of idol worship in this new nation by setting up golden calves at Bethel and Dan (1 Kin. 12:25–33). These were symbols of the fertility religion of Baal. His strategy was to mix this false religion with worship of the one true God in an attempt to win the loyalty and good will of the people and bind them together as a distinctive nation.

This act of idolatry was condemned by the writer of 1 and 2 Kings. Each succeeding king of Israel was measured against the standard of Jeroboam's idolatry. Of each king who led the people astray, it was written, "He did not depart from the sins of Jeroboam the son of Nebat, who had made Israel sin" (2 Kin. 15:9).

Just as Jeroboam was used as a bad example by the writer of 1 and 2 Kings, King David was used as a standard of righteousness and justice. In spite of David's moral lapses, he became the measure of righteousness for all kings who followed him. The Northern Kingdom was marked by rebellion and strife as opposing factions struggled for the right to reign, but the house of David continued in the Kingdom of Judah without interruption for nearly four centuries. The writer explained that the evils of kings such as Abijam (or Abijah) did not cancel out the love and mercy that God had promised to the house of David: "Nevertheless for David's sake the Lord his God gave him a lamp in Jerusalem, by setting up his son after him and by establishing Jerusalem; because David did what was right in the eyes of the Lord" (1 Kin. 15:4–5).

Special Considerations.

The writer of 1 Kings reported that Solomon had "seven hundred wives, princesses, and three hundred concubines" (1 Kin. 11:3). In the ancient world, the number of wives held by a ruler symbolized his might and power. Rulers also took on wives to seal political alliances and trade agreements. But Solomon cannot be totally excused for his excesses because of these cultural factors. According to the writer of 1 Kings, he let his foreign wives turn away his heart from worshiping the one true God (1 Kin. 11:1–3). This was a fatal flaw in his character that eventually led to rebellion and the separation of Solomon's empire into two opposing nations (1 Kin. 11:11–13).

The Books of 1 and 2 Kings describe several miracles wrought by God through the prophets Elijah and Elisha. In addition to proving God's power, these miracles are also direct attacks on the pagan worship practices of the followers of Baal. Elijah's encounter with the prophets of Baal on Mount Carmel, for example, was a test of the power of Baal—whether he could send fire from heaven (lightning bolts) to ignite the sacrifice and bring the rains that were needed to end the drought. Baal was silent, but God thundered—and the rains came, as Elijah had predicted (1 Kin. 18:20–46).

LAMA [LAH muh]—a Hebrew word meaning "why." It is found twice in the New Testament (Matt. 27:46; Mark 15:34), as one of Jesus' "seven words" from the cross: "My God, My God, why have You forsaken Me?"—a quotation from Psalm 22:1.

LAMENTATIONS, BOOK OF—a short Old Testament book, written in poetic form, that expresses deep grief over the destruction of the city of Jerusalem and the temple. Its English title comes from a Greek verb meaning "to cry aloud," which accurately describes the contents of the book.

Structure of the Book.

The book consists of five poems, one for each chapter. The first, second, and fourth poems are written as acrostics, with each successive verse beginning with the next letter of the Hebrew alphabet. The third poem is also an acrostic, although in an expanded form giving three verses to each of the 22 letters of the Hebrew alphabet. The fifth poem departs from the acrostic pattern, but it contains 22 verses, the same number as poems one, two, and four.

It is clear that the writer of Lamentations went to much trouble to compose this book. He wove several literary devices together, under the inspiration of God's Spirit, to give these poems a somber tone. Nothing less could express his deep sorrow over the plight of Jerusalem at the hands of the invading Babylonians.

Authorship and Date.

Lamentations itself gives no clue concerning its author, but many conservative Bible scholars agree on the prophet Jeremiah as the most likely candidate. The book is realistic in its portrayal of conditions in Jerusalem just before its fall, suggesting that the author was an eyewitness of these events. This supports Jeremiah's authorship, since he prophesied in Jerusalem during this period of his nation's history. In addition, the Septuagint (an ancient Greek translation of the Old Testament) attributes the authorship of Lamentations to Jeremiah.

Some of the language in Lamentations and the Book of Jeremiah is also similar. For example, the phrase "daughter of" appears about 20 times in each book. In addition, Jeremiah was a very sensitive prophet who expressed his feelings about his nation's sins and approaching doom in rich symbols and metaphors. A deep outpouring of sorrow is characteristic of Lamentations as well as some sections of Jeremiah. All this evidence supports the view that the prophet wrote the Book of Lamentations. The date of the writing was probably some time shortly after the fall of the city in 586 B.C.

Historical Setting.

The fall of Jerusalem to Babylonian forces under Nebuchadnezzar was one of Israel's most bitter experiences. Many of the nation's leading citizens were carried into captivity in Babylonia and lived there for almost 50 years. Their idolatry and unfaithfulness had resulted in the loss of two of the focal points of their faith: Jerusalem and the temple. Jeremiah must have expressed their collective shock and sorrow as he wrote this poetic book.

Theological Contribution.

Why was there such despondency over the destruction of a city? The reasons become clear when we sense the importance of Jerusalem in the purpose of God.

Jerusalem was more than the capital of the nation or the city of Israel's beloved King David. Jerusalem was the site of the Temple of God, the place where God's presence dwelt and where sacrifice could be made to him. In later years Jerusalem became the focal point of God's final work of salvation in the person of Jesus Christ. Lamentations reminds us of the central role that this city has always played in God's work of redemption in the world.

Special Considerations.

Lamentations has many strange expressions such as "daughter of Zion" (2:1), "daughter of Judah" (2:5), and "daughter of Jerusalem" (2:15). These do not refer to daughters of these cities but to the cities themselves as daughters of the Lord. In this context, these phrases refer to supreme grief. As such they remind us of the profound sorrow associated with God's judgment of His sinful people; yet, since they remain daughters, these cities speak of great hope during desperate times.

L ANGUAGES OF THE BIBLE—the languages in which the Bible was originally written. The most famous of these are Hebrew, the original language of most of the Old Testament, and Greek, used in the writing of most of the New Testament. But several other languages also had a bearing on the writing or transmission of the original texts of the Bible.

Aramaic.

Spoken from at least about 2000 B.C., Aramaic eventually replaced many of the languages of the ancient world in popularity and usage. Parts of the books of Ezra (4:8–6:18; 7:12–26) and of Daniel (2:46–7:28) were written in Aramaic. Aramaic was the language spoken in Palestine in the time of Jesus. While the New Testament was written in the Greek language, the language Jesus spoke was probably Aramaic. "Talitha, cumi" (Mark 5:41) and "Ephphatha" (Mark 7:34) are two Aramaic phrases spoken by Jesus that have been preserved in English versions of the New Testament. Another name for the Aramaic dialect is Syriac.

Latin.

The New Testament also refers to Latin, the language that sprang from ancient Rome (Luke 23:38; John 19:20). Most of the Roman Empire also used Greek in Jesus' day. But as Roman power spread throughout the ancient world, Latin also expanded in use. The influence of Latin on the Mediterranean world in the time of Jesus is shown by the occurrence of such Latin words as "denarii" (Matt. 18:28) and "praetorian" (Phil. 1:13, imperial guard, NRSV, NASB; palace guard, NIV) in the New Testament.

Persian.

This language was spoken by the people who settled the area east of the Tigris River in what is now western Iran. When the Jewish people were taken as captives to Babylon in 586 B.C., they may have been exposed to this distinctive language form, which used a combination of pictorial and phonetic signs in its alphabet. Several words derived from Persian are found in the Old Testament (for example, satrap; Dan. 6:1–2).

LAW—an orderly system of rules and regulations by which a society is governed. In the Bible, particularly the Old Testament, a unique law code was established by direct revelation from God to direct His people in their worship, in their relationship to Him, and in their social relationships with one another.

Israel was not the only nation to have a law code. Such collections were common among the countries of the ancient world. These law codes generally began with an explanation that the gods gave the king the power to reign, along with a pronouncement about how good and capable he was. Then came the king's laws grouped by subject. The code generally closed with a series of curses and blessings.

The biblical law code, or the Mosaic Law, was different from other ancient Near Eastern law codes in several ways. Biblical law was different, first of all, in its origin. Throughout the ancient world, the laws of most nations were believed to originate with the gods, but they were considered intensely personal and subjective in the way they were applied. Even the gods were under the law, and they could suffer punishment if they violated it—unless, of course, they were powerful and able to conquer the punishers. The king ruled under the god whose temple and property he oversaw. Although he did not live under a written law code, he had a personal relationship to the god. Therefore, law was decided case by case and at the king's discretion. For most of a king's lifetime, his laws were kept secret.

By contrast, the biblical concept was that law comes from God, issues from His nature, and is holy, righteous, and good. Furthermore, at the outset of God's ruling over Israel at Sinai, God the great King gave His laws. These laws were binding on His people, and He upheld them. Furthermore, His laws were universal. Ancient oriental kings often tried to outdo their predecessors in image, economic power, and political influence. This was often their motivation in setting forth law codes. God, however, depicts His law as an expression of His love for His people (Ex. 19:5–6).

In Israel all crimes were crimes against God (1 Sam. 12:9–10). Consequently, He expected all His people to love and serve Him (Amos 5:21–24). As the final judge, He disciplined those who violated His law (Ex. 22:21–24; Deut. 10:18; 19:17). The nation or community was responsible for upholding the law and insuring that justice was done (Deut. 13:6–10; 17:7; Num. 15:32–36).

God's law, unlike those of other nations of the ancient world, also viewed all human life as especially valuable, because people are created in God's image. Thus, biblical law was more humane. It avoided mutilations and other savage punishments. Victims could not inflict more injury than they had received. Neither could criminals restore less than they had taken or stolen simply because of a class distinction. Everyone was equal before God's law.

The "eye for eye" requirement of the Mosaic Law was not a harsh statement that required cruel punishment. Instead, it was a mandate for equality before the law (Ex. 21:24). Each criminal had to pay for his own crime (Num. 35:31). Under the law codes of some pagan nations, the rich often could buy their way out of punishment. God's law especially protected the defenseless widow, fatherless child, slave, and stranger from injustice (Ex. 21:2, 20–21; 22:21–23).

Some scholars refer to Leviticus 17–26 as the "holiness code." Although it does not contain all of God's directions for ceremonial holiness, it does set forth much of what God requires. These chapters contain moral and ritual specifications regarding the tabernacle and public worship as well as the command to love one's neighbor as oneself (19:18). The nation of Israel was to be characterized by separation from other nations. Several of these laws prohibited pagan worship. Because God is holy (21:8), Israel was to be holy and separated from other nations (20:26).

The Book of Deuteronomy is sometimes called the Deuteronomic Code. This book contains the command to love God with all one's heart, soul, and might (Deut. 6:5) as well as a second record of the Ten Commandments (Deuteronomy 5).

Biblical law is more than a record of human law. It is an expression of what God requires of people. It rests on the eternal moral principles that are consistent with the very nature of God Himself. Therefore, biblical law (the Ten Commandments) is the summary of moral law. As such it sets forth fundamental and universal moral principles.

What is often called the civil law includes those laws in the Pentateuch (first five books of the Old Testament) that regulate civil and social behavior. All laws are fundamentally religious since God is the lawgiver and ruler over everything. There are eight distinct categories of civil law in the Old Testament: (1) laws regulating leaders, (2) laws regulating the army, (3) laws respecting criminals, (4) laws dealing with crimes against property, (5) laws relating to humane treatment, (6) laws about personal and family rights, (7) laws about property rights, and (8) laws regulating other social behavior.

Laws Regulating Leaders.
Several different types of laws in this category of civil law were designed to keep Israel's leadership strong and free of graft and corruption.

Exclusion laws—God commanded that several categories of people not be allowed to vote or serve in office. These included the physically handicapped, sexually maimed, those of illegitimate birth, and those of foreign extraction, such as Moabite or Ammonite (Deut. 23:1–3). These laws were another of the attempts by God to teach Israel in a concrete manner that they were to be spiritually clean and perfect before Him.

Laws about the king—Long before Israel had a human king, God specified that if a king were to be appointed, he should follow all the laws God had given. Other specifications were that he should be a true Israelite, that he should not trust in a large army for protection, and that he should not be a polygamist or a greedy person (Deut. 17:14–20). The judges of the Book of Judges functioned as temporary military leaders. They also handled some of the functions of a modern judge. Israel's kings were different from these judges, in that they were permanent and they maintained a standing army, a governmental network, and a royal court supported by taxation.

Laws about judges—Judges were of two classes, priestly and non-priestly (elders). The priestly judges presided over religious lawsuits, and elders presided over civil lawsuits (Deut. 17:8–13; 2 Chr. 19:8, 11). Judges, also called elders, were to be elected from among heads of households (Ex. 18:13–26).

Laws about the judicial system—God commanded Israel to organize its ruling system into layers of courts (Ex. 18:21–22; Deut. 1:15), with lesser matters decided by lesser courts and greater matters decided by greater courts (Deut. 16:18). Matters that involved foundational principles or that were too hard for the lower courts were brought to the highest courts or the chief judge (2 Chr. 19:10–11). The highest court was God Himself (Ex. 22:21–24; Deut. 10:18).

Judges were charged not to be partial in favor of the rich or against the poor, widows, aliens, or others who might be helpless (Ex. 23:6–9; Deut. 16:18–20; 27:19). Consequently, they were to hear the witnesses carefully, examine the evidence, and make their decisions on the basis of what God had revealed in His written law. They also presided over making or nullifying all contracts.

Laws about witnesses—Witnesses were charged by God to tell the truth (Lev. 19:16). If they did not do so, they were judged by Him. If their deception was discovered, they were to bear the penalty involved in the case (Ex. 23:1–3; Deut. 19:15–19). Conviction of serious crimes required two or more witnesses (Num. 35:30). Indeed, no one could be convicted on the testimony of one witness. Written documents and other testimony could be used as evidence against the accused (Deut. 17:6; 19:18).

Laws about law enforcement—Refusal to comply with what the court decided (contempt of court) brought a sentence of death (Deut. 17:12–13). The citizens of ancient Israel were the policemen, bailiffs, etc. (Deut. 16:18). Usually executions were in the hands of the citizens (Deut. 13:9–10; 15:16). Later, the king's private army enforced his will, while Levites also served as policemen (2 Chr. 19:11).

Laws about refuge cities—Judges controlled the entrance into the refuge cities. These were the cities where those who had committed accidental murder (manslaughter) could flee to safety. When the high priest of the nation died, refugees were free to go home without penalty (Ex. 21:12–14; Deut. 19:1–13). Israel was responsible for keeping the roads to such cities as safe as possible so the fugitive could outrun the avenger—the relative responsible for the fugitive's execution to repay the kinsman's death.

Laws about prophets—God's law strictly prohibited idolatry and provided for the death of those who would lead Israel into idolatry. The test of a true prophet was not his ability to work miracles but his faithfulness to God and His revelation (Deut. 18:14–22). On the other hand, Israel was to obey the words of true prophets. If they did not do so, God Himself would punish the people.

Laws Regulating the Army.

The second category of civil law consisted of laws regulating the army. All Palestine belonged to God. Within its borders His people were commanded to wage war to gain and maintain the territory. To this end all Israelite males 20 years of age and older formed a militia (Num. 1:21–43), with 50 probably being the exemption age (Num. 4:3, 23). If only a small-scale war was being fought, a selective service system operated by the casting of lots (Num. 31:3–6). Kings were to maintain only small standing armies. Their first defense from outside attack was to be the Lord Himself (Deut. 17:16; 23:9–14).

Certain citizens were exempt from the military: priests and Levites (Num. 1:48–49), the man who had not yet dedicated his newly built home (Deut. 20:5), anyone who had not gathered the first harvest from a field or vineyard (Deut. 20:6), a groom who had not yet consummated his recent marriage (Deut. 20:7), or any man who had been married within a year of the call to arms (Deut. 24:5).

All war was holy war—that is, it was fought under the lordship of God. Therefore, God promised to protect and fight for His army (Deut. 20:1–4), keeping them from harm and marshaling the forces of nature against the enemy (Josh. 10:11; 24:7). But God's protection required ritualistic separation from sin and death, dedication to God, and the following of His direction about the battle (Deut. 23:9–14). God was the commander-in-chief and the one to whom thanksgiving was due for the victory (Num. 10:9–10).

Within Palestine every non-Israelite was to be killed and all their possessions and goods offered to God (Deut. 20:16–18; 2:34; 3:6). Thus, they were to purify the territory and guard themselves from Canaanite idolatry. When the Israelites were fighting outside Palestine, the city being attacked was to be offered peace before the attack. Refusal triggered the attack. All the citizens and goods of that city then became rightful slaves and booty (Deut. 20:10–15).

Laws Respecting Criminals.

The third category of civil law consisted of laws against specific criminal offenses. In His law God defined what a criminal offense was and what the proper punishment for each offense was to be. All crimes were sins, or offenses, against God's law. Since there were degrees of punishments, there were degrees of sin under the law. God prohibited the Israelites from punishing criminals excessively (Deut. 25:1–3).

Crimes against God—Under God's law, all of life was religious, but some crimes were considered especially directed against the worship system God had established. Conviction in these cases resulted in death, because such crimes struck out pointedly against God and life itself.

These crimes against God included worshiping other gods alongside God (Ex. 22:20; 34:14); turning from God to worship other gods (Deut. 13:1–18); seeking to control other people and future events by magic or sorcery (Ex. 22:18; Deut. 18:9–14); sacrificing children to false gods (Lev. 18:21; 20:2–5); blasphemy (Lev. 24:16); false prophecy (Deut. 18:18–20); and Sabbath labor other than that permitted by God (Ex. 35:2, 3; Matt. 12:1–8).

Crimes against society—Certain crimes struck at society as a whole. Among these were the perversion of justice through bribery, torture of witnesses, and false testimony or perjury (Ex. 23:1–7; Deut. 19:16–21). Judges were commanded to treat all people equally.

Crimes against sexual morality—Biblical law relating to sexual morality protected and sanctified the family. The sexual union of two persons made them one flesh, and this was the only such union they were to experience.

1. Fornication. In Israel the sexual union was most sacred. A newly married woman charged with premarital sex with a man other than her husband was to be put to death if the charge was proven. If the charge was not proven, her husband had to pay a large fine and keep her as his wife. Also, he could never divorce her (Deut. 22:13–21).

2. Adultery. Under God's law adultery was a serious crime, perhaps because tearing apart the two who had become one amounted to murder. Those convicted of adultery were to be put to death (Lev. 20:10–12; Deut. 22:22). A betrothed woman (virgin) was protected by the law, but she was also considered to be married in some cases. If she and some man other than her betrothed had sexual union, they were to be put to death (Deut. 22:23–24).

3. Homosexuality. Sodomy or male homosexuality was pointedly condemned and prohibited. It brought death under God's law (Lev. 20:13). By implication, the same penalty was probably also meted out for female homosexuality, or lesbianism.

4. Prostitution. Prostitutes of every guise (male or female, cultic or non-cultic) were to be put to death (Gen. 38:24; Lev. 19:29; 21:9).

5. Incest. Sexual union with one's own offspring or near relative was to result in death (Lev. 20:11–14).

6. Bestiality. Having sex with a beast (a common feature of Canaanite worship) was an offense punishable by death (Ex. 22:19; Lev. 18:23; Deut. 27:21).

7. Transvestiture. The distinction between the sexes was to be retained in their outward appearance. Hence, transvestiture (wearing the clothing of the opposite sex) was forbidden.

Crimes against an individual's person—Crimes of violence against others were serious criminal offenses. The following crimes are cited in biblical law.

1. Murder. The willful and premeditated taking of a human life was punishable by death. Accidental killing, killing as an act of war, and lawful executions were not considered murder (Ex. 21:12–14; Num. 35:14–34). The sixth commandment is, "You shall not murder." Jesus pointed to the spirit of this commandment when He expanded it to forbid hatred, anger, bitter insults, and cursing (Matt. 5:21–22).

2. Assault and battery. God's law expected people to live at peace with one another. But realizing that offenses might occur, God provided legislation about assault and battery. If injuring a person caused the victim to lose time but no further harm was done, the offender had to pay his victim for the time lost. Presumably the courts established the fine in such cases (Ex. 21:18–19). If someone maimed his foe in a struggle, he would pay for the lost time; but he would also suffer the same disfigurement at the hands of the court (Lev. 24:19). Some important exceptions to this punishment should be noted.

If the victim were a slave, disfigurement resulted in his freedom (a very heavy financial loss to the guilty party). If the slave died, the offender was to die. If the slave survived and was not disfigured, there was no penalty on the master, except that exacted for loss of time (Ex. 21:20–21, 26–27).

If a son or daughter attacked either parent, the attacker was to be put to death (Ex. 21:15). One law called for the severing of the hand of a woman who attacked a man's genitals, even though she may have been trying to protect her husband (Deut. 25:11–12).

3. Miscarriage. Miscarriage, or the death of the mother resulting from a blow by someone in a fight, brought death upon the attacker. Premature birth caused by this offense required a money fine determined by the husband as governed by the courts (Ex. 21:22).

4. Rape and seduction. A man who raped a betrothed woman was to be put to death (Deut. 22:25–27). However, if he raped or seduced an unattached woman, he was to pay a large fine and propose marriage. A girl's father could refuse the marriage and keep the money; but if he approved, the rapist had to marry the girl and could never divorce her (Ex. 22:16–17; Deut. 2:28–29). If the seduced girl was a betrothed slave, she was considered unattached (for she had not yet been released from slavery). Consequently, the attacker was not put to death. But the man had to bring a guilt offering before God to make restitution for his sin.

5. Oppression. In Israel the defenseless were to be defended. Those without rights or power to enforce their rights were protected by God. These included the alien passing through the area and the alien who was a permanent resident. The widow, fatherless child, deaf, blind, slave, hired hand, and poor were to be given just wages, paid immediately, given interest-free loans (except aliens) in emergencies, gifts of food at festivals, and the privilege of gleaning, etc. (Ex. 22:21–24; Lev. 19:14, 33; Deut. 24:14; 27:18–19).

6. Kidnapping. Capturing a person to sell or use him as a slave was a capital offense (Deut. 24:7). This prohibition

extended to foreigners (unless they were prisoners of war; Ex. 22:21-24), the blind and deaf (Lev. 19:14), and all people (Deut. 27:19).

7. Slander. Slander (making malicious statements about another person) was strictly forbidden and punished if the crime was committed during a trial (Ex. 23:1). This was viewed as a mortal attack on a person (Lev. 19:16).

Laws Dealing with Crimes Against Property.

Biblical law, unlike other ancient near Eastern codes, placed a higher value on human life than on possessions. But it also allowed people to have private possessions by protecting them from theft and fraud. The following crimes against property are dealt with in the Bible.

Stealing—God prohibited anyone from stealing from another. Heavy financial penalties were levied upon the thief. If he could not pay, he was required to serve as an indentured servant to pay the restitution price in labor (Ex. 22:1–3).

Blackmail and loan fraud—God's law counted these crimes as a kind of theft, mandating heavy penalties and possible indentured service as penalties (Ex. 22:1–3; Lev. 6:1–7).

Weights and measures—Ancient Israel did not use money; transactions were in measured, or weighed, precious metal. God prohibited anyone from juggling weights so the goods or metals would be measured out to favor the thief. Such a thief had to repay his victims (Lev. 19:35–36; Deut. 25:13–16).

Lost animals—"Finders, keepers" did not hold in ancient Israel. Straying animals were to be returned to the owner or cared for until claimed; "If you meet your enemy's ox or his donkey going astray, you shall surely bring it back to him again," (Ex. 23:4–5; Deut. 22:1–4).

Boundaries—The land was marked into sections by ancient landmarks, according to the allotments made shortly after it was conquered. To move these landmarks resulted in God's curse. This act was considered stealing from one's neighbor as well as rebellion against God the great landowner (Deut. 19:14; 27:17).

Laws Relating to Humane Treatment.

God's law regulated treatment of otherwise defenseless animals and people.

Protection of animals—Some of these laws were also environmental laws. For example, Israel was commanded not to work the land on the seventh year. Whatever grain or fruit grew up was to be left for the animals and the poor. This forced a crop rotation system on the Hebrew people so they would have some harvest every year (Ex. 23:11–12; Lev. 25:5–7). They were allowed to eat certain wild beasts and birds but were forbidden to take a mother. Presumably, they could take the young or the eggs, but they were required to let the mother live (Deut. 22:6–7). An ox or any working beast (or human being) was to be fed adequately to give him strength for doing the work (Deut. 25:4). Animals were not to be cruelly beaten or overloaded. They were to be rested on the Sabbath (Ex. 20:8–11; 23:12; Deut. 22:1–4).

Protection of human beings—The poor, widow, fatherless child, alien, sojourner, blind, deaf, etc., were to receive humane treatment from God's people (Ex. 22:21–25). To preserve their self-respect, they were given opportunities to earn a living by gleaning and working for wages. They were also to be paid properly (Deut. 24:14–15, 19–22).

The respectable and responsible poor were to be extended interest-free loans (Lev. 25:35–37). Their cloaks, which they used at night as blankets, could not be taken as collateral. Neither could a creditor forcibly enter a person's house to collect the debt (Deut. 24:10–13).

The elderly were to be respected, cared for, and protected (Lev. 19:32). Travelers could enter fields to gather a meal for themselves, but they were forbidden to take more than they could eat (Deut. 23:24–25). If these provisions did not satisfy the needs of the poor, they could sell themselves into indentured service (temporary servitude). In cases like this, the law demanded that they be treated humanely (Lev. 25:39–43). In general, treatment of others was to be governed by the law of love (Lev. 19:18) or the Golden Rule (Matt. 7:12).

Laws About Personal and Family Rights.

Another broad category of civil law dealt with personal and family rights. The following situations were covered by these statutes.

Parents and children—The law of God assumed that parents would act responsibly and feed and clothe their children even as God fed and clothed them. Parents also were to discipline and teach their children (Deut. 6:6–7). A father was responsible for circumcising his sons (Gen. 12–13) redeeming his firstborn from God (Num. 18:15–16), and finding his children proper marriage partners (Gen. 24:4).

Children were commanded to respect and obey their parents (Ex. 20:12). Disrespect in the form of striking or cursing a parent and delinquency (stubbornness and disobedience expressed in gluttony and drunkenness) were punishable by death (Ex. 21:15, 17; Deut. 21:18–21). Minor children were under their parents' authority and could not make binding vows. Unmarried girls were not allowed to make binding vows without their fathers' or their male guardians' agreement (Num. 30:3–5).

Marriage—God prohibited the Israelites from marrying near relatives and members of their own immediate family (Lev. 18:6–18; Deut. 27:20–23). He also forbade intermarriage with the Canaanites because these pagans would lead their mates into idolatry (Deut. 7:1–4). But if Canaanites converted and became Israelites (members of God's covenantal community), no legal and religious bar prevented marriage with them. A man could marry a woman prisoner of war after she mourned her parents' deaths for a month. This did not necessarily mean her parents were actually dead, but only that this woman now became an Israelite. If her husband divorced her, she had to be set free. Her marriage had made her a full citizen under the law—an Israelite.

Special laws also regulated the marriage of priests. A priest was not to marry a former harlot, a woman who had been previously married, or one who had previously had sexual relations. His bride had to be a virgin Israelitess (Lev. 21:7, 13–15).

Within the marriage bond, women were protected from undue male harshness by the laws relating to the dowry, the large sum of money given to the girl and held in part by her father in case of their divorce or the husband's death. Laws also called for severe penalties for violent crimes (usually perpetrated by men), as well as severe penalties for the beating and maiming of household members. God also admonished the man to love the woman as his own body and to treat her accordingly (Deut. 21:10–14).

The wife and mother was to be honored by the children (Ex. 20:12). Sexual relations were forbidden during a woman's menstrual period—perhaps for sanitary reasons, but certainly to emphasize the sanctity of life and the life-giving process (Lev. 18:19; 20:18). A woman of child-bearing age left childless at the death of her husband was to be married to one of his surviving near relatives so she could bear children to carry on the family name (Deut. 25:5–10). This also provided her with an advocate and protector in the civil court (Deut. 22:13–19) and a representative before God's altar (Deut. 16:16).

The husband was given primary authority in the family. His wife was under his authority in all matters. Obviously, this did not reduce her to a slave status or to an inferior position, since the two had become one. It did, however, establish a clear authority structure that minimized internal familial struggles and allowed the family to function socially, economically, and religiously (Num. 30:6–15).

Infidelity was punishable by death. Divorce was granted under certain circumstances (Deut. 24:1–4). When a man wrongfully accused his wife of infidelity "Then the elders of that city shall take that man and punish him" (Deut. 22:17–19); he could not divorce her.

Hired servants—God especially protected the poor from the ravages of the rich. One such measure was the law requiring employers to pay their hired help a just and fair wage and to do so at the end of each work day (Lev. 19:13; Deut. 24:14).

Slaves—Slaves were of two classes, indentured and permanent. Hebrews who were unable to pay debts were indentured, or committed to temporary servitude. The indenture lasted only six years or until the year of Jubilee. He might be given a wife while in this state, but the wife and children resulting from the union were bound to the master. Such a man could bind himself permanently to the master either for the master's sake or for that of his family (Ex. 21:2–6).

An Israelite indentured because of poverty was not to be thought of or treated as a slave. He could not be treated with the rigor of slavery. He was to be treated as a hired servant. For example, he was to be paid (Deut. 15:12–14). He could be bought out of the situation by his relatives, or by himself—presumably by savings resulting from his wages while indentured (Lev. 25:39–43, 47–55).

A woman sold to a man as a wife was especially protected. She could be redeemed by her family if the master was not satisfied with her. She could not be sold as a slave to foreign people. She was to be treated as a daughter and provided for in the same way as other wives. If these laws were disobeyed, her freedom was granted (Ex. 21:2–6).

Permanent slaves could be acquired by purchase or as prisoners of war. They were only to be taken from the nations and peoples outside Palestine (Lev. 25:44–46). Fugitive slaves were not to be returned to their owners or treated as slaves—a provision that worked to force masters to treat slaves humanely (Deut. 23:15–16).

Slaves were considered permanent members of their master's household, circumcised, and admitted to Passover (Ex. 12:43–44) and all the special meals eaten before the Lord, except the guilt offering (Deut. 12:17–18; 16:10–11). A slave could be forced to work; but if beaten severely, he was to be freed (Ex. 21:20–32). If a slave was killed, the master was to be put to death (Ex. 21:20).

Aliens—Aliens could convert to Judaism, be circumcised, and become full members of the covenant (Num. 9:14; 15:12–15). Even if aliens temporarily or permanently living as free people in Israel did not convert, they were to receive full privileges under the civil law (Num. 15:29–30). Unlike Israelites, aliens ate foods declared unclean by God; such foods could be sold or given to them (Deut. 14:21).

Israelites were forbidden to take advantage of the poor Israelite by charging him interest for the loan of food, clothing, money, or anything else (Ex. 22:25; Lev. 25:35–37). But the poor and desperate alien could be charged interest, perhaps because the Israelites considered his state a result of God's judgment (Deut. 23:20).

Laws Regulating Property Rights.

Another broad category of civil law consisted of those laws that regulated property rights. The following situations were covered by these laws.

Lost property—Under Mosaic law, all lost property was to be returned to its owner if the owner was known or to be held until claimed by him (Deut. 22:1–4).

Damaged property—Property held in trust was protected under the law. A person caught stealing had to restore to the owner double the value of the goods stolen. If the goods were stolen through carelessness by a trustee of the property, the trustee had to repay the full amount missing. If the loss was accidental or not due to the trustee's carelessness, that trustee was not liable for the loss, provided he was willing to swear before God that the loss was not his fault (Ex. 22:7–13). Borrowed goods had to be returned. If they were damaged or lost while borrowed, they had to be replaced by the borrower (Ex. 22:14–15).

Unsafe property—Owners were held responsible for unsafe property. Thus, if someone was hurt because of an owner's property, the owner had to pay a penalty. In the case of death, the owner of the property lost his life (Ex. 21:28–36; Deut. 22:8).

Land ownership—Ultimately, God owned all the land (Lev. 25:23). He demanded that His tenants rest the land every seventh year by not planting a crop (Lev. 25:1–7). During this seventh year, all travelers and the poor were allowed to eat of the produce of the land without paying for it. All parcels of land were assigned permanently to certain families; they reverted back to those original owners or their heirs every 50th year (Lev. 25:8–24). The land could also be purchased by those owners at its original selling price (Lev. 25:29–31) in the interim. Furthermore, it was a serious matter to move the ancient markers that designated the boundaries of the land. Within walled cities, only Levites owned houses in a permanent sense (Lev. 25:32–34).

Inheritance laws—Normally only legitimate sons were to inherit all the family's property. The first-born son received twice as much as the others (Deut. 21:15–17; 25:6). He was responsible for caring for elderly family members and providing a respectable burial for them. A wicked son could be disinherited. If no sons were born to a family, legitimate daughters were to inherit the property (Num. 27:7–8). Such heiresses had to marry within their own tribe or lose the inheritance (Num. 36:1–12).

Laws Regulating Other Social Behavior.

The final category of civil law included those statutes that regulated specific social behavior. God commanded the

Hebrew people to keep themselves from pagan religious and cultic practices (Ex. 20:3–5; Lev. 19:27). Among these practices were boiling a kid in its mother's milk (Deut. 14:21), shaving one's head in a particular way (Lev. 13:33; 21:5), worshiping idols (Deut. 7:5, 25; 12:2–3), sacrificing children (Lev. 20:2), participating in homosexuality and temple prostitution (Lev. 19:29), slashing or tattooing one's body (Lev. 19:28), and practicing magic, sorcery, or divination (Lev. 19:26, 31).

God's people were to preserve and study the Lord's law (Deut. 4:2; 6:6–7), revere His name (Deut. 8:6; 10:12), be grateful and thankful (Deut. 8:10), and obey, love, and serve their redeemer God (Deut. 10:14–16; 6:4–5; 11:1, 13–14).

LETTERS—written messages between persons separated by distance. In the Old Testament David wrote a letter to Joab, sending Uriah the Hittite into the heat of battle and insuring his death. In Bible times, letters were written on sheets of parchment, or animal skins; fragments of pottery; papyrus; and clay tablets.

In the New Testament, Saul of Tarsus went to the high priest in Jerusalem and secured letters from him to the synagogues of Damascus. These letters authorized Saul to arrest Christians and bring them to Jerusalem (Acts 9:2; 22:5). The Jerusalem Council also sent a letter to Christians expressing their decision (Acts 15:23, 30).

LEVITICUS, BOOK OF—an Old Testament book filled with worship instructions for God's Chosen People, Israel. The Levites, members of the tribe of Levi, were the priestly family of the nation; the title of the book seems to indicate that its instructions were given specifically for them. Because of its emphasis on holiness, sacrifice, and atonement, the book has an important message for modern believers.

Structure of the Book.

Leviticus is difficult reading for most Bible students. It contains page after page of detailed instructions about strange worship rituals that seem to have no clear organizing principle. But with careful analysis, the book breaks down into two main divisions.

The first several chapters of the book contain instructions about the ritual of sacrifice, including animal sacrifice, or the burnt offering—a key ingredient of Old Testament worship. Other segments of the book deal with the consecration of the priesthood, personal purification and dietary laws, laws of atonement, holiness of the people, and the redemption of tithes and vows.

Authorship and Date.

Most conservative Bible students acknowledge Moses as the author of the Book of Leviticus. But some scholars insist the book was pulled together from many different sources by an unknown editor several centuries after Moses' death. This theory overlooks the dozens of instances in Leviticus where God spoke directly to Moses and Moses wrote down His instructions to be passed along to the people (4:1; 6:1; 8:1; 11:1).

In addition, nothing was more important to the nation of Israel in its earliest years than the development of its system of worship. Thus, worship rules would have been established at a very early stage in Israel's history. This argues convincingly for the early writing of these rules at the hand of Moses, probably about 1400 B.C.

Historical Setting.

The Book of Leviticus belongs to the period in Israel's history when the people were encamped at Mount Sinai following their miraculous deliverance from slavery in Egypt. At Sinai Moses received the Ten Commandments and other parts of the Law directly from God. He also built and furnished the tabernacle as a place where the people could worship God (Exodus 40). Just after the tabernacle was filled with God's glory, Moses received instructions for the people regarding worship of God in this holy place. It is these instructions that we find in the Book of Leviticus.

Theological Contribution.

The Book of Leviticus is important because of its clear teachings on three vital spiritual truths: atonement, sacrifice, and holiness. Without the background of these concepts in Leviticus, we could not understand their later fulfillment in the life and ministry of Jesus.

Atonement—Chapter 16 of Leviticus contains God's instructions for observing the Day of Atonement. On that day the high priest of Israel entered the most sacred place in the tabernacle and offered an animal sacrifice to atone for his own sins. Then he killed another animal and sprinkled its blood on the altar to atone for the sins of the people. New Testament writers later compared this familiar picture to the sacrifice of Jesus on our behalf. But unlike a human priest, Jesus did not have to offer sacrifices, "first for His own sins and then for the people's, for this He did once for all when He offered up Himself" (Heb. 7:27).

Sacrifice—The Book of Leviticus instructs the Covenant People to bring many types of sacrifices or offerings to God: burnt offerings, grain offerings, peace offerings, sin offerings, and guilt or trespass offerings. These were considered gifts by which a worshiper expressed his loyalty and devotion to God. But a blood offering—presenting the blood of a sacrificed animal to God—went beyond the idea of a gift. It symbolized that the worshiper was offering his own life to God, since the Hebrews believed that "the life of the flesh is in the blood" (Lev. 17:11). Again, this familiar teaching assumed deeper meaning in the New Testament when applied to Jesus. He gave

His life on our behalf when He shed His blood to take away our sins.

Holiness—The basic meaning of holiness as presented in the Book of Leviticus is that God demands absolute obedience of His people. The root meaning of the word is "separation." God's people were to be separate from, and different than, the surrounding pagan peoples. This is actually the reason for God's instruction that His people were not to eat certain unclean foods. Only a clean, undefiled people could be used by Him to bring about His purpose of world redemption. Leviticus also makes it clear that the holiness demanded by God extended to the daily behavior of His people. They were expected to practice kindness, honesty, and justice and to show compassion toward the poor (Lev. 19:9–18).

Special Considerations.

The blood of bulls and goats so prominent in Leviticus had no power to take away sin. But each of these rituals was "a shadow of the good things to come" (Heb. 10:1). They pointed forward to God's ultimate sacrifice, given freely on our behalf: "So Christ was offered once to bear the sins of many" (Heb. 9:28).

LUKE, GOSPEL OF—the third gospel, in which the great truths of Jesus are communicated primarily through vivid stories. Luke is the first of a two-part work. In this work, the history of the gospel is traced from its beginnings in the life of Jesus (the Gospel of Luke) to the founding of the early church (the Acts of the Apostles).

The author of the Gospel of Luke is more interested in persons, especially those in trouble, than in ideas. He also is a skilled writer, and the literary quality of the Gospel of Luke is the highest of all four gospels. Luke often is the most interesting gospel to read. But he is also a serious historian who places Jesus within the context of world history. He presents Jesus and the church as the fulfillment of the history of salvation.

Structure of the Gospel.

The literary structure of the Gospel of Luke is constructed primarily around Jesus' ministry in Galilee and in Jerusalem.

The first two chapters of the gospel could be entitled "Introduction and Infancy." Here Luke declares his purpose in writing (1:1–4), and he tells the immortal stories of the births of John the Baptist and Jesus. The ministry of Jesus begins with a note of expectation in chapter 3. The rulers of the Roman world at that time are named. Next, accounts are given of the preaching of John the Baptist and of Jesus' baptism, genealogy, and temptation (3:1–4:13).

Between His Temptation and Transfiguration (4:14–9:28), Jesus conducted His ministry in Galilee. Convinced of His approaching death (9:21–27, 43–45), Jesus steadfastly set His face to go to Jerusalem (9:51) where, like the prophets before Him, He would accept His fate. This journey occupies the central part of Luke (9:51–19:27). The reader is kept in dramatic tension as Jesus moves to Jerusalem and the shadow of the cross darkens His pathway. The cross, however, is not simply unlucky fate; on the contrary, "the Son of Man goes as it has been determined" (22:22) to fulfill the divine plan for which He came (note the use of "must" in 2:49; 4:43; 9:22; 17:25; 22:37; 24:7, 44).

Like Moses, Jesus accomplished for His people a deliverance—a deliverance from sin to salvation. The events of Jesus' final week in Jerusalem (19:28–24:53) conclude the gospel, and the ascension serves as a transition from the end of Luke to the beginning of Acts.

Authorship and Date.

The author does not identify himself by name, but he does tell us a good deal about himself. Although not an eyewitness of the events he reports, he has followed them closely enough to write an orderly, reliable narrative (1:1–4). He is an educated man with the best command of Greek of any New Testament writer. He counts among his acquaintances a person of high social standing, the "most excellent" Theophilus, to whom he addresses both Luke (1:3) and Acts (1:1). As a Gentile, the author is interested in Gentiles; he is equally disinterested in matters purely Jewish. At some point in his life he joined the apostle Paul. His experiences with Paul served as a firsthand source for his sequel to the Gospel of Luke.

For the author's name we are dependent on later tradition. Writing about A.D. 175, Irenaeus, bishop of Lyon, identified the author as Luke, the companion of Paul. Eusebius agreed, adding that Luke was a native of Antioch. The importance of Antioch in Acts (13:1–3) lends credibility to Eusebius' statement. The few glimpses we get of Luke from Paul's epistles—a physician, both beloved and compassionate (Col. 4:14) who was with Paul during his Roman imprisonment (Philem. 24; 2 Tim. 4:11)—parallels what we gather from him in Luke–Acts. The logical conclusion is that Luke wrote Luke–Acts.

The date of Luke's writing can only be guessed from inferences. Luke tells us that he drew upon earlier accounts, some of which were written (1:2). It is likely that two such accounts were Q (about A.D. 50) and the Gospel of Mark (about A.D. 60). The Gospel of Luke probably was written sometime shortly after A.D. 70.

Historical Setting.

Luke was written by a Gentile for Gentiles. The author substitutes Greek expressions for nearly all Jewish expressions (*amen* is one of the few exceptions), and he seldom appeals to Old Testament prophecy. When Luke occasionally quotes from the Old Testament, he usually uses quotations that show that "all flesh [Gentiles as well as Jews] shall see the salvation of God" (3:6). Furthermore, we know that Christianity encountered increasingly hostile opposition in the 50s and 60s. One ancient writer referred to "a class hatred for their abominations, called Christians." It appears that Luke intended to supply influential

Romans, like Theophilus, with the solid truth about Christians. Luke shows that in every instance where Christians were suspected of sedition against Rome they were judged innocent (Luke 23:4, 14, 22; Acts 16:39; 17:9; 18:15–16; 19:37; 23:29; 25:25; 26:31).

Although Christianity was regarded by many pagans as a "mischievous superstition" that thrived on secrecy, Luke shows that Jesus associated with all sorts of people and that the early church openly proclaimed the gospel (Acts 2:14; 17:22). The truths of the Christian message did not happen in a corner (Acts 26:26), argued the apostle Paul. An implicit argument of Luke–Acts is that if Judaism had earned the toleration of the Roman Empire, then Christianity, which was the fulfillment of the Old Testament, should be granted the same status. It is reasonably certain that one of Luke's reasons for writing his gospel was to show that Christianity was neither superstitious nor subversive.

Theological Contributions.

Luke has the most universal outlook of all the gospels; he portrays Jesus as a man with compassion for all peoples. Whereas Matthew traces Jesus' genealogy back to Abraham, the father of the Hebrew people (1:2), Luke traces it back to Adam, the father of the human race (3:38). In Matthew Jesus sends his disciples "to the lost sheep of the house of Israel" (10:6) only, but Luke omits this limitation.

Luke is also the most socially-minded of the gospels. When He was in the synagogue at Nazareth, Jesus gave the keynote of His ministry by reading from Isaiah:

"The Spirit of the Lord is upon Me, Because He has anointed Me to preach the gospel to the poor. He has sent Me to heal the brokenhearted, To preach deliverance to the captives and recovery of sight to the blind, To set at liberty those who are oppressed, To preach the acceptable year of the LORD" (Is. 61:1–2).

In Luke, Jesus' life is presented as a commentary on this passage of Scripture. He blesses the poor, the hungry, those who weep, and the excluded (6:20–23). In one parable He takes the side of a beggar who sits outside the gate of a rich man (16:19–31); and in another parable He celebrates a tax collector who shies away from the Temple because of his sinfulness (18:9–14). Jesus reaches out to a widowed mother who had lost her only son (7:11–17) and to a sinful woman (7:36–50). In another parable the hero of mercy is a despised Samaritan (10:25–37); and after a healing, a Samaritan is praised for his gratitude (17:11–19). The open arms of the Father, as in the parable of the Prodigal Son (15:11–32), await all who return to Him. Jesus' identification with sinners leads Him to open His arms to them on the cross, where "He was numbered with the transgressors" (22:37).

Jesus also criticizes the rich. "Woe to you who are rich" (6:24), He says; for the tables will turn. The rich are fools because they think life consists of possessing things (12:13–21). Those wealthy enough to throw dinner parties ought to invite those who cannot repay—"the poor, the maimed, the lame, the blind"—for God will repay "at the resurrection of the just" (14:13–14).

Special Considerations.

For Luke the coming of Christ is good news; and his gospel is one of joy. The births of John and Jesus are echoed by songs of praise from Mary (1:46–55), Zacharias (1:67–79), the angels (2:14), and Simeon (2:29–32). Even the unborn leap for joy (1:44). Sad and cruel scenes will follow, but the note of joy that rings from Gabriel at the Annunciation (1:32–33) is repeated by the apostles at the end of the gospel (24:52–53).

Second, Luke is a gospel of the Holy Spirit. Unlike the other evangelists, Luke emphasizes the activity of the Spirit in the ministry of Jesus. John the Baptist and his parents are filled with the Spirit (1:15, 41, 67), as is Simeon (2:25–35). Jesus begins His ministry "in the power of the Spirit" (4:14; also 4:1, 18; 10:21), and He promises the Spirit to His disciples in their hour of need

(12:12). Jesus is not alone; the Spirit is always with Him, within Him, empowering Him to accomplish God's purpose.

Third, Luke is a gospel of prayer. The multitude prays as Zacharias serves at the altar (1:10). Mary prays at the news of salvation (1:46–55). Jesus prays at His baptism (3:21), when He chooses His disciples (6:12), at Peter's confession (9:18), and at His transfiguration (9:29). In the solitude of prayer Jesus takes the first steps of ministry (5:16) and falls to His knees on the Mount of Olives (22:39–46). He gives His final breath back to God in prayer, "Father, into Your hands I commend My spirit" (23:46).

LXX—the abbreviation for the Septuagint, the Greek translation of the Hebrew Old Testament.

MALACHI, BOOK OF—a short prophetic book of the Old Testament written to rebuke the people of Israel for their shallow worship practices. The name comes from the Hebrew word *malachi* (1:1), meaning "my messenger" or "messenger of the LORD."

Structure of the Book.

Portions of Malachi are written in the format of a debate, unlike any other book of the Bible. God first makes a statement of truth that is then denied by the people. God then refutes their argument in great detail, restating and proving the truth of His original statement (1:2–7; 2:10–17; 3:7–10). Malachi also uses questions and answers freely to focus his accusations toward the priesthood as well as the people. These features make Malachi one of the most argumentative books of the Bible.

Authorship and Date.

Some scholars believe the word "Malachi" should be interpreted as a description ("my messenger") rather than as the name of a specific person. This line of reasoning concludes that the book was written by an unknown author. But no other book of prophecy in the Old Testament was written anonymously. Although nothing else is known about this person, the weight of tradition has assumed the book was written by a prophet named Malachi. The prophecy can be specifically dated at about 450 B.C.

Historical Setting.

Malachi was addressed to the nation of Judah almost 100 years after its return from captivity in Babylon. At first the people had been enthusiastic about rebuilding Jerusalem and the temple and restoring their system of worship. But their zeal soon began to wane. They wondered about God's love for them as His Chosen People. They began to offer defective animals as sacrifices and to withhold their tithes and offerings. Malachi was written to call the people back to authentic worship of their Redeemer God.

Theological Contributions.

The prophecy of Malachi is noted for its vivid portrayal of the love of God as well as His might and power. Israel needed to be reminded of these truths at a time when widespread doubt had dashed its expectations of the Messiah.

Special Considerations.

Malachi leaves us with the feeling that the story is not yet finished, that God still has promises to fulfill on behalf of His people. After Malachi came 400 long years of silence. But when the time was right, heaven would burst forth in song at the arrival of the Messiah.

MARANATHA [mar a NATH a] (*Our Lord, come!*)—an Aramaic expression written by the apostle Paul as he concluded his first letter to the Corinthians (1 Cor. 16:22, KJV). The meaning seems to be, "Our Lord is coming soon, and he will judge all those who do not love him." The fact that Paul used an Aramaic expression in addressing the Gentile Christians of Corinth indicates that "maranatha" had become a familiar expression of Christian hope—a watchword of the imminent Second Coming of the Lord.

MARK, GOSPEL OF—the second book of the New Testament and the earliest of the four gospels, according to most New Testament scholars. The Gospel of Mark portrays the person of Jesus more by what He does than by what He says. It is characterized by a vivid, direct style that leaves the impression of familiarity with the original events.

Although Mark is the shortest of the four gospels, it pays close attention to matters of human interest. Mark is fond of linking the episodes of Jesus' ministry together with catchwords (for example, "immediately," "then"), rather than editorial comment; and frequently he interrupts a longer story by inserting a smaller one within it (Mark 5:21–43; 6:6–30; 11:12–25; 14:1–11).

Structure of the Gospel.

The Gospel of Mark can be divided roughly into two parts: Jesus' ministry in Galilee (chaps. 1–9) and Jesus' ministry in Judea and Jerusalem (chaps. 10–16). Mark begins his gospel with the appearance of John the Baptist (1:2–8), followed by the baptism of Jesus (1:9–11). He comments on the temptation of Jesus only briefly (1:12–13) and concludes his introduction by a capsule of Jesus' message, "The time is fulfilled, and the kingdom of God is at hand. Repent, and believe in the gospel" (1:15). Then follows a series of 14 brief stories depicting Jesus as a teacher, healer, and exorcist in and around His hometown of Capernaum. In these stories Jesus often is in conflict with the Jewish authorities of His day.

In chapter four Mark assembles a number of Jesus' parables. In each parable Jesus uses common experiences to tell who God is and what human beings can become. Mark then resumes the activities of Jesus as an open-air preacher and healer with a series of 17 more episodes (4:35–8:26).

The first half of the gospel reaches a climax when Jesus is en route to Caesarea Philippi and asks His disciples, "Who do men say that I am?" (8:27). Peter responds, "You are the Christ" (8:29); and Jesus then shocks the disciples by explaining that the Christ must suffer and die, and whoever desires to be His disciple must be prepared for the same (8:31–9:1). A glorious Transfiguration of Jesus immediately follows this pronouncement; it shows that the Father in heaven confirms Jesus' role as a suffering Messiah (9:2–13). Then follows another series of 23 stories as Jesus journeys to Jerusalem for the Passover.

In the various encounters included in the Gospel of Mark, Jesus tries to drive home the truth He taught at Peter's confession—that messiahship and discipleship involve suffering: "Whoever desires to become great among you shall be your servant.... For even the Son of Man did not come to be served, but to serve, and to give His life a ransom for many" (10:43, 45).

Chapter 13 contains a discourse of Jesus on the end of the age. Chapters 14–15 conclude the passion story, with accounts of Jesus' betrayal (14:1–11), His last supper with His disciples (14:12–31), His arrest (14:32–52), trial (14:53–15:20), and crucifixion (15:21–41). At the end, Jesus suffers passively "as a sheep before its shearers is silent" (Is. 53:7). In the oldest manuscripts the gospel ends with an angel announcing the resurrection of Jesus (16:1–8).

Authorship and Date.

The Gospel of Mark nowhere mentions the name of its author. The earliest witness to identify the author was Papias (A.D. 60–130), a bishop of Hierapolis in Asia Minor (Turkey). Papias called him Mark, an interpreter of Peter. Papias then added that Mark had not followed Jesus during His lifetime, but later had written down Peter's recollections accurately, although not always in their proper order. Subsequent tradition unanimously agrees with Papias in ascribing this gospel to Mark.

The Mark believed to have written this gospel is John Mark. He was a native of Jerusalem (Acts 12:12), and later became an associate of both Peter (1 Pet. 5:13) and Paul (2 Tim. 4:11). Eusebius tells us that Mark composed his gospel in Rome while in the services of Peter. There are good reasons to accept this report. The gospel has many characteristics of an eyewitness account, for which Peter would have been responsible (1:29–31). Moreover, it is unlikely that the early church would have assigned a gospel to a minor figure like John Mark unless he in fact were its author, since the books of the New Testament normally required authorship by an apostle to qualify for acceptance in the Canon. It may be that as a youth Mark was present at the arrest of Jesus and that he has left an anonymous signature in the story of the young man who fled naked (14:51–52). If Mark composed his gospel while in the services of Peter, and Peter died in Rome between A.D. 64 and A.D. 68, then the gospel would have been written in Italy in the early 60's.

Historical Setting.

The Gospel of Mark is evidently written for Gentiles, and for Romans in particular. Mark translates Aramaic and Hebrew phrases (3:17; 5:41; 7:34; 14:36); he transliterates familiar Latin expressions into Greek, for example, *legio* (5:9), *quadrans* (12:42), *praetorium* (15:16), *centurio* (15:39). Moreover, Mark presents Romans in a neutral (12:17; 15:1–10), and sometimes favorable (15:39), light. The emphasis on suffering in the gospel may indicate that Mark composed his gospel in order to strengthen Christians in Rome who were undergoing persecutions under Nero.

Theological Contribution.

Mark begins his gospel with the statement, "The beginning of the gospel [good news] of Jesus Christ, the Son of God" (1:1); and the last human to speak in the gospel is the centurion who confesses at the cross, "Truly this Man was the Son of God!"

(15:39). One of Mark's key objectives is to portray Jesus as God's Son. At decisive points in his story, he reveals the mystery of Jesus' person. At the baptism (1:11) and transfiguration (9:7) the Father in heaven calls Jesus "My beloved Son," thus indicating that Jesus shares a unique relationship with the Father. Demons recognize Jesus as God's Son, too (1:24; 3:11; 5:7), testifying that Jesus is equipped with God's authority and power.

Mark, however, is careful to avoid portraying Jesus as an unrealistic superstar whose feet do not touch the ground. The Son of God is not immune from the problems of life, but enters fully into them. He must be obedient to the will of the Father, even to death on a cross. Mark portrays Jesus according to the model of the Suffering Servant of Isaiah. Thus, Jesus tells a parable, which ultimately reflects His own fate: the only son of the owner of a vineyard suffers rejection and death at the hands of rebellious tenant farmers (12:1–12).

Furthermore, Mark does not emphasize Jesus' deity at the expense of His humanity. Jesus appears sorrowful (14:34), disappointed (8:12), displeased (10:14), angry (11:15–17), amazed (6:6), and fatigued (4:38). In no other gospel is Jesus' humanity presented as strongly as in the Gospel of Mark.

For Mark, faith and discipleship have no meaning apart from following the suffering Son of God. Faith is not a magic that works independently of the believer's participation (6:1–6); rather, it draws the believer into intimate union with Jesus as Lord (9:14–29). Jesus' disciples are to be with Him as He is with the Father, and they are given the same tasks of proclamation and power over the forces of evil as He had (3:13–15; 6:7).

As the Son of Man serves in self-abasement, so too must His disciples serve (10:42–45). Discipleship with Christ leads to self-denial and suffering: "Whoever desires to come after Me, let him deny himself, and take up his cross, and follow Me" (8:34). This, however, is not a matter of a religious desire to suffer; rather, when we lose our lives, we find them in Christ (8:35).

Thus, we can only know and confess Jesus as God's Son from the vantage point of the cross (15:39). It is only through the Son of God who suffers and dies that we may see into the heart of God (symbolized by the tearing of the temple curtain, thus exposing the Holy of Holies) and enter into fellowship with the Father.

Special Considerations.

The ending of the Gospel of Mark poses a problem. The two oldest and most important manuscripts of the Greek New Testament (Sinaiticus and Vaticanus) end with the words, "For they were afraid" (16:8). Other manuscripts add, in whole or in part, the material making up verses 9–20. This longer ending, however, is unlike Mark 1:1–16:8 in style and content; it contains material presented exactly as it is in Matthew and Luke. It has long been debated whether Mark intended to end his gospel at 16:8, or whether the original ending was lost and a secondary ending (vv. 9–20) was later added.

The following observations suggest that Mark originally did not end at 16:8, and that the original ending was either lost (for example, the final section of a scroll or codex misplaced or destroyed) or left unfinished (for example, due to Mark's death).

First, it seems unlikely that, having begun the gospel with a bold introduction (1:10) Mark would end it on a note of fear (16:8). Considering the centrality of Jesus throughout the gospel, one would expect an appearance of the resurrected Christ rather than just an announcement of His resurrection.

Second, Mark's Gospel conforms in broad outline to the preaching pattern of the early church—except for the shorter ending at 16:8. It would seem logical that one who drafted a gospel along the lines of the early Christian preaching would not have omitted a central feature like the resurrection (1 Cor. 15:3–26).

Third, the longer, later ending (vv. 9–20) testifies that the early tradition was dissatisfied with the shorter ending of Mark.

Finally, why would Matthew and Luke, both of whom normally follow Mark's report, depart from him at the resurrection appearances unless the ending of Mark was somehow defective? These reasons suggest that the shorter ending of Mark (at 16:8) is not the original (or intended) ending—for whatever reason—and that verses 9–20 are a later addition supplied to compensate for the omission.

Another feature of Mark's Gospel concerns the "messianic secret." Often following a miracle, Jesus commands persons healed, onlookers, disciples, and even demons to silence (1:34; 1:44; 3:12; 5:43; 7:36; 8:26; 8:30; 9:9). It has long puzzled readers why Jesus, who came into the world to make Himself known, would work at cross-purposes with His mission by trying to remain hidden.

The puzzle can be explained in part by realizing that Jesus' command to silence was intended to protect Himself from false expectations of the Messiah that were current at that time. For most of Jesus' contemporaries, "messiah" brought up pictures of a military hero overthrowing the Roman rule of Palestine. Jesus had no intention to take up the warrior's sword; rather, He took up the servant's towel.

Another reason why Jesus tried to conceal His miraculous power was because He realized that faith could not be forced upon people by a spectacle (Matt. 4:5–7). Not sight but insight into Jesus' life and purpose could evoke true faith.

Finally, Jesus demanded silence because no title or label could convey Him adequately. Saving knowledge of Jesus needed to come through personal experience with Him. Indeed, until Jesus died on the cross He could not rightly be known as God incognito who reveals Himself to those who are willing to deny self and follow Him in costly discipleship.

MATTHEW, GOSPEL OF—the opening book of the New Testament. Matthew has had perhaps a greater influence on Christian worship and literature than any other New Testament writing. For 17 centuries the church took its readings for Sundays and Holy Days from Matthew, drawing from the other gospels only where it felt Matthew was insufficient.

Matthew offers the most systematic arrangement of Jesus' teaching in the New Testament, and the early church used it heavily for its instruction of converts. Because of its emphasis on the fulfillment of Old Testament prophecy, Matthew is well suited as the opening book of the New Testament. In it the promises of God are recalled and their fulfillment in Jesus Christ is announced.

Structure of the Gospel.

The Gospel of Matthew contains five main sections. Each section consists of stories of Jesus' life, samples of His preaching and teaching, and a concluding refrain, "When Jesus had ended" (7:28; 11:1; 13:53; 19:1; 26:1). The story of Jesus' birth (chaps. 1–2) and the account of his betrayal, trial, and crucifixion (chaps. 26–28) stand outside this framework; they introduce and conclude the story of Jesus.

Section one begins with Jesus' baptism by John, His temptation, and the beginnings of His Galilean ministry (chaps. 3–4). The Sermon on the Mount (chaps. 5–7) follows; in it Jesus sets forth a new system of ethics, both individual and social, for the kingdom. Throughout the Sermon, Jesus contrasts the law, which was given by Moses, with the kingdom, which is present in Himself—showing the superiority of the kingdom. He highlights the contrast with two recurring phrases, "You have heard that it was said to those of old ... but I say to you."

Section two begins with a series of miracles by Jesus (chaps. 8–9), continues with Jesus' teaching to His disciples concerning mission and suffering (chap. 10), and ends with the refrain (11:1). Section three contains stories that emphasize the difference between the ways of the kingdom and the ways of the world (chaps. 11–12) and parables on the nature of the kingdom (chap. 13). The refrain is repeated in 13:53, thus concluding the section.

Section four features further miracles, debates, and conflicts from Jesus' ministry (chaps. 14–17). It concludes with words of counsel directed by Jesus to His disciples about the Christian life (chap. 18). The section ends at 19:1.

Section five is set in Jerusalem, and it recounts clashes between Jesus and the religious leaders (chaps. 19–22). In the discourses which follow, Jesus denounces the scribes and Pharisees (chap. 23), teaches of the end times (chap. 24), and tells three parables on judgment (chap. 25). The final refrain occurs in 26:1, and leads into the account of the betrayal, arrest, crucifixion, and resurrection of Jesus (chaps. 26–28).

The Gospel of Matthew concludes with Jesus' command to go into all the world and make disciples, baptizing and teaching them in His name. He leaves His disciples with this assurance: "Lo, I am with you always, even to the end of the age" (28:20).

Authorship and Date.

Matthew is an anonymous gospel. Like other gospel titles, the title was added in the second century A.D. and reflects the tradition of a later time. How, then, did the gospel acquire its name? Writing about A.D. 130, Papias, bishop of Hierapolis in Asia Minor (modern Turkey), records, "Matthew collected the oracles in the Hebrew (that is, Aramaic) language, and each interpreted them as best he could." Until comparative studies of the gospels in modern times, the church understood "oracles" to refer to the first gospel and considered Matthew, the apostle and former tax collector (9:9; 10:3), to be the author.

This conclusion, however, is full of problems. Our Gospel of Matthew is written in Greek, not Aramaic (as Papias records); and no copy of an Aramaic original of the gospel has ever been found. The Greek of the gospel cannot readily be translated back into Aramaic; and this strongly indicates that the gospel is not a Greek translation of an Aramaic original. It is now generally agreed that Mark is the earliest of the four gospels and that the author of Matthew substantially used the Gospel of Mark in writing this gospel.

If the apostle Matthew wrote the gospel, one would wonder why he quoted so extensively from Mark (601 of Mark's 678 verses appear in Matthew), who was not a disciple of Jesus. Such observations virtually eliminate the possibility of the apostle Matthew being the author of the gospel.

The most promising way out of this dead-end street is to understand the "oracles" mentioned by Papias, not as the Gospel of Matthew, but as a collection of Jesus' sayings collected by the apostle Matthew. Later these sayings were used by an unknown author as a source for the present Gospel. The actual author probably was a Palestinian Jew who used the Gospel of Mark, plus a Greek translation of Matthew's Aramaic "oracles," and composed the gospel in Greek. The name of the gospel, therefore, stems from the apostle Matthew on whom the author draws, in part, to compose his work. This interpretation has the benefit of paying Papias' testimony the respect it deserves, as well as honoring the problems mentioned above.

Historical Setting.

The Gospel of Matthew is full of clues that it was written to convince Jewish readers that Jesus is the Messiah. First, the author makes no attempt to translate or explain Jewish words and practices. Also, the gospel quotes more frequently from the Old Testament than does any other gospel. Most important, however, Jesus is portrayed as a physical and/or spiritual descendant of the three greatest personalities of the Old Testament, although he surpasses them. Matthew traces Jesus' genealogy back to Abraham (1:2), the father of the faith.

In the Sermon on the Mount (chaps. 5–7), Jesus appears as a royal teacher whose authority exceeds that of Moses, the founder of the faith. And Jesus fulfills the hopes of David, the greatest king of Israel. He is born in Bethlehem (mentioned five times in chap. 2), and like David he appears as a king (19:28). He is frequently recognized as "the son of David" (9:27; 12:23; 15:22; 21:9; 21:15), although in truth He is David's "Lord" (22:41–46).

Matthew appealed to a Jewish audience, but not exclusively. The visit of the wise men from the (Gentile) East (2:1–12) hints of the gospel's rejection by the Jews and its acceptance by the Gentiles (21:43; also 4:15–16; 8:5–13; 12:18–21; 13:38). Furthermore the Great Commission—the command to "make disciples of all the nations" (28:19)—indicates an interest beyond the confines of Judaism. We can conclude that Matthew was written to Jews and Jewish Christians to show that Jesus is the promised Messiah of the Old Testament. It also shows that the gospel does not lead to narrow Jewish concerns (chap. 23), but out into the Gentile world.

Theological Significance.

Matthew's main subject is the "kingdom of heaven" or "kingdom of God." This kingdom is mentioned 51 times in the Gospel of Matthew, twice as often as in any other gospel. The kingdom is already here in Jesus (12:28), but it is not yet fulfilled (13:43; 25:34). The kingdom cannot be earned (19:23); it can be received only by those who recognize that they do not deserve it (5:3; 21:31). The kingdom extends like a fishing net, gathering people from every part of society (13:47), offering new life in the life-changing presence of God (8:11). The kingdom is more valuable than a precious gem (13:45–46), and it excludes any and all competitors for its allegiance (6:33).

The kingdom of God means the rule or reign of God—in the entire universe, in the world, and in our hearts. The primary indication of the presence of the kingdom in the world is the transformation of life, both individually and socially. A person enters the kingdom not by saying the right words, but by doing "the will of My father in heaven" (7:21).

Special Considerations.

The Gospel of Matthew has at least five special considerations that will be mentioned briefly here:

1. Matthew sought to prove to the Jews that Jesus was the Christ, the fulfillment of Old Testament prophecy. A recurring statement that occurs in this gospel is, "All this was done that it might be fulfilled which was spoken by the Lord through the prophet" (1:22; also 2:15, 17, 23).

2. Matthew has a special interest in the church, which by the time this gospel was written had become the dominant factor in the lives of Christians. Indeed, Matthew is the only gospel to mention the word "church" (16:18; 18:17).

3. Matthew has a strong interest in eschatology (the doctrine of last things)—that is, in the second coming of Jesus, the end of the age, and the final judgment (chaps. 24–25).

4. Matthew has a great interest in the teachings of Jesus, especially concerning the kingdom of God (chaps. 5–7; 10; 13; 18; 24–25).

5. Matthew writes to show that Jesus is the King to whom God has given power and authority to redeem and to judge mankind (1:1–17; 2:2; 21:1–11; 27:11, 37; 28:18).

MENE, MENE, TEKEL, UPHARSIN [MEE neh, MEE neh, TEK uhl, ue FAR sin] (*numbered, numbered, weighed, and divided*)—a puzzling inscription that appeared on the wall of the palace of Belshazzar, king of Babylon, during a drunken feast (Dan. 5:1–29). The king had just ordered that the gold and silver vessels Nebuchadnezzar had stolen from the temple in Jerusalem be used in the revelry. When the fingers of a man's hand had written the words, Belshazzar called his wise men, but they could neither read the inscription nor interpret its meaning. Daniel was then summoned. He deciphered the message and told the king what it meant.

The words of the inscription refer to three Babylonian weights of decreasing size and their equivalent monetary values. In his interpretation of this inscription, Daniel used a play on words to give the message God had for Belshazzar and Babylon.

"Mene: God has numbered your kingdom, and finished it." God had counted the days allotted to Belshazzar's rule and his time had run out. "Tekel: You have been weighed in the balances and found wanting." Belshazzar's character, his moral values and spiritual worth, had been evaluated and he was found to be deficient. "Peres: Your kingdom has been divided, and given to the Medes and Persians." Belshazzar's empire had been broken into bits and pieces, dissolved and destroyed.

Some scholars have suggested that in referring to three weights listed in declining order, Daniel may have been referring to the declining worth of various Babylonian kings. Thus, the great king Nebuchadnezzar perhaps was symbolized by the mina, Evil-Merodach by the shekel (in other words, only one 50th as great as Nebuchadnezzar), and Nabonidus and Belshazzar (father and son respectively, who reigned as co-regents) were half-shekels—implying that it took two "half-regents" to equal one Evil-Merodach.

The overall impact of Daniel's double meaning in these words was to point out that the degeneration of the rulers of Babylon cried out for God's judgment. That very night Belshazzar was killed and Babylon was conquered by the Persians.

MICAH, BOOK OF—a brief prophetic book of the Old Testament, known for its condemnation of the rich because of their exploitation of the poor. Micah also contains a clear prediction of the Messiah's birth in Bethlehem, centuries before Jesus was actually born in this humble little village. The book takes its title from its author, the prophet Micah, whose name means, "Who is like the Lord?"

Structure of the Book.

Micah is a short book of only seven chapters, but it stands as a classic example of the work to which the Old Testament prophets were called. Over and over again, Micah sounds the theme of God's judgment against his homeland, Judah, as well as her sister nation, Israel, because of their moral decline. Micah watched as the Assyrians grew in strength and marched their armies throughout the ancient world. It was clear to him that this pagan nation would serve as the instrument of God's judgment unless Judah and Israel turned back to God.

Micah also is known as the champion of the oppressed. He condemns wealthy landowners for taking the land of the poor (2:2). He also attacks dishonest merchants for using false weights, bribing judges, and charging excessive interest rates. Even the priests and prophets seemed to be caught up in this tidal wave of greed and dishonesty that swept his country. To a people more concerned about observing rituals than living a life of righteousness, Micah thundered, "He has shown you, O man, what is good; and what does the LORD require of you but to do justly, to love mercy, and to walk humbly with your God?" (6:8). This is one of the greatest passages in the Old Testament. It expresses the timeless truth that authentic worship consists of following God's will and dealing justly with other people.

In addition to the theme of judgment, Micah also emphasizes the reality of God's love. Practically every passage about God's wrath is balanced with a promise of God's blessing. The greatest promise in the book is a prophecy of the birth of the Messiah: "But you, Bethlehem Ephrathah, though you are little among the thousands of Judah, yet out of you shall come forth to Me the One to be ruler in Israel" (5:2). This messianic verse is stunning in its accuracy because it names the specific town where the Messiah was born—the village of Bethlehem in the territory of the tribe of Judah. This prophecy was fulfilled about 700 years after Micah's time with the birth of Jesus in Bethlehem.

The final two chapters of Micah's book are presented in the form of a debate between God and His people. God invites the nations of Israel and Judah to reason with Him on the subject of their conduct. He convinces them that their sin is deep and grievous, but He assures them of His presence in spite of their unworthiness.

Authorship and Date.

This book was written by the prophet Micah, a native of the village of Moresheth (1:1) in southern Judah near the Philistine city of Gath. Since Micah championed the rights of the poor, he was probably a humble farmer or herdsman himself, although he shows a remarkable knowledge of Jerusalem and Samaria, the capital cities of the nations of Judah and Israel. Micah also tells us that he prophesied "in the days of Jotham, Ahaz, and Hezekiah, kings of Judah" (1:1). The reigns of these three kings stretched from about 750 B.C. to 687 B.C.; so his book was probably written sometime during this period.

Historical Setting.

The Book of Micah belongs to that turbulent period during which the Assyrians launched their drive for supremacy throughout the ancient world. Micah probably saw his prophecy of judgment against Israel fulfilled, since the Assyrians defeated this nation in 722 B.C.

The fall of Israel to the north must have stunned the citizens of Judah. Would they be the next to fall before the conquering armies of this pagan nation? Still, the religious leaders retreated into a false confidence that no evil would befall them because the Temple was situated in their capital city of Jerusalem (3:11). Micah warned there was no magical saving power in their Temple or their rituals (3:12). They needed to turn back to God as their source of strength and power.

Theological Contribution.

The mixture of judgment and promise in the Book of Micah is a striking characteristic of the Old Testament prophets. These contrasting passages give real insight into the character of God. In His wrath He remembers mercy; He cannot maintain His anger forever. Judgment with love is the ironic, but essential, work of the Lord. In the darkest days of impending judgment on Israel and Judah, there always was the possibility that a remnant would be spared. God was determined to maintain His holiness, and so He acted in judgment on those who had broken His covenant. But He was just as determined to fulfill the promises He had made to Abraham centuries earlier. This compelled Him to point to the fulfillment of the covenant in the kingdom to come.

Perhaps the greatest contribution of the Book of Micah is its clear prediction of a coming Savior. The future Messiah is referred to indirectly in some of the prophetic books of the Old Testament. But He is mentioned directly in the Book of Micah.

This prophecy of the Messiah's birth is remarkable when we think of the circumstances that were necessary to bring it to fulfillment. Although they were residents of Nazareth, Mary and Joseph happened to be in Bethlehem at the right time when the Messiah was born about 700 years after Micah's prediction. This is a valuable lesson on the providence of God. He always manages to work His will through a unique combination of forces and events.

Special Considerations.

Micah begins his words of judgment with calls for the people to come to court. God is portrayed as the prosecuting attorney, the witness for the prosecution, and the sentencing judge. God is a witness against His people (1:2); He demands justice (3:1); He even calls upon the elements of creation to be His witnesses, since He has a legal dispute against His people (6:1–2). This type of language is also found in the Book of Isaiah (Is. 1:2). It is likely that Isaiah and Micah drew this terminology from the Book of Deuteronomy (Deut. 31:28). The clear implication is that God has the right to hold His people accountable for their behavior.

God insists that His people keep their part of the covenant agreement. But even while making His demands, He holds out the possibility of grace and forgiveness. This leads his Covenant People to declare: "You will cast all our sins into the depths of the sea. You will give truth to Jacob and mercy to Abraham, which You have sworn to our fathers from days of old" (7:19–20).

MIDRASH [MID rash] (*inquiry*)—any of a group of Jewish commentaries on the Hebrew Scriptures written between A.D. 400 and A.D. 1200. The word Midrash is based on a Hebrew word that means "to search out." The implication is that of discovering a thought or truth not seen on the surface—therefore a study, commentary, or homiletical exposition.

Midrashim (plural of Midrash) are a collection of public sermons, stories, legal discussions, and meditations on the books of the Bible used during the festivals for public worship in the synagogues. Midrashim were written in Israel and Babylon by the rabbis. Some Mid-rashim are contained in the Babylonian Talmud; others are part of independent collections of commentaries.

There are two types of Midrash: Halakah ("law" or "tradition"), an interpretation of the laws of the Scriptures, and Haggadah ("narration"), the nonlegal, or homiletical, part of the Talmud.

MISHNA [MISH nah] (*repetition*)—the first, and basic, part of the Talmud and the written basis of religious authority for traditional Judaism. The Mishna contains a written collection of traditional laws (halakoth) handed down orally from teacher to student. It was compiled across a period of about 335 years, from 200 B.C. to A.D. 135.

The Mishna is grouped into 63 treaties, or tractates, that deal with all areas of Jewish life—legal, theological, social, and religious—as taught in the schools of Palestine. Soon after the Mishna was compiled, it became known as the "iron pillar of the Torah," since it preserves the way a Jew can follow the Torah.

For many Jews, the Mishna ranks second only to the canon of the Hebrew Scriptures. Indeed, many Jews consider it part of the Torah. Because it is the core for both the Jerusalem and Babylonian Talmuds, the Mishna serves as a link between Jews in the land of Israel and Jews scattered around the world.

N

N AHUM, BOOK OF—a short prophetic book of the Old Testament that foretells the destruction of the nation of Assyria and its capital city, Nineveh.

Structure of the Book.

The book opens with a brief identification of the prophet Nahum. Then it launches into a psalm of praise that celebrates the power and goodness of God. This comforting picture is contrasted with the evil deeds of the Assyrians. With graphic language, Nahum presents a prophetic picture of the coming judgment of God. He informs the nation of Assyria that its days as a world power are drawing to a close. In an oracle of woe, the prophet describes Nineveh as a "bloody city, full of lies and robbery" (3:1). But soon the city of Nineveh will be laid waste, and Assyria will crumble before the judgment of God.

Authorship and Date.

This book was written by a prophet known as "Nahum the Elkoshite" (1:1). This brief identification tells us all we know about this spokesman for the Lord. Even the location of his home, Elkosh, is uncertain, although some scholars believe he may have lived in northern Judah. The book can be dated with reasonable accuracy. Nineveh fell, as Nahum predicted, about

612 B.C. Therefore, the book was probably written shortly before this time.

Historical Setting.

For more than 100 years before Nahum's day, Assyria had been one of the dominant powers of the ancient world. The northern kingdom of Israel fell to Assyrian forces in 722 B.C. Some prophets taught that this pagan nation was used as an instrument of God's judgment against His wayward people. But now it was Assyria's turn to feel the force of God's wrath. The armies of Nabopolassar of Babylon stormed Nineveh in 612 B.C.

The entire Assyrian Empire crumbled three years later under the relentless assault of this aggressive Babylonian ruler. Thus, as Nahum prophesied, Assyria's day of dominance ended with their humiliation by a foreign power.

Theological Contribution.

This book teaches the sure judgment of God against those who oppose His will and abuse His people. Acts of inhumanity are acts against God, and He will serve as the ultimate and final judge. God sometimes uses a pagan nation as an instrument of His judgment, just as He used the Assyrians against the nation of Israel. But this does not excuse the pagan nation from God's laws and requirements. It will be judged by the same standards of righteousness and holiness that God applies to all the other people of the world.

Special Considerations.

By a strange irony, the city in Galilee most closely associated with the ministry of Jesus was Capernaum. The name Capernaum in the Hebrew language means "the village of Nahum."

Some people wonder about the gloomy, pessimistic tone of the Book of Nahum. How can this picture of God's wrath and judgment be reconciled with the God of grace and love whom we meet in the New Testament? As the sovereign, all-powerful God, He has the right to work His purpose in the world. Judgment against sin is a part of the work He must do in order to remain a just and holy God.

Nahum's announcement of God's approaching judgment also carries a call for holy living and faithful proclamation by God's Covenant People. Our work is to carry the message of His salvation to those who are surely doomed unless they turn to God in repentance and faith.

NEHEMIAH, BOOK OF—a historical book of the Old Testament that describes the rebuilding of the city walls around Jerusalem. The book is named for its major personality, a Jewish servant of a Persian king and effective leader, who organized and guided the building project.

Structure of the Book.

Nehemiah was serving as cupbearer to the Persian king Artaxerxes (1:11–2:1) in 445 B.C., when he received distressing news about his native land. Jerusalem's wall was still in ruins, although the project to rebuild the city and its beautiful Temple had been under way for many years. So Nehemiah went to Jerusalem himself on special assignment from the king to oversee the building project. In spite of harassment by their enemies, Nehemiah rallied the people to the challenge and completed the wall in less than two months.

Nehemiah remained as Persian governor of Jerusalem for the next 12 years, leading the people in several important religious reforms. The priest Ezra assisted Nehemiah in interpreting God's Law for His people. He had accompanied a group of captives back to Jerusalem about 13 years before Nehemiah arrived on the scene.

Authorship and Date.

As written originally in the Hebrew language, Nehemiah was connected to the books of First and Second Chronicles and Ezra. The material in these books formed one unbroken book, perhaps written by the priest Ezra. The purpose of this work was to show how God's blessings sustained his Covenant People after they returned to their native land following the years of captivity in Babylonia and Persia. Most conservative scholars, however, believe Nehemiah contributed some of the material that appears in the book that bears his name. This is the only logical explanation for chapters 1–7 and 11–13, which are written by Nehemiah as a first-person report. Ezra could have picked up these passages from Nehemiah's personal diary.

Historical Setting.

The Book of Nehemiah is set in that crucial time in Jewish history known as the postexilic period. These were the years after the return of the Covenant People to their homeland in 538 B.C. following 70 years of Captivity in Babylonia and Persia. At first the exiles were excited about rebuilding their lives and restoring their city; but the work was slow and tiring, and the living conditions were primitive. Their enemies often exploited them in their plight. These were the desperate circumstances that motivated Nehemiah to return to Jerusalem to encourage his countrymen.

Theological Contribution.

Nehemiah is an excellent case study in courageous, resourceful leadership. Against overwhelming odds, he encouraged the people to "rise up and build" (2:18). Their rapid completion of the wall has been an inspiration to countless Christians across the centuries who have faced the challenge of completing some major task to the glory of God.

Nehemiah also teaches that prayer is an important part of the faith of every follower of God. At several crucial points in his book, he prayed for God's direction (1:5–11; 2:1–20; 4:1–14; 6:9–14). If this courageous leader needed to claim God's strength and guidance through prayer, how much more fervently should we pray for God's will to be done through us as we face the important decisions of life! Nehemiah is an excellent object lesson on the power of prayer for all believers.

Special Considerations.

Scholars have debated who returned to Jerusalem first, Ezra or Nehemiah. But the Bible makes it plain that Ezra arrived about 13 years before Nehemiah. Ezra went back to Jerusalem in the seventh year of King Artaxerxes' reign (Ezra 7:8), while Nehemiah returned during this Persian king's 20th year (Neh. 2:1). The debate arises because of the account of the religious revival under Ezra, which is inserted as chapters 8–10 of Nehemiah.

Perhaps there is a simple reason why this "Ezra story" was included in the Book of Nehemiah. It was used to emphasize the truth that rebuilding the Law of God in the hearts of the people was just as important as rebuilding a wall of stone around the nation's capital city. This was a spiritual, lifesustaining wall that no enemy could batter down.

NEW TESTAMENT—the second major division of the Bible. It tells of the life and ministry of Jesus and the growth of the early church. The word "testament" is best translated as "covenant." The New Testament embodies the new covenant of which Jesus was Mediator (Jer. 31:31–34; Heb. 9:15). This new covenant was sealed with the atoning death of Jesus Christ.

The 27 books of the New Testament were formally adopted as the New Testament canon by the Synod of Carthage in A.D. 397, thus confirming three centuries of usage by spiritually sensitive members of various Christian communities.

NUMBERS, BOOK OF—an Old Testament book that traces the Israelites through their long period of wandering in the wilderness as they prepared to enter the Promised

Land. Numbers takes its name from the two censuses or "numberings" of the people recorded in the book (chaps. 1 and 26). But Numbers contains a great deal more than a listing of names and figures.

Structure of the Book.

Numbers is actually a sequel to the Book of Exodus. Exodus follows the Hebrew people as they escape from slavery in Egypt and cross the wilderness, arriving finally at Mount Sinai, where they receive the Ten Commandments and other parts of God's Law. The Book of Numbers picks up this story with the people still encamped at Sinai. It follows their wanderings through the Wilderness of Sinai for the next 40 years until they finally arrive at Moab on the eastern side of the Jordan River, ready to occupy the land of Canaan. Thus, the books of Exodus and Numbers together show how an enslaved people were prepared to take possession of the land that God himself had promised many centuries earlier to Abraham and his descendants.

Just as Moses is the central figure in Exodus, he also is the dominant personality in Numbers. His leadership ability is pushed to the limit in Numbers as the people grumble about everything from the food they have to eat to the water supply. Time after time God supplied their needs by sending manna, quail, and water; but still they cried out in a stubborn spirit. Finally, in exasperation, Moses struck a rock with his rod to produce drinking water. This was a clear violation of God's command, since He had instructed Moses to speak to the rock, not strike it. Because of his disobedience, Moses was not allowed to enter the Promised Land. He died shortly after viewing the land at a distance from atop Mount Nebo in Moab (Deuteronomy 34).

Historical Setting.

The events in the Book of Numbers cover a span of about 39 or 40 years in Israel's history—from 1445 B.C., when they left their encampment at Mount Sinai, to 1405 B.C., when they entered the land of Canaan by crossing the Jordan River near Jericho. These were years of preparation as well as punishment. Their harsh life in the desert wilderness prepared them for the task of pushing out the Canaanites.

The Book of Numbers clearly shows why the Israelites did not proceed immediately to take the land after leaving Mount Sinai. Moses chose 12 spies or scouts and sent them into Canaan along its southern border to explore the land and check its defenses. Ten of them returned with a pessimistic report about the war-like Canaanites who held the land. But two of the spies, Joshua and Caleb, encouraged the people to take the land; for God had promised to prepare the way. When the Israelites refused, God sentenced them to two generations of aimless wandering in the wilderness before they could enter the Promised Land (Num. 14:1–38).

Authorship and Date.

Numbers is one of the first five books of the Old Testament—books that have traditionally been assigned to Moses as author. He is the central personality of the book, and it is reasonable to assume that he wrote about these events in which he played such a prominent role. One passage in Numbers states, "Now Moses wrote down the starting points of their journeys at the command of the Lord" (33:2). Other similar references to Moses' writings are found throughout Numbers, giving strong support to the conviction that he wrote the book.

Moses must have written Numbers some time just before his death as the Hebrew people prepared to enter the land. This would place the time of writing at about 1404 B.C.

Theological Contribution.

The Book of Numbers presents the concept of God's correcting wrath upon His own disobedient people. Through their rebellion, the Hebrews had broken the covenant. Even Moses was not exempt from God's wrath when he disobeyed God.

But even in His wrath, God did not give up on His people. While He might punish them in the present, He was still determined to bless them and bring them ultimately into a land of their own. Even the false prophet Balaam recognized this truth about God's sovereign purpose. Balaam declared: "God is not a man, that He should lie, nor a son of man, that He should repent. Has He said, and will He not do it? Or has He spoken, and will He not make it good?" (23:19).

Special Considerations.

The Israelite warriors counted in the two censuses in the Book of Numbers have been a puzzle to Bible scholars (see chaps. 1 and 26). In each case, they add up to an army of more than 600,000. If this is correct, then the total Israelite population must have been more than 2,000,000 people. Such a figure seems out of line for this period of ancient history when most nations were small.

One explanation is that the word translated "thousands" in English meant something like units, tents, or clans in the Hebrew language. If so, a much smaller number was in mind. But other scholars believe there is no reason to question the numbers, since the Israelites did increase dramatically during their years of enslavement (Ex. 1:7–12).

OBADIAH, BOOK OF—a brief prophetic book of the Old Testament that pronounces God's judgment against the Edomites, ancient enemies of Israel. The book is the shortest in the Old Testament, containing one chapter of only 21 verses.

Structure of the Book.

In a brief introduction, the author reveals himself as the prophet Obadiah, a name meaning "servant of the Lord" or "worshiper of the Lord." He makes it clear that he has received this message directly from God. The Lord has announced that He will destroy the Edomites because they have sinned against Israel. They mocked God's Covenant People in their hour of misfortune and even participated in the destruction and looting of the capital city, Jerusalem, when it fell to a foreign power. Because of this great sin, Edom will be destroyed. But Israel, the prophet declares, will be blessed by God and restored to its native land.

Authorship and Date.

The author clearly identifies himself as the prophet Obadiah, but this is all we know about him. Several Obadiahs are mentioned in the Old Testament (1 Kin. 18:3; Ezra 8:9; Neh. 12:25), but none of these can be identified for sure as the author of this book. But at least his prophecy can be dated with greater certainty. Most scholars believe the great humiliation of Israel that the prophet mentions was the siege of Jerusalem by the Babylonians, beginning in 605 B.C. and ending with its final destruction in 586 B.C. Thus, the book must have been written shortly after the fall of the city, perhaps while the Jews were still in Captivity in Babylonia.

Historical Setting.

This book's condemnation of the Edomites is understandable when we consider the bitter feelings that had always existed between these two nations. It began centuries earlier when the twin brothers, Jacob and Esau, went their separate ways (Genesis 27; 36). Esau's descendants settled south of the Dead Sea and became known as the Edomites. Jacob's descendants settled farther north, eventually developing into the Covenant People known as the nation of Israel. The Bible reports many clashes between these two factions.

One notable example was the refusal of the Edomites to let the Israelites cross their land as they traveled toward the land of Canaan (Num. 20:14–21). But the final insult to Israel must have been Edom's participation in the looting of Jerusalem after the city fell to the Babylonians. This led the prophet Obadiah to declare, "For your violence against your brother Jacob, shame shall cover you, and you shall be cut off forever" (v. 10).

Theological Contribution.

The Book of Obadiah makes it clear that God takes His promises to His Covenant People seriously. He declared in the Book of Genesis that He would bless the rest of the world through Abraham and his descendants. He also promised to protect His special people against any who would try to do them harm (Gen. 12:1–3). This promise is affirmed in the Book of Obadiah. God is determined to keep faith with His people, in spite of their unworthiness and disobedience.

Special Considerations.

Verses 1–9 of Obadiah and Jeremiah 49:7–22 express essentially the same idea. Many of the words and phrases in these two passages are exactly alike. Some scholars believe Jeremiah drew from the Obadiah passage to emphasize God's impending judgment on Edom. If this is true, it indicates the little Book of Obadiah was taken seriously by Jeremiah, one of the great prophetic figures in Israel's history.

OLD TESTAMENT—the first of the two major sections into which the Bible is divided, the other being the New Testament. The title "Old Testament" apparently came from the writings of the apostle Paul, who declared, "For until this day the same veil remains unlifted in the reading of the Old Testament, because the veil is taken away in Christ" (2 Cor. 3:14).

The word testament is best translated "covenant." God called a people, the nation of Israel, to live in covenant with Him. The Old Testament begins with God's creation of the universe and continues by describing the mighty acts of God in and through His people. It closes about 400 years before the coming of Jesus Christ, who established a New Covenant as prophesied by the prophet Jeremiah (Jer. 31:31–34).

OMEGA [oh MAY gah]—the last letter of the Greek alphabet, used figuratively in the phrase "the Alpha and the Omega" as a title describing both God the Father and the Lord Jesus Christ (Rev. 1:8, 11).

ORACLE [OR uh cull]—a prophetic speech, utterance, or declaration. In Greek religion, an oracle was a response given by a pagan god to a human question. Oracles were uttered by persons entranced, by those who interpreted dreams, and by those who saw or heard patterns in nature. The most famous oracle, in this sense, was the Oracle at Delphi. Delphi was the shrine of Apollo—the Greek god of the sun, prophecy, music, medicine, and poetry.

The word "oracle" is used in several ways in the Bible. In the Book of Numbers it is used to describe the prophecies of Balaam the son of Beor, the soothsayer (Numbers 23–24; Josh. 13:22). The Hebrew word translated "oracle" means a "similitude, parable, or proverb." In 2 Samuel 16:23 the word "oracle" is a translation of a Hebrew word that means "word" or "utterance." It refers to a communication from God given for man's guidance.

A different Hebrew word is translated "oracle" in Jeremiah 23:33–38 (burden, KJV). This word means "a thing lifted up"; it can refer to a prophetic utterance as well as a physical burden. Jeremiah plays upon this double meaning and speaks of the prophetic oracle as a burden that is difficult to bear.

When the New Testament speaks of oracles, it sometimes refers to the Old Testament or some portion of it (Acts 7:38; Rom. 3:2). Hebrews 5:12 uses the term to speak of both the Old Testament revelation and the Word made flesh, Jesus Christ. First Peter 4:11 warns that the teacher of Christian truths must speak as one who utters oracles of God—a message from God and not his own opinions.

PARABLE—a short, simple story designed to communicate a spiritual truth, religious principle, or moral lesson; a figure of speech in which truth is illustrated by a comparison or example drawn from everyday experiences.

A parable is often no more than an extended metaphor or simile, using figurative language in the form of a story to illustrate a particular truth. The Greek word for "parable" literally means "a laying by the side of" or "a casting alongside," thus "a comparison or likeness." In a parable something is placed alongside something else, in order that one may throw light on the other. A familiar custom or incident is used to illustrate some truth less familiar.

Although Jesus was the master of the parabolic form, He was not the first to use parables. Examples of the effective use of parables are found in the Old Testament. Perhaps the best known of these is Nathan's parable of the rich man who took the one little ewe lamb that belonged to a poor man (2 Sam. 12:1–4). By means of this parable, Nathan reproved King David and convicted him of his sin of committing adultery with Bathsheba (2 Sam. 12:5–15). A wise woman of Tekoa also used a parable (2 Sam. 14:5–7) to convince King David to let his son return to Jerusalem.

Jesus' characteristic method of teaching was through parables. His two most famous parables are the parable of the lost son (Luke 15:11–32) and the parable of the Good Samaritan (Luke 10:25–37). Both parables illustrate God's love for sinners and God's command that we show compassion to all people. Actually, the parable of the lost son (sometimes called the parable of the prodigal son or the parable of the loving father) is the story of two lost sons: the younger son (typical of tax collectors and prostitutes) who wasted possessions with indulgent living, and the older son (typical of the self-righteous scribes and Pharisees) who remained at home but was a stranger to his father's heart.

Some entire chapters in the Gospels are devoted to Jesus' parables; for instance, Matthew 13—which contains the parables of the sower (vv. 1–23), the wheat and the tares (vv. 24–30), the mustard seed (vv. 31–32), the leaven (vv. 33), the hidden treasure (v. 44), the pearl of great price (vv. 45–46), and the dragnet (vv. 47–52).

Although parables are often memorable stories, impressing the listener with a clear picture of the truth, even the disciples were sometimes confused as to the meaning of parables. For instance, after Jesus told the parable of the wheat and the tares (Matt. 13:24–30), the disciples needed interpretation in order to understand its meaning (Matt. 13:36–43). Jesus sometimes used the parabolic form of teaching to reveal the truth to those who followed Him and to conceal the truth from those who did not (Matt. 13:10–17; Mark 4:10–12; Luke 8:9–10). His parables thus fulfilled the prophecy of Isaiah 6:9–10. Like a double-edged sword, they cut two ways—enlightening those who sought the truth and blinding those who were disobedient.

Most of Jesus' parables have one central point. Thus, Bible students should not resort to fanciful interpretations that find "spiritual truth" in every minute detail of the parable. The central point of the parable of the Good Samaritan is that a "hated"

Samaritan proved to be a neighbor to the wounded man. He showed the traveler the mercy and compassion denied to him by the priest and the Levite, representatives of the established religion. The one central point of this parable is that we should also extend compassion to others—even those who are not of our own nationality, race, or religion (Luke 10:25–37).

In finding the central meaning of a parable, the Bible student needs to discover the meaning the parable had in the time of Jesus. We need to relate the parable to Jesus' proclamation of the kingdom of God and to His miracles. This means that parables are more than simple folk stories; they are expressions of Jesus' view of God, people, salvation, and the new age that dawned in His ministry. A good example of this approach are the parables dealing with the four "lost" things in Luke 15:3–32: the lost sheep, the lost coin, and the two lost sons. The historical context is found in Luke 15:1–2: Jesus had table fellowship with tax collectors and sinners. The Pharisees and scribes, the "religious experts" of Jesus' day, saw such action as disgusting because, in their view, it transgressed God's holiness. If Jesus truly were a righteous man, they reasoned, then He would not associate with such people; He would keep Himself pure and separate from sinners.

In response to their murmuring, Jesus told them these parables. God rejoices more, He said, over the repentance of one sinner (those sitting with Him at table) than over "ninety-nine just persons who need no repentance" (Luke 15:7)—that is, than over the religious professionals who congratulate themselves over their own self-achieved "goodness" (see the parable of the Pharisee and the tax collector; Luke 18:9–14). Likewise, the prodigal son (Luke 15:11–24) represents the tax collectors and sinners; the older son (Luke 15:25–32) represents the scribes and Pharisees.

A major theme in Jesus' parables is the demand of following Him in authentic discipleship. In the parable of the great supper (Luke 14:15–24), Jesus showed clearly that the time for decision is now. In the parable of the unfinished tower and the king going to war (Luke 14:28–32), Jesus demanded that His followers be prepared to give up all. In the parables of the hidden treasure and the pearl of great price (Matt. 13:44–46), Jesus stated that the kingdom of heaven is of such value that all other treasures in life are of secondary worth. Jesus' parables are a call to a radical decision to follow Him.

PASTORAL EPISTLES—the name given to three letters of the apostle Paul: 1 Timothy, 2 Timothy, and Titus. They are called the pastoral epistles because they clearly show Paul's love and concern as pastor and administrator of several local churches.

Historical Setting.

The occasion for Paul's writing these three letters was the need to maintain the faith and to insure the faithfulness of the church. He charged the young pastor Timothy, "Guard what was committed to your trust" (1 Tim. 6:20). This declaration is the heart of the pastoral epistles. Here Timothy, with all the church, is charged to keep the deposit of faith—the written record or message to be carried on by the indwelling power of the Holy Spirit.

The more immediate need of the first two epistles—1 Timothy and Titus—lay in the fact that many things in Ephesus and Crete, where Timothy was serving, needed adjustment and correction. Paul, intending to advise Timothy and Titus in the faith, determined to advise others at the same time. Paul charged them to avoid heresy, hold to sound doctrine, and maintain purity and piety of life.

Authorship.

In the 19th century doubts were expressed about whether Paul actually wrote these three letters. Scholars noted alleged differences in style and vocabulary, church organization, heresies, biographical and historical situations, and theology from those found in the letters that were undisputedly written by Paul.

Linguistic objections to Pauline authorship of the pastoral epistles include certain words, phrases, or forms that appear about twice as often in the pastorals as in Paul's other letters. But this argument is inconclusive because it is impossible to prove. Paul may have chosen to speak in a different vocabulary because he was writing on other subjects and to specific church situations.

Theological objections point to an emphasis on works in the pastorals rather than on grace and faith and an apparent attack on second-century Gnosticism. Good works, however, are mentioned as the "fruit" (the natural outgrowth) of the "tree" of faith, and grace is celebrated in several passages (1 Tim. 1:14; 2 Tim. 1:9; Titus 2:11–3:7). Moreover, it is reasonable to assume that in these epistles Paul may not have been fighting a Gnosticism as advanced as some have argued.

Ecclesiastical objections have also been raised to the view that Paul wrote the pastorals. Some scholars charge that a highly structured hierarchical organization, later than the time of Paul, is reflected in the pastoral epistles. However, the elements of church organization found in the pastorals are also described elsewhere in the New Testament (Acts 20:28; Phil. 1:1).

Chronological objections revolve around the discrepancies that supposedly exist between the pastoral epistles and the Book of Acts, with the assumption that Paul was put to death at the end of his one-and-only Roman imprisonment. The charge is a very good reason for extending the life of Paul beyond the events recorded in Acts. The pastoral epistles would then be the product of Paul's fourth missionary journey and second imprisonment (1 Tim. 3:14; 2 Tim. 1:8, 16).

All the pastorals are to be taken as written by Paul because their internal evidence reflects the character and temperament of the great apostle. The evidence of the writings themselves indicates that Paul is the writer, since his name appears in the salutation of each letter (1 Tim. 1:1; 2 Tim. 1:1; Titus 1:1).

Date.

The first letter to Timothy and the one to Titus were written during travel and missionary work between Paul's two Roman imprisonments. A date somewhere between A.D. 61 and 63 can be set, because the Second Epistle to Timothy contains Paul's farewell address (2 Tim. 4:6–8), the last words from the apostle shortly before his martyrdom, generally set between A.D. 65 and 68.

Summary of Theme.

The purpose of the pastoral epistles is to admonish, instruct, and direct the recipients in their pastoral duties. These letters deal with the care and the organization of the church, the flock of God. They contain common injunctions to guard the Christian faith, to appoint qualified officials, to conduct proper worship, and to maintain discipline both personally and in the churches. They give instructions in the work of the church and show how threats to the doctrinal and moral purity of Christians should be overcome.

PENTATEUCH [PEN tuh tuke]—a Greek term meaning "five-volumed" which refers to the first five books of the Old Testament. The Jews traditionally refer to this collection as "the Book of the Law," or simply "the Law." Another word for this collection, "Torah," means "instruction, teaching, or doctrine." It describes such basic sections of the Pentateuch as parts of Exodus, Leviticus, and Deuteronomy.

This ancient division of the Law into five sections is supported by the Septuagint, a third-century B.C. translation of the

Hebrew Old Testament into Greek, and also by the Samaritan Pentateuch, which is even earlier.

The five books together present a history of humanity from creation to the death of Moses, with particular attention to the development of the Hebrew people. The activity of God receives special emphasis throughout, and the Pentateuch reveals a great deal about God's nature and His purposes for mankind.

The Pentateuch is generally divided into six major sections: (1) the creation of the world and its inhabitants (Genesis 1–11); (2) the period from Abraham to Joseph (Genesis 12–50); (3) Moses and the departure of the Israelites from Egypt (Exodus 1–18); (4) God's revelation at Sinai (Exodus 19—Numbers 10); (5) the wilderness wanderings (Numbers 11–36); and (6) the addresses of Moses (Deuteronomy 1–34).

From the time it was written, the Pentateuch was consistently accepted as the work of Moses. His specific writing or compiling activity is mentioned in the Pentateuch (Ex. 17:14; 24:4; 34:27), while in the post-exilic writings the Law, or Torah, was often attributed directly to Moses (Neh. 8:1; 2 Chr. 25:4; 35:12). This tradition was supported by Christ in New Testament times (Mark 12:26; John 7:23).

The Pentateuch was also called the Law of the Lord (2 Chr. 31:3; Luke 2:23–24) and "the Book of the Law of God" (Neh. 8:18). The word "book" should not be understood in its modern sense, for several different writing materials were used by Old Testament scribes, including papyrus and leather scrolls or sheets, pieces of broken pottery, clay tablets, and stone. The word "book" has two important usages in connection with the Law. First, it indicates that the material referred to was in written form at an early period. Second, it shows the combination of divine authorship and human transmission that gave the Law its supreme authority and made it "The Book" for the ancient Hebrews.

The Mosaic authorship of the Pentateuch was accepted without question for centuries by both Jews and Christians. Occasionally, the account of Moses' death (Deut. 34:5–8) was questioned, but in the Jewish Talmud, a collection of rabbinical laws and interpretations of the Torah, the section was said to have been written by Joshua. In the Middle Ages Jewish and Christian scholars began to point to supposed contradictions and insertions in the Law, some of the latter being credited to Ezra.

In spite of these objections, most people believed unquestioningly in Moses as the author; but criticism took on a new appearance in 1753 with a theory by Jean Astruc, a French physician, that Moses had used two principal literary sources from which he composed the Book of Genesis: one contained the divine name Elohim ("God") and the other contained the divine name Jehovah or Yahweh ("the LORD").

With the expansion of this suggestion by later authors came the increasing abandonment of belief in Mosaic authorship, and support for the view that the Pentateuch was compiled by unknown editors from a number of documents. It became common to attribute sections of the Pentateuch to late periods in Israel's history. Even the main documents from which the Pentateuch had supposedly been compiled were assigned to periods long after the time of Moses.

In the 19th century the Book of Deuteronomy began to be regarded as the law-scroll found in the time of Joshua (2 Kin. 22:8–10), and written at about that time, according to many scholars.

While more conservative thinkers rejected these conclusions, the liberal humanism of the day pushed forward with its suppositions. Allied with the views of organic evolutionists, it presented its opinions about the authorship of Genesis as "scientific." Actually, these liberal scholars were using procedures that were the exact opposite of true scientific method. But this did not prevent them from making pronouncements that amounted to rewriting history. Thus, all priestly materials in the Pentateuch were assigned to one main documentary source and regarded as late rather than early.

According to the liberal view, the tabernacle could no longer be dated in the days of Moses. It was regarded instead as a much later invention, based on the design of the Jerusalem temple, that had been put back into the Mosaic period by an anonymous compiler or editor. Israelite religion was interpreted in evolutionary terms as originating in the worship of spirits in nature, then advancing slowly from simple family sacrifices to the high view of God as the one and only true God.

This type of approach was aided by the 19th century emphasis on evolution. The liberal view found its fullest development in the supposition that the Pentateuch was compiled from four principal documents, none of which was in writing before about 850 B.C. This theory of composition, popularized by Julius Wellhausen in 1878, is still held by liberal scholars, but with slight changes in emphasis because of the pressure of more recent discoveries.

This view of the compilation of the Pentateuch has had its critics at every stage. Some of the presuppositions of the liberal position are incorrect. One example is the notion that writing was only invented about the time of David (about 1000 B.C.). Evidence to the contrary already existed in Wellhausen's day, but it was ignored. Most recently, the Ebla Tablet discoveries show that a sophisticated language was in use in the ancient world about 2400 B.C.

It is now known that all priestly pronouncements dealing with social organization in the ancient world are always early rather than late, because priests were originally responsible for such matters. Furthermore, exhaustive comparative studies have shown that no other composition of the ancient Near East was assembled in the manner that liberal scholars claimed was the case with the Pentateuch. Archaeological and linguistic studies have confirmed many old customs recorded in the Pentateuch. These discoveries have provided an excellent background against which we can understand the Law of Moses.

To date, no articles that would prove the existence of such persons as Abraham, Isaac, and Jacob have been recovered. But if the traditions about the nature and location of the cave of Machpelah (Gen. 23:17) are correct, we know the actual burial place of Abraham, Sarah, Isaac, Rebekah, and Jacob.

Studies in Genesis have shown that the book was compiled from genuine literary sources. But these are vastly different from those imagined by liberal scholarship. Generally speaking, the liberal view has failed to take account of ancient methods of compiling and transmitting information. Liberal scholars have supposed that Western editorial methods can be applied equally well to Near Eastern compositions, which is simply not true.

Whereas the 19th-century critics relied heavily upon the handing down of material by word of mouth, subsequent studies have shown that anything of importance in the ancient world was written down when it happened or shortly afterward. Furthermore, this record was quite independent of any verbal accounts passed on to later generations. Not all written or spoken material survived, of course; but enough did to provide us with the Pentateuch, as well as other Scriptures.

Finally, any suggestion that the five books of Moses are basically fraudulent in nature, not actually having been compiled or written by Moses, is contrary to Jewish tradition, as well as the nature of God as revealed in the Torah.

The five books of the Pentateuch can be described as follows:

Genesis.

This "book of beginnings" contains very ancient material, describing mankind's place in God's creation and the unfolding of human history. It begins with an account of how the universe came into existence (1:1–2:4), followed by narratives about Adam and Eve and their sin of disobedience (2:5–3:24). The descendants of Adam are described (4:1–5:32), and after this the reasons for a disastrous flood and its consequences (6:1–9:29). Nations spread across the Near East after the Flood (10:1–11:32), and Abraham became prominent after obeying God's call (12:1–25:11). Thereafter the narratives continue with Ishmael, Isaac, and Jacob (25:12–36:43), concluding with the story of Joseph's career (37:1–50:26).

Genesis is important for its theology of creation, sin, and the divine plan of salvation because it provides answers about these matters. If Scripture did not begin in this way, New Testament theology would have little foundation in history. Genesis deals with real people. Near Eastern archaeological discoveries provide an important background to the narratives that describe their activities. The covenants between God and persons such as Noah and Abraham point forward to the covenant under Moses at Mount Sinai. They also point to the new covenant in Jesus Christ.

No author is named for the Book of Genesis, although it has always been regarded as a cornerstone of the Law, and therefore probably written by Moses. In contrast to the artificial sources proposed by liberal criticism, genuine blocks of source material can be recognized in the narratives. Eleven such units can be recovered by observing the phrase "These are the generations [that is, family histories] of" at the headings of major sections. Genesis was apparently compiled by placing these units end to end.

Exodus.

This book deals with the miracle of Israel's deliverance from Egypt and with God's covenant relationship with the Israelites at Mount Sinai. Preliminaries to the departure from Egypt (Ex. 1:1–4:28) are followed by the circumstances leading up to the Exodus, including the ten plagues of Egypt and the celebrating of the first Passover (4:29–12:36). The deliverance from Egypt and the subsequent journey to Sinai (12:37–19:2) precede the giving of the Law of God through Moses (19:3–31:8), in spite of intervals of idolatry (32:1–33:23). A renewal of the covenant relationship is followed by narratives describing the construction of the tabernacle (34:1–40:38).

The Book of Exodus continues Hebrew history from the death of Joseph, showing how the sons of Jacob became a distinctive nation. The covenant was central to this event. It bound God and Israel in an agreement by which God undertook to provide for all His people's mate-rial needs, including a land in which to live, if they would worship Him alone as the one true God and live as a holy community. Central to the rules of the covenant were the Ten Commandments, which are still fundamental to any relationship with God. The tabernacle was a portable place of worship that was placed in the center of Israel's wilderness encampment, symbolizing God's presence in their midst.

Leviticus.

This is a book primarily for priests. The priests were responsible for teaching the Law to the people, conducting sacrificial worship in the tabernacle according to the directions given by God, and ordering the life of the community. Because Israel was meant to live as a holy people (Ex. 19:6), Leviticus contained regulations for both the spiritual and material aspects of life. These rules can be divided into five sections: (1) sacrificial laws (Leviticus 1–7); (2) laws governing ordination (Leviticus 8–10); (3) laws about impurities (Leviticus 11–16); (4) laws about holiness (Leviticus 17–26); and (5) rules governing vows (Leviticus 27).

All this material was divinely revealed to the nation of Israel directly from God. No part of it has been adopted from any other nation. The Year of Jubilee legislation (Lev. 25:8–17) is unique in the Near East. Leviticus continues the narrative of Exodus, but it emphasizes the way in which God is to be worshiped and the manner in which His people are to live. Holiness must govern the community (Lev. 11:44); and this must be reflected by everyone, not just the priesthood.

Numbers.

This book follows the lead given by Leviticus in emphasizing the holiness of Israel. All the various elements that make up the book bear upon this important concept. The book can be divided into three broad sections: (1) the departure from Sinai (1:1–10:10); (2) the journey to Kadesh (10:11–20:21); and (3) the journey from Kadesh to Moab (20:22–30:13). The holiness of the tabernacle is central, as is the important place that the Levites occupied (8:5–26) in relation to the Aaronic priesthood. The description of the wilderness wanderings shows how quickly divine blessing could turn to severe judgment whenever God's commandments were broken.

The disobedience and idolatry of the Israelites is a sad theme in Numbers. Even Moses was not totally obedient to God. Although he brought Israel to Moab and within sight of the Promised Land, he was not privileged to lead the nation across the Jordan River. The book ends with the nation looking forward to the settlement of Canaan.

Deuteronomy.

This book may be described as a covenant-renewal document that begins with a review of Israel's departure from Sinai (1:1–4:40); describes the religious foundation of the nation (4:44–26:19); reestablishes the covenant (27:1–30:20); and narrates the final days of Moses (31:1–34:12). In Deuteronomy Moses looks back upon God's blessing and provision while looking forward to the time when Israel will occupy the Promised Land.

The language of the book is noble oratory that glorifies the righteous and faithful God of Sinai and encourages the response of His people in obedience and faithfulness. The God revealed in Moses' addresses is not only the Judge of all the earth, but also the loving Father of mankind. Israel is reminded that the privileges of covenant relationship with Him also carry responsibilities. Moses predicts a dark future for the nation if it does not follow the covenant principles and remain faithful to God.

PERES [**PEA rez**] (*divided*)—one of the mysterious words that appeared in the handwriting on the wall in King Belshazzar's palace in Babylon (Dan. 5:28). Daniel interpreted this word to mean that Belshazzar's kingdom had been "divided" (*peres*) and given to the Medes and "Persians." This play on words is reflected in "Upharsin" (Dan. 5:25), which means "and Parsin" (the plural of Peres).

PETER, EPISTLES OF—two New Testament epistles bearing the name of "Peter, an apostle of Jesus Christ" (1 Pet. 1:1) and "Simon Peter, a servant and apostle of Jesus Christ" (2 Pet. 1:1), though otherwise having little in common.

First Peter, the longer of the two epistles, is written in fine Greek and refers frequently to the Old Testament. It is an epistle for the downhearted, written to give encouragement in times of trial and disappointment. First Peter anchors the Christian's hope not on logic or persuasion, but on the matchless sacrifice of Jesus Christ, who "suffered for us, leaving us an example, that you should follow His steps" (2:21).

In contrast to 1 Peter, 2 Peter is briefer and written in a forced style. It rails against false teachers, while reminding believers of their election by God and assuring them of Christ's return.

Structure of the Epistles.

Following a greeting (1:1–2), 1 Peter begins on a positive note, praising God for the blessings of a "living hope" that He has reserved for believers (1:3–12). This doxology of praise sets a triumphant tone for the remainder of the letter, which can be divided into three parts: blessings, duties, and trials. The blessings extend from 1:3 to 2:10. Because of the "inheritance incorruptible and undefiled … reserved in heaven for you" (1:4), Peter calls on his readers to live a life holy and blameless, reminding them that they are a "holy nation, His [God's] own special people" (2:9).

The second part of 1 Peter extends from 2:11 to 3:22. This section consists of guidance for social duties. The Christian's lifestyle ought to be a testimony to nonbelievers (2:11–17); slaves ought to obey their masters—even unjust ones—bearing their humiliation as Christ bore His (2:18–25); the silent example of a Christian wife has great effect on a non-Christian husband (3:1–6); Christian husbands are to treat their wives as joint-heirs of the grace of life (3:7). In all things, let a blameless lifestyle bring shame on whoever would show opposition (3:8–22).

The third and final part of 1 Peter addresses the question of trials (4:1–5:11). In light of the nearness of the end, Christians must be "good stewards of the manifold grace of God" (4:1–11). They can rejoice in sharing Christ's sufferings because of the glory that awaits them (4:12–19). In their pastoral duties, church elders are to follow the example of Jesus, who perfects, establishes, and strengthens the flock (5:1–11). The epistle closes with mention of Silvanus, the secretary who wrote the letter, and with greetings from "Babylon" (5:12–14).

Second Peter begins with a greeting (1:1–2), enjoining believers, because they have been chosen by God, to develop noble characters (1:3–14). Recognizing that his own death is near, the author sees in the transfiguration of Jesus a forecast of the brilliant day when Christ will come again (1:15–21). Chapter two is a condensation of material from the letter of Jude, condemning false teachers and prophets. The final chapter deals with the future coming of the Lord and the reasons for its delay (3:1–18).

Authorship and Date.

First Peter identifies its author as "Peter, an apostle of Jesus Christ" (1:1). His frequent references to Christ's suffering (2:21–24; 3:18; 4:1; 5:1) show that the profile of the Suffering Servant was etched deeply upon his memory. He calls Mark his "son" (5:13), recalling his affection for the young man and family mentioned in Acts 12:12. These facts lead naturally to the assumption that the apostle Peter wrote this letter.

Authorship of the epistle by the apostle Peter has been challenged, however, on the following grounds: (1) no official persecutions of the church took place during Peter's lifetime; (2) the epistle echoes some of Paul's teachings; and (3) the literary quality of the Greek seems too refined for a Galilean fisherman.

Valid as these objections are, they do not seriously challenge Peter's authorship of the epistle. The sufferings mentioned in the epistle need not refer to official persecutions, which did not begin until the time of the Roman emperor Domitian (A.D. 81–96), but to earlier local incidents. The last two questions are neatly resolved by recognizing the role that Silvanus (5:12) played in composing the epistle.

As a former associate of the apostle Paul, and as one who doubtless came to the Greek language as a native, Silvanus may have played an important role in bringing this epistle to completion. We might say of 1 Peter that the ideas came from Peter, but the design from Silvanus. The reference to "Babylon" (5:13), a common image for civil power opposed to God, indicates that the epistle was written from Rome.

The question of authorship of 2 Peter is more difficult. Although the epistle claims to come from the apostle Peter (1:1; 3:1–2), who witnessed the transfiguration of Christ (1:18) and at the time of writing was nearing his death (1:14), few scholars believe Peter wrote the letter. Reasons for this judgment stem from a number of factors.

The style of 2 Peter is inferior to that of 1 Peter. Nearly the whole of Jude 4–18 has been reproduced in the second chapter; if Jude were not written until late in the first century, then 2 Peter obviously could not have been written before it. Again, 2 Peter refers to Paul's epistles as a part of "the Scriptures" (3:16). This suggests a date, perhaps early in the second century, when Paul's epistles had reached a level of authority in the early church. Finally, the Epistle of 2 Peter seems to have been unknown to the early church, and it was one of the last books to be included in the New Testament. These factors suggest that 2 Peter was written by an anonymous author but attributed by someone to the apostle Peter in order to assure a hearing for a message in a time well after Peter's death.

On the other hand, most of the above objections are removed if we assume an earlier date for Jude and an earlier acceptance of a few of Paul's letters into a developing Christian canon. In short, 2 Peter was probably written by Peter just before his martyrdom during the reign of Nero (about A.D. 65).

Historical Setting.

First Peter is addressed to Christians living in "Pontus, Galatia, Cappadocia, Asia, and Bithynia" (1:1)—places in the northern and western parts of Asia Minor (modern Turkey). The readers appear to have been Gentiles (1:14, 18; 2:10; 4:3), although they probably had not been evangelized by Peter himself (1:12). The letter was obviously written to believers undergoing trials and persecutions, to give them courage in the face of their adversities (5:10).

Since it makes no mention of its audience, 2 Peter was probably intended for a general readership. Its primary purpose was to combat false teachers. Widespread in the ancient world was the view that sparks of eternal light lay trapped within the prisons of human bodies. These sparks of light, which longed to return to their primal home, could be liberated only by *gnosis,* or knowledge. Second Peter uses "knowledge" (1:5–6; 3:18) to show that only in Jesus Christ is the knowledge of God and salvation fully revealed. These false teachers also must have been critical of the delay in Christ's return. To this challenge the author devoted the entire third chapter.

Theological Contribution.

First Peter was written by one who sensed the triumphant outcome of God's purpose for the world (1:4). The triumph of the future depends in no way on what we have done but on the resurrection of Jesus Christ. Because God has raised Jesus from the dead, God is deserving of praise; for "His abundant mercy has begotten us again to a living hope" (1:3).

The unshakableness of our hope in Jesus Christ, which awaits us in heaven, resounds like a clap of thunder throughout this epistle. Because Christ has been raised from the dead, His suffering and death have meaning. The believer can gain courage in present adversity by looking to the example of Christ in His suffering. We have a sure hope for the future because of Christ's resurrection. This truly is a "living hope," for it is one we can live by, even in the midst of "various trials" (1:6).

If 1 Peter is an epistle of hope, the accent falls not on wishful thinking, but on present help. No biblical writer shows the connection between faith and conduct in a clearer manner than does Peter. "Conduct," in fact, is a key word in this epistle (1:15, 17–18; 2:12; 3:1–2, 16). For Peter, practice is the most important thing.

The conduct Peter describes is the result of a life reclaimed by the perfect power of Jesus Christ. Christ has redeemed believers (1:18–19); Christ upholds and guides them (1:8; 2:25); and Christ will reward them (5:4). Christ is both the model and goal of the redeemed life. Consequently, believers may move forward on the pilgrim way, confident that the end will rise up to meet them with joy and salvation (2:11; 4:13–14).

Jesus said, "Blessed are those who are persecuted for righteousness' sake, for theirs is the kingdom of heaven" (Matt. 5:10).

There is no better commentary on this Beatitude than the Epistle of 1 Peter. Here, too, Jesus is our sole help and our sure Lord, "who for the joy that was set before Him endured the cross" (Heb. 12:2).

Second Peter shifts the emphasis from a hope by which one can live to a hope on which one can count. The epistle speaks to the assurance of salvation in chapter one by making the extraordinary claim that Christians are "partakers of the divine nature" (1:4).

The second chapter deals with false teachers. The unique contribution of 2 Peter, however, comes in chapter three. In chapter three the "day of the Lord" (3:10) or the "day of God" (3:12) breaks through the gloom of the doubters who taunt the hopeful (3:4). Such persons may be assured that God does not delay in coming because he lacks power or concern. Rather, what the unfaithful interpret as delay, the faithful know to be patience; for God is "not willing that any should perish but that all should come to repentance" (3:9).

PHILEMON, EPISTLE TO—the shortest and most personal of Paul's epistles. Philemon tells the story of the conversion of a runaway slave, Onesimus, and the appeal to his owner, Philemon, to accept him back. The letter is warm and masterful, reminding us that the presence of Christ drastically changes every relationship in life.

Structure of the Epistle.

Philemon consists of one chapter of 25 verses. A greeting, addressed to Philemon and the church that meets in his house (vv. 1–3), is followed by four verses in praise of Philemon's love and faith (vv. 4–7). Paul comes to his point in verses 8–16, where he tells of his affection for Onesimus and entreats Philemon to receive him back as a "beloved brother" (v. 16). Paul is so confident that Philemon will do even more than he asks that he offers to pay any expenses Philemon has incurred and asks him to prepare the guest room for a forthcoming visit (vv. 17–22). Final greetings conclude the letter (vv. 23–25).

Authorship, Date, and Historical Setting.

The Epistle to Philemon is a companion to the Epistle to the Colossians. Both were written during Paul's imprisonment, probably in Rome (Col. 4:18; Philem. 9). They contain the names of the same greeters (compare Col. 4:7–17 with Philem. 23–25) and were delivered at the same time by Tychicus and Onesimus (Col. 4:7–9). The date for the two letters is the late 50s or early 60s.

Theological Contribution.

The Epistle to Philemon is a lesson in the art of Christian relationships. No finer example of "speaking the truth in love" (Eph. 4:15) exists than this beautiful letter. While it was Philemon's legal right in the ancient world to punish or even kill a runaway slave, Paul hoped—indeed expected (v. 19)— that Philemon would receive Onesimus back as a brother in the Lord, not as a slave (v. 16). From beginning to end Paul addresses Philemon as a trusted friend rather than as an adversary (v. 22); he appeals to the best in his character (vv. 4–7, 13–14, 17, 21). In spite of Paul's subtle pressures for Philemon to restore Onesimus, he is careful not to force Philemon to do what is right; he helps him choose it for himself (vv. 8–9, 14).

Special Considerations.

Although Paul never, so far as we know, called for an end to slavery, the Epistle to Philemon laid the ax at the root of that cruel and deformed institution—and to every way of treating individuals as property instead of persons. If there is "one God and Father of all" (Eph. 4:6), and if all are debtors to Him (Rom. 3:21–26), then people cannot look on another person as something to be used for their own ends. In Christ that person has become a "beloved brother."

PHILIPPIANS, EPISTLE TO THE—one of four shorter epistles written by the apostle Paul while he was in prison. The others are Ephesians, Colossians, and Philemon. Paul founded the church at Philippi (Acts 16:12–40). Throughout his life the Philippians held a special place in his heart. Paul writes to them with affection, and the epistle breathes a note of joy throughout. When Paul first came to Philippi, he was thrown in jail. In the deep of the night, bound and beaten, he sang a hymn to God (Acts 16:25). A decade later Paul was again in prison, and he still was celebrating the Christian's joy in the midst of suffering, "Rejoice in the Lord always. Again I will say, rejoice!" (Phil. 4:4).

Structure of the Epistle.

Paul begins the epistle by giving thanks for the love of the Philippians and by praying for its increase (1:1–11). Even though Paul is in prison, the gospel is not confined; on the contrary, it is increasing. Whether Paul lives or dies, "Christ is preached" (1:18); and this results in salvation (1:12–26). Following these reflections, Paul introduces a series of exhortations: to remain faithful in suffering (1:27–30); to remain considerate of others, as Jesus Christ was (2:1–11); and to avoid evil and live blamelessly (2:12–18).

Paul then turns to news of two companions. Once a decision has been reached about his trial, Paul will send Timothy to the Philippians with the news (2:19–24). For the present, he is sending back Epaphroditus, who had brought the Philippians' gift to him and who in the meantime has been critically ill (2:25–30). In chapter 3 Paul discusses the difference between true and false righteousness. Whereas the Judaizers would say, "If you do not live rightly you will not be saved," Paul teaches, "If you do not live rightly you have not been saved."

The final chapter summarizes several miscellaneous matters. Paul exhorts quarrelsome church members to rise above their differences (4:1–5). He also leaves two important lessons, on substituting thankful prayer for anxiety (4:6–7), and on the characteristics of a noble and godly life (4:8–9). He concludes with thanks for the Philippians' gift and includes final greetings (4:10–23).

Authorship.

There can be little doubt that Philippians comes from Paul. The entire epistle bears the stamp of his language and style; the setting pictures Paul's imprisonments; and the recipients correspond with what we know of the church at Philippi.

During his second missionary journey, in A.D. 49, Paul sensed the Lord calling him to visit Macedonia (Acts 16:6–10). At Philippi he founded the first Christian congregation on European soil (Acts 16:11–40). A lifelong suppor-tive relationship developed between the Philippians and Paul (Phil. 1:5; 4:15). He visited the church again during his third missionary journey (Acts 20:1, 6).

At the time he wrote Philippians, Paul was in prison awaiting trial (Phil. 1:7). The Philippian Christians came to Paul's aid by sending a gift, perhaps of money, through Epaphroditus (4:18). During his stay with Paul, Epaphroditus fell desperately ill. But he recovered, and Paul sent him back to Philippi. He sent this letter with him to relieve the anxiety of the Philippians over their beloved fellow worker (2:25–30).

Historical Setting and Date.

The location of Paul's imprisonment has been long debated. Much can be said for Ephesus or Caesarea but still more for Rome. Paul refers to "the whole palace guard" (1:13), and he even sends greetings from "Caesar's household" (4:22). These references suggest Rome, as does the description of his confinement in 1:12–18. This description is similar to Clement's description of Paul's Roman imprisonment written near the close of the first century. Paul also considers the possibility of his death (1:23). This prospect was more likely toward the end of his life in Rome than earlier. The epistle, therefore, should probably be dated about A.D. 60.

Theological Contribution.

The focus of Paul's thoughts in this epistle is the Christcentered life, the hallmark of which is joy. Paul has surrendered everything to Christ and can say, "For to me, to live is Christ" (1:21), "to be a prisoner for Christ" (1:13), "to live and die in Christ" (1:20), "and to give up all to win Christ" (3:7–8)." Christ has laid hold of Paul (3:12), and Paul's sole passion is to glorify Christ (3:8–9). Paul longs for his experience of Christ to be repeated in the lives of the Philippians. He prays that they will abound in the love of Christ (1:9), will lay hold of the mind of Christ (2:5–11), and, like himself, will know the experience of Christ—His sufferings, death, and resurrection (3:10–11).

Because Paul's only motive is to "know Him" (3:10), he shares in the power of Christ and "can do all things through Christ," who is his joy and strength (4:13). Several times in the epistle Paul exhorts the Philippians to translate their relationship with Christ into daily life by being "like-minded" with Christ or "setting their minds on Christ." In the face of opposition, Paul tells them to "stand fast ... with one mind striving together for the faith of the gospel" (1:27).

Differences between Christians can be overcome when the parties have "the same mind in the Lord" (4:2). Paul exhorts the believers to set their mind on the high calling of God in Jesus Christ (3:14–15) and to meditate on whatever is true, noble, just, pure, lovely, and of good report (4:8). To have the mind of Christ is to see life from Christ's perspective and to act toward other people with the intentions of Christ.

Special Considerations.

Nowhere is the mind of Christ presented to the Christian more strongly than in Philippians 2:1–11. Appealing to the Philippians to be of "one mind" (2:2) in pursuing humility, Paul cites the example of the incarnation of God in Jesus Christ. "Let this mind be in you which was also in Christ Jesus" (2:5), urges Paul. Unlike Adam, who sought to be equal with God (Gen. 3:5), Christ did not try to grasp for equality with God. Instead, being God, He poured Himself out and took upon Himself the form of a slave, to the point of dying the death of a common criminal. "Therefore," glories Paul, "God … has highly exalted Him, and given Him the name which is above every name" (2:9).

This is the Christ whose attitude and intention all believers must share. To be identified with Christ in humility and obedience is the noblest achievement to which anyone can aspire.

POETRY—lofty thought or impassioned feeling expressed in imaginative words. Beautiful poetry occurs in both the Old Testament and the New Testament of the Bible.

Poetry in the Old Testament.

At a very early date poetry became part of the written literature of the Hebrew people. Many scholars believe the song of Moses and the song of Miriam (Ex. 15:1–21), celebrating the destruction of Pharaoh's army in the sea, is the oldest existing Hebrew hymn or poetic work, dating perhaps from the 12th century B.C.

Three of the greatest poetic masterpieces of the Old Testament are the Song of Deborah (Judges 5); the Song of the Bow—David's lament over the death of Saul and Jonathan (2 Sam. 1:17–27)—and the Burden of Nineveh (Nah. 1:10–3:19).

Approximately forty percent of the Old Testament is written in poetry. This includes entire books (except for short prose sections), such as Job, Psalms, Proverbs, the Song of Solomon, and Lamentations. Large portions of Isaiah, Jeremiah, and the Minor Prophets are also poetic in form and content. Many scholars consider the Book of Job to be not only the greatest poem in the Old Testament but also one of the greatest poems in all literature.

The three main divisions of the Old Testament—the Law, the Prophets, and the Writings—contain poetry in successively greater amounts. Only seven Old Testament books—Leviticus, Ruth, Ezra, Nehemiah, Esther, Haggai, and Malachi—appear to have no poetic lines.

Poetic elements such as assonance, alliteration, meter, and rhyme—so common to poetry as we know it today—occur rarely in Hebrew poetry; these are not essential ingredients of Old Testament poetry. Instead, the essential formal characteristic of Hebrew poetry is parallelism. This is a construction in which the content of one line is repeated, contrasted, or advanced by the content of the next—a type of sense rhythm characterized by thought arrangement rather than by word arrangement or rhyme. The three main types of parallelism in biblical poetry are synonymous, antithetic, and synthetic.

Synonymous parallelism—A parallel segment repeats an idea found in the previous segment. With this technique a kind of paraphrase is involved; line two restates the same thought found in line one, by using equivalent expressions. Examples of synonymous parallelism are found in Genesis 4:23: "Adah and Zillah, hear my voice;/Wives of Lamech, listen to my speech!/For I have killed a man for wounding me/Even a young man for hurting me." Another example is found in Psalm 2:4: "He who sits in the heavens shall laugh;/The Lord shall hold them in derision." Yet a third example is Psalm 51:2–3: "Wash me thoroughly from my iniquityAnd cleanse me from my sin./For I acknowledge my transgressions,/And my sin is always before me." (Also see Ps. 24:1–3; 103:3, 7–10; Jer. 17:10; Zech. 9:9.)

Antithetic parallelism—By means of this poetic construction, the thought of the first line is made clearer by contrast—by the opposition expressed in the second line. Examples of antithetic parallelism may be found in Psalm 1:6: "The Lord knows the way of the righteous,/But the way of the ungodly shall perish"; in Psalm 34:10: "The young lions lack and suffer hunger;/But those who seek the Lord shall not lack any good thing"; and in Proverbs 14:20: "The poor man is hated even by his own neighbor,/ But the rich has many friends."

Synthetic parallelism—Also referred to as climactic or cumulative parallelism, this poetic construction expands the idea in line one by the idea in line two. In synthetic parallelism, therefore, there is an ascending (or descending) progression, a building up of thought, with each succeeding line adding to the first.

Here is one good example of this poetic technique: "He shall be like a tree/Planted by the rivers of water,/That brings forth its fruit in its season,/Whose leaf also shall not wither;/And whatever he does shall prosper" (Ps. 1:3).

Another poetic form found in the Old Testament is the alphabetical acrostic, a form used often in the Book of Psalms (Psalms 9–10; 25; 34; 37; 111; 112; 119; 145). In the alphabetical psalms the first line begins with the first letter of the Hebrew alphabet, the next with the second, and so on, until all the letters of the alphabet have been used. Thus, Psalm 119 consists of 22 groups of eight verses each. The number of groups equals the number of letters in the Hebrew alphabet. The first letter of each verse in a group is (in the original Hebrew text) that letter of the alphabet that corresponds to its position in the group.

Many of the subtleties of Hebrew poetry, such as puns and various plays on words, are virtually untranslatable into English and may be fully appreciated only by an accomplished Hebrew scholar. Fortunately, many good commentaries are available to explain to the layperson these riches of Hebrew thought.

The Bible is full of numerous figures of speech, such as metaphors and similes. For example, the psalmist metaphorically described God by saying, "The Lord is my rock and my fortress and my deliverer; My God, my strength, in whom I will trust; My shield and the horn of my salvation, my stronghold" (Ps. 18:2).

Moses gave this remarkable simile describing God's care of Israel in the wilderness: "As an eagle stirs up its nest,/Hovers over its young,/Spreading out its wings, taking them up,/Carrying them on its wings,/So the Lord alone led him" (Deut. 32:11–12).

Such figures of speech are not to be interpreted literally but as poetic symbolism for God. He is the firm ground of life and a solid defense against evil. The worshiper sings for joy because of His protecting presence and the soaring power of His loving care.

Poetry in the New Testament.

Very little poetry is found in the New Testament, except poetry quoted from the Old Testament or hymns that were included in the worship services of the early church. The Beatitudes (Matt. 5:3–10; Luke 6:20–26) have a definite poetic form. The Gospel of Luke contains several long poems: Zacharias' prophecy, known as the *Benedictus* (Luke 1:68–79); the song of Mary, known as the *Magnificat* (Luke 1:46–55); the song of the heavenly host, known as the *Gloria* in Excelsis (Luke 2:14); and the blessing of Simeon, known as the *Nunc* Dimittis (Luke 2:29–32). Examples of parallelism may be found in the New Testament. For instance, synonymous parallelism occurs in Matthew 7:6: "Do not give what is holy to the dogs, nor cast your pearls before swine." Antithetic parallelism occurs in Matthew 8:20: "Foxes have holes and birds of the air have nests, but the Son of Man has nowhere to lay His head." Synthetic parallelism occurs in John 6:32–33: "Moses did not give you the bread from heaven, but My Father gives you the true bread from heaven. For the bread of God is He who comes down from heaven and gives life to the world."

In the writings of the apostle Paul several poetic passages may be found: his lyrical celebration of God's everlasting love (Rom. 8:31–39); his classic hymn to love (1 Corinthians 13); his glorious faith in the triumph of the resurrection (1 Cor. 15:51–58); and his thoughts on the humbled and exalted Christ (Phil. 2:5–11).

Who can deny the poetic passion in Paul's words to the Corinthians? "We are hard pressed on every side, yet not crushed;/we are perplexed, but not in despair;/persecuted, but not forsaken;/struck down, but not destroyed" (2 Cor. 4:8–9).

PROPHECY—predictions about the future and the end-time; special messages from God, often uttered through human spokesmen, which indicate the divine will for mankind on earth and in heaven.

The focus of all prophetic truth is Jesus Christ (Heb. 1:2; Luke 24:25–27), who was destined to be the greatest prophet (Deut. 18:15–18). He declared God's truth in this age (John 3:31–33) and the age to come (Is. 2:2–4). As the embodiment of truth (John 1:1), Christ fully radiated the brilliance of God, which the earlier prophets reflected only partially.

Earlier prophets anticipated Jesus Christ by reflecting His person and message in their own life and ministry (Ex. 34:29–35; 1 Kin. 19:10; 2 Chr. 24:20–21). Each contributed a portion of the truth, sharing in the Spirit that would be completely expressed in Jesus Christ (John 6:68).

Prophecy was technically the task of the prophet. But all truth or revelation is prophetic, pointing to some future person, event, or thing. The full panorama of God's will takes many forms; it may be expressed through people, events, and objects. Historical events such as the Passover anticipated Jesus Christ (1 Cor. 5:7), as did various objects in the tabernacle, including manna (John 6:31–35) and the inner veil (Matt. 27:51; Heb. 10:20).

Prophecy may also be expressed in many different forms through the prophet himself, whether by his mouth or some bodily action. The prophets received God's messages from the voice of an angel (Gen. 22:15–19), the voice of God, a dream (Daniel 2), or a vision (Ezek. 40:2ff.). The prophetic speech might range from the somber reading of a father's last will (Genesis 49) to an exultant anthem to be sung in the Temple (Ps. 96:1, 13).

Sometimes a prophet acted out his message symbolically. Isaiah's nakedness (Isaiah 20) foretold the exile of the Egyptians and the Cushites. Hosea's marriage symbolized God's patience with an unfaithful wife, the nation of Israel. Ahijah divided his garment to foretell the division of the monarchy (1 Kin. 11:30–31). Even the names of some of the prophets are symbolic, matching their message. Hosea means "salvation"; Nahum, "comfort"; Zephaniah, "the Lord hides"; and Zechariah, "the Lord remembers."

Prophecy declared God's word for all time, so the time of fulfillment of a prophecy is rarely indicated in the Bible. Exceptions to this rule include the timetable assigned to Daniel's seventy weeks' prophecy (Dan. 9:24–27), the prophecy of Peter's denial (Matt. 26:34), and predictions of someone's death (Jer. 28:16–17). The common problem of knowing the time for the fulfillment of a prophecy is acknowledged by Peter (2 Pet. 1:11). This problem is due to several factors. First, some prophecies appear together, as if they would be fulfilled simultaneously. For example, Isaiah 61:1–2a has already been fulfilled, according to Luke 4:18–19; but Isaiah 61:2b, which adjoins it, awaits fulfillment. The same is true of Zechariah 9:9–10. The prophets saw the mountain peaks of prophetic events but not the valleys of time in between.

Another factor that complicates the problem is the ambiguity of tenses in the Hebrew language, which distinguishes type of action but usually not time of action. The prophets focused on the reality of their prophecies and not the time of their fulfillment. In their minds their prophecies were already accomplished, primarily because they knew God was in charge of history.

Finally, since the prophets' messages had eternal force, it is often difficult to tell whether they applied their messages to their day or the future. For example, Isaiah 7:14 promised a son who could be a contemporary of Isaiah (perhaps the prophet's son in 8:3 or the son of Hezekiah the king in Isaiah 36–39), or Jesus (Matt. 1:23), or both.

Several questions are raised when there appear to be more than one possible fulfillment for a prophecy. Does a primary fulfillment in one passage rule out a secondary application to another passage? Not necessarily. Did the author intend both fulfillments with one as an analogy or illustration for the other? Did the author intend a dual fulfillment for two different audiences at two different times?

Joel 2:30, speaking about signs on the earth, was applied by the apostle Peter to the tongues of fire at Pentecost (Acts 2:3–4, 18–19). But Jesus seemed to apply this prophecy to His Second Coming (Mark 13:24; Luke 11:25). In the same way, the destruction of Gog and Magog in Ezekiel 38 and 39 may be fulfilled in Revelation 20:8 after the Millennium. But similarities of this prophecy to earlier invasions from the north before the millennium seem to allow for its multiple fulfillment. The earlier parallels with Ezekiel 38 and 39 are two invasions from the north in Daniel 11:40, 44 and a third in Revelation 19:17–18, where the birds consume the carcasses as in Ezekiel 39:17–20.

The problem of understanding when a prophecy is fulfilled is compounded if the modern reader has a theological bias about who is to fulfill a prophecy. For example, premillennialists believe that a 1,000-year reign by Christ (Rev. 20:2–7) will exalt the nation of Israel and the Jewish people in the future (Rom. 11:24–26). But amillennialists believe the promises to Israel in the Old Testament have been taken from Israel and transferred to the church (Gal. 6:16). Such a disagreement does not deny that Abraham's descendants will inherit Palestine from the River of Egypt to the Euphrates River (Gen. 15:18). But the premillennialist looks for a future revival of Israel as a nation (Ezek. 37:11–28), while the amillennialist claims the promise of the land was fulfilled in the past in the days of Joshua (Josh. 21:43–44) or Solomon (2 Chr. 9:26).

Prophecy presents volumes about the future kingdom of God, particularly information about the Messiah and His chosen people, Israel. Much prophecy also foretells the destiny of the nations and their relationship to the kingdom of God. The New Testament identifies Jesus as the King (John 1:49) who spends much of His ministry describing His kingdom and its establishment (Matthew 13; 24–25). The battleground is the world; and the arch-foe of Christ is Satan, whose intrigue in Eden gave him control of the nations (Matt. 4:9). Most prophecy is concerned with undoing Satan's work; it elaborates upon the initial promise of Genesis 3:15, which announced that Christ, the seed of the woman (Gal. 4:4), would crush the great Serpent, the Devil (Rom. 16:20; Rev. 20:2). All prophecy testifies about Jesus (Rev. 19:10).

Over 300 prophecies in the Bible speak of Jesus Christ. Specific details given by these prophecies include His tribe (Gen. 49:10), His birthplace (Mic. 5:2), dates of His birth and death (Dan. 9:25–26), His forerunner John the Baptist (Mal. 3:1; 4:5; Matt. 11:10), His career and ministry (Is. 52:13–53:12), His crucifixion (Ps. 22:1–18), His resurrection (Ps. 16:8–11; Acts 2:25–28), His ascension (Psalm 2; Acts 13:33), and His exaltation as a priest-king (Psalm 110; Acts 2:34). The kingly magnificence of His second coming is also graphically portrayed.

Psalms 2, 45, and 110 picture His conquest and dominion over the nations. His kingdom is characterized in Psalm 72. Events leading up to and including the first and second advents of Christ are described in the two burdens of the prophet Zechariah (Zechariah 9–11, 12–14).

Premillennialists point to many Bible passages to support their belief in the national resurrection of Israel. Many prophecies graphically portray Israel's history (Leviticus 26; Deuteronomy 27–28; Amos 6–9). Her bounty as a nation is prophesied in Deuteronomy 30 and Isaiah 35 . Just as the nation had received a double punishment (Jer. 16:18), so it would receive a double blessing (Is. 61:7). Temple worship would be restored (Ezekiel 40–48); Israel would be the center of world government (Zechariah 1–6); and the Davidic line would be set up as a permanent dynasty (2 Sam. 7:12–16; Luke 1:32–33).

Much controversy surrounds the roles of the church and Israel in the final days preceding Christ's Second Coming, known as the "day of Jacob's trouble" (Jer. 30:7), "the great tribulation" (Matt. 24:21), or "the great day of His wrath" (Rev. 6:17). This will be a period of seven years (9:27) with the most intense trial in the last three and one-half years of this time (Dan. 12:11–12; Rev. 12:6; 13:5).

As Christ's Second Coming approaches, many difficult prophecies about the Tribulation will be understood more clearly (Jer. 30:24; Dan. 11:32–35; 12:3, 9–10). Premillennialists point to the establishment of the state of Israel in 1948 as just one of these signs of Christ's approaching return.

While premillennialists agree upon the restoration of Israel in the earthly reign of Jesus Christ, many are divided over the relation of Israel to the church, particularly just before Christ's appearance at the end of the Tribulation. Covenant theologians see Israel and the church as one people who go through the Tribulation together. Some dispensational theologians believe Israel and the church are always separated in the Bible. As a result, they believe the church will not join Israel in its days of tribulation, but will be transported to heaven before it begins, at the beginning of the seven years.

Among premillennialists, theories exist about the time of the church's departure to meet the Lord in the air (1 Thess. 4:13–17): the pre-tribulational rapture, the mid-tribulational rapture, and the post-tribulational rapture. These three theories place the rapture at the time of John's ascension to heaven (Rev. 4:1), at the time when the two prophets ascend to heaven (Rev. 11:11–12), and at the end of the series of seven bowls (Rev. 16:15), respectively.

PROVERB—a short, pithy statement about human nature and life. In the Bible Solomon is singled out for his use of proverbs (1 Kin. 4:32). His wisdom was shown by his ability to make clear, true commentaries upon the nature of things. The Hebrew word most frequently translated as proverb means literally "a similitude," or loosely, "a representation." So when God declared that Israel would be "a proverb ... among all peoples" (1 Kin. 9:7), He implied that the name Israel would come to symbolize disobedience. Proverbs are designed to make God's truth accessible to all people, so they might direct their lives in accordance with His will.

PROVERBS, BOOK OF—one of the "wisdom books" of the Old Testament, containing instructions on many of the practical matters of daily life. The Proverbs was a familiar literary form in all ancient cultures; it was a very suitable device for collecting and summarizing the wisdom of the centuries. But the Book of Proverbs has one important difference: it points the believer to God with instructions on how to live a holy, upright life.

Structure of the Book.

The Book of Proverbs has the longest title of any Old Testament book, covering the first six verses of chapter one. The author introduces himself as a teacher, one of the wise men of Israel, who has written this book as a manual of instruction on the ways of wisdom. His declaration, "The fear of the Lord is the beginning of knowledge" (1:7), summarizes the theme of

Proverbs, a point he emphasizes again and again throughout the book.

In its 31 chapters, Proverbs discusses many practical matters to help believers live in harmony with God as well as their neighbors. Subjects covered in this wise and realistic book include how to choose the right kind of friends, the perils of adultery, the value of hard work, dealing justly with others in business, the dangers of strong drink, treating the poor with compassion, the values of strong family ties, the folly of pride and anger, and the characteristics of genuine friendship.

Scholars agree that Proverbs is a compilation of material from several different sources. This gives the book a unique internal structure. But the book itself tells us which parts were written by one author and which came from another's hand.

Authorship and Date.

The name of Sol-omon as author is associated with the Book of Proverbs from the very beginning. Verse 1 of chapter 1 states: "The proverbs of Solomon the son of David." We also know that Solomon was noted throughout the ancient world for his superior wisdom (1 Kin. 4:29–34). Additional evidence of his authorship is found within the book itself, where Solomon is identified as author of the section from 10:1–22:16 as well as writer of chapters 25–29.

But what about those portions of Proverbs that clearly are attributed to other writers, such as "the wise" (22:17), Agur (30:1), and King Lemuel (31:1)? Although Solomon wrote a major portion of Proverbs, he did not write the entire book. Many scholars believe he wrote the basic core of Proverbs but that some writings were later added from other sources.

Another interesting fact about this book and its writing is that the second collection of proverbs attributed to Solomon (chaps. 25–29) was not added to the book until more than 200 years after his death. The heading over this material reads: "These also are proverbs of Solomon which the men of Hezekiah king of Judah copied" (25:1). Perhaps these writings of Solomon were not discovered and inserted into the book until Hezekiah's time.

Because of the strong evidence that the Book of Proverbs is, indeed, a compilation, some scholars dismiss the idea that Solomon wrote any of the material. But evidence for his authorship of some sections is too strong to be dismissed that lightly. In its original version the book must have been written by Solomon some time during his reign from 970 B.C. to 931 B.C. Then, about 720 B.C. or later the non-Solomonic sections were added to the book.

Historical Setting.

The Book of Proverbs is the classical example of the type of writing in the Old Testament known as Wisdom Literature. Other books so categorized are Job, Ecclesiastes, and the Song of Solomon. These books are called wisdom writings because they were written by a distinctive group of people in Israel's history who grappled with some of the eternal questions of life. This type of writing flourished especially during Solomon's time, and he was known as the wisest of the wise throughout the ancient world. "Thus Solomon's wisdom excelled the wisdom of all the men of the East and all the wisdom of Egypt. For he was wiser than all men ... and his fame was in all the surrounding nations" (1 Kin. 4:30–31).

Theological Contribution.

Israel's distinctive contribution to the thinking of the wise men of all nations and times is that true wisdom is centered in respect and reverence for God. This is the great underlying theme of the Book of Proverbs.

Special Considerations.

In reading the Book of Proverbs, we need to make sure we do not turn these wise sayings into literal promises. Proverbs are statements of the way things generally turn out in God's world. For example, it is generally true that those who keep God's commandments will enjoy "length of days and long life" (3:2). But this should not be interpreted as an ironclad guarantee. It is important to keep God's laws, no matter how long or short our earthly life may be.

PSALMS, BOOK OF—a collection of prayers, poems, and hymns that focus the worshiper's thoughts on God in praise and adoration. Parts of this book were used as a hymnal in the worship services of ancient Israel. The musical heritage of the Psalms is demonstrated by its title. It comes from a Greek word that means "a song sung to the accompaniment of a musical instrument."

Structure of the Book.

With 150 individual psalms, this book has the most chapters of any in the Bible. It is also one of the most diverse, since the psalms deal with such subjects as God and His creation, war, worship, wisdom, sin and evil, judgment, justice, and the coming of the Messiah.

In the original Hebrew manuscripts, this long collection of 150 psalms was divided into five sections: book 1 (1–41); Book 2 (42–72); Book 3 (73–89); Book 4 (90–106); and Book 5 (107–150). Each of these major sections closes with a brief prayer of praise.

Scholars are not sure exactly why the Book of Psalms was organized in this manner. One theory is that it was divided into five sections as a sort of parallel to the Pentateuch—the first five books of the Old Testament (Genesis, Exodus, Leviticus, Numbers, and Deuteronomy). But other scholars believe the five sections were different collections of psalms that circulated at different times in Israel's history. These five small collections were finally placed together, they believe, to form the large compilation which we know today as the Book of Psalms.

The second theory does not seem to make sense when we examine the content of the psalms themselves. Individual psalms attributed to David appear in all five sections of the Book. Within these five sections, different types of psalms also appear. These include songs of thanksgiving, hymns of praise, psalms of repentance and confession, psalms that invoke evil upon one's enemies, messianic psalms, and songs sung by pilgrims as they traveled to Jerusalem to observe one of the great festivals of their faith. Such variety among the psalms within these five sections may indicate they were complete collections within themselves before they were placed with other groups of psalms to form this larger body of material.

But no matter how the present arrangement of the book came about, these individual psalms were clearly inspired by God's Spirit. Through these hymns of praise, we come face to face with our Maker and Redeemer. In the glory of His presence, we are compelled to exclaim along with the psalmist, "O LORD, our Lord, how excellent is Your name in all the earth!" (8:1).

Authorship and Date.

Most people automatically think of David when they consider the question of who wrote the Book of Psalms. A shepherd boy who rose to become the most famous king of Judah, he was also known as "the sweet psalmist of Israel" (2 Sam. 23:1). He lived during the most creative age of Hebrew song and poetry. As king, he organized the services of worship in the tabernacle, appointing priests and Levites for the specific purpose of providing songs and music. So it is not surprising that his name should be clearly associated with this beautiful book of praise.

The brief descriptions that introduce the psalms have David listed in them in 73 instances. But some scholars believe the phrase, "A psalm of David," should not be interpreted as a certain indication that David actually wrote all these psalms. They point out the Hebrew word translated as "of" can also be translated "to" or "for." Thus, these psalms could have been written by anonymous authors and dedicated to David or even written on his behalf (for David) and added to a special collection of his material already being used in the sanctuary.

While this is an interesting theory, there is no compelling reason to question the traditional view that David actually wrote most or all the psalms that bear his name. David's personality and identity are clearly stamped on many of these psalms. For example, Psalm 18 is a psalm of David that sings praises to God as the sovereign Savior. The title indicates it was written after David was delivered "from the hand of all his enemies and from the hand of Saul." The same psalm in almost identical wording appears in 2 Samuel 22. This passage indicates that David sang this song after the death of Saul.

While it is clear that David wrote many of the individual psalms, he is definitely not the author of the entire collection. Two of the psalms (72 and 127) are attributed to Solomon, David's son and successor. Psalm 90 is a prayer assigned to Moses. Another group of 12 psalms (50 and 73–83) is ascribed to the family of Asaph. The sons of Korah wrote 11 psalms (42, 44–49, 84–85, 87–88). Psalm 88 is attributed to Heman, while Psalm 89 is assigned to Ethan the Ezrahite. With the exception of Solomon and Moses, all these additional authors were priests or Levites who were responsible for providing music for sanctuary worship during David's reign. Many of the psalms designate no specific person as author. They were probably written by many different people.

A careful examination of the authorship question, as well as the subject matter covered by the psalms themselves, reveal they span a period of many centuries. The oldest psalm in the collection may be the prayer of Moses (90). One of the latest psalms is 137, a song of lament clearly written during the days when the Jews were being held captive by the Babylonians, from about 586 to 538 B.C.

It is clear that the 150 individual psalms were written by many different people across a period of a thousand years in Israel's history. They must have been compiled and put together in their present form by some unknown editor shortly after the Captivity ended about 538 B.C.

Historical Setting.

Some of the psalms written by David grew out of specific experiences in his life. For example, Psalm 3 is described as "a Psalm of David when he fled from Absalom his son" (see also 51, 52, 54, 56, 57, 59). But others seem to be general psalms that arose from no specific life situation (53, 55, 58). Knowing the particular historical background of a psalm can help the student interpret it correctly and apply its message to life today.

Theological Contribution.

We may think of the psalms as a description of our human response to God. At times God is presented in all His majesty and glory. Our response is wonder, awe, and fear: "Sing to God, you kingdoms of the earth" (68:32). But other psalms portray God as a loving Lord who is involved in our lives. Our response in these cases is to draw close to His comfort and security: "I will fear no evil; for You are with me" (23:4).

God is the same Lord in both these psalms. But we respond to Him in different ways, according to the specific needs of our lives. What a marvelous God we worship, the psalmist declares—One who is high and lifted up beyond our human experiences but also one who is close enough to touch and who walks beside us along life's way.

Other psalms might be described as outcries against God and the circumstances of life rather than responses to God because of His glory and His presence in our lives. The psalmist admits he sometimes feels abandoned by God as well as his human friends (88). He agonizes over the lies directed against him by his false accusers (109). He calls upon God to deliver him from his enemies and to wipe them out with His wrath (59). Whatever else we may say about the psalms, we must admit they are realistic about human feelings and the way we sometimes respond to the problems and inequities of life.

But even in these strong psalms of lament, the psalmist is never totally engulfed by a feeling of despair. The fact that he uttered his protest to the Lord is a sign of hope in God and His sense of justice. This has a significant message for all believers. We can bring all our feelings to God, no matter how negative or complaining they may be. And we can rest assured that He will hear and understand. The psalmist teaches us that the most profound prayer of all is a cry for help as we find ourselves overwhelmed by the problems of life.

The psalms also have a great deal to say about the person and work of Christ. Psalm 22 contains a remarkable prophecy of the crucifixion of the Savior. Jesus quoted from this psalm as He was dying on the cross (Ps. 22:1; Matt. 27:46; Mark 15:34). Other statements about the Messiah from the psalms that were fulfilled in the life of Jesus include these predictions: He would be a priest like Melchizedek (Ps. 110:4; Heb. 5:6); He would pray for His enemies (Ps. 109:4; Luke 23:34); and His throne would be established forever (Ps. 45:6; Heb. 1:8).

Special Considerations.

The Book of Psalms is the best example in the Bible of the nature of Hebrew poetry. The principle upon which this poetry is based is not rhythm or rhyme but parallelism. In parallelism, one phrase is followed by another that says essentially the same thing but in a more creative, expressive way. Here is a good example of this poetic technique:

> The Lord of hosts is with us;
> The God of Jacob is our refuge (46:11).

This example is known as synonymous parallelism because the second phrase expresses the same thought as the first. But sometimes the succeeding line introduces a thought that is directly opposite to the first idea. This is known as antithetic parallelism. Here is a familiar couplet that demonstrates this form:

> For the Lord knows the way of the righteous,
>> But the way of the ungodly shall perish (1:6).

A third kind of parallelism in Hebrew poetry may be called progressive, or climbing—in which part of the first line is repeated in the second, but also something more is added. For example:

> The floods have lifted up, O Lord,
>> The floods have lifted up their voice (93:3).

Another literary device the Hebrew writers used to give their psalms a peculiar style and rhythm was the alphabetical acrostic. The best example of this technique is Psalm 119—the longest in the collection—which contains 22 different sections of eight verses each. Each major section is headed by a different letter of the Hebrew alphabet. In the original language, each verse in these major divisions of the psalm begins with the Hebrew letter that appears as the heading for that section. Many modern translations of the Bible include these Hebrew letters as a part of the structure of this psalm. Writing this poem with such a structure required a high degree of literary skill.

The peculiar poetic structure of the 150 psalms makes them ideal for believers who like to create their own devotional exercises. You can easily combine the lines from many different psalms into a fresh, authentic expression of praise to God. Here is an example of such a combined psalm:

> Oh, give thanks to the
>> Lord, for He is good!
>>> For His mercy endures forever (136:1).

> He has not dealt with us according to our sins,
>> Nor punished us according to our iniquities (103:10).

For You, O God, have heard my vows;
    You have given me the heritage of those who fear
    Your name (61:5).

Your testimonies are very sure;
    Holiness adorns Your house, O LORD, forever (93:5).

So teach us to number our days,
    That we may gain a heart of wisdom (90:12).

The fear of the Lord is the beginning of wisdom;
    A good understanding have all those who do His
    commandments (111:10).

Oh, give thanks to the God of heaven!
    For His mercy endures forever (136:26).

PSEUDEPIGRAPHA—a collection of Jewish books containing various forms of literature, using names of famous people in Israel's history for the titles of the books. The real authors are unknown. Such names as Ezra, Baruch, Enoch, Solomon, Moses, and Adam are used to add authority to the writing.

A few of these books are folk tales or sacred legends. These include the Letter of Aristeas, the Book of Adam and Eve, and the Martyrdom of Isaiah. One book of psalms, the Psalms of Solomon, has been included in the Pseudepigrapha. Ethical and wisdom writings are also part of this collection.

One problem addressed by the pseudepigraphal books is, Why do the wicked seem to prosper and the righteous suffer? Books like Jubilees, Enoch, and IV Ezra develop a careful scheme of history that shows the power of the world in the hands of the ruler of this age. The ruler of this age is Satan or Belial. The present age will end with God as Lord of all nations.

The books in the Pseudepigrapha were written by pious Jews living in either Palestine or Egypt. They were concerned that the Jews live according to the Law of Moses.

The Book of Jubilees describes a conversation that took place on Mt. Sinai between Moses and an angel of the Lord. The Martyrdom of Isaiah reports the sad news of the death of the great prophet. Through this story, the writer (using Isaiah's name) emphasizes how far Israel has gone astray. To protest against the growing secularization of the Pharisees, The Assumption of Moses was written around A.D. 7 to 29.

The Book of Adam and Eve, written in the middle of the first Christian century, is probably a protest against Christians. It tells about the future resurrection that was promised to Adam. The Testament of the Twelve Patriarchs is a book with many sub-books, describing the patriarch Jacob blessing his twelve sons before his death. Written about 105 B.C.

by a Pharisee, it tells about the intense hope for a Messiah held by some Jews during this period. The value of this book is the contribution it makes to an understanding of forgiveness, the two great commandments, the Messianic expectation, the resurrection, the Antichrist, demonology, and other teachings that were later developed in the New Testament.

Some collections of pseudepigraphal works include The Sayings of the Fathers. This work is actually a collection of wisdom sayings from the rabbis that is included in the Mishnah and Talmud.

Q—the letter Q (from the German word *Quelle,* meaning "source") refers to a hypothetical document that contained material from which Matthew and Luke drew as they wrote certain sections of their gospels. This document supposedly consisted mostly of sayings of Jesus in narrative form. Not all scholars accept the existence of Q as a background document to these gospels.

QUOTATIONS IN THE NEW TESTAMENT. Several different kinds of quotations appear in the New Testament. It includes quotations of pagan authors (Acts 17:28; 1 Cor. 15:33; Titus 1:12) and at least one quotation of a statement of Jesus that is not recorded in any of the four gospels (Acts 20:35).

The New Testament also contains statements that parallel noncanonical literature from the New Testament era. For example, Jude 14 and 15 parallel 1 Enoch 1:9, a book of the Apocrypha. The New Testament also quotes itself (Luke 10:7; 1 Tim. 5:18). But more than anything else, it quotes the Old Testament. This indicates how important each testament is for an understanding of the other.

The number of quotations from and allusions to the Old Testament in the New varies with the counter. Direct quotations have been numbered from less than 150 to more than 300. When allusions are added to this number, the total number rises to anywhere from 600 to more than 4,000, again according to the person doing the counting.

A number of verses from the Old Testament are quoted more than once in the New Testament. The majority of quotations are taken from the Septuagint, the Greek translation of the Old Testament.

The New Testament authors used the Old Testament Scriptures to do several things: (1) to provide authority for their statements or conclusions, (2) to answer questions or to rebuke opponents' claims, (3) to provide further interpretations of the Old Testament, (4) to call attention to parallel situations, (5) to show continuity in the revelation of God, and (6) to demonstrate that the Old Testament predicted the coming of Jesus the Messiah.

The New Testament authors used the Old Testament Scriptures to do several things: (1) to provide authority for their statements or conclusions, (2) to answer questions or to rebuke opponents' claims, (3) to provide further interpretations of the Old Testament, (4) to call attention to parallel situations, (5) to show continuity in the revelation of God, and (6) to demonstrate that the Old Testament predicted the coming of Jesus the Messiah.

The New Testament authors used the Old Testament Scriptures to do several things: (1) to provide authority for their statements or conclusions, (2) to answer questions or to rebuke opponents' claims, (3) to provide further interpretations of the Old Testament, (4) to call attention to parallel situations, (5) to show continuity in the revelation of God, and (6) to demonstrate that the Old Testament predicted the coming of Jesus the Messiah.

R EVELATION—God's communication to people concerning Himself, His moral standards, and His plan of salvation.

God is a personal Spirit distinct from the world; He is absolutely holy and is invisible to the view of physical, finite, sinful minds. Although people, on their own, can never create truth about God, God has graciously unveiled and manifested Himself to mankind. Other religions and philosophies result from the endless human quest for God; Christianity results from God's quest for lost mankind.

God has made Himself known to all people everywhere in the marvels of nature and in the human conscience, which is able to distinguish right from wrong. Because this knowledge is universal and continuous, by it God has displayed His glory to everyone (Ps. 19:1–6).

Some Christians think that only believers can see God's revelation in nature, but the apostle Paul said that unbelievers know truth about God: The unrighteous must have the truth to "suppress" it (Rom. 1:18); they "clearly see" it (Rom. 1:20); knowing God, they fail to worship Him as God (Rom. 1:21); they alter the truth (Rom. 1:25); they do not retain God in their knowledge (Rom. 1:28); and knowing the righteous judgment (moral law) of God, they disobey it (Rom. 1:32). The reason the ungodly are "inexcusable" (Rom. 2:1) before God's righteous judgment is that they possessed but rejected the truth God gave them.

What can be known of God from nature? God's universal revelation makes it clear that God exists (Rom. 1:20), and that God, the Creator of the mountains, oceans, vegetation, animals, and mankind, is wise (Ps. 104:24) and powerful (Psalm 29; 93; Rom. 1:20). People aware of their own moral responsibility, who know the difference between right and wrong conduct and who have a sense of guilt when they do wrong, reflect the requirements of God's moral law (the Ten Commandments) that is written on their hearts (Rom. 2:14–15).

What is the result of divine revelation in nature? If people lived up to that knowledge by loving and obeying God every day of their lives, they would be right with God and would not need salvation. However, people do not love God with all that is in them. Nor do they love their neighbors as themselves. People worship and serve things in creation rather than the Creator (Rom. 1:25). The problem does not lie with the revelation, which like the Law is holy, just, and good (Rom. 7:12); the problem is with the sinfulness of human lives (Rom. 8:3). The best human being (other than Jesus Christ) comes short of the uprightness God requires.

Because of God's universal revelation in nature, the philosopher Immanuel Kant could say, "Two things fill the mind with ever new and increasing admiration and awe ... the starry heavens above me and the moral law within me."

When Christians defend justice, honesty, and decency in schools, homes, neighborhoods, businesses, and governments, they do not impose their special beliefs upon others. They merely point to universal principles that all sinners know but suppress in their unrighteousness (Rom. 1:18).

As valuable as general revelation is for justice, honesty, and decency in the world today, it is not enough. It must be completed by the good news of God's mercy and His gracious gift of perfect righteousness. Nature does not show God's plan for saving those who do wrong: that Jesus was the Son of God, that He died for our sins, and that He rose again from among the dead. The message of salvation was seen dimly through Old Testament sacrifices and ceremonies. It was seen more clearly as God redeemed the Israelites from enslavement in Egypt and as God disclosed to prophets the redemptive significance of His mighty acts of deliverance.

The full and final revelation of God has occurred in Jesus Christ. "God, who at various times and in different ways spoke in time past to the fathers by the prophets, has in these last days spoken to us by His Son, whom He has appointed heir of all things, through whom also He made the worlds" (Heb. 1:1–2). Christ has "declared" God to us personally (John 1:18). To see Christ is to see the Father (John 14:9). Christ gave us the words the Father gave Him (John 17:8). At the cross Jesus revealed supremely God's self-giving love. There He died, "the just for the unjust, that He might bring us to God" (1 Pet. 3:18). And the good news is not complete until we hear that He rose again triumphantly over sin, Satan, and the grave, and is alive forevermore.

Christ chose apostles and trained them to teach the meaning of His death and resurrection, to build the church, and to write the New Testament Scriptures. We are to remember the words of these eyewitnesses to Christ's resurrection. The content of God's special revelation concerning salvation, given to specially gifted spokesmen and supremely revealed in Christ, is found in "the words which were spoken before by the holy prophets, and of the commandment of ... the apostles of the Lord and Savior" (2 Pet. 3:2). "The Holy Scriptures ... are able to make you wise for salvation through faith which is in Christ Jesus" (2 Tim. 3:15).

R EVELATION OF JOHN—the last book of the Bible, and the only book of Apocalyptic Literature in the New Testament. *Apocalypsis,* the title of this book in the original Greek, means "unveiling" or "disclosure" of hidden things known only to God. Other examples of apocalyptic literature can be found in the Old Testament in Daniel (chaps. 7–12), Isaiah (chaps. 24–27), Ezekiel (chaps. 37–41), and Zech-ariah (chaps. 9–12).

Like its counterparts, the Book of Revelation depicts the end of the present age and the coming of God's future kingdom through symbols, images, and numbers. These symbols include an angel whose legs are pillars of fire, men who ride on horses while smiting the earth with plagues of destruction, and a fiery red dragon with seven heads and ten horns who crouches before a heavenly woman about to deliver a child.

Why was apocalyptic literature written in such imagery? One reason is that these books were written in dangerous times when it was safer to hide one's message in images than to speak plainly. Moreover, the symbolism preserved an element of mystery about details of time and place. The purpose of such symbolism, however, was not to confuse, but to inform and strengthen believers in the face of persecution.

Although the keys to some symbols have been lost, the overall message of this book is clear: God is all-powerful. No countermoves of the devil, no matter how strong, can frustrate the righteous purposes of God.

Structure of the Book.

The Book of Revelation contains seven visions.

The first vision (chaps. 1–3) is of Christ Almighty exhorting His earthly church to remain loyal against all hostile attacks.

The second vision (chaps. 4–7) is of Christ the Lamb standing with a sealed scroll before God in heaven. As the Lamb opens each of the seven seals, which symbolize knowledge of the destinies of individuals and nations, a series of disasters befalls the earth.

A series of seven angels blowing seven trumpets forms vision three (chaps. 8–11). At the sound of these trumpets more disasters occur.

The fourth vision (chaps. 12–14) consists of the persecution of the church—symbolized by a heavenly woman and by two witnesses (Moses and Elijah)—by Satan and the beast.

Vision five (chaps. 15–16) is another series of seven: seven bowls pouring out God's wrath.

The judgment of Babylon (a symbol for Rome) forms the sixth vision (chaps. 17:1–19:10).

The final victory, final judgment, and final blessedness form the seventh and final vision (chap. 19:11–21).

The consummation of God's eternal kingdom finds expression in the word "new." Christ comes with the promise to make all things new: a new heaven, a new earth, and a new Jerusalem (chap. 21). The book closes with the sigh and longing of all Christians, "Come, Lord Jesus!" (22:20).

Authorship and Date.

The author identifies himself as John (1:4, 9; 21:2; 22:8), a prophet (1:1–4; 22:6–7). He was familiar enough with his readers to call himself their "brother and companion in tribulation" (1:9). He indicates that he was exiled to the island of Patmos (1:9) off the west coast of Asia Minor (modern Turkey) and that on the "Lord's Day" (Sunday) he was caught up "in the Spirit" (1:10) and saw the visions recorded in his book. An examination of the Greek language of the book of Revelation reveals that it has some strong similarities with the Gospel and Epistles of John, but also some striking stylistic differences. The author seems to think in Hebrew and write in Greek.

As a whole, this evidence points to John the Apostle, who spent his latter years in Ephesus or on the island of Patmos. The earliest church tradition was unanimous in attributing the Book of Revelation to John. Although later voices have found problems with this identification, the apostle John remains the strongest candidate for authorship. The Book was probably written during the latter years of the reign of the Roman Emperor Domitian (A.D. 81–96).

Historical Setting.

John tells us, "The seven heads [of the beast] are seven mountains" (17:9), undoubtedly a reference to the famed seven hills of Rome. Chapter 13 tells us that the dragon (Satan) gave authority to the beast (Rome) to exact worship from its inhabitants (v. 4). The first Roman emperor to demand that his subjects address him as "Lord and God" on an empire-wide basis was Domitian. It was under Domitian that the apostle John was banished to Patmos. Christians, of course, were forbidden by the First Commandment (Ex. 20:3) to worship anyone other than God. In the Book of Revelation, John sounded the trumpet alert to Domitian's challenge.

Theological Contribution.

The grand theme of the Book of Revelation is that of two warring powers, God and Satan, and of God's ultimate victory. It would be a mistake to consider the two powers as equal in might. God is stronger than Satan, and Satan continues his scheming plots only because God permits him to do so. Thus, at the final battle Satan and his followers are utterly destroyed— without a contest—by fire from heaven (20:7–10).

John portrays God's majesty and power through two key words. The first is the image of the throne. Elsewhere in the New Testament this word is found 15 times, but in Revelation it occurs 42 times. The throne stands for the rightful reign of God over the course of history. Angelic choruses bow before God's throne and chant, "Holy, holy, holy, Lord God Almighty" (4:8).

The second term is "Almighty." Outside Revelation this term is found only once in the New Testament (2 Cor. 6:18), but here it occurs nine times (once as Omnipotent in 19:6). Almighty means "without contenders." No matter how fierce and wicked

Satan may be, he cannot defeat God. In God's time and in His way He will fulfill His promises and accomplish His sovereign purpose in history.

The central figure in the army of God the King is Jesus Christ. The Book of Revelation begins with the words, "The Revelation of Jesus Christ" (1:1). This is not a book of revelations, but of one revelation—Jesus Christ. John's first vision is of Christ standing in the midst of His churches with eyes like fire (all-seeing), feet like fine brass (all-powerful), hair like wool, white as snow (eternal and all-knowing), and with a sharp two-edged sword coming out of His mouth (the word of truth). Christ is "the First and the Last" (1:11; 22:13), whose final promise is "Surely I am coming quickly" (22:20).

Throughout the Book of Revelation Christ appears in various images, each illuminating a special function or characteristic. He appears as a lion (5:5), representing royal power. As a root (5:5; 22:16), He represents Davidic lineage. As the rider on a white horse (19:11), He symbolizes victory over evil. Most important is the symbol of the Lamb who was slain (5:6). By His sacrifice on the cross, Christ has redeemed humankind (1:5). Because of His humble obedience to the will of the Father, He alone is worthy to open the sealed book that discloses events to come (5:6–10).

This Lamb is victorious. He shares in the power of God's throne (7:17). At the end of time, He will come in judgment (19:11). Then He will reveal Himself as the Lord of the world who was foretold in the Old Testament (2:26; 12:5; 19:15) and the source of new life with God in the heavenly Jerusalem (21:22; 22:1).

In its own way, each metaphor tells an important truth about Christ. Christ is before all things, and all things were created in Him and for Him. This is the abiding message of Revelation: Jesus Christ is the fulfillment of the hopes of believers, no matter how grim circumstances may appear.

Special Considerations.

Revelation was written originally for first-century Christians who faced severe trials under a totalitarian political system. Its imagery reflects the historical realities of that time. This is not to say, however, that it is not also addressing succeeding generations, including our own. As is true of all biblical prophecy, God's Word comes to a particular situation; but it yields a harvest to later generations as they receive it. Thus, Revelation assures us that God is present, purposeful, and powerful today, no matter what forms the beast may take.

One of the unique characteristics of Revelation is its use of four, twelve, and seven. Thus, we find four living creatures, four horsemen, and four angels; twelve elders, twelve gates to the city of God, twelve foundations, and twelve varieties of fruit on the tree of life; and seven churches, seven spirits of God, seven thunders, seven seals, seven trumpets, seven bowls, and seven beatitudes. In apocalyptic literature these numbers represent completeness and perfection. Conversely, 3 1/2 is a number frequently associated with Satan (11:2; 13:5; 42 months or 3 1/2 years); this number symbolizes a fracturing and diminishing of God's unity.

With this in mind, the 144,000 elect in chapter seven should not be taken literally. Immediately following this passage (v. 9), John mentions that he saw "a great multitude [of the redeemed] which no one could number." Actually, the 144,000 refers to martyrs—12,000 from each of the twelve tribes of Israel. One hundred and forty-four thousand (a multiple of 12,000 times 12) stands for totality. This means that no martyr will fail to see God's reward.

Finally, the number of the beast, 666 (Rev. 13:18), probably refers to Nero, or more specifically to the idea that Nero would return alive to lead the armies of Satan against God. In Hebrew and Greek, letters of the alphabet also served as numbers, and in this case the numerical value of "Nero Caesar" amounts to 666, the number of the beast.

R OMANS, EPISTLE TO THE—the most formal and systematic of Paul's epistles. The main theme of Romans is that righteousness comes as a free gift of God and is receivable by faith alone. Romans stands at the head of the Pauline epistles because it is the longest of his letters, but it is also Paul's most important epistle.

Repeatedly in its history, the church has found in this epistle a catalyst for reform and new life. In the fourth century a troubled young man, sensing a divine command to open the Bible and read the first passage he came to, read these words: "Not in revelry and drunkenness, not in licentiousness and lewdness, not in strife and envy. But put on the Lord Jesus Christ, and make no provision for the flesh, to fulfill its lusts" (13:13–14).

"In an instant," says St. Augustine, "the light of confidence flooded into my heart and all the darkness of doubt was dispelled." In the 16th century a young monk found release from his struggles with God by claiming salvation by grace through faith (Rom. 1:17; 3:24). This truth caused Martin Luther to launch the greatest reform the church has ever known. Romans, perhaps more than any single book of the Bible, has exerted a powerful influence on the history of Christianity.

Structure of the Epistle.

The Epistle to the Romans consists of two halves, a doctrinal section (chaps. 1–8) and a practical section (chaps. 12–16), separated by three chapters on the place of Israel in the history of salvation (chaps. 9–11).

Paul declares his main theme in the first chapter—that the gospel is the power of salvation to everyone who believes (1:16–17). This declaration is then held in suspension until 3:21, while Paul digresses to show that all peoples are in need of salvation:

the Gentiles have broken the law of conscience, and the Jews the law of Moses (1:18–3:20).

Paul then returns to his opening theme. In a classic statement of the Christian gospel, he explains that righteousness comes by the grace of God through people's trust in the saving work of Christ (3:21–31). The example of Abraham testifies that the promise of God is realized through faith (4:1–25). The benefits of justification are peace and confidence before God (5:1–11). Thus, Christ's ability to save is greater than Adam's ability to corrupt (5:12–21).

Paul then takes up the problem of sin in the Christian life. Rather than acting as a stimulus to sin, grace draws us into a loyal union with Christ (6:1–14). Christ has freed us from slavery to sin so that we may become slaves of righteousness (6:15–7:6). Paul admits that the law brings sin to light, but sin convinces us of our need for a Savior (7:7–25). Paul concludes the doctrinal section by one of the most triumphant chapters in all the Bible: believers are not condemned by God, but are raised by the power of the Holy Spirit to face all adversity through the redeeming love of God (8:1–39). In chapters 9–11 Paul discusses the question of why Israel rejected the Savior sent to them.

Paul then discusses a number of practical consequences of the gospel. A proper response involves the sacrifice of one's entire life to the gospel (12:1–2). The gifts of grace to the church are complementary, not competitive or uniform (12:3–8). He lists insights for Christian conduct (12:9–21). Christians are instructed on the attitudes they should have toward the government (13:1–7), neighbors (13:8–10), the Second Coming (13:11–14), and judging (14:1–12) and cooperating with others (14:13–15:13). Paul closes with his travel plans (15:14–33) and a long list of greetings (16:1–27).

Authorship and Date.

There can be no doubt that Romans is an exposition of the content of the gospel by the strongest thinker in the early church—the apostle Paul. The epistle bears Paul's name as author (1:1). Throughout, it reflects Paul's deep involvement with the gospel. Paul most likely wrote the epistle during his third missionary journey as he finalized plans to visit Rome (Acts 19:21). His three-month stay in Corinth, probably in the spring of A.D. 56 or 57, would have provided the extended, uninterrupted time needed to compose such a reasoned commentary on the Christian faith.

Historical Setting.

Romans was written to a church that Paul did not found and had not visited. He wrote the letter to give an account of his gospel in preparation for a personal visit (1:11). Paul wrote most probably from Corinth, where he was completing the collection of money from the Macedonian and Achaian Christians for the "poor saints" in Jerusalem. After delivering the money, he planned to visit Rome and, with the Romans' support, to travel to Spain. The epistle, therefore, served as an advanced good-will ambassador for Paul's visit to Rome and his later mission to Spain (15:22–33).

Theological Contribution.

The great theme of Romans is God's power to save. The Romans understood power; when Paul wrote this epistle to the capital of the ancient world, Rome ruled supreme. The gospel, however, is nothing to be ashamed of in comparison; for it, too, is power—indeed the "power of God to salvation for everyone" (1:16). In the gospel both Jews and Gentiles find access to God, not on the basis of human achievement, but because of God's free grace bestowed on those who accept it in faith.

Paul emphasizes that everyone stands in need of God's grace. This was apparent in the case of the Gentiles, who, instead of worshiping the Creator, worshiped the things created (1:25). But the Jews, in spite of their belief that they were superior to Gentiles, were also bankrupt. The Jews knew the revealed will of God and they judged others by it; but they failed to see they were condemned by the very law under which they passed judgments (2:1–3:8). Thus, "there is no difference, for all have sinned and fall short of the glory of God" (3:22–23).

But "good news" is that God's love is so great that it reaches humankind even in their sin. The form it took was the death of the beloved Son of God on the cross. The righteous one, Jesus, died on behalf of the unrighteous. Therefore, God pronounces persons justified, not when they have attained a certain level of goodness—thus excluding justification by works—but in the midst of their sin and rebellion (5:8–10). Such grace can be received only by grateful and trusting surrender, which is faith. In light of this magnificent salvation, Paul urged the Romans not to return to their old human nature, which always stands under condemnation of the law. Rather, he called on them to live free from sin and death through the power of the indwelling presence of the Holy Spirit (8:10–11).

Special Considerations.

Romans reflects Paul's deep concern with the relation between Jew and Gentile (chaps. 9–11). The Jews are indeed God's Chosen People, although their history is one of rebellion against God. Their rejection of Christ is consistent with their history, although a remnant does remain faithful. The rejection of the Jews, ironically, has increased the truly faithful because the cutting off of the native olive branch (Israel) has allowed a wild branch (Gentiles) to be grafted onto the tree (11:13).

Paul also declared that the inclusion of the Gentiles in the household of God aroused the Jews to jealousy, moving them to claim God's promised blessings. Thus, the hardened response of the Jews to the gospel is only temporary, until the Gentiles are fully included into the faith. At some future time the Jews will change and, like the remnant, "all Israel will be saved" (11:26).

Paul's wrestling with this problem caused him not to doubt or condemn God, but to marvel at God's wisdom (11:33). This marvelous epistle has kindled the same response in Christians of all generations.

R UTH, BOOK OF—a short Old Testament book about a devoted Gentile woman, Ruth of Moab, who became an ancestor of King David of Israel.

Structure of the Book.

The Book of Ruth tells the story of a Moabite woman who married into a family of Israelites. But her husband and all the other men of the family died, leaving Ruth and her mother-in-law Naomi in a desperate situation. Ruth accompanied Naomi back to Judah, where they scratched out an existence by gathering leftover grain in the fields. This led to Ruth's encounter with Boaz, a wealthy Israelite and distant kinsman of Naomi, who eventually married the Moabite woman. Their son became the father of David's father, making Ruth and Boaz the great-grandparents of Judah's most famous king.

Authorship and Date.

The author of Ruth is unknown, although some scholars credit it to the prophet Samuel. The book had to be written some time after David became king of Judah, since it refers to his administration. This would place its writing at some time around 990 B.C.

Historical Setting.

The events in the book occurred at a dark time in Israel's history—in "the days when the judges ruled" (1:1), according to the historical introduction. This was a period when the nation lapsed again and again into worship of false gods. What a contrast this is to Ruth, who remained faithful to God, although she was a Moabite by birth—one considered an alien by God's Chosen People!

Theological Contribution.

Ruth's life gives us a beautiful example of the providence of God. He brought Ruth to precisely the right field where she could meet Boaz. God is also portrayed in the book as the model of loyal and abiding love (2:20).

Special Considerations.

The name Ruth means "friendship," and this book contains one of the most touching examples of friendship in the Bible. Ruth's words to her mother-in-law are quoted often as a pledge of love and devotion. "Entreat me not to leave you, or to turn back from following after you; for wherever you go, I will go; wherever you lodge, I will lodge; your people shall be my people, and your God, my God" (1:16).

S

SABACHTHANI [**suh BAHK thuh nigh**]—one of the final words spoken by Jesus from the cross (Matt. 27:46; Mark 15:34), an Aramaic phrase meaning "you have forsaken me."

SACRIFICE—the ritual through which the Hebrew people offered the blood or the flesh of an animal to God as a substitute payment for their sin. Sacrifice and sacrificing originated in the Garden of Eden soon after the Fall of mankind. Various principles of sacrifice are confirmed in the account of Cain and Abel (Gen. 4:3–5). Abel offered a better sacrifice than Cain for two reasons. First, he gave the best that he had, whereas Cain simply offered whatever happened to be available. Second, Abel's offering demonstrated that he was motivated by faith in God and that his attitude was pleasing to God (Gen. 4:4–5; Heb. 11:4). Cain, by contrast, would soon demonstrate that his attitude was displeasing to God. He would become selfish, angry, and deceitful. He would then murder his brother, lie to God, and refuse to confess his sin or show remorse.

It is a serious mistake to affirm that Abel's sacrifice was acceptable to God because it was an animal sacrifice and that Cain's sacrifice was unacceptable because he did not bring an animal. Genesis 4 makes no mention of offerings for the atonement of sin, and therefore to insist that the blood of an animal is mandated here is to read more into the account than is warranted. Attitude on the part of the offerer, not the nature of the offering, is in the forefront of the author's concern in Genesis 4. Nor is it helpful to claim that God's provision of animal skins in Genesis 3, in contrast to the fig leaves used by Adam and Eve, presupposes the slaughter of a sacrificial animal. Warmth and comfort are in view, not atonement.

When Noah came out of the ark, his first act was to build an altar upon which he sacrificed animals to God. This pleased God not because God was hungry but because Noah's act was a recognition that God understood his sinfulness, its penalty, and the necessity of blood sacrifice as a divine provision (Heb. 11:39–40). Noah represented all mankind who now recognized God's gracious provision and promise. God pledged never again to curse the ground (Gen. 8:20–22), and He blessed Noah because of his faith.

Eventually, God called Abraham, who rejoiced in anticipation of the appearance of a promised redeemer (John 8:56). Abraham regularly worshiped God by offering sacrifices to Him. God taught Abraham that the ultimate sacrifice would be the sacrifice of a human being, one of Adam's descendants—an only son provided miraculously by God.

The fullest explanation of the concept of sacrifice is found in the Mosaic Law. In this code sacrifice has three central ideas: consecration, expiation (covering of sin), and propitiation (satisfaction of divine anger). Only consecration had a kind of sacrifice which spoke of it alone. This was the vegetable or grain offerings. These could not be brought to God, however, unless they were preceded by an expiatory offering, or an animal or bloody sacrifice. There was no consecration (commitment) to God apart from expiation (dealing with the penalty and guilt of sin). People could not approach God and be right with Him without the shedding of blood.

The general word for sacrifices in the Mosaic Law was *qorban*—literally "that which is brought near." The fuller designation of these sacrifices was a gift of holiness (Ezek. 20:40). The word *qorban* was used of anything given or devoted to God (Mark 7:11), so it included more than sacrifices presented at the altar. Sacrifice, however, referred to items placed on the altar to be consumed by God. Hence, there was no sacrifice apart from the altar.

The Old Testament also referred to sacrifices as food for the Lord (Lev. 3:11, 16; 22:7) and an offering made by the fire for the satisfaction of the Lord (Lev. 2:2, 9). As a spiritual being, God did not need physical food. Nevertheless, He did insist that these sacrifices be given to Him. Sacrifice as worship is people giving back to God what God has previously given them as a means of grace. Ultimately, these sacrifices speak of the one final and perfect sacrifice of Jesus Christ (Heb. 10:11–18).

The gift aspect of sacrifice was emphasized by the many divine regulations determining what was acceptable to God. For people to determine what pleased God would put them in the place of God. Therefore, God determined what was pleasing to Him. Whatever was offered had to be "clean" (acceptable, or symbolically without sin). Not everything designated "clean," however, was to be offered as a sacrifice. Of the clean animals, only oxen, sheep, goats, and pigeons were acceptable offerings. Likewise, of the clean vegetables, only grain, wine, and oil were proper.

These materials were selected perhaps to teach that people should give to God from that which sustains their lives. In short, people were required to give God the gift of their lives. Therefore, God repeatedly emphasized that He did not need or desire food and sacrifices themselves. He wants our love, commitment, and service (Deut. 6:5; 1 Sam. 15:22).

Both the Old Testament and the New Testament confirm that sacrifices were presented as a symbolic gesture. People were obligated, because of their sins, to present offerings by which they gave another life in place of their own. These substitutes pointed forward to the ultimate substitute, Jesus Christ (Heb. 10:1–18).

According to God's command, the animal sacrificed had to be physically perfect in age and condition. Through the perfection of this animal, perfection was presented to God. Ultimately, this symbolized the necessity for people to present themselves perfect before God by presenting the perfect one in their place (1 Pet. 1:18–19). The true Lamb of God, innocent of all sin, took away sin (John 1:29).

After the animal was selected and presented at the altar, the first act was the laying on of hands by the person presenting the offering. By this act the worshipers symbolically transferred their sin and guilt to the sacrificial animal that stood in their place. The sacrifice symbolically pointed to the Savior who would do for the believers what they could not do for themselves. He would take upon Himself sin and guilt and accomplish redemption for His people (Is. 53:4–12; Matt. 1:21).

In the festival of the Day of Atonement, two goats depicted this redemptive act. One goat died, its death symbolizing how the ultimate sacrifice in the future would pay the penalty for the believer's sin. Its blood was applied to the Mercy Seat in the Holy of Holies, symbolizing how the great sacrifice would cover people's sin, bring them into God's presence, and make full restitution to God. To the head of the second goat the priest symbolically transferred the sin of God's people. Then this goat, known as the scapegoat, was sent into the wilderness to symbolize the removal of the people's sin (Leviticus 16).

SACRIFICIAL OFFERINGS—offerings brought periodically (sometimes daily; Ex. 29:38; Heb. 10:11) to God in Old Testament times by which people hoped to atone for their sins and restore fellowship with God. The Bible depicts us as sinners abiding in death and destined for death. We abide in death because we are separated from fellowship with God and unable to restore that life-giving fellowship (Rom. 5:12; 8). The sentence of death hangs over us because of our identity with Adam's fall (Rom. 5:14), our enmity toward God, and our constant sinning (Gen. 6:5; 8:21; Rom. 3:10). Ultimately, this will result in physical death and eternal suffering in hell.

God, however, provided a method by which our penalty can be paid and fellowship with God can be restored. This method is the sacrificial offering of Jesus Christ (Hebrews 9–10). This perfect offering was anticipated throughout the Old Testament by various sacrificial offerings. These Old Testament sacrifices were effective only when offered in faith in the promised sacrifice (Gen. 3:15; Heb. 9:8–9; 10:8–9, 16–17).

The first sacrifices were the offerings of Cain and Abel. Only Abel's offering was a true sacrifice made in faith because Abel recognized his unworthiness and the divine promise of a true and perfect redeemer (Gen. 4:3–5; Heb. 1:4). The sacrifice of Christ is most clearly and fully anticipated in the Mosaic system of sacrificial offerings. The following specific sacrificial offerings were provided for in the Mosaic Law:

Burnt Offering.

This kind of offering was described as "that which goes up (to God)." It was termed "whole" (Lev. 6:22) because the entire offering was to be burnt upon the altar. It was termed "continual" (Ex. 29:38–42) to teach the nation of Israel that their sinfulness required a complete and continual atonement and consecration. This sacrifice, offered every morning and evening, pointed to Christ's atoning death for sinners (2 Cor. 5:21) and His total consecration to God (Luke 2:49). The burnt offering spoke of Christ's passive obedience and His submission to the penalty required by human sinfulness. It also refers to His perfect obedience to God's law by which He did for us what we are unable to do for ourselves.

Cereal Offering (**see** *Meal Offering*).

Drink Offering.
    An offering of liquid, such as wine (Ex. 29:40).

Fellowship Offering (**see** *Peace Offering*).

Grain Offering (**see** *Meal Offering*).

Guilt Offering (**see** *Sin Offering*).

Heave Offering (**see** *Peace Offering*).

Meal Offering.
    This offering is translated meat offering in some versions, but since this offering was bloodless and meatless, it is more meaningfully rendered meal (NKJV) or grain (NIV); sin offering (NRSV) cereal offering. Meal offerings were prepared and presented to God as a meal, symbolically presenting the best fruits of human living to God to be consumed or used as He desired (Heb. 10:5–10). A notable exception to this is that poor people could present meal offerings as sin offerings.
    In the meal offering a person presented to God a vicarious consecration of the perfect life and total property of another (Christ). There is no ground in this offering for human boasting as though the offerer were received by God on the grounds of human effort. Rather, the recognition of the person's unworthiness is emphasized by the fact that meal offerings must be accompanied by a whole burnt offering or a peace offering (Lev. 2:1; Num. 15:1–16). Both offerings were made to atone for human sin.

Meat Offering (**see** *Meal Offering*).

Peace Offering.
    This sacrificial offering was also called a heave offering and a wave offering. This was a bloody offering presented to God (Lev. 3:1; fellowship offering, NIV). Part of the offering was eaten by the priest (representing God's acceptance) and part

was eaten by worshipers and their guests (nonofficiating priests or Levites and the poor, Deut. 12:18; 16:11). Thus, God hosted the meal, communing with the worshiper and other participants. This sacrifice celebrated covering of sin, forgiveness by God, and the restoration of a right and meaningful relationship with God and with life itself (Judg. 20:26; 21:4).

There were three kinds of peace offerings: (1) thank offerings in response to an unsolicited special divine blessing; (2) votive (vowed) offerings in pursuit of making a request or pledge to God; and (3) freewill offerings spontaneously presented in worship and praise.

Sin Offering.

This bloody offering, also known as a guilt offering, was presented for unintentional or intentional sins for which there was no possible restitution (Lev. 4:5–13; 6:24–30). If the offering was not accompanied by repentance, divine forgiveness was withheld (Num. 15:30). Expiation or covering (forgiveness) of sin was represented by the blood smeared on the horns of the altar of incense or burnt offering and poured out at the base of the altar.

The size and sex of the beast offered depended on the rank of the offerers. The higher their post the more responsibility they bore. The penalty for all sin, death, was vicariously inflicted on the animal. Guilt for the worshiper's sin was transferred symbolically through the laying on of the offerer's hands.

Thank Offering (**see** *Peace Offering*).

Trespass Offering.

This was a bloody offering presented for unintentional or intentional sins of a lesser degree and for which the violater could make restitution (Lev. 5:15). The sprinkling of the blood on the sides of the altar rather than on its horns gave further evidence that this offering addressed sins of a lesser degree.

Special provisions were made for the poor by allowing less valuable offerings to be substituted in this kind of sacrifice.

The amount of restitution (money paid) was determined by the officiating priest. Restitution declared that the debt incurred was paid. Significantly, Christ was declared a trespass offering in

Isaiah 53:10 (guilt offering, NIV). He not only bore the sinner's penalty and guilt but made restitution, restoring the sinner to right standing with God.

Wave Offering (**see** *Peace Offering*).

SAMARITAN PENTATEUCH—an ancient version of the first five books of the Old Testament as preserved by the Samaritans. The manuscript copies of the Samaritan Pentateuch use a form of letters similar to that which was in general use before the Captivity—the old Hebrew, or "Phoenician" script. The origin of this version of the Law is difficult to determine, but the events recorded in 2 Kings 17:24–28 suggest that the Law was the basis of the instruction given by the exiled priest that enabled the newly settled Samaritans to worship the God of Israel.

Since only the Pentateuch (the first five books of the Old Testament) was accepted as authentic Scripture by the Samaritans, it must have been available in complete form as early as 681 B.C. Some scholars claim that the Samaritans had no copy of the Law before about 450 B.C. But there is no reason why copies of the Law should not have been circulating in Israel during Jeroboam II's rule (about 793–753 B.C.). This means they could have been taken to Assyria when the citizens of Samaria were deported by this pagan nation in 722 B.C. Nor is there any difficulty in supposing that the priest who returned to Samaria brought with him a copy of the Law for traditional teaching purposes.

Because of their differences with the pure Hebrew tradition, the Samaritans occasionally changed the wording of their books of the Law to give preference to Mount Gerizim to show that their temple there was the authentic place for worship. In other respects the Samaritans promoted their own ceremonies and beliefs, but they emphasized the place of Moses as the lawgiver who acted by direct divine command. Despite scribal additions and variations in spelling, the Samaritan Pentateuch is very similar to the Hebrew Pentateuch.

Several fragments related to the text of the Samaritan Pentateuch were discovered among the Dead Sea Scrolls. These prove that this text was handed down in Samaritan circles in the same way that the Hebrew Law and other parts of the Old Testament were preserved by the Jews. Certain groups among the Samaritans probably made copies of individual books as well as the entire Pentateuch. These valuable manuscript fragments support the idea of such activity without actually indicating that the Samaritan Pentateuch's text was earlier than that of the traditional Hebrew Bible.

SAMUEL, BOOKS OF—two historical books of the Old Testament that cover the nation of Israel's transition from a loose tribal form of government to a united kingship under Saul and David. The books are named for the prophet Samuel, who anointed these two leaders.

Structure of the Books.

In the Bible used by the Hebrew people during Old Testament days, the books of Samuel consisted of one continuous narrative. This long book was divided into 1 and 2 Samuel when the Hebrew Bible was translated into the Greek language in the second century b.c. All Bibles since that time have followed the two-book pattern.

First Samuel covers the lives of the prophet Samuel and King Saul, introducing David as a warrior and a successor to the throne. Second Samuel focuses on David's career as Israel's greatest king.

Some of the most dramatic stories in the Bible are found in these two Old Testament books. First Samuel reports Samuel's own experience as a boy when he heard God's call to a prophetic ministry (chap. 2). It also reveals that David was a shepherd boy destined for greatness when he defeated the Philistine giant Goliath with nothing but a slingshot and a stone (1 Sam. 17:19–51).

Contrast this triumphant moment, however, with David's great sin, when he committed adultery with Bathsheba, then arranged for the killing of her husband, Uriah (2 Samuel 11). David repented of his sin and claimed God's forgiveness, but from that day on his fortunes were clouded and his family was troubled.

Authorship and Date.

Since the name of the great prophet Samuel is associated with these books, it is logical to assume that he wrote 1 and 2 Samuel. But the problem with this theory is that all of 2 Samuel and a major portion of 1 Samuel deal with events that happened after Samuel's death. However, there is strong support for Samuel's authorship of some of the material, since the Book of 1 Chronicles refers to "the book of Samuel the seer" (1 Chr. 29:29).

Before Samuel's death about 1000 B.C., he must have written accounts of the kingship of Saul and the early life of David that appear as part of 1 Samuel. Many scholars believe that Abiathar the priest wrote those parts of these two books that deal with the court life of David. He served as a priest during David's administration; so he may have had access to the royal records that provided the historical facts for these accounts.

Historical Setting.

The Books of 1 and 2 Samuel describe a turning point in Israel's history. This was a time when the people became dissatisfied with their loose tribal form of organization and insisted on a united kingdom under the ruling authority of a king. For hundreds of years they had existed as a tribal society, with each tribe living on its own portion of the land and minding its own affairs. If a superior enemy threatened the entire nation, they depended on deliverance at the hands of Judges, those military leaders described in the Book of Judges, who would raise a volunteer army to make their borders secure.

This system of defense, however, proved woefully inadequate when the Philistines began to flex their muscles against the nation with renewed intensity about 1100 B.C. These warlike people boasted of iron chariots, a wellorganized army, and other superior weapons that they used with military precision against the poorly organized Israelites. The threat of this superior force led the nation to clamor for a king—a ruler who could unite all the tribes against a common enemy.

Saul was anointed by Samuel about 1050 B.C. to serve as first king of the nation. A gifted young man of great promise, he ruled for 40 years (Acts 13:21) before taking his life by falling on his own sword when the Philistines prevailed against him in a decisive battle (1 Sam. 31:1–7). David, his successor, also ruled 40 years (2 Sam. 5:4; 1 Chr. 29:27), from 1010 to 970 B.C. Building on Saul's beginning, David succeeded in driving out the Philistines, unifying the people, and conquering or establishing peaceful relationships with surrounding nations.

Theological Contribution.

The major theological contribution of 1 and 2 Samuel is the negative and positive views of the kingship that they present. On the negative side, the books make it clear that in calling for a king the people were rejecting God's rule. Because Israel was unable to live under God's rule through the judges, God gave in to their demands and granted them a king. But He also warned them about the dangers of the kingship (1 Sam. 8:9–21).

On the positive side, 1 and 2 Samuel portray the kingship as established through David as a clear picture of God's purpose for His people. The covenant that God established with David demonstrated God's purpose through David's family line; David's ancestors would be adopted as the sons of God in a special sense (2 Samuel 7). David's line would continue through the centuries, and his throne would be established forever (2 Sam. 7:13). In the person of Jesus Christ the Messiah, this great covenant came to its fulfillment.

Special Considerations.

The story of David and Goliath (1 Samuel 17) presents more than a dramatic encounter between two warriors. It also points up the contrast between David and Saul. Since he was tall himself, Saul should have been the one to face the giant (1 Sam. 9:2). By his failure to meet Goliath, Saul demonstrated both his folly and his inability to rule. By rising to the challenge, David demonstrated his wisdom and faith, proving that he was God's man for the throne of Israel.

In addition to its stories, the books of 1 and 2 Samuel contain several poems, or psalms of praise and lament. One such poem is the lovely prayer of Hannah (1 Samuel 2), in which Hannah rejoices in God's goodness in allowing her to conceive. The dramatic Psalm of the Bow (2 Samuel 1), in which David laments the death of Saul and Jonathan, is another of these poems.

SCRIPTURE—the Old and New Testaments, which make up the Bible, God's written Word. God gave to the world His living Word, Jesus Christ, and His written Word, the Scriptures. Although the Bible was written by prophets and apostles, the Bible originated not with their wills, but with God's (2 Pet. 1:20–21). "All Scripture," Paul wrote, "is given by inspiration of God" (2 Tim. 3:16).

After Jesus, God's living Word, returned to heaven, the Bible, God's written Word, remained on earth as God's eternal guide for mankind. The written Word is durable and universally available and has remained essentially unchanged in its message since it was first inspired by God.

Because the Bible is God's inspired Word, it is able to make us "wise for salvation through faith which is in Christ Jesus" (2 Tim. 3:15). The Scriptures testify of Christ (John 5:39) and are understood and received as He opens our understanding to the revealed will of His Father (Luke 24:27). Like the Berean Christians, we should search the Scriptures daily (Acts 17:11) to discover God's message for our lives.

S CROLL—a roll of papyrus, leather, or parchment on which an ancient document—particularly a text of the Bible—was written (Ezra 6:2). Rolled up on a stick, a scroll was usually about 11 meters (35 feet) long—the size required, for instance, for the Book of Luke or the Book of Acts. Longer books of the Bible required two or more scrolls.

One of the scrolls written by the prophet Jeremiah was read in the Temple and in the king's palace, then destroyed by King Jehoiakim. The king cut it into pieces and threw it into the fire to show his contempt for God's prophet. But Jeremiah promptly rewrote the scroll through his scribe, Baruch (Jer. 36:1–32).

Books did not exist until the second or third century A.D., when the codex was introduced. The codex had a page arrangement much like our modern books.

S HEMA, THE [shuh MAH] (hear thou)—the Jewish confession of faith that begins, "Hear, O Israel: The Lord our God, the LORD is one!" (Deut. 6:4). The complete Shema is found in three passages from the Old Testament: Numbers 15:37–41, Deuteronomy 6:4–9 and 11:13–21.

The first of these passages stresses the unity of God and the importance of loving Him and valuing His commands. The second passage promises blessing or punishment according to a person's obedience of God's will. The third passage commands that a fringe be worn on the edge of one's garments as a continual reminder of God's laws. These verses make up one of the most ancient features of worship among the Jewish people. Jesus quoted from the Shema during a dispute with the scribes (Mark 12:28–30).

SHIBBOLETH [SHIBB oh lehth]—the password used by the Gileadites at the fords of the Jordan River to detect the fleeing Ephraimites (Judg. 12:6). In a conflict between the people of Ephraim, who lived west of the Jordan, and the people of Gilead, who lived east of the Jordan, the Gileadites were victorious. Led by the judge Jephthah, the Gileadites seized the fords of the Jordan, where they met the fleeing invaders and asked them to say "Shibboleth."

Because of a difference in dialect, an Ephraimite "could not pronounce it right" (v. 6), saying "Sibboleth" instead. Betrayed by his own speech, the unlucky Ephraimite was then killed at the fords of the Jordan by Jephthah and his men.

SONG OF SOLOMON, THE—an Old Testament book written in the form of a lyrical love song. Some interpreters believe this song speaks symbolically of the love of God for the nation of Israel. But others insist it should be interpreted literally—as a healthy expression of romantic love between a man and a woman. No matter how the book is interpreted, it is certainly one of the most unusual in the Bible. Its title, "the song of songs" (1:1), implies it was the loveliest and best-known of all the songs of Solomon.

Structure of the Book.

The Song of Solomon is a brief book of only eight chapters. But in spite of its brevity, it has a complicated structure that sometimes confuses the reader. Several different characters or personalities have speaking parts within this long lyrical poem. In most translations of the Bible, these speakers change abruptly with no identification to help the reader follow the narrative. But the NKJV clears up this confusion by publishing identification lines within the text. This helps the reader gain a clearer understanding of this beautiful song.

The three main parties with speaking parts in this long poem are: (1) the groom, King Solomon; (2) the bride, a woman referred to as "the Shulamite" (6:13); and (3) the "daughters of Jerusalem" (2:7). These women of Jerusalem may have been royal servants who served as attendants to Solomon's Shulamite bride. In this love song, they serve as a chorus to echo the sentiments of the Shulamite, emphasizing her love and affection for Solomon.

In addition to these main personalities, the brothers of the Shulamite bride are also mentioned in the poem (8:8–9). These may have been her stepbrothers. The poem indicates she worked under their command as "the keeper of the vineyards" (1:6).

This beautiful love song falls naturally into two major sections of about equal length—the beginning of love (chaps. 1–4) and the broadening of love (chaps. 5–8).

In the first section, the Shulamite tells about Solomon's visit to her home in the country in the springtime (2:8–17). She also recalls the many happy experiences of their courtship when she visited Solomon in his palace in Jerusalem (2:4–7). She thinks about the painful separations from his love during this time (3:1–5), as well as the joyous wedding procession to Jerusalem to become the king's bride (3:6–11). Solomon also praises his bride-to-be in a beautiful poem on the magic and wonder of love (chap. 4).

In the second section of the book, the love of the Shulamite and Solomon for each other continues to deepen after their marriage. She has a troubled dream when he seems distant and unconcerned (5:2–8). But Solomon assures her of his love and praises her beauty (6:4–7:9). Longing to visit her country home (7:10–8:4), she finally makes the trip with Solomon; and their love grows even stronger (8:5–7). The song closes with an assurance of each to the other that they will always remain close in their love.

Authorship and Date.

Traditionally, authorship of the Song of Solomon has been assigned to Solomon, since the book itself makes this claim (1:1). But some scholars reject this theory. They insist it was a later collection of songs attributed to Solomon because of his reputation as a writer of psalms and proverbs (1 Kin. 4:32). A careful analysis of the internal evidence, however, gives support to the view that Solomon wrote the book.

Solomon is mentioned by name several times in the song (1:1, 5; 3:7, 9, 11; 8:11–12), and he is specifically identified as the groom. The book also gives evidence of wealth, luxury, and exotic imported goods (3:6–11)—a characteristic of his administration. The groom of the song also assures the Shulamite bride that she is "the only one" (6:9) among his "sixty queens and eighty concubines" (6:8)—probably a reference by Solomon to his royal harem. At the height of his power and influence, Solomon was known to have 700 wives and 300 concubines (1 Kin. 11:3).

This internal evidence supports the traditional view that Solomon himself wrote this song that bears his name. It must have been written early in his reign, probably about 965 B.C.

Historical Setting.

With his large harem, how could King Solomon write such a beautiful love song to one specific wife? Perhaps his union with the Shulamite woman was the only authentic marriage relationship Solomon ever knew. Most of his marriages were political arrangements, designed to seal treaties and trade agreements with other nations. In contrast, the Shulamite woman was not a cultured princess but a lowly vineyard keeper whose skin had been darkened by her long exposure to the sun (1:6). Yet, she was the bride to whom Solomon declared, "How much better than wine is your love, and the scent of your perfumes than all spices!" (4:10).

This has a real message about the nature of true love. Authentic love is much more than a surface relationship; it extends to the very core of one's being. Love like this cannot be bought and sold like some commodity on the open market. Solomon had many wives, but the Shulamite may have been the only one with whom he enjoyed a warm, enriching relationship.

Theological Contribution.

The great message of the Song of Solomon is the beauty of love between a man and a woman as experienced in the relationship of marriage. In its frank but beautiful language, the song praises the mutual love that husband and wife feel toward each other in this highest of all human relationships.

The sexual and physical side of marriage is a natural and proper part of God's plan, reflecting His purpose and desire for the human race. This is the same truth so evident at the beginning of time in the Creation itself. God created man and woman and brought them together to serve as companions and to share their lives with one another: "Therefore a man shall leave his father and mother and be joined to his wife, and they shall become one flesh" (Gen. 2:24). Like the Book of Genesis, the Song of Solomon says a bold "yes" to the beauty and sanctity of married love.

But this book also points beyond human love to the great Author of love. Authentic love is possible in the world because God brought love into being and planted that emotion in the hearts of His people. Even husbands and wives should remember that the love they share for one another is not a product of their human goodness or kindness. We are able to love because the love of God is working in our lives: "In this is love, not that we loved God, but that He loved us and sent His Son to be the propitiation for our sins. Beloved, if God so loved us, we also ought to love one another" (1 John 4:10–11).

Special Considerations.

The symbols and images that the groom uses to describe the beauty of his Shulamite bride may seem strange to modern readers. He portrays her hair as "a flock of goats, going down from Mount Gilead" (4:1). Her neck, he says, is like "the tower of David, built for an armory, on which hang a thousand bucklers" (4:4).

In his use of these symbols, the groom is reflecting the cultural patterns of the ancient world. To those who lived in Solomon's time, the rippling effect of a flock of goats moving down a hillside was, indeed, a thing of beauty. And a stately tower atop a city wall reflected an aura of stability and nobility. The Shulamite woman would have been very pleased at such creative compliments from her poetic groom.

Scholars are not certain of the exact meaning of the phrase, "the Shulamite" (6:13), which has come to be used as a title for the bride in this song. Since the word is a feminine form of the Hebrew word for "Solomon," perhaps Shulamite simply means "Solomon's bride." Because the poem makes several references to Lebanon (3:9; 4:8, 11, 15; 5:15; 7:4), some scholars believe she came from this mountainous territory along the Mediterranean coast in northwestern Palestine.

TALITHA CUMI [TAL uh thuh KOO migh]—an Aramaic
phrase spoken by Jesus when He raised the daughter of
Jairus from the dead. The phrase means, "Little girl, arise"
(Mark 5:41).

TALMUD—a collection of books and commentary compiled
by Jewish rabbis from A.D. 250–500. The Hebrew word *talmud* means "study" or "learning." This is a fitting title for a
work that is a library of Jewish wisdom, philosophy, history,
legend, astronomy, dietary laws, scientific debates, medicine,
and mathematics.

The Talmud is made up of interpretation and commentary
of the Mosaic and rabbinic law contained in the Mishna, an
exhaustive collection of laws and guidelines for observing the
law of Moses. As a guide to following the law, the Talmud also
serves as a basis for spiritual formation. More than 2,000 scholars or rabbis worked across a period of 250 years to understand
the meaning of God's word for their particular situation. Out of
these efforts they produced the Talmud.

The wide variety and comprehensive detail of the Talmud's
subject matter conveys a deep thirst for learning. Questions as
minute as why God created a gnat and as universal as the origin

of the universe filled the teachers of Israel with wonder. A passion for truth and understanding led the Jewish teachers deep into the marvels of the human experience.

The Pharisees were the first to give greater attention to the laws of Moses. The Roman historian Josephus reported that their oral tradition included regulations that were not recorded in the Mosaic Law at all. The Mishna collected all of these oral regulations into one permanent record. In response to the Mishna, wide discussions concerning its content and meaning began, resulting in the Talmud.

The centers for these learned discussions were the academies in Babylonia and Israel. As a result, two Talmuds, the Babylonian Talmud and the Jerusalem Talmud, were created. Because the Babylonian rabbis were far more thorough in word-by-word interpretation of the Mishna than were the rabbis in Israel, the Babylonian Talmud is much more complete. An English edition of this work fills 36 volumes and almost 36,000 pages.

The Talmud is divided into six major sections. The first of these deals with agriculture and crops and the offerings, tithes, and prayers associated with them. The second section is about holidays and festivals such as the Sabbath, Passover, Rosh Hashanah and others. A third section discusses laws about marriage, divorce, property, and related subjects. Another section concerns the rules governing the courts. The next section deals with the laws pertaining to the Temple and the sacrifices and Jewish foods. The final section discusses the laws of ritual purity.

At some points during Jewish history, traditions and the Talmud have been considered equal to or better than the Scripture itself. Jesus encountered such an attitude among the Pharisees even before the existence of the Talmud (Matt. 15:3). Christians must be careful not to make the same mistake in regard to our own traditions.

TARGUM—translations of the Old Testament from the Hebrew language into Aramaic. The word "Targum" is related to a Hebrew term meaning "translation." These translations were sometimes literal and exact, but often were paraphrased. Many translators took the opportunity to comment upon the Hebrew texts. In a sense, some Targumim (plural) are a form of commentary on the Bible.

Scholars question when and why the Old Testament was first translated into Aramaic. Some suggest that the Hebrew language had changed so much that an explanation of Mosaic Law helped the Israelites understand its true meanings. Ezra sometimes provided such explanations (Neh. 8:8). Other scholars think the Israelites adopted the Aramaic language during the Babylonian Captivity. The Targumim, then, translated the Old Testament into a more understandable language.

By the time of Christ, Aramaic was the common language in Israel. During a synagogue service, one verse of the Hebrew text was read, followed by a translation and explanation in Aramaic. By the second or third century A.D., the common practice was to read only the Aramaic translation.

The best-known Targum was probably the Targum Onkelos, which translated the Pentateuch quite literally. The Targumim are helpful today in understanding ancient Jewish interpretations of the Old Testament. Because they are paraphrased, they cannot be used to attest the original Hebrew reading of a Bible passage.

TESTAMENT—a written document that provides for the disposition of one's personal property after death; a bequest. The word "testament" occurs only two times in the NKJV (2 Cor. 3:14; Heb. 9:16–17). In the KJV the word appears in several additional places (Matt. 26:28; 2 Cor. 3:6; Rev. 11:19)—translated in all these cases as "covenant" by the NKJV. The word "testament" also refers to either of the two main divisions of the Bible: the

Old Testament and the New Testament, or, more accurately, the Old Covenant and the New Covenant (2 Cor. 3:14).

THESSALONIANS, EPISTLES TO THE—two letters written by the apostle Paul, which are among the earliest of Paul and of the New Testament. The major theological theme of 1 and 2 Thessalonians is the return of Christ to earth. Important as this theme is, however, the Thessalonian letters leave the reader wide awake to the responsibilities of the present, not gazing into the future. Both epistles aim to establish and strengthen a young church in a stormy setting (1 Thess. 3:2, 13; 2 Thess. 2:17; 3:3). In neither epistle does Paul fight any grave errors in the church. In both epistles the reader feels the heartbeat of Paul the pastor as he identifies with a young congregation taking its first steps in faith.

Structure of the Epistles.

Paul begins the first epistle by thanking God for the faith, hope, and love of the Thessalonians, and marveling that they have become "examples to all in Macedonia and Achaia" (chap. 1). Paul recalls his sacrificial labor for the gospel (2:1–12), and the suffering the Thessalonians endured (2:13–16). Longing to see them again (2:17–3:5), Paul expresses his relief and encouragement upon hearing Timothy's report of their well-being (3:6–10). He prays for their growth in the gospel (3:11–13).

In chapters four and five Paul addresses three concerns. He reminds his converts that in sexual matters a Christian must conduct himself differently from a pagan (4:1–8). He adds a gentle reminder to work diligently and thus earn the respect of "those who are outside" (non-Christians, 4:9–12). Paul then devotes extended consideration to the most pressing questions in Thessalonica, the Second Coming of Christ (4:13–5:11).

The first letter concludes with a number of memorable exhortations and a charge to read the epistle "to all the holy brethren" (5:12–28).

Second Thessalonians is both shorter and simpler than 1 Thessalonians. Paul follows a nearly identical opening (1:1) with an assurance that when Christ returns He will punish those who persecute the Thessalonians (chap. 1). Chapter two brings Paul to the purpose of the letter—to clarify and expand his teaching on the Second Coming (1 Thess. 4:13–5:11). Certain signs will precede the return of Christ, in particular, an outbreaking of lawlessness, followed by the appearance of "the man of sin," or "lawless one" (Antichrist), who will escort to their doom those who have no love for the truth (2 Thess. 2:1–12). In contrast to those who are perishing, believers can give thanks to God for their call to salvation (2:13–17).

Paul concludes by requesting the prayers of the Thessalonians (3:1–5) and encouraging idlers to earn their living rather than live off their neighbors (3:6–15). He ends with a benediction in his own hand (3:16–18).

Authorship and Date.

The vocabulary, style, and thought of the Thessalonian correspondence are genuinely Pauline. In 1 Thessalonians 2:1–3:10 Paul shares his point of view on some of the events described in Acts 16:16–18:7, thus supporting Luke's description of Paul's ministry in Acts. Both letters bear Paul's name as author (1 Tess. 1:1; 2 Thess. 1:1). Paul's co-workers, Silvanus (Silas) and Timothy, are both mentioned along with Paul in the opening greeting of both epistles.

It is possible to date the Thessalonian letters with some precision. Paul wrote both from Corinth (1 Thess. 1:1; 2 Thess. 1:1; Acts 18:5) while Gallio was proconsul (governor of a Roman province) of Achaia. We know from an inscription discovered at Delphi that Gallio ruled in Corinth from May, A.D. 51, to April, A.D. 52. If Paul spent 18 months in Corinth (Acts 18:11), and yet was brought to trial before Gallio (Acts 18:12–17), he must have arrived in Corinth before Gallio became proconsul. If he wrote to the Thessalonians shortly after leaving them, which seems probable, the letters would have to be dated in late A.D. 50 or early A.D. 51.

Historical Setting.

Paul founded the church at Thessalonica in A.D. 49 or 50 during his second missionary journey (Acts 17:1–9). The church consisted of a few Jewish converts and a larger number of former pagans (1 Thess. 1:9; Acts 17:4). Desiring not to handicap the young church, Paul worked at his own job as a tentmaker—and at some sacrifice to himself, he adds (1 Thess. 2:7–12)—twice receiving aid from the ever-faithful Philippians (Phil. 4:16).

Paul's stay in Thessalonica was cut short, however, when the Jews gathered some local troublemakers and accused him before the city fathers of "turning the world upside down" by favoring Jesus as king instead of Caesar (Acts 17:1–7). This accusation was no small matter; it was a matter of treason, which in the Roman Empire was punishable by death. Not surprisingly, an uproar broke out; and Paul was escorted out of town, leaving Timothy to patch up the work (Acts 17:10, 15). Separated so suddenly from the infant church, Paul describes his feelings as one who had been "orphaned" (Greek text, 1 Thess. 2:17).

Once he was safe in Athens, Paul sent Timothy (who apparently had since rejoined him) back to Thessalonica to strengthen and encourage the believers (1 Thess. 3:2). When Timothy returned to Paul, who had since moved on to Corinth (Acts 18:1–5), he brought news of the love and faith of the Thessalonians. Paul was greatly relieved at this news.

In response to Timothy's encouraging report, Paul wrote the first epistle to Thessalonica. Evidently the Thessalonians were unsettled over the Second Coming of Christ, because Paul discusses the issue in both letters. In the first letter he informs them that at Christ's coming the dead in Christ must be raised first, then the living (1 Thess. 4:13–18). Since the time of Christ's coming will be as secretive as a thief's, Paul admonishes the believers to keep alert and be watchful (1 Thess. 5:1–11). Some, however, may have been too watchful, assuming that Christ would come any moment. In his second letter, therefore, Paul reminds the Thessalonians that certain events, namely, a rebellion against faith and the appearance of a "lawless one" (Antichrist), must happen before Christ returns (2 Thess. 2:8–9). In the meantime, Paul tells them to get back to work: "If anyone will not work, neither shall he eat" (2 Thess. 3:10).

Theological Contributions.

Three themes appear in the Thessalonian correspondence: thanksgiving for their faith and example in the past; encouragement for those undergoing persecution in the present; and exhortation to further work and growth in the future.

Paul writes the epistles in the spirit of a true pastor. He is overjoyed with their enthusiastic response to the gospel (1 Thess. 1). He longs for the day when they will stand with him in the presence of the Lord Jesus (1 Thess. 2:19–20). At the same time, Paul is grieved at unjust charges leveled against him that his gospel is more talk than action (1 Thess. 1:5; 2:1–8). Cut off from his flock, he is anxious for their well-being (1 Thess. 2:17–3:5).

Paul compares himself to a nursing mother caring for her children (1 Thess. 2:7), and to a father working in behalf of his family (1 Thess. 2:9–12). He gives himself body and soul to the Thessalonians (1 Thess. 2:8) and dares to hope that they will give themselves likewise to God (1 Thess. 5:23). Such is the concern of a dedicated pastor.

Paul addresses the question of the return of Christ as a concerned pastor. He reminds them that confidence in Christ's return enables believers to be patient (1 Thess. 1:10), creates hope and joy (1 Thess. 2:19), and spurs them to pursue pure and blameless lives (1 Thess. 3:13; 5:23). Uncertainty as to when Christ will return demands alertness and watchfulness (1 Thess. 5:1–11), but the certainty that He will return makes present trials and sufferings bearable (2 Thess. 1:3–11). His return will come as a surprise, like a thief in the night (1 Thess. 5:4); but it will not be disorderly: those who have died first in Christ will proceed first to Christ, followed by the living, "And thus we shall always be with the Lord" (1 Thess. 4:17).

There is no mention in either letter of a Millennium, followed by a battle between Christ and Satan (Rev. 20:1–10). Paul simply states that at His coming Jesus will destroy the "lawless one" and will judge the unrighteous (2 Thess. 2:8–12). The end, however, will follow widespread rebellion and abandonment of the faith. Paul appeals for them to be levelheaded during the time of trouble and warns Christians not to despair when they see the Antichrist pretending to be God (2 Thess. 2:4). The schemes of "the man of sin" or "man of lawlessness" (2 Thess. 2:6, NIV) will be restrained until his treachery is fully disclosed, and then Christ will utterly destroy him (2 Thess. 2:8).

On the subject of the Second Coming, Paul assures the Thessalonians what will happen, but not when it will happen. His discussion throughout is dominated by an emphasis on practical living, rather than on speculation. The best way to prepare for Christ's return is to live faithfully and obediently now.

TIMOTHY, EPISTLES TO—two letters of the apostle Paul, which, along with the Epistle to Titus, form a trilogy called the Pastoral Epistles. These letters are called Pastoral Epistles because they deal with matters affecting pastors and congregations. In these letters to Timothy, Paul's primary concern is to instruct his young associate to guard the spiritual heritage that he has received (1 Tim. 6:20; 2 Tim. 1:12–14; 2:2) by establishing sound doctrine in the church.

Structure of the Epistles.

First Timothy begins with a warning against false doctrine (1:1–11) and a reminder of God's mercy, illustrated by Paul's experience of salvation (1:12–20). This is followed by instructions on church practices: on prayer (2:1–8), on public worship (2:9–15), and on the qualifications of bishops (3:1–7) and deacons (3:8–13). A salute to Christ concludes the section (3:14–16).

Continuing with Timothy's responsibilities, Paul warns that false teachers will infiltrate the church (4:1–5). He instructs Timothy on the characteristics of a fit minister of the gospel (4:6–16), as well as his duties toward others (5:1–2), widows (5:3–16), elders (5:17–25), and servants (6:1–2). Following another warning against false teaching (6:3–10), Paul exhorts Timothy to "fight the good fight of faith" (6:11–21).

After a brief greeting (1:1–2), the second Epistle to Timothy begins by recalling Timothy's spiritual heritage (1:3–7), exhorting him to be strong under adversity and to keep the faith (1:8–18). In chapter two Paul uses the metaphors of soldier (2:3–5), farmer (2:6), experienced worker (2:15), and household utensils (2:20–21) as models for Timothy to imitate as a strong and worthy servant of the gospel. Paul declares what people will be like in the last days (3:1–9), although Timothy can take encouragement in the face of adversity from Paul's example and from the Scriptures (3:10–17).

The final chapter of 2 Timothy takes on a solemn tone as Paul appeals to Timothy to press forward in fulfilling his pastoral calling (4:1–5). Writing in the shadow of his impending death (4:6–8), Paul closes with personal greetings (4:9–22).

Authorship and Date.

The authorship and date of the Pastoral Epistles remain an unresolved question in New Testament studies. On the one hand, the epistles bear the name of Paul as author (1 Tim. 1:1; 2 Tim. 1:1; Titus 1:1) and preserve personal references to him (1 Tim. 1:3, 12–16; 2 Tim. 4:9–22; Titus 1:5; 3:12–13). Other considerations, however, pose problems for Paul's authorship of the Pastorals. These can be listed under the following categories:

Historical—The Book of Acts makes no mention of a situation in which Paul goes to Macedonia, leaving Timothy behind in Ephesus (1 Tim. 1:3), or Titus in Crete (Titus 1:5).

Ecclesiastical—The description of church order in the Pastorals (for example, bishops, elders, deacons, an enlistment of widows) appears rather advanced for Paul's time.

Theological—Some ideas in the Pastorals differ from Paul's thought. For example, "faith" (Titus 1:13; 2:2) suggests orthodoxy or "sound doctrine," rather than a saving relationship with Christ; "righteousness" (Titus 3:5) suggests "good deeds," rather than a status of being justified before God. Likewise, the understanding of law (1 Tim. 1:8–11) differs from Paul's usual teaching on the subject (compare Rom. 3:19–20).

Literary—The vocabulary and style of the Pastorals differ from Paul's other writings. A significant number of words that appear in the Pastorals are not found in Paul's genuine letters, and the tone of the letters is uncharacteristically harsh at places (for example, Titus 1:12–13).

Each of these objections is not of equal weight, although taken as a whole they are impressive. If one assumes, as church tradition often has, that Paul was released following the Roman imprisonment mentioned in Acts 28 (2 Tim. 4:16) and later went to Spain (1 Clement 5, writing about A.D. 96), or revisited points eastward, many of the problems listed above are lessened. In this view, the circumstances of the Pastorals would fall after the events described in Acts. Thus, confronted by a rise in false teaching and by a need to increase church discipline and order, Paul could have written the Pastorals with the help of a secretary who expressed Paul's ideas in somewhat un-Pauline ways. This would date the letters between Paul's first and second Roman imprisonments, or about A.D. 65.

On the other hand, some feel that an admirer of Paul, using genuine notes or letters of the apostle, drafted the Pastorals to address the problems of a later day in the spirit of Paul. This view would date the letters at the close of the first century.

Historical Setting.

First and Second Timothy differ in historical context. In the first epistle Paul writes from Macedonia to young Timothy (1 Tim. 4:12), who has been left in Ephesus to oversee the congregation (1 Tim. 1:3). The second epistle, also written to Timothy in Ephesus (2 Tim. 1:18), comes from Rome where Paul is undergoing a second (2 Tim. 4:16) and harsher imprisonment (2 Tim. 1:16, 18; 2:9). Paul is alone (except for Luke, 2 Tim. 4:11), and he knows the end of his life will come soon (2 Tim. 4:6). One can almost hear the plaintive echo of the apostle's voice as he bids Timothy to "come quickly before winter" (2 Tim. 4:9, 21).

The occasion for both epistles is much the same. Paul is deeply troubled by false teaching (1 Tim. 1:3–11; 2 Tim. 2:23) and apostasy (1 Tim. 1:6; 4:1; 2 Tim. 3:1–9), which endanger the church at Ephesus. He warns Timothy to beware of fables and endless genealogies (1 Tim. 1:4; 4:7; 2 Tim. 4:4), idle gossip (1 Tim. 5:13; 2 Tim. 2:16), rigid lifestyles based on the denial of things (1 Tim. 4:3), the snares of wealth (1 Tim. 6:9–10, 17–19), and religious speculations (1 Tim. 6:20). He warns that apostasy, in whatever form, will spread like cancer (2 Tim. 2:17). Paul urges Timothy to combat its malignant growth by teaching sound doctrine, promoting good works, and accepting one's share of suffering for the sake of the gospel (2 Tim. 1:8; 2:3, 11–13).

Theological Contribution.

The message of 1 and 2 Timothy can be summed up by words like remember (2 Tim. 2:8), guard (1 Tim. 6:20), be strong (2 Tim. 2:1), and commit (1 Tim. 1:18; 2:2). For Paul, the best medicine for false teaching and apostasy is "sound doctrine" (1 Tim. 1:10; 4:3). The gospel is a spiritual inheritance to be received from faithful witnesses and passed on to such (2 Tim.

2:2). It brings about wholeness or health (which is the meaning of "sound" in Greek), not only in belief, but also in good deeds. So vital is sound doctrine to the health of the church that it is something to be pursued (1 Tim. 6:11), fought for (1 Tim. 6:12), and even suffered for (2 Tim. 1:8; 2:3, 11–13).

Special Consideration.

The Epistles to Timothy might be considered our earliest manual of church organization. Within them we find guidelines for the selection of church leaders (1 Tim. 3:1–13). They also reveal an awareness of the need for standard forms of expressing the faith. For example, the words, "This is a faithful saying," appear four times in the epistles (1 Tim. 1:15; 3:1; 4:9; 2 Tim. 2:11). Two creeds, or perhaps hymns, also appear (1 Tim. 3:16; 2 Tim. 2:11–13). Finally, 2 Timothy presents the first (and only) pronouncement in the New Testament on the Bible as "Scripture" (referring to the Old Testament, 2 Tim. 3:14–17).

In Greek, the word for "inspiration" (2 Tim. 3:16) means "breathed into by God." As God breathed life into Adam (Gen. 2:7), so He breathes life into the written word, making it useful for teaching, reproof, and correction. Paul leaves us, therefore, not with a theory about Scripture, but with a description of its purpose and its power for salvation (2 Tim. 3:15).

TITUS, EPISTLE TO—one of three Pastoral Epistles among Paul's writings, the others being 1 and 2 Timothy. The Pastoral Epistles are so named because they deal with matters concerning pastors and congregations. They are the only letters of Paul addressed to individuals (Philemon is addressed "to the church in your house," 1:2). The purpose of the epistle to Titus was to warn against false teaching and to provide guidance for one of Paul's younger associates on sound doctrine and good works.

Structure of the Epistle.

Following an extended greeting (1:1–4), Paul advises Titus on the qualifications for church elders or bishops (1:5–9) and warns against false teachers (1:10–16). He proceeds to list ideal characteristics of older men (2:1–2), older women (2:3–5), younger men (2:6–8), and slaves (2:9–10) in the church. The grace of God as it is shown in Jesus Christ provides the foundation for such qualities of life (2:11–15). The final chapter lists ideal characteristics for Christians in society as a whole (3:1–2), again based on the goodness and grace of God (3:3–7); right beliefs thus lead to right actions (3:8–11). The letter closes with personal news and greetings (3:12–15).

Authorship and Date.

The circumstances were the same as those under which the apostle Paul wrote the letters to Timothy.

Historical Setting.

According to Titus 1:5, Paul left Titus on the island of Crete to continue establishing churches by appointing "elders in every city." As soon as Artemas or Tychicus relieved him, Titus was to meet Paul in Nicopolis (on the west coast of Greece) where the apostle planned to spend the winter (Titus 3:12).

The occasion for the letter was clear enough—to warn against false teachers (1:10–16). The precise nature of the teaching was less clear, although it included "Jewish fables," legalism, and disputes over genealogies (1:10, 14; 3:9–10). Paul urged Titus to avoid such traps, for people associated with them would get caught in their own schemes (3:11).

Theological Contribution.

Titus emphasizes sound doctrine (1:9; 2:8, 10) and challenges believers to good works (1:16; 2:14; 3:14). Paul summons Titus "to affirm constantly that those who have believed in God should be careful to maintain good works" (3:8). This letter will allow no separation between belief and action. We often hear it said that it makes no difference what we believe, as long as we do what is right. The truth, however, is that we become what we think, and all action is shaped by belief.

Two passages (2:11–14; 3:4–7) remind us of this truth. In a world such as ours, we cannot be reminded too often to hold fast to the truth of the gospel of our salvation.

TORAH [toe RAH]—guidance or direction from God to His people. In earlier times, the term Torah referred directly to the five books of Moses, or the Pentateuch. Moses told the people, "Command your children to observe to do all the words of this law." While the English word "law" does not suggest this, both the hearing and the doing of the law made the Torah. It was a manner of life, a way to live based upon the covenant that God made with His people.

Later the Hebrew Old Testament included both the books of wisdom and the prophets, but this entire collection was spoken of as the Torah. Jesus quoted Psalm 82:6, calling it a part of the law (John 10:34). Following the return from Babylon, the development of the synagogue gave rise to interpretations of the law by leading rabbis, which after a time were collected into 613 precepts. Considered part of the Torah, they were as binding as the law itself. Jesus referred to these additions to the original law of Moses as "the traditions of men."

The Torah, both then and now for Jewish people, should be seen as a total way of life. It requires complete dedication because it is seen as God's direction for living the covenant relationship.

TRANSLITERATION—the process by which letters or words are spelled in the corresponding characters of another alphabet. For example, Hades is a transliteration of a Greek word meaning "the unseen world" (Matt. 11:23; Luke

10:15; Acts 2:27). Amen is the transliteration of a Hebrew word meaning "so be it" or "let it be so" (Num. 5:22).

TYPE—a figure, representation, or symbol of something to come, as an event in the Old Testament foreshadows another in the New Testament. Types generally find their fulfillment in the person and ministry of Christ, but they sometimes relate to God, His people, or some other reality.

Scholars using typology range over a wide spectrum of interpretation. On the one extreme is the method that makes practically every item in the Old Testament find a greater fulfillment in the New Testament. At the other extreme are those scholars who insist on the word "type" being explicitly mentioned in the New Testament before they recognize any Old Testament type. Between those extremes, many scholars feel that there are some Old Testament correspondences to New Testament truths that are indeed typical, although the word "type" is not specifically used.

For instance, Melchizedek, the king-priest of Salem (Gen. 14:18–20 and Ps. 110:4), is said to be typical of Christ (Heb. 6:20). Jesus said the bronze serpent in the wilderness (Num. 21:4–9) was in some sense typical of His own crucifixion (John 3:14–15). The writer of Hebrews (Hebrews 9–10) pointed out that the tabernacle typically foreshadowed the person and work of Jesus Christ.

The NKJV uses the word "type" in only one place; in Romans 5:14 the apostle Paul mentions Adam as "a type of Him [Jesus] who was to come" (pattern, NIV).

U

UNCLEAN, UNCLEANNESS—defiled, foul, unfit. To be unclean refers to foods that are unfit, to defilement of a moral or religious character, and to spiritual impurity. The Old Testament distinguishes between what is clean and helpful and what is unclean and unacceptable (Lev. 10:10; 11:47). The priest was to teach the people the difference (Ezek. 44:23).

The teaching about uncleanness springs from the concept of God's holiness (Lev. 11:44–45). Freedom from uncleanness and guilt is possible through God's gracious work (Ps. 51:7). Holiness within, purity of heart, is possible through the exercise of faith in Christ's redemption (Titus 2:14; 1 Pet. 1:2) and obedience to His word of truth (John 15:3; 17:17; 1 Pet. 1:22).

There were different kinds of uncleanness. One type was unclean food. Several kinds of birds—such as ravens and vultures—and certain animals—such as swine, camels, and hares—were labeled unclean (Lev. 11:1–19). Besides foods, persons were designated unclean under certain conditions. Through a discharge or because of menstruation, men and women were considered unclean (Lev. 15:2–13, 19–24). Body emissions from open sores also rendered the person unclean. A leprous person was unclean (Lev. 13:11).

Serious uncleanness was connected with dead bodies, including both humans and animals (Lev. 11:25–31). Anything on which a dead thing fell would become unclean (Lev. 11:32). Severe defilement came from a dead human body: "He who touches the dead body of anyone shall be unclean seven days" (Num. 19:11). Indeed, when a person died in a tent, the whole tent was regarded as unclean (Num. 19:14). To be unclean was to be disqualified for divine worship.

The land could be defiled through idolatry (Ezek. 36:18) or through the sacrifice of innocent children (Ps. 106:38). God's Temple was defiled because of the entry of pagans (Ps. 79:1). The prophet Haggai used the notion of uncleanness of things to speak of immoral behavior of people (Hag. 2:13–14).

In the gospels, the word "unclean" describes those who are possessed by undesirable or even demonic spirits. Jesus exercised command over these unclean spirits (Luke 4:36) and effectively rebuked them (Luke 9:42). The disciples were also given power over unclean spirits (Mark 6:7; Acts 5:16). Jesus often cast out unclean spirits (Mark 1:23, 26–27; 5:2).

The word defilement described a sinful and unfit condition (Is. 6:5). Because of sin, "we are all like an unclean thing" (Is. 64:6). The New Testament lists uncleanness or moral defilement along with fornication and other sins, such as covetousness, as works of the flesh (Gal. 5:19; Col. 3:5). Believers are not called to uncleanness, but they are to live in holiness (1 Thess. 4:7). They are not to yield their members to uncleanness but to righteousness and holiness (Rom. 6:19).

Unclean things and people can be purified. Temple articles were purified through sprinkling of blood (Lev. 16:19). For those who touched dead bodies, washing with water provided cleansing (Lev. 15:27). Sprinkling with hyssop and water made clean the tent in which someone had died (Num. 19:18). For a woman with an issue of blood, a priest could offer sacrifice and make atonement (Lev. 15:30).

The uncleanness of sin to which the prophet Isaiah referred (Is. 6:5) is an uncleanness that is removed through God's actions. To Isaiah's lips the angel applied coals of fire and said, "Your iniquity is taken away" (Is. 6:7). John explained that the blood of Jesus Christ, God's Son, cleanses us from the defilement of sin (1 John 1:7). God fully provides for the cleansing of that which is unclean.

The reason why food and other things were designated unclean is not always fully clear. But there was a connection between the regulations about uncleanness and God's holiness. Following the list of unclean foods, God declared, "You shall be holy; for I am holy" (Lev. 11:44).

The great concern for dead things causing uncleanness may point to the notion that dead things were the very opposite of God. He is the living God. Death and dead things are opposite to who God is and what He desires. Thus, to be in contact with dead bodies was to be defiled. The human corpse represents an absence of life, and thus an absence of God. The laws about uncleanness are a powerful statement of the living God of the universe. Those made clean through His provision, however, will enjoy eternal life.

URIM AND THUMMIM [YOU rim, THUME em]—gems or stones carried by the high priest and used by him to determine God's will in certain matters. Many scholars believe these gems were lots that were cast, much as dice are thrown, to aid the high priest in making important decisions.

The Urim and Thummim were either on, by, or in the high priest's breastplate. For this reason the breastplate is often called the breastplate of judgment, or decision. In the instructions for making the breastplate, the linen was to be doubled to form a square (Ex. 28:16). If the top edge was not stitched together, the breastplate would be an envelope or pouch. Many scholars believe the Urim and Thummim were kept in this pouch and were stones or gems with engraved symbols that signified yes-no or true-false. By these the high priest reached a decision, according to this theory.

The Jewish historian Josephus (about A.D. 37–100), a contemporary of the apostle John, believed that the Urim and Thummim had to do with the flashing of the precious stones in the breastplate. Later Jewish writers believed that the letters in the names of the twelve tribes of Israel engraved on the stones stood out or flashed in succession to spell out God's answer. This theory does imply that the Urim and Thummim could produce answers to questions that called for more than a mere yes or no reply. Another theory is that by staring at the Urim and Thummim, the high priest went into a state of ecstasy or trance during which God spoke to him.

The student or Bible teacher should bear in mind that all of these theories are pure guesswork. No one knows the exact nature of the Urim and Thummim or precisely how they were used.

There are few allusions to the Urim and Thummim in the Bible. They are first mentioned in the description of the breastplate of judgment (Ex. 28:30; Lev. 8:8). When Joshua succeeded Moses, he was to have answers from the Urim through Eleazar the priest (Num. 27:21). They are next mentioned in Moses' dying blessing upon Levi (Deut. 33:8). There are places in the Bible where Urim and Thummim may be implied but are not named (Josh. 7:14–18; 1 Sam. 14:37–45; 2 Sam. 21:1).

Saul sought direction from the witch of Endor when he could receive no answer from the Lord, "either by dreams or by Urim or by the prophets" (1 Sam. 28:6). Another interesting reference to the Urim and Thummim occurred during the period after the return of the Jewish people from their years in captivity by the Babylonians. The Persian governor of Jerusalem denied the people permission to observe some of their ancient Jewish food laws until "a priest could consult with the Urim and Thummim" (Ezra 2:63).

VISIONS—experiences similar to dreams through which supernatural insight or awareness is given by revelation. But the difference between a dream and a vision is that dreams occur only during sleep, while visions can happen while a person is awake (Dan. 10:7).

In the Bible, people who had visions were filled with a special consciousness of God. The most noteworthy examples in the Old Testament of recipients of visions are Ezekiel and Daniel. Visions in the New Testament are most prominent in the Gospel of Luke, the Book of Acts, and the Book of Revelation.

The purpose of visions was to give guidance and direction to God's servants and to foretell the future. Daniel's vision, for example, told of the coming of the Messiah (Dan. 8:1, 17).

WANDERINGS OF ISRAEL—the activities of the Israelite tribes during the period between their departure from Egypt under Moses and the time when they were encamped by the Jordan River, ready to be led into Canaan by Joshua. The period of time covered by these events is traditionally 40 years, much of which was spent in the area of Kadesh–barnea.

The Israelite journeyings are commonly spoken of as "wilderness wanderings," because they took the people through some areas that were known as wilderness. In order to understand the nature of the wanderings, it is important to realize the difference between a wilderness and a desert. A desert is best imagined as a barren expanse of sand dunes or a rocky area that does not support any vegetation.

Although a wilderness may also have barren areas, it has grassy upland plains, oases, springs, and vegetation such as flowers, shrubs, and trees that can support a surprising variety of animal life. The Sinai Mountain range where the Hebrew people wandered appears rugged and inhospitable when viewed from the air. But when approached by land, it shows it has a few grassy areas and upland plains.

Even the central Sinai area is not completely lacking in surface water. The Wadi el-Arish, which is most probably the Old

Testament "brook of Egypt," is a seasonal watercourse. South and west of that wadi is another prominent watercourse, the Wadi Feiran, which leads to the best oasis in Sinai. It sustains a considerable amount of vegetation. Thus, it was possible for the Israelites to survive and feed their flocks under wilderness conditions.

The wanderings of the Hebrew people began with the crossing of the Red Sea, a papyrus-reed marsh probably situated in the region of the Bitter Lakes. Immediately thereafter they entered the Wilderness of Shur, an area in northwest Sinai lying south of the coastal road from Egypt to Philistia and bounded on the east by the Wadi el-Arish. This was the first stage of the journey to Mount Sinai (Ex. 15:22), which was probably followed in a southeasterly direction along the east coast of the Gulf of Suez. In this region the water table is high and many springs and wells are available. In spite of this, the Israelites experienced many difficulties (Ex. 15:23–25). They were relieved when they arrived at the oasis of Elim.

It is extremely difficult to identify most of the encampments of the wilderness period. This is partly because many of the names may have been given to the locations by the Israelites themselves as a result of specific happenings (for example, Marah, Ex. 15:23; Taberah, Num. 11:3), and not because those were the local names. Even if they had been named before the Hebrews arrived, only the most important of them would have survived in modern Arabic. An example of one place name that has survived is Jebel Musa ("Mountain of Moses") as one possible location of Mount Sinai. This imposing peak in the Sinai range is the traditional site of the covenant with Israel, although two other locations, Jebel Serbal and Ras es-Safsafeh, have also been suggested.

The Israelites encamped in the Wilderness of Sin at Rephidim, possibly the Wadi Refayid in southwest Sinai, and drove off an Amalekite attack (Ex. 17:8–16) before reaching

Mount Sinai. There they received the Law, and settled for nearly a year (Num. 1:1; 10:11) while Moses worked at organizing the new nation. At this stage of the wanderings the construction of the tabernacle and the regulations governing its use were given careful attention because of their importance for the future life of the Israelites.

Even these precautions, however, were not enough to stop dissatisfaction among the wandering Israelites as they traveled toward Kadesh. The people complained about the lack of food in the wilderness. Even when God provided manna, they soon began to dislike it. To punish them God sent a flock of quail for food, which made the people ill and caused many deaths (Num. 11:32–33).

From the Wilderness of Paran Moses sent spies into Canaan, but they returned with discouraging reports about the inhabitants (Num. 13:32–33). The people then refused to enter Canaan and rebelled against their leaders. God was angry with them. With the exception of Joshua and Caleb, all the people alive at that time were condemned to spend the rest of their lives in the wilderness. Korah, Dathan, and Abiram accused Moses and Aaron of assuming too much priestly authority. They were punished by being swallowed up in a spectacular earthquake (Num. 16:32–33). The Israelites became angry at this, and God would have killed them all if Moses had not interceded on their behalf.

Because of an act of disobedience at Kadesh (Num. 20:8–12), Moses and Aaron were forbidden to enter the Promised Land. Nevertheless, they and the Israelites attempted to go to Canaan along the King's Highway which passed through Edomite territory. But they were refused permission. The people then journeyed to Mount Hor on the border of Edom, where Aaron died (Num. 20:28). A skirmish with the Canaanite king of Arad took place before the Hebrews moved toward the wilderness area east of Moab (Num. 21:1–3). When the Amorite King Sihon refused them access to the King's Highway, he was defeated in battle (Num. 21:21–32). Shortly afterwards Og, king of Bashan, suffered the same fate (Num. 21:33–35).

The Israelites now occupied a large area of territory in Transjordan. This alarmed Balak, king of Moab. He hired Balaam, a Mesopotamian soothsayer, to curse the Israelites, but by divine intervention he blessed them instead (Numbers 22–24). Unfortunately the Israelites committed sin with the Moabite women, and this was to prove an indication of what lay ahead in Canaan.

While the people were in the plains of Moab, across the Jordan River from Jericho, a second census of the people was taken, apparently in preparation for the crossing into Canaan, for which Joshua was appointed leader (Num. 27:18–23). Perhaps because of the immorality with the Moabite women, Moses proclaimed a series of regulations involving offerings and festivals that would be observed once the Israelites were in Canaan (Numbers 28–29).

The hold of the Israelites on Transjordanian territory was consolidated by a successful attack upon the Midianites. This resulted in a great deal of plunder. The conquered lands were ideal for raising herds and flocks, so the tribes of Gad and Reuben and half of the tribe of Manasseh were given that territory as their own. Moses then issued instructions for the conquest of Canaan, and appointed leaders who would divide the land among the tribes.

After reviewing Israel's wilderness wanderings (Num. 33:1–49) and composing a victory song (Deut. 32:1–43), Moses climbed Mount Nebo to see the land that he had been forbidden to enter. With a final blessing upon Israel, Moses died on Mount Nebo. With his death the wilderness wanderings ended and the occupation of Canaan began.

WISDOM—ability to judge correctly and to follow the best course of action, based on knowledge and understanding.

The apostle Paul declared that the message of the cross is foolishness to the Greeks and a stumbling block to the Jews. But to those who believe, said Paul, this "foolishness of God" is "the wisdom of God" (1 Cor. 1:18–25).

Against the wisdom of God Paul contrasted "the wisdom of this world" (1 Cor. 1:20; 3:19), "human wisdom" (1 Cor. 2:4), "the wisdom of men" (1 Cor. 2:5), "the wisdom of this age" (1 Cor. 2:6), and "man's wisdom" (1 Cor. 2:13).

The biblical concept of wisdom, therefore, is quite different from the classical view of wisdom, which sought through philosophy and human rational thought to determine the mysteries of existence and the universe. The first principle of biblical wisdom is that people should humble themselves before God in reverence and worship, obedient to His commands. This idea is found especially in the Wisdom Literature: the books of Job, Proverbs, and Ecclesiastes.

In the Old Testament, the best example of a "wise man" is King Solomon (1 Kin. 10:4, 6–8; 2 Chr. 1:7–12). And yet the same book that heaps such lavish, warm, and glowing praise upon Solomon for his reputed wisdom (1 Kin. 4:29–34) also points out how Solomon's heart turned away from the Lord (1 Kin. 11:1–13).

WISDOM LITERATURE—a type of literature, common to the peoples of the ancient world, that included ethical and philosophical works. The wisdom literature of the Old Testament consists of the books of Job, Proverbs, and Ecclesiastes, and certain of the psalms (Psalm 1; 19; 37; 49; 104; 107; 112; 119; 127; 128; 133; 147; 148).

In general, two principal types of wisdom are found in the wisdom literature of the Old Testament—practical and speculative. Practical wisdom consists mainly of wise sayings that offer guidelines for a successful and happy life. These are maxims of commonsense insight and observation about how intelligent people should conduct themselves.

The Book of Proverbs is a good example of practical wisdom; it encourages the pursuit of wisdom and the practice of strict discipline, hard work, and high moral standards as the way to happiness and success. Proverbs is an optimistic book. It assumes that wisdom is attainable by all who seek and follow it. The book also declares that those who keep God's moral and ethical laws will be rewarded with long life, health, possessions, respect, security, and self-control.

Speculative wisdom, such as that found in the books of Job and Ecclesiastes, goes beyond practical maxims about daily conduct. It reflects upon the deeper issues of the meaning of life, the worth and value of life, and the existence of evil in the world.

The Book of Job seeks to explain the ways of God to humankind. One of the themes of the book is the suffering of the righteous and the apparent prosperity of the wicked. The answer to such questions is that the prosperity of the wicked is brief and illusory (Job 15:21–29; 24:24) while the righteous, although presently suffering, will eventually receive God's reward.

Like the Book of Proverbs, the Book of Ecclesiastes also contains rules for living and sayings of practical wisdom. But Ecclesiastes is more than a collection of discourses and observations designed to instruct people on how to conduct their lives. Because of its skeptical and pessimistic tone, the Book of Ecclesiastes is the most "philosophical" book of the Bible. As such, it must be classified among the works of speculative wisdom.

The wisdom psalms are similar in tone and content to the books of Job and Proverbs. Some of these psalms struggle with the problem of evil and sin in the world. Others give practical advice for daily living.

WORD, THE—a theological phrase that expresses the absolute, eternal, and ultimate being of Jesus Christ (John 1:1–14; 1 John 1:1; Rev. 19:13). The Old Testament spoke of the word of God as the divine agent in the creation of the universe: "By the word of the Lord the heavens were made" (Ps. 33:6). In the New Testament, the Gospel of John declared, "And the Word became flesh and dwelt among us" (John 1:14). Through the incarnation of Christ, God has come to dwell in our midst. Through the life and ministry of Jesus, a unique and final revelation of God has been given—one superior to the revelation given through the Law and the Prophets. In Christ, the Word of God, God's plan and purpose for mankind is clearly revealed (2 Cor. 4:4; Heb. 1:1–3).

WORD OF GOD—the means by which God makes Himself known, declares His will, and brings about His purposes. Phrases such as "word of God," and "word of the Lord" are applied to the commanding word of God that brought creation into existence (Genesis 1; 2 Pet. 3:5) and also destroyed that same world through the waters of the Flood (2 Pet. 3:6); to God's announcement of an impending or future act of judgment (Ex. 9:20–21; 1 Kin. 2:27); to the word that declares God's commitment and promises His blessing (Gen. 15:1, 4); and to a particular instruction from God (Josh. 8:27).

The term "word of God" is also used of the Ten Commandments given from Mount Sinai (Deut. 5:5); of the whole Mosaic Law (Is. 2:3); of specific parts of the Old Testament (Rom. 9:6; 1 Tim. 4:5); of a more personal communication from God (1 Sam. 3:21; 15:10); of the directive of God that set in motion John the Baptist's ministry (Luke 3:2); of Jesus' message of the kingdom of God (Luke 8:11); of the gospel as preached in the early church (Acts 4:31); and finally of the Lord Jesus Christ Himself (Rev. 19:13).

God's word is the primary means by which He is present and working in the world. He is not Himself part of this world, but He acts in it by means of His word. He becomes personally known through His word (1 Sam. 3:21). His word is powerfully creative (Ezek. 37:4) and its purposes are irresistible (Is. 55:11; Jer. 23:29). God's word is totally dependable; it represents His permanent commitment (Is. 40:8). When heard and responded to, His word meets deep needs in the human heart and provides joy, satisfaction, and confident direction that can be achieved in no other manner (Deut. 8:3; Ps. 119:162; Jer. 15:16). God's word has the power to penetrate all pretense and discern "the thoughts and intents of the heart" (Heb. 4:12).

God's speaking of His word reaches a culmination in the sending of His Son (John 1:1, 14; Heb. 1:1–2). All that is true of God's earlier word is supremely true of Jesus. The gospel of Jesus Christ is, in a special way, the word of God as it makes known and brings into operation the reconciliation with God that is His purpose for mankind (2 Cor. 5:18–19). So central is the gospel to the purpose of God in this world that the successful spread of the gospel is the growth of the word of God (Acts 12:24).

Not only Jesus' message but also all that He is communicates God to us. He Himself is described as the Word of God (John 1:1; Rev. 19:13). Jesus brings the presence of God to a new level—the personal presence of God in the world in a human life.

WRITING—language symbols or characters written or imprinted on a surface with a marking instrument. Archaeological discoveries of the last century or so have revolutionized our knowledge of ancient writing methods and the materials that were used.

Development of Writing.

The art of writing was practiced in the ancient world as early as 3300 B.C. This art developed through a number of stages before the use of a written alphabet emerged. Early Egyptian writing was done in hieroglyphics, or the use of symbols and pictures to represent words.

Early alphabetic inscriptions, although fragmentary and damaged, were discovered in temple ruins at Serabit el-Khadem in the Sinaitic Peninsula. These were dated at about 1500 B.C. The text was the work of laborers who had been employed to work an Egyptian turquoise mine. Many of the signs used in this writing show a distinct resemblance to Egyptian picture writing. The signs are too few in number to serve as a full alphabet.

Later excavations at Gezer and Shechem yielded potsherds belonging to the same period or slightly earlier. Digging at Lachish produced inscriptions on a dagger blade. The writing had many of the same letters that were discovered at Serabit in the Sinai Peninsula. Four pieces of pottery found at Lachish, dated at about 1250 B.C., bore the same kind of writing. From Byblos (Gebal) on the coast north of Beirut came inscriptions about kings who lived there from the thirteenth to the ninth centuries B.C.

All this evidence indicates that alphabetic writing, with a recognizable continuous script, was in use in and near Palestine at about the same time that Egyptian hieroglyphics and Babylonian cuneiform were also being used.

A calendar from the archaeological dig at Gezer is the oldest important Israelite document as well as the earliest completely intelligible Hebrew text found on Palestinian soil. It presents a "farmer's almanac" of agricultural operations by months. This calendar has been dated to the tenth century B.C.

Another celebrated discovery was the Moabite Stone. When it was found (1868), it was the earliest known example of the

Phoenician alphabetic script. This small stela of black basalt records the story of Mesha's wars against the kings of Israel and Judah. It is virtually the only surviving record of the ancient Moabites and their kingdoms.

The Siloam Inscription, carved in the tunnel connecting the Gihon Spring with the Pool of Siloam in Jerusalem, comes from the reign of King Hezekiah of Judah (about 700 B.C.). Discovered in 1880, it describes the successful junction made when opposite ends of the work were joined.

Finally, there are the Lachish Letters discovered in 1935 and 1938. These were potsherds containing part of the military correspondence between the governor of Lachish and an officer of an Israelite outpost when Babylon's army was overrunning the ancient world in 587–586 B.C.

The Canaanite or Old Semitic (Phoenician) alphabet was widely used among the countries between the Nile and the Euphrates Rivers. The model on which it was built probably came from Egypt. The Phoenicians exploited and perfected this alphabet, then carried it to Greece in their shipping and trading activities.

Several significant archaeological finds have yielded valuable information about ancient writing and how it developed.

The Ras Shamra Tablets.

Ras Shamra is a site on the coast of northwest Syria opposite Cyprus. The site was identified as the ancient city of Ugarit, a Canaanite city that served as a gateway of commerce between Asia and the Mediterranean lands as early as about 2000 B.C. Among its buildings was an extensive library of clay tablets of cuneiform writing. The building also included a writing school for scribes. The language of most of the texts found was similar to the Hebrew language.

Several items found at this site were dictionaries and lexicons, including some written in Sumerian-Babylonian (Akkadian) and Hurrian (Horite) vocabularies. In that day Sumerian was used only by scholars; Babylonian was the diplomatic and commercial language. Inscriptions in Egyptian hieroglyphics, Hittite and Cypriot were also discovered. Commercial, medical, legal, diplomatic, and private documents were discovered, although the greatest part of the find consisted of religious writings.

The religious tablets were written in an alphabetic script of 29 or 30 letters. The words are written from left to right. This evidence shows the Ugaritic alphabet was invented by people who were aware of the Phoenician or a similar alphabetic system. They adapted this system into an alphabet.

The Dead Sea Scrolls.

These scrolls are the greatest archaeological discovery about the text of the Bible ever made. The earliest of them have been dated at about three centuries before Christ. The first find included two scrolls of Isaiah, the Manual of Discipline of the Essene community, the Habakkuk Commentary, The War Scroll, and Thanksgiving Psalms. Later finds yielded a palimpsest written in Phoenician script, fragments of the Minor Prophets, phylacteries, and parts of two letters from the Jewish revolutionary Simon Bar Kochba. In addition a copper scroll and thousands of manuscript fragments were found. Their importance includes a firsthand view of what a Hebrew scroll looked like at the beginning of the Christian era.

The Nag Hammadi Documents.

An entire library of papyrus documents was accidentally discovered by peasants north of Luxor, Egypt, in 1946. These manuscripts were written in the Sahidic dialect of the Coptic language. The leather covers in which they were wrapped probably account for their excellent preservation. The find included 13 codices with nearly 1,000 pages. They have been dated to the third and fourth centuries A.D. Originally produced by a sect known as the Gnostics, these manuscripts represent a wide variety of literature, including a number of otherwise unre-corded sayings of Jesus. Many quotations are genuinely biblical. These writings show familiarity with the New Testament, but they contain little of abiding spiritual or moral value. Their understanding of the person and work of Christ is not in agree-ment with the teaching of the New Testament.

The Eblaite Discoveries.

A group of tablets discovered beginning in 1974 represents the royal archives in a civilization that flourished in northwest-ern Syria around 2500 B.C. Seventy-five percent of their contents deal with economic and administrative matters. This culture rivaled those of Egypt and Sumer during the same period. The language was apparently an early form of Canaanite belonging to the same linguistic branch as Hebrew. They used the char-acters of Sumerian but wrote in an old Phoenician language. This discovery has helped Old Testament scholars determine the meaning of certain words in the Hebrew texts of the Old Testament. These tablets also show that the world of the 25th century B.C. was not primitive but highly urbanized, cosmo-politan, and literate.

Study of all these ancient writings reinforces our confidence in the history and culture of the Old Testament.

WRITING MATERIALS—ancient surfaces, such as ani-mal skins and stone, on which information was recorded in Bible times. The earliest writing materials were clay tablets or stone (Ex. 32:16; Job 19:23–24). An engraving tool or a chisel was used to write on stone, bricks, and tablets (Is. 8:1). A reed pen (3 John 13), a metal pen, or a brushlike tool was used to write on softer materials (Job 19:24; Jer. 17:1).

The ink used was black, sometimes of metallic content. Usually it was made of soot, mixed with oil and gum of balsam. This permitted erasure by a water-bearing sponge. Inkhorns were carried by scribes. Inkwells discovered at Qumran were of brass and earthenware.

Many materials were used throughout the ancient world to receive writing—stone, ivory, leaves, bark, wood, metals, linen, baked clay, wax, and potsherds. But the three main materials on which the text of the Bible was written were skins, papyrus, and vellum. Prepared skins were used to record state documents as early as 3000 B.C.

The ancient Persians used leather as a writing material; so did the Assyrians in the eighth century B.C. Jeremiah's scroll, cut up by King Jehoiakim, was leather (Jer. 36:23).

Papyrus met the needs of the Greco-Roman world for nearly a thousand years. The Phoenicians used Egyptian papyrus in the tenth century B.C. It was easily obtained, relatively inexpensive, and durable. Unfortunately, it becomes brittle with age. The first papyrus document, an employee list, was not found until 1778. The bulk of papyrus discoveries took place near the turn of this century.

Vellum (parchment) is a material prepared from the skin of cattle, sheep, goats, and sometimes deer. However, papyrus was the preferred material for books until vellum replaced it in the fourth century A.D. (2 Tim. 4:13).

Christian Scriptures in Greek were written in capital letters, separately formed often without spaces between words. These were called uncial letters. The word uncial probably means "inch high." In the ninth century A.D. a new style known as miniscule, or cursive, came into general use. The letters were smaller and often more quickly formed than the uncial characters. The Scriptures continued to be reproduced in this smaller script until the invention of printing.

Z

ZECHARIAH, BOOK OF—an Old Testament prophetic book that portrays the coming glory of the Messiah. Many scholars describe Zechariah as "the most Messianic of all the Old Testament books" because it contains eight specific references to the Messiah in its brief 14 chapters.

Structure of the Book.

The 14 chapters of Zechariah fall naturally into two major sections: chapters 1–8, the prophet's encouragement to the people to finish the work of rebuilding the Temple, and chapters 9–14, Zechariah's picture of Israel's glorious future and the coming of the Messiah.

In the first section, Zechariah introduces himself as God's prophet and calls the people to repent and turn from their evil ways. Part of their sin was their failure to finish the work of rebuilding the Temple after returning from the Captivity in Babylon. In a series of eight symbolic night visions that came to the prophet (1:7–6:8), Zechariah encourages the people to finish this important task. These visions are followed by a coronation scene (6:9–15), in which a high priest named Joshua is crowned as priest and king, symbolizing the Messiah who is to come. This is considered one of the classic Messianic prophecies of the Old Testament. Chapters 7 and 8 also continue another important element of the Messianic hope: the One to come will reign in justice from Zion, the city of Jerusalem (8:3, 15–16).

The second major section of Zechariah's book, chapters 9–14, contains God's promises for the new age to come. Chapter 9 has a remarkable description of the manner in which the ruling Messiah will enter the city of Jerusalem: "Behold, your King is coming to you; He is just and having salvation, lowly and riding on a donkey, a colt, the foal of a donkey" (9:9). These were the words used by Matthew and John to describe Jesus' triumphant entry into Jerusalem more than 500 years after Zechariah made this startling prediction (Matt. 21:5; John 12:15).

Other promises for the future in this section of the book include the restoration of the nation of Israel (chap. 10) and Jerusalem's deliverance from her enemies (chap. 12), as well as her purification as the holy city (chap. 13). Like the Book of Revelation, Zechariah closes on the theme of the universal reign of God. All nations will come to worship Him as He extends His rule throughout the world (chap. 14).

Authorship and Date.

Most conservative scholars agree that the entire book of Zechariah was written by the prophet of that name, who identifies himself in the book's introduction as "the son of Berechiah" (1:1). But some scholars insist the second major section of the book, chapters 9–14, was written by an unknown author. These scholars believe this section was added to the book about 30 or 40 years after Zechariah the prophet wrote chapters 1–8.

It is true that these two sections of the Book have their own unique characteristics. In the first section Zechariah encourages the people to finish the Temple, while in the second section he is more concerned about the glorious age of the future. The language and style of these two sections of Zechariah are also quite different. And the prophecies in these two sections seem to be set in different times.

Chapters 1–8, Zechariah tells us, were delivered as prophecies "in the eighth month of the second year of Darius" (1:1), and "in the fourth year of King Darius" (7:1). These references to Darius I of Persia (ruled 522–486 B.C.) date these prophecies clearly from 520 to 518 B.C. But chapters 9–14 contain a reference to Greece (9:13), probably indicating it was written after 480 B.C., when the balance of world power was shifting from the Persians to the Greeks. How can these major differences between these two sections of the book be explained unless we accept the theory that they were written by two different people?

One possible explanation is that Zechariah was a young man when he delivered his prophecies in the first section of the book. The book itself contains a clue that this may have been the case. In one of his visions, two angels speak to one another about the prophet, referring to him as "this young man" (2:4). Thus, it is quite possible that Zechariah could have encouraged the Jewish captives in Jerusalem in the early part of his ministry and could have delivered the messages about the future, contained in the second section of the book, during his final years as a prophet.

After all the evidence is examined, there is no convincing reason to dispute the traditional view that Zechariah the prophet wrote the entire book that bears his name. These prophecies were first delivered and then reduced to writing over a period of about 45 years—from 520 to 475 B.C.

As for the prophet himself, very little is known about him beyond the few facts he reveals in his book. He was a descendant, perhaps the grandson, of Iddo the priest (1:1)—one of the family leaders who returned from the Captivity in Babylon (Neh. 12:16). This means that Zechariah probably was a priest as well as a prophet—an unusual circumstance because most of the prophets of Israel spoke out against the priestly class. Since he was a young man when he began to prophesy in 520 B.C.,

Zechariah was probably born in Babylonia while the Jewish people were in captivity. He probably returned with his family with the first wave of captives who reached Jerusalem under Zerubbabel about 538 B.C.

Historical Setting.

The setting at the beginning of the Book is the same as the setting of the Book of Haggai. The prophet Haggai spoke directly to the issue of the rebuilding of the Temple, encouraging those who returned from captivity in Babylon to finish the task. Zechariah spoke to that issue as well, according to the Book of Ezra (Ezra 5:1). But Zechariah wished to bring about a complete spiritual renewal through faith and hope in God. He spoke about the nature of God's Law and of the hope that God promised to those who were faithful to Him.

The second portion of Zechariah was written in the period between the times of the prophets Haggai (520 B.C.) and Malachi (450 B.C.). The Persian Empire was ruled by two great kings during these years, Darius I (522–486 B.C.) and Xerxes I (485–465 B.C.). This was a period when the Jewish people in Jerusalem were settled in their new land with a walled city and their beloved Temple. But they were unhappy and dissatisfied. Some of the people had expected that Zerubbabel, governor of Jerusalem, might be the Messiah, but this had proven to be false. The people needed a new word concerning God's future for them. This message from God was given in a most dramatic fashion by the great prophet Zechariah.

Theological Contribution.

One of the greatest contributions of the Book of Zechariah is the merger of the best from the priestly and prophetic elements in Israel's history. Zechariah realized the need for both these elements in an authentic faith. He called the people to turn from their sins. He also realized that the Temple and religious ritual played an important role in keeping the people close to God. Because he brought these elements together in his own ministry, Zechariah helped prepare the way for the Christian community's understanding of Christ as both priest and prophet.

Zechariah is also noted for his development of an apocalyptic-prophetic style—highly symbolized and visionary language concerning the events of the end-time. In this, his writing resembles the Books of Daniel and Revelation. The visions of lampstands and olive trees, horsemen and chariots, measuring lines and horns place him and these other two books in a class by themselves. Zechariah also has a great deal to say about the concept of God as warrior. While this was a well-established image among biblical writers, Zechariah ties this idea to the concept of the Day of the Lord (see Joel 2). His description of the return of Christ to earth as the great Warrior in the Day of the Lord (14:1–9) is one of the most stirring prophecies of the Old Testament.

On that day, according to Zechariah, Christ will place His feet on the Mount of Olives, causing violent changes throughout the land (14:3–4). The day will be changed to darkness and the darkness to light (14:5–8). The entire world will worship Him as the Lord spreads His rule as King "over all the earth" (14:9).

Special Considerations.

Zechariah 12:10 is a remarkable verse that speaks of the response of the nation of Israel to Jesus Christ as Savior and Lord. It describes a day in the future when the Jewish people (the house of David and the inhabitants of Jerusalem) will recognize the significance of the death of Jesus. This recognition will lead to mourning, repentance, and salvation (compare Rom. 11:25–27).

But the most startling thing about this verse is the phrase, "Then they will look on Me whom they have pierced." In speaking through the prophet Zechariah, the Lord identifies Himself as the one who will be pierced. Along with Psalm 22 and Isaiah 53, these words are a wonder of inspiration as they describe the result of Jesus' death as well as the manner in which He died to deliver us from our sins.

ZEPHANIAH, BOOK OF—a brief prophetic book of the Old Testament that emphasizes the certainty of God's judgment and the preservation of a remnant, a small group of people who will continue to serve as God's faithful servants in the world. The book takes its title from its author, the prophet Zephaniah, whose name means "the Lord has hidden."

Structure of the Book.

Zephaniah contains only three short chapters, but these chapters are filled with some of the most vivid pictures of God's judgment to be found in the Bible. After a brief introduction of himself as God's spokesman, the prophet launches immediately into a description of God's approaching wrath. He portrays this great "day of the Lord" as a time of "trouble and distress," "darkness and gloominess," "trumpet and alarm" (1:14–15).

Zephaniah's prophecy makes it clear that the nation of Judah, as well as surrounding countries, will feel the sting of God's wrath. Judah's capital city, Jerusalem, is soundly condemned for its wickedness, rebellion, and injustice. The prophet even portrays God with searchlamps as He exposes the corruption of the city and marks it for His certain judgment (1:12).

In spite of its underlying theme of judgment and punishment, the Book of Zephaniah closes on a positive note. After God judges the wayward nations, the prophet announces He will raise up a remnant of the faithful who will continue to serve as His Covenant People in the world. The book ends with a glorious promise for the future, a time when God will "quiet you in His love" and "rejoice over you with singing" (3:17).

Authorship and Date.

Scholars are in general agreement that Zephaniah the prophet wrote this book that bears his name. In his introduction (1:1), the author traces his ancestry back four generations to Hezekiah, a former king of Judah noted for his faithfulness to God. Zephaniah must have been proud that he was the great-great-grandson of this beloved ruler, who had led his people back to worship of the one true God.

The book also tells how Zephaniah the prophet ministered during the days of Josiah, a godly king who reigned over the nation of Judah from about 640 to about 609 B.C. Most scholars place the writing of the book at about 627 B.C.

Historical Setting.

This book belongs to a dark period in Judah's history. About 100 years before Zephaniah's time, Judah's sister nation, the northern kingdom of Israel, had fallen to a foreign power because of its sin and idolatry. Zephaniah sensed that the same thing was about to happen to the southern kingdom of Judah— and for precisely the same reason.

Under the leadership of two successive evil kings, Manasseh and Amon, the people of Judah had fallen into worship of false gods. Zephaniah delivered his prophecy and wrote this book to warn the people of God's approaching wrath and judgment. As Zephaniah predicted, God punished His people and the surrounding pagan nations through a superior foreign power. Not even a brief religious renewal under the good king Josiah was enough to turn the tide of paganism and false worship that carried Judah toward certain destruction. Judgment came to the nation in 586 B.C., when the invading Babylonians destroyed the city of Jerusalem and carried its leading citizens into Captivity in Babylon.

Theological Contribution.

The judgment of the Lord portrayed by the prophet Zephaniah springs from His nature as a God of holiness. Because God demands holiness and righteousness in His people, He will judge those who continue to sin and rebel (1:17). But the Lord also is merciful and faithful to His promise. To the committed remnant He offers encouragement and protection from the approaching dark day (2:1–3). And to the righteous He promises the final realization of the covenant He sealed with Abraham hundreds of years earlier. People of all nations will gather to worship the Lord (2:11; 3:9). His own people will be renewed in righteousness (3:11–13). And the King of kings Himself will rule in their midst (3:15).

Special Considerations.

The prophet Zephaniah shows keen familiarity with the city of Jerusalem (1:10–11). Since he was a member of the royal line, he was probably a resident of Jerusalem. It must have troubled him deeply to pronounce God's prophecies of judgment against his beloved city.

One of the most beautiful passages in the book is the description of the joy of the Lord (3:8–20). His song of joy will join the happy singing of His people. The dark day of doom will not last. A happy day is coming for those who, like Zephaniah, are "hidden in the day of the Lord's anger" (2:3).